Forgiveness and Its Moral Dimensions

Forgiveness and Its Moral Dimensions

Edited by

BRANDON WARMKE, DANA KAY NELKIN,
AND MICHAEL MCKENNA

OXFORD
UNIVERSITY PRESS

OXFORD
UNIVERSITY PRESS

Oxford University Press is a department of the University of Oxford. It furthers
the University's objective of excellence in research, scholarship, and education
by publishing worldwide. Oxford is a registered trade mark of Oxford University
Press in the UK and certain other countries.

Published in the United States of America by Oxford University Press
198 Madison Avenue, New York, NY 10016, United States of America.

Library of Congress Cataloging-in-Publication Data
Names: Warmke, Brandon, editor. | Nelkin, Dana Kay, 1966– editor. |
McKenna, Michael, 1963– editor.
Title: Forgiveness and its moral dimensions / editors Brandon Warmke,
Dana Kay Nelkin, Michael McKenna.
Description: New York : Oxford University Press, [2021] |
Includes bibliographical references and index.| Contents: The forgiven /
David Shoemaker—Institutional apologies and forgiveness / Angela Smith—Forgiveness
and consequences / Richard Arneson.
Identifiers: LCCN 2020051763 (print) | LCCN 2020051764 (ebook) |
ISBN 9780190602154 (paperback) | ISBN 9780190602147 (hardback) |
ISBN 9780190602178 (oso) | ISBN 9780190602161 (updf) | ISBN 9780197578032 (epub)
Subjects: LCSH: Forgiveness—Moral and ethical aspects.
Classification: LCC BJ1476 .F66 2021 (print) | LCC BJ1476 (ebook) | DDC 179/.9—dc23
LC record available at https://lccn.loc.gov/2020051763
LC ebook record available at https://lccn.loc.gov/2020051764

DOI: 10.1093/oso/9780190602147.001.0001

1 3 5 7 9 8 6 4 2

Paperback printed by Marquis, Canada
Hardback printed by Bridgeport National Bindery, Inc., United States of America

Contents

Preface

The original idea for this volume on forgiveness first came together when the three of us realized we had a shared interest in bringing together new work on this topic, one that had fallen out of fashion but just recently reemerged. Brandon was a graduate student at the time, and Michael his supervisor. Dana had recently given Brandon some excellent advice on one of his own articles. While we shared agreement on several matters, we realized that a good deal was up for debate. So we resolved to work together to help bring the topic even more into the spotlight. While forgiveness is a pervasive part of our ethical lives, there is considerable disagreement about what it is and what norms govern it. A pervasive view is that forgiveness most fundamentally involves forswearing resentment or anger directed at the culpable. But others dispute this. As for normative issues, some contend that forgiveness is inappropriate when the guilty do not forswear their wrongdoing or do not experience remorse. Others deny this, arguing that unconditional forgiveness is morally defensible. Naturally, some develop these views in the context of religious beliefs, while others explore the matter without considering these broader assumptions. Yet a further issue concerns forgiveness in wider, collective contexts, such as South Africa's response to apartheid. The chapters in this volume represent a diversity of views on these issues by leading philosophers who have offered us new insights into this aspect of our ethical lives.

We continue to find forgiveness a fascinating and philosophically challenging topic. There is much unexplored terrain, and we believe these new chapters will take our conversations in new and fruitful directions. We hope you'll join those discussions, too.

Acknowledgments

We would like to thank the authors for their contributions to this volume, and for their patience with our efforts to bring this book to print. We are especially indebted to Peter Ohlin for his support and guidance.

Author Bios

Lucy Allais is professor of philosophy at the University of the Witwatersrand, Johannesburg, and Henry Allison Chair of the History of Philosophy at the University of California, San Diego. She has published work on Kant, forgiveness, moral responsibility, and punishment, and she is working on freedom of the will.

Richard Arneson holds the Valtz Family Chair in Philosophy at the University of California, San Diego, where he has taught since 1973. He teaches moral and political philosophy and writes mainly on theories of social justice and on act consequentialism and its critics. He also does work on applied philosophy topics.

Eve Garrard is a moral philosopher who is currently Honorary Research Fellow in the Department of Philosophy at Manchester University. Her research interests are in moral theory, bioethics, and philosophical issues connected with the concepts of evil and forgiveness. She has coedited (with Geoffrey Scarre) *Moral Philosophy and the Holocaust* (2003), coauthored (with David McNaughton) *Forgiveness* (2010), and has published various papers on aspects of forgiveness and of evil. She is currently doing further work on the idea of evil. She has published several papers on bioethical issues, and in the past she sat on various Ethics Committees, including the Royal College of Pathology Ethics Committee, and has been involved in GP ethics and clinical ethics training.

Ishtiyaque Haji is professor of philosophy at the University of Calgary. He has research interests in ethical theory, philosophy of action, metaphysics, and philosophical psychology. He is the author of *Moral Appraisability* (1998), *Deontic Morality and Control* (2002), (with Stefaan Cuypers) *Moral Responsibility, Authenticity, and Education* (2008), *Freedom and Value* (2009), *Incompatibilism's Allure* (2009), *Reason's Debt to Freedom* (2012), *Luck's Mischief* (2016), and *The Obligation Dilemma* (2019).

Margaret R. Holmgren is associate professor of philosophy emeritus at Iowa State University. She is the author of *Forgiveness and Retribution: Responding to Wrongdoing* (Cambridge University Press, 2012) and of a number of articles in the areas of ethics, philosophy of law, and moral epistemology. With Heimir Geirsson, she also coedited the anthology *Ethical Theory*, which is now in its third edition, with Broadview Press. Before coming to Iowa State University, she taught at Oberlin College and Wellesley College.

Michael McKenna (PhD, Virginia) is a professor of philosophy at the University of Arizona. His areas of research are mostly devoted to free will and moral responsibility but also include issues in moral psychology, action theory, ethics, and metaphysics.

He is the author of *Conversation and Responsibility* (Oxford University Press), the coauthor with Derk Pereboom of *Free Will: A Contemporary Introduction* (Routledge Press), and has also written numerous articles, most of which would impress you if you were to read them. He is also coeditor of *Moral Responsibility and Alternative Possibilities*, *Free Will and Reactive Attitudes*, and *The Nature of Moral Responsibility*. He has a boundless lust for life, and he often drinks to excess.

David McNaughton is retired and lives in Edinburgh with his wife, Rosa, and their two dogs. He is Emeritus Professor of Philosophy at both Keele and Florida State Universities, and he is currently Honorary Professor of Philosophy at Edinburgh University. He is the author of *Moral Vision* (1988) and (with Eve Garrard) of *Forgiveness* (2010), and of a number of papers on ethics, philosophy of religion, and the relations between the two. His edition of Joseph Butler's *Fifteen Sermons* came out in 2017 with Oxford University Press, and he is currently editing Butler's *Analogy of Religion*. He and Piers Rawling are also writing a book on their approach to practical reasons.

Dana Kay Nelkin (PhD, UCLA) is a professor of philosophy at the University of California, San Diego, and an affiliate professor at the University of San Diego School of Law. Her areas of research include moral psychology, ethics, bioethics, and philosophy of law. She is the author of *Making Sense of Freedom and Responsibility* (Oxford University Press) and a number of articles on a variety of topics, including self-deception, friendship, the lottery paradox, moral luck, psychopathy, forgiveness, and praise and blame. She is also a coeditor of the *The Ethics and Law of Omissions* and *The Oxford Handbook of Moral Responsibility*. Her work in moral psychology includes participation in an interdisciplinary research collaboration of philosophers and psychologists, The Moral Judgements Project, which brings together normative and descriptive enquiries about the use of moral principles such as the Doctrine of Doing and Allowing and the Doctrine of Double Effect.

Derk Pereboom is the Susan Linn Sage Professor in the Philosophy Department at Cornell University. He is the author of *Living without Free Will* (Cambridge University Press, 2001), *Consciousness and the Prospects of Physicalism* (Oxford University Press, 2011), *Free Will, Agency, and Meaning in Life* (Oxford University Press, 2014), and of articles on free will, philosophy of mind, and in the history of modern philosophy.

Glen Pettigrove holds the Chair in Moral Philosophy at the University of Glasgow. Before joining the Glasgow department, he taught at the University of Auckland. He specializes in moral psychology, normative ethics, and early modern philosophy. He has a particular interest in the role of the emotions in our personal and collective lives and has written on anger, cheerfulness, forgiveness, guilt, love, and shame. He is the author of *Forgiveness and Love* (Oxford University Press, 2012) as well as numerous articles on virtue, religious ethics, and group attitudes.

David Shoemaker is a professor in the Department of Philosophy and the Murphy Institute of Political Economy at Tulane University. He has written or edited numerous books and articles on topics in moral psychology, agency and responsibility, personal identity and ethics, and social/political philosophy. He is a recurring visiting researcher at Lund University, associate editor of *Ethics*, general editor of the series *Oxford Studies in Agency and Responsibility*, and, with David Sobel, the coeditor of the long-running ethics blog PEA Soup.

Angela M. Smith is a Distinguished Scholar in the Department of Philosophy at Washington and Lee University. She is the coeditor (with Randolph Clarke and Michael McKenna) of *The Nature of Moral Responsibility: New Essays* (Oxford University Press, 2015) and has published extensively on topics related to moral agency, moral responsibility, and moral blame.

Eleonore Stump is the Robert J. Henle Professor of Philosophy at Saint Louis University. She is also honorary professor at Wuhan University and at the Logos Institute, St. Andrews, and a professorial fellow at Australian Catholic University. She has published extensively in philosophy of religion, contemporary metaphysics, and medieval philosophy. Her books include *Aquinas* (2003), *Wandering in Darkness: Narrative and the Problem of Suffering* (2010), and *Atonement* (2018). She has given the Gifford Lectures at Aberdeen (2003), the Wilde lectures at Oxford (2006), the Stewart lectures at Princeton (2009), and the Stanton lectures at Cambridge (2018). She is past president of the Society of Christian Philosophers, the American Catholic Philosophical Association, and the American Philosophical Association, Central Division; and she is a member of the American Academy of Arts and Sciences.

Christine Swanton is at the Philosophy Department at the University of Auckland, New Zealand. She has recently published *The Virtue Ethics of Hume and Nietzsche* (Wiley Blackwell, 2015). *Virtue Ethics: A Pluralistic View* was published with Oxford University Press in 2003. Recent work incudes *Perspectives in Role Ethics Routledge* (with Tim Dare, ed.) and a book manuscript *Target Centred Virtue Ethics* (Oxford University Press, forthcoming).

Richard Swinburne is a Fellow of the British Academy. He was professor of the philosophy of religion at the University of Oxford from 1985 until 2002. He is best known for his trilogy on the philosophy of theism (*The Coherence of Theism, The Existence of God*, and *Faith and Reason*), second editions of all of which have been published recently, and for the short "popular" book, *Is There a God?* which summarizes them. He is the author of several books, including *Responsibility and Atonement*, on the meaning and justification of central Christian doctrines. He is also known for his defense of substance dualism, developed in *Mind, Brain, and Free Will* and (in a more "popular" version) in his latest book *Are We Bodies or Souls?*

Brandon Warmke (PhD, Arizona) is assistant professor of philosophy at Bowling Green State University. He works in ethics, social philosophy, moral psychology, and political philosophy. He is the author of several philosophical and empirical papers on public discourse and moral responsibility, and over a dozen papers on forgiveness. With Justin Tosi, he is the author of *Grandstanding: The Use and Abuse of Moral Talk* (Oxford University Press, 2020). His work has been featured in *The Atlantic*, *HuffPost*, *Scientific American*, *The Guardian*, *Slate*, *The New York Times Magazine*, and *Vox*.

1

Forgiveness

An Introduction

Brandon Warmke, Dana Kay Nelkin, and Michael McKenna

We are in the midst of a rich resurgence of philosophical interest in forgiveness. This interest reflects, at least in part, a large body of new work
in psychology, several new and newsworthy cases of institutional apology
and forgiveness, and intense and increased attention to the practices surrounding responsibility, blame, and praise. While until recently the negatively valenced elements of blame and attitudes such as resentment and
indignation took center stage in discussions of responsibility practices,
there has been much new recent work on positively valenced elements,
such as praise, gratitude, and perhaps especially forgiveness. Questions
concerning forgiveness can be broadly divided into those concerning the
nature of forgiveness, and those concerning its norms, or the conditions,
if any, under which it is permissible, obligatory, forbidden, supererogatory,
good, admirable, and so on.

But before such questions can even be addressed, it is important to acknowledge that they appear to presuppose a single phenomenon picked
out by a unitary concept when it is possible that there are instead multiple
phenomena picked out by overlapping notions. In fact, there is not agreement even about exactly which cases fix the phenomenon to be investi-
gated, reinforcing the challenge to confirm that debates are real and not
merely apparent. Still, theorists have tended to agree about at least a significant set of paradigm cases, and it will help to have some cases in mind as
we go forward. Among the most often discussed are cases within ongoing
personal relationships, such as ones in which spouses who have had affairs
repent and profusely apologize and are then forgiven by their partners who
had been angry and resentful, followed by reconciliation. But forgiveness
has also been thought by many not to be confined to personal relationships.

Brandon Warmke, Dana Kay Nelkin, and Michael McKenna, *Forgiveness* In: *Forgiveness and Its Moral Dimensions*.
Edited by: Brandon Warmke, Dana Kay Nelkin, and Michael McKenna, Oxford University Press. © Oxford University Press
2021. DOI: 10.1093/oso/9780190602147.003.0001

So, for many, it makes sense to say that one can forgive the person who recklessly caused an accident on the freeway causing one to be late to pick up one's child after finding out more about the situation and reflecting on it. And moving even beyond cases of forgiveness between strangers, we find that institutional apology and forgiveness appear often at the heart of complex and complicated political relations. For example, an ongoing source of tension between Japan and Korea concerns whether there has been an adequate apology on the part of Japan for their treatment of Korean "comfort women" during World War II, and what it would take to achieve forgiveness.[1]

Now the cases of interpersonal forgiveness in which spouses have broken a promise, profusely apologized to their partners who were justifiably resentful, and were forgiven in response to their expressed remorse are almost universally agreed to be central cases of forgiveness. There is less consensus about cases that deviate in any of a whole host of ways, including, for example, those that lack initial resentment on the part of the victim or apology on the part of the offender, as well as those involving strangers or institutions like governments, as we will see. But it will be helpful to keep these different kinds of cases in mind as ones that commonly go under the label "forgiveness" and that are highlighted by many theorists as we distinguish various questions about the nature and norms of forgiveness, and introduce the chapters to follow.

The Nature of Forgiveness

What is forgiveness? The question is, as you can perhaps already see, more complicated than it might appear. We begin by highlighting some commonly accepted preconditions on forgiveness—facts that must obtain if someone is to be in a position to forgive at all. We will then move on to discuss various proposed accounts of the nature of forgiveness itself.

---

[1] Koichi Nakano, a political scientist at Sophia University in Tokyo, said the 2015 agreement was flawed because it was made between government leaders and did not include the voices of the victims. "When you are talking about victims of human rights abuses, you can't come to a resolution without their presence and consent," he said. "As long as there are people who are not convinced that the apologies are heartfelt or that the compensation is adequate, then of course the aggressor would continue to ask for forgiveness and atonement." ("Japan Balks at Calls for New Apology over "Comfort Women," *New York Times*, January 18, 2018).

Moral Badness or Wrongdoing

It is commonplace to think that to be forgiven, an agent must have done something morally bad or wrong.[2] For if one did nothing wrong, then one's conduct is *justified*. And if one's conduct is morally justified, then it cannot be forgiven. If one is morally "in the clear" as it were, there is nothing to forgive. As Margaret Holmgren puts it, "Where there is no wrongdoing, there is nothing for the injured person to forgive, although there may be much for her to accept. . . . Forgiveness is an issue only when a moral agent commits an offense, without justification, and in the absence of an exculpating excuse" (2012: 35). While Holmgren focuses on wrongdoing, it may be possible to forgive others for behavior that is merely bad, perhaps because it was motivated by morally bad motives, or because it had bad consequences. And while most philosophers have focused on forgiving people for their conduct, it may also be possible to forgive them for their moral character, for who they are (Bell 2008). The precise nature of those things for which we can be forgiven is still a matter of debate.

The objective requirement that one must have done something morally bad or wrong to be forgiven can be challenged. Suppose you believe you forgive someone for something that all relevant parties justifiably believe was morally wrong. Yet years later all parties discover that it wasn't morally wrong after all. An objective requirement on wrongdoing means that although all parties thought you had forgiven, you had not.

Are there alternatives to this objective requirement? One option is a merely subjective requirement on forgiveness: to forgive, the forgiver must believe that the forgiven has done something wrong. Indeed, virtually all parties to the literature on forgiveness affirm at least this much.[3] A mere subjective requirement would enable forgiveness to be given in the earlier case but also in any case in which we believe someone has done wrong, even if there was no wrong. A modified version of the subjective requirement might add that forgiveness itself requires only that we believe someone has done wrong, but that forgiveness is *appropriate* only when the conduct is objectively wrong. On this view, even though someone could forgive an objectively innocent person, this would not be an appropriate thing to do.

---

[2] See, for example, Murphy and Hampton (1988: 20), Holmgren (2012: 35), Haber (1991: 32), and Bash (2007: 5).

[3] See, e.g., Haber (1991) and Hieronymi (2001).

These considerations make clear that there is much work yet to be done in articulating both the specific nature of that for which one can be forgiven, and to what extent there must be objective wrongdoing in order to forgive. We will proceed on the assumption that, minimally, the forgiver must judge the forgiven to have done something morally bad or wrong.

Moral Responsibility and Blameworthiness

In addition to wrongdoing, it is common to hold that forgiveness requires that the forgiven must be morally responsible and blameworthy for her conduct.[4] In other words, to be a candidate for forgiveness, one's behavior must not be excused. In an early and important essay on forgiveness, Jeffrie Murphy wrote that "we may forgive only what is initially proper to resent, and if a person has done nothing wrong or was not responsible for what he did, there is *nothing to resent*" (1988: 20, emphasis original). According to this common assumption, if one has a valid excuse for one's conduct, then one cannot be forgiven for it. Furthermore, if a person is not a morally responsible agent at all—that is, not an agent that could act freely and responsibly, perhaps due to mental illness or injury—then she cannot be forgiven for any of her conduct. This is why forgiving very young children or the mentally disabled strikes many as out of place, a kind of category error.

As with wrongdoing, however, we might doubt whether a person needs to be morally responsible and blameworthy for conduct to be forgiven for it. Perhaps instead the forgiver only needs to believe that the wrongdoer is morally responsible and blameworthy. Indeed, most parties to the literature affirm at least this much. A subjective requirement also follows from a more general observation that forgiveness is to be distinguished from excusing. To excuse behavior involves judging that someone has done wrong, but that she is not responsible or blameworthy for it, perhaps due to nonculpable ignorance, or having been drugged or brainwashed. When we forgive, however, we continue to judge that the wrongdoer has done something for which she is morally responsible and blameworthy.[5] And even if it is possible to forgive those we falsely believe to be responsible, it may still be inappropriate in some relevant sense to do so.

[4] Holmgren (2012: 35); Murphy and Hampton (1988: 20); Haber (1991: 33).
[5] Hieronymi (2001); Allais (2008).

Furthermore, a forgiver may not merely need to judge that the wrongdoer is blameworthy; she may also be required to hold her blameworthy, by being disposed or prepared to blame her. This feature of forgiveness distinguishes forgiveness from condonation, a kind of "putting up with" bad behavior that is distinct from forgiveness (Murphy and Hampton 1988: 40; Griswold 2007: 46–47).

As we noted, it is widely assumed that, minimally, the forgiver must judge the wrongdoer to be morally responsible and blameworthy. But even this assumption can be challenged. Suppose that, as Baruch Spinoza and other modern-day "free will skeptics" have argued, no one is ever morally responsible for anything we do, even though most of us think we are responsible. If no one is free and responsible, then no one is morally blameworthy for his or her actions, and presumably, we shouldn't judge or hold people morally responsible and blameworthy for those actions either. Perhaps, then, an account of forgiveness should not require judging or holding blameworthy at all. Forgiveness can promote pro-sociality and foreclose moral protest after wrongdoing even if forgivers refrain from judging wrongdoers morally responsible and blameworthy.[6]

Standing

Who can forgive? Suppose that you are mean to your spouse. Your neighbor, who overheard your yelling, calls up to say that she forgives you for being so unkind. Is it possible your neighbor could forgive you for this? Many philosophers say no. Your neighbor, they say, lacks the standing to forgive.

We must note that the term "standing" has been used differently in the literature on forgiveness than it has been used in the literature on blame (Nelkin 2016; Warmke 2017). This can cause confusion. In the blame literature, "standing to blame" is typically taken to mean *moral standing*. To lack standing to blame means that one's blame is inappropriate. Perhaps you *could* blame a friend for repeatedly lying, but since you are also such a liar, it would be *hypocritical* for you to do so. You could not blame appropriately and therefore lack the standing to forgive. But when philosophers say someone lacks the "standing to forgive," they mean that one cannot forgive *at all*. For someone who lacks the standing to forgive, forgiveness—morally

---

[6] Pereboom (2014); see Chapter 4, this volume.

appropriate or not—is not an option. For this reason, the "standing to for-give" can be thought of as a metaphysical standing, and not a moral one. With respect to our example of the "forgiving" neighbor, the thought is not simply that the neighbor could forgive but that it would be morally inappro-priate for her to do so. Rather, it is that she cannot forgive at all because she lacks standing. Of course, we can talk about the "moral standing" to forgive as well, and we will address some questions regarding the norms of forgive-ness later in this chapter.

Who, then, has "metaphysical standing" to forgive? And how does one get it? This is a matter of debate, and we will only briefly survey the terrain here. It is sometimes claimed that only the victim (in some relevant sense of "victim") of a wrongdoing has the standing to forgive the wrongdoer for that wrong.[7] This is why, it might be thought, your neighbor lacked standing to forgive you for being unkind to your spouse: you were not the victim. A victim has *direct standing* to forgive someone when she has been directly wronged by that person. When your spouse directly wrongs you, for ex-ample, you have the direct standing to forgive her.[8]

It is controversial whether direct standing is the only way to have standing to forgive. There are arguably four other general varieties of standing. When one has *indirect standing*, she can forgive a wrongdoer for what has happened to her even though she was not directly wronged. Suppose Betty lies to you, and this causes you to be late to pick up your brother. Your brother may have indirect standing to forgive Betty, even though she did not wrong him di-rectly. One has *proxy standing* when one can forgive a wrongdoer for what she did to the victim on behalf of the victim.[9] Suppose Ted's adult daughter is killed by a drunk driver. If Ted can forgive the driver on behalf of Maria, he does so in virtue of possessing proxy standing. Even if proxy standing is possible, it is often claimed that the proxy forgiver must stand in some spe-cial relationship with the person on whose behalf he forgives.[10] *Third-party standing*, perhaps the most controversial of the group, involves the forgiver forgiving a wrongdoer for what the wrongdoer did to someone else.[11] A bit more precisely, these are scenarios in which "*A* forgives the offender *B* for

---

[7] Jeffrie Murphy defended this "victim-only" view in his early work (Murphy and Hampton 1988: 12), but he has since repudiated it (2012: 185). Walker (2013) defends the victim's exclusive right to forgive.

[8] There are several varieties of direct standing, but we will ignore them here. See Warmke (2017).

[9] Although he labels it "third party," proxy standing is what Griswold has in mind (2007: 119).

[10] Griswold (2007: 119).

[11] Pettigove (2009: 591); Walker (2013: 495).

something B did to the victim C, where A is not plausibly seen as a fellow victim, and where A forgives B on A's on behalf, not on behalf of C or anyone else who might be a victim of the wrong" (Walker 2013: 495). You might, for example, forgive your brother for being rude to your mother. Or your neighbor might call to forgive you for being unkind to your spouse. There is an ongoing debate as to whether third-party forgiveness is possible and, if so, under what conditions.[12]

The aforementioned varieties all involve standing to forgive others. But is it possible to forgive oneself? Some argue it is.[13] If so, one might need a special kind of standing. Self-forgiveness might happen in two ways. First, you might forgive yourself for something you did to yourself, say the self-infliction of a wound. This may be best understood as an interesting case of direct standing: the victim and wrongdoer just happen to be the same person. Self-forgiveness may instead involve forgiving yourself for what you have done to another, which is perhaps to be understood as a nonstandard variety of third-party forgiveness.[14]

Accounting for the standing to forgive poses a unique challenge when constructing a full theory of the nature and norms of forgiveness. Recall that "standing to blame" is used as a moral notion. One *can* blame even if one does not have the moral standing to do so appropriately. This allows theorists to give an account of the nature of blame and then explore the situations in which one's blame would be morally inappropriate, that is, when one lacks standing. "Standing to forgive," however, is not used as a moral notion, but as a metaphysical one. How, then, does a theorist account for the conditions of standing in relation to an account of the nature of forgiveness itself?

We see two main options. First, one might say that there are conditions on possessing standing to forgive, but that these restrictions are given by the constitutive conditions on forgiving itself. This approach builds standing into the nature of forgiveness. Here's one way that strategy might proceed. Suppose you thought that (1) forgiveness requires the overcoming of resentment; (2) only victims of wrongdoing can experience resentment; and (3) only victims of wrongdoing can forgive that wrongdoer. On such a view,

---

[12] For arguments against, see Walker (2013), and for arguments in favor, see Pettigrove (2009, 2012), MacLachlan (2007), and Chaplin (2019).
[13] Milam (2015).
[14] Norlock (2009).

the constitutive conditions themselves limit the class of potential forgivers. Only those who can meet the constitutive conditions therefore have the standing to forgive.

On a different approach, the class of persons who can meet the constitutive conditions on forgiveness is wider than the class of persons who have standing to forgive. A separate account is then required, detailing the conditions on the standing to forgive. Suppose you thought that forgiveness is the overcoming of hostile attitudes. Virtually anyone can do this, but not just anyone can do so and thereby forgive, it might be thought. In order to forgive, one must also have standing, and therefore a further account of standing would be required. Which of these two strategies is preferable for capturing both the standing to forgive and the constitutive conditions of forgiveness is an open question.

Thus concludes our discussion of some commonly held preconditions on forgiveness. Although there is ongoing debate, we proceed assuming, minimally, that in order to forgive, one must (1) judge that someone has done wrong; (2) judge and hold that person morally blameworthy; and (3) have standing to forgive that person.

We now turn our attention to accounts of the nature of forgiveness itself. What is to forgive? As you might imagine, there is a diversity of philosophical accounts of the nature of forgiveness. To simplify, we will package them into a handful of different approaches to the nature of forgiveness. Each of these general accounts should be thought of as a family of closely related claims about the nature of forgiveness. By necessity, and with apology, we do not canvass every extant theory, and hope our colleagues will forgive us for this.

Emotion Accounts

Emotion accounts of forgiveness are joined in their conviction that to forgive is to do something with one's emotions. This family of views traces its lineage to English philosopher Joseph Butler's two sermons on forgiveness and resentment, published in 1726[15] (although the details of that lineage have been challenged in recent years[16]). According to emotion accounts, forgiveness is thought to be, in the words of Jeffrie Murphy, "primarily a matter of how

---

[15] Butler (2017).
[16] See, e.g., Garcia (2011).

I *feel* about you (not how I treat you)" (Murphy and Hampton 1988: 21; see also Hughes 1993: 108). Since such views have, at least until recently, dominated the forgiveness literature, we will dwell on them longer than others. Defenders of emotion accounts themselves disagree about the two main aspects of the account: (1) which specific emotions are involved in forgiveness; and (2) the nature of the relevant emotional change. We briefly discuss each of these in turn.

For decades, it has been commonplace to hold that forgiveness crucially implicates *resentment*, where resentment is understood to be a negative morally reactive attitude that one experiences when one believes one has been unjustifiably wronged by someone who is morally responsible. The thought has been that forgiving a wrongdoer requires doing something with your resentment of her for what she did to you. While many philosophers still defend a resentment-based view, emotion accounts have witnessed two trends in the past decade.

First, there has been a trend toward permissiveness regarding the set of emotions that may be implicated in forgiveness. This is most clearly seen in the evolution in Jeffrie Murphy's own emotion account. While in his landmark 1988 book with Jean Hampton, he defined forgiveness narrowly as the overcoming of resentment, by the release of his 2003 book, he loosened up a bit, encouraging us to "think of forgiveness as overcoming a variety of negative feelings that one might have toward a wrongdoer—resentment, yes, but also such feelings as anger, hatred, loathing, contempt, indifference, disappointment, or even sadness" (2003: 59).

The second trend involves a dawning realization over the years that there is no consensus about how resentment is to be characterized. Some think of resentment as a "hostile feeling" (Garrard and McNaughton 2002), while others think of it as a kind of "moral protest" (Hieronymi 2001), while still others think of resentment as the paradigmatic sort of "moral anger" (Hughes 1993). Some describe resentment as a "vindictive passion" (Murphy 2003: 16). Others claim that resentment "need not entail motivation to retaliate for the wrong" (Holmgren 2012: 31). Some classify resentment as a "feeling of insult" (Blustein 2014: 33; see also Murphy and Hampton 1988: 44–45). Even among those who defend resentment-based emotion accounts, there is more diversity than first appears.

Given both the move away from *resentment*-based emotion accounts to more inclusive ones and the diversity of resentment-based accounts themselves, it will be helpful to have a way of classifying the various emotions thought to be implicated in forgiveness. We can break them down into three broad categories.

Narrow Emotionalism: Forgiveness responds to a narrow set of emotions: only "hostile retributive feelings," attitudes whose aim is to see the offender suffer for what she has done (Garrard and McNaughton 2002: 44). Examples of such emotions include malice, spite, or ill will. One can retain many other nonhostile negative emotions and still forgive.

Moderate Emotionalism: Forgiveness responds both to hostile retributive emotions and to what we may call moral anger. Some moral anger, it is thought, doesn't involve wishing that someone suffer. But this moral anger must also be dealt with in one's forgiveness. One need not overcome all negative emotions about the event in question, though. For a view in this vein, see Griswold (2007).

Expansive Emotionalism: Forgiveness responds to all negative emotions that the victim has toward the wrongdoer on account of the wrongdoing in question (Richards 1988: 79). Examples include sadness, disappointment, contempt, bitterness, and loathing (Blustein 2014; Holmgren 1993; Murphy 2003).

Emotion-based accounts say that forgiveness crucially implicates a change in emotion. But what kind of change? This, too, has been a vexed question. Many writers speak of "overcoming" resentment or other attitudes (e.g., Murphy 2003; Holmgren 1993). But others talk about forgiveness as abandoning (Richards 1988), forbearing or withdrawing (Darwall 2006), letting go (Griswold 2007), or eliminating (Lauritzen 1987) the relevant emotion(s). Some philosophers have proposed more precise explanations of *how* the emotions are overcome or otherwise dealt with. Pamela Hieronymi (2001) argues that in forgiving, resentment is overcome by revising one of the judgments that undergirds it. Jeffrey Blustein (2014) argues that forgiving involves a certain kind of forgetting which moderates or eliminates the relevant emotions. Santiago Amaya (2019) argues that forgiveness involves a process he calls emotional distancing.

In addition, some philosophers have argued that purging negative emotions, even if necessary for forgiveness, is not also sufficient. Forgiveness requires more than mere indifference to one's wrongdoer. Rather, the forgiver must also take up some kind of positive attitude toward one's wrongdoer. Jean Hampton, for example, argues that the forgiver must "reapprove" the wrongdoer (Murphy and Hampton 1988: 83), deciding to see him "in a new, more favorable light" (84), and "revising her judgement of the person himself" (85). Eve Garrard and David McNaughton argue that the forgiver, in addition to overcoming hostile attitudes, takes up a well-wishing attitude, one of good will, toward one's wrongdoer (2010). And according to Eleonore Stump (2018), the negative, blaming attitude toward one's wrongdoer can actually remain in forgiveness; to forgive, it is sufficient to love one's wrongdoer, and this is compatible with blame. In a similar vein, Jada Twedt Strabbing (2017) argues that forgiveness crucially requires openness to reconciliation with the wrongdoer, though this "openness" may not be best described as an emotion, and so may not properly be counted as an emotion account.

Setting aside the finer details, philosophers who defend emotion-based accounts tend to agree on two points. First, the change in emotion involves some kind of action or process that is done for reasons, perhaps even specifically moral reasons (Murphy 2003; Griswold 2007). Were your resentment to abate because you fell and hit your head, for example, this would not qualify as forgiveness (Horsbrugh 1974). Defenders of emotion-based views also seem to agree that the emotional change must not be only done for reasons, but with what Marilyn McCord Adams called "agent effort" (1991). Suppose you could take a pill that eliminated your resentment. Even if you took the resentment-eliminating pill for reasons ("She apologized, no reason to keep blaming her"), this kind of elimination has struck some philosophers as being of the wrong sort. It's difficult to say exactly why this couldn't be forgiveness, though. (Maybe you think it could be.) Perhaps forgiveness cannot be so easy, or it must "pass through" one's moral agency in a "deeper" way. However, perhaps it is possible to simply discover, upon waking up one day, that one has forgiven an old grievance, through no desire, effort, or intention to do so.

We must note that there is also a strand of emotion-based accounts that stresses the *forswearing* of resentment or other emotions. P. F. Strawson, for example, claimed that to forgive is, in part, to forswear resentment (1962). Sometimes in the forgiveness literature "forswearing" is conflated with "overcoming." But as early as 1991, Marilyn McCord Adams distinguished the two. She characterized the forswearing of resentment as a "deliberate act," and the overcoming of resentment, as we saw earlier, as involving "agent effort." Her idea seemed to be that one can forswear resentment by making a certain decision or commitment straightaway, but in doing so, one need not thereby overcome resentment.

Many questions about emotion-based accounts remain. Here are a few:

- Which emotions may or must be responded to or dealt with in forgiveness?
- Are emotion-based accounts of forgiveness committed to any specific account of the nature of emotion to begin with?
- What must be done with these emotions and what is the nature of this process?
- What happens if the emotions come back or flare up? Does one become unforgiven? Must one overcome them again?
- What kind of control do we have over the relevant emotions? Is this the kind of control we have over forgiveness?
- How active must a person be in bringing about forgiveness? Must one forswear one's negative attitudes, or could the requisite emotional changes occur passively, perhaps over months or years, resulting in forgiveness?

Revenge and Punishment Forbearance Accounts

Other philosophers defend views according to which forgiveness is centrally the forswearing and forbearance of revenge or punishment. Punishment forbearance views claim that "forgiveness is deliberately to refuse to punish" (Zaibert 2009: 368).[17] This might be thought of as either a necessary or sufficient constitutive condition on forgiveness.[18] Others have argued for the closely related but distinct normative claim that if you forgive someone you should not then punish her (Swinburne 1989: 87n8; Bash 2015: 53).[19] This normative claim should be assessed independently from the metaphysical or conceptual claim about the constitutive conditions on forgiveness.

---

[17] For similar views, see Enright et al. (1992: 88), Wolterstorff (2009: 203), Londey (1986: 4–5), and Russell (2016).

[18] For further discussion of this claim, see Haber (1991), Murphy (2003: 101), O'Shaughnessy (1967), Griswold (2007: 32–33), Pettigrove (2012: 117–121), and Warmke (2011, 2013).

[19] For discussion of this claim, see Tosi and Warmke (2017).

Similar accounts of forgiveness claim that forgiveness is centrally the for-swearing and forbearance of revenge. Though matters are complicated, this is how some commentators have interpreted Bishop Joseph Butler's account of forgiveness, noted earlier, found in two of his *Fifteen Sermons Preached at Rolls Chapel* (1726), "Upon Resentment" and "Upon Forgiveness of Injuries."[20] According to Charles Griswold, for example, Butler thinks that forgiveness involves the forswearing of revenge and the moderation of any excessive resentment (2007: 36).

Notice that what distinguishes these views from the emotion views discussed earlier is that they do not identify forgiveness as emotional change—they do not claim that forgiveness is, as Murphy put it, primarily a matter of how I feel about you. This is because neither punishment nor revenge as such are emotions (attitudes may be described as punitive or vengeful, but those attitudes are not the same as punishing or taking revenge). These views stress that forgiveness is primarily a matter of renouncing some treatment of the wrongdoer and then forbearing to treat the wrongdoing in those ways. Here are some additional questions:

- How should we think of the differences between revenge, punishment, and blame?
- Does Joseph Butler have a consistent view of forgiveness to begin with?
- What does it mean to forswear or forbear punishment or revenge?

Performative Accounts

All the views canvassed thus far conceive of forgiveness as more or less a pri-vate affair. Another family of approaches, however, conceive of forgiveness as something performed. According to these views, to forgive is to engage in social (or at least overt) behavior. A bit of background can bring these views into relief. In his 1991 book on forgiveness, Joram Graf Haber argued that the question "What is forgiveness?" is best answered "in the context of what speakers mean when" they say things like "I forgive you" (29, 40, 53). For Haber, the key to understanding forgiveness was wrapped up in the question of what speakers do when they say "I forgive you." It should be noted that

---

[20] Butler (2017).

Haber was not the first to focus on the performative nature of forgiveness. William Neblett (1974), Richard Swinburne (1989), and Marilyn McCord Adams (1991) articulated performative accounts, arguing that one can forgive by saying "I forgive you." But Haber was the first to construct a detailed framework for seeing how forgiveness could be a performative. He utilized the Austinian notion of illocutionary to force explain how saying "I forgive you" can be a social, communicative act that also had an effect beyond the mere utterance (i.e., the locutionary act). In addition to this mere utterance, we can perform a further, illocutionary act. For example, uttering "where is the cheese" also has the illocutionary force of asking a question. For Haber, the illocutionary force of "I forgive you" is behabitive. That is, this social act reveals to our communicant that we have taken up a certain attitudinal stance. It expresses an attitude much like "I applaud you" or "I welcome you." On Haber's own account, "I forgive you" is the clearest way to forgive, and expresses a forgiving attitude, crucially, that I've overcome my resentment or at least that I'm willing to try to do so (1991: 40).

Glen Pettigrove extended Haber's account by arguing that paradigmatically, utterances like "I forgive you" possess both behabitive and commissive force (2004, 2012). For Pettigrove, the commissive force of forgiveness commits the speaker to forswear hostile reactive attitudes and retaliation toward the wrongdoer and to treat her with an appropriate level of benevolence (2004: 385).

Not to be outdone, Brandon Warmke extended the account even further, arguing that paradigmatic cases of forgiveness possess behabitive, commissive, and declarative force (2016a, 2016b). Declaratives, to put it crudely "change reality." "I christen this ship" or "I hereby find you guilty" are examples of statements possessing declarative force when sincerely uttered by persons with the appropriate authority. On this view, to sincerely tell your wrongdoer "I forgive you" is to alter reality in some way. How does this happen, though? What part of reality is "changed"?

Here, several philosophers have relied on an analogy between the cancellation of a financial debt and moral forgiveness (Swinburne 1989; Nelkin 2013; Warmke 2016a). When you cancel someone's debt through some performative action, you give up a right to demand payment and you relieve them from a duty to repay. Debt cancellation thereby alters the operative norms of interaction. Similarly, forgiveness "alters the norms of interaction between the victim and the wrongdoer in certain characteristic ways" and so can be thought of as the exercise of a normative power (Warmke 2016b; see also Bennett 2018). For the wrongdoer, forgiveness can effect a release of certain personal obligations to the victim (e.g., to apologize, show remorse, offer restitution) (Nelkin 2013). For the victim, forgiveness relinquishes her right or license to regard or treat the wrongdoer in certain ways (e.g., ways constitutive of private or overt blame) (Warmke 2016a, 2016b). It is not clear, however, whether these norm alterations must be accomplished with an overt act or could instead be done privately. One might, for example, be able to release someone from a debt without engaging in any overt or communicative acts. And while extant performative accounts have focused on utterances like "I forgive you," some argue that forgiveness may be performed with other kinds of social acts, such as gestures or facial expressions (Swinburne 1989: 85).[21]

Here are some further questions about performative accounts:

- Can performative accounts also allow for a kind of forgiveness of the heart?
- Must all performances of forgiveness function the same way?
- Can any of the norm-altering functions of overt acts of forgiveness be accomplished privately?
- Is it possible to engage in a performative act of forgiveness yet still maintain hostile, resentful attitudes?

Monist versus Pluralist Accounts

The accounts forgiveness just surveyed might be taken as attempts to identify the one thing that is forgiveness, wherever it is found. Call these monist accounts of forgiveness. But these extant accounts need not be understood that way. Many philosophers have been impressed with the idea that forgiveness is a diverse and diffuse practice and that there is no one thing that forgiveness is. Nick Smith gives voice to this thought, writing that "notions of forgiveness seem to identify a loose constellation of interrelated meanings among various beliefs, judgments, emotions and actions" (2008: 134). Many accounts of forgiveness are plausible in their own right. Are we forced to choose the *one* thing forgiveness is? How would we go about settling that issue? However, if we conceive of forgiveness as a diverse practice, new methodological

---

[21] For more on performative accounts see Warmke (forthcoming).

possibilities emerge. According to pluralist accounts of forgiveness, the constitutive conditions on forgiveness vary from situation to situation, person to person. Indeed, there may be very little that is always the same in every case of forgiveness (Neblett 1974: 273).

A common distinction made by forgiveness pluralists is between overt modes of forgiveness and private modes of forgiveness. Marilyn McCord Adams, for example, distinguished "performative forgiveness" from "forgiveness from the heart" (1991; see also Zaibert 2009; Warmke and McKenna 2013). Forgiveness from the heart involves a process of letting go of one's own point of view (regarding the situation, one's self and/or the victim, and the offender), which will typically "involve many changes in feelings, attitudes, judgments and desires" (Adams 1991: 294–295). Performative forgiveness, however, "focuses on externals (material compensations or behavior) and the formal structures of relationships, not on inner attitudes or feelings" (294).

A pluralist account of forgiveness may be developed further by attending to the ways that moral blame is also commonly thought to be a diverse practice. Various philosophers have noted that blame may be manifested in different modes and so distinguished private blame from overt blame.[22] Private blame involves *regarding* the wrongdoer in a certain way. This might mean manifesting one of the so-called reactive attitudes, such as resentment, indignation, or disapprobation,[23] or judging that the wrongdoer has a "discredit" or "debit" in her "ledger," a negative mark that diminishes her moral standing.[24] Private blame therefore involves adopting a blaming attitude (whatever that attitude comes to) toward someone, but concealing (perhaps intentionally, perhaps not) the characteristic outward behavioral manifestations of that attitude.

Sometimes, however, we do not keep our blame to ourselves. We may not merely *regard* the wrongdoer in a certain way; we may also *express* how we regard the wrongdoer. In doing so, one can engage in overt blame. Overt blame is therefore blame's outward manifestation, for it involves adopting a blaming attitude *and* making it manifest in one's conduct. But not all overt blame is, as it were, directed at the blamed party. One might, for example, go out of one's way to avoid the wrongdoer, which is an outward manifestation

---

[22] See Coates and Tognazzini (2012), Haji (1998), McKenna (2012), Wallace (1994), and Zimmerman (1988).

[23] See, e.g., Fischer and Ravizza (1998), Russell (1995), Fischer (1994), Wallace (1994), and Strawson (1962).

[24] See Zimmerman (1988: 38).

of a blaming attitude, but not an expression of blame communicated directly to the wrongdoer. Or perhaps one blames overtly in the absence of the wrongdoer by complaining about the wrongdoer's behavior to a third party, speaking ill of her in any manner of ways: "Ralph is such a pig for telling that joke; who does he think he is, anyway!?" Seeing that we can express our blame without directing it at the blamed party, McKenna (2013) introduced a further mode of blaming, what he called *directed blame*. Directed blame is aimed at addressing the blamed party. Examples of directed blaming might include reproach, censure, shunning, outright denunciation, and other expressions of anger, hostility, or disapproval, such as a disapproving facial grimace, a gentle reprimand, or a heartfelt request for apology or reparations.

These resources developed by McKenna and others can help us make sense of the diversity of our forgiveness practices. Just like there is a private mode of blame, there is a private mode of forgiveness. Private forgiveness—much like Adams's forgiveness from the heart—involves taking up a forgiving attitude toward the wrongdoer. And just like blame can be overtly expressed, so can forgiveness. In some cases, one takes up a forgiving attitude *and* overtly expresses one's forgiveness directly to the wrongdoer (by saying "I forgive you," for instance). We can call these cases of *directed forgiveness*. In other cases, we may take up a forgiving attitude and overtly express our forgiveness, but not to the wrongdoer herself (perhaps because she is dead or otherwise absent). Call these cases of indirect forgiveness. And finally, hollow forgiveness involves engaging in overt aspects of forgiving, but lacking in, to some significant degree or another, the interior aspects of forgiveness.[25] Hollow forgiveness, too, can be directed either at the wrongdoer or instead toward others. This division of forgiveness practices into modes is one way to countenance the pluralism of forgiveness. But even within these modes, forgiveness can be diverse. There may be, for instance, distinct ways to forgive "from the heart." A few other issues include:

- What are the theoretical and practical costs and benefits of both monist and pluralist views?
- What philosophical methodology should be employed to settle disputes about what forgiveness is?
- On monist accounts, how are we to explain the apparent diversity of forgiveness practices?

[25] The term "hollow forgiveness" is from Baumeister et al. (1998).

- On pluralist accounts, what fixes the "paradigmatic" cases? If there are no such cases, how do we circumscribe the practice of forgiveness at all?

The Norms of Forgiveness

What is the moral status of forgiveness? Answers to this question depend in no small part on what you take forgiveness to be, as well as your preferred normative ethical theory. Here, we will set these matters aside and focus on one of the primary debates regarding the morality of forgiveness. We will then look at a few skeptics of the morality of forgiveness.

Let's use the term "positive moral status" to refer to an instance of forgiveness that is morally permissible, morally good, morally virtuous, morally right, or morally supererogatory. Debates regarding when an individual instance of forgiveness has positive moral status have generally been about whether certain conditions have been met. These conditions are usually divided into two kinds. To simplify matters, we will focus on what Charles Griswold (2007) calls the "paradigmatic scene," in which a victim of wrongdoing forgives the wrongdoer for a direct wrong done against the victim by the wrongdoer. *Victim-dependent* conditions require that the victim of wrongdoing meet certain conditions if her forgiveness is to have positive moral status. *Wrongdoer-dependent* conditions require that the wrongdoer meet certain conditions if one is to appropriately forgive her. We can say a bit about each of these kinds of conditions.

It is commonly accepted that the victim must meet certain conditions if her forgiveness is to have positive moral status. Typically, these conditions focus on the victim's motivating reasons for forgiving. Jeffrie Murphy, for example, writes that the "acceptable grounds for forgiveness must be compatible with self-respect, respect for others as moral agents, and respect for the rules of morality and the moral order" (1988: 24; see also Haber 1991: 90; Garrard and McNaughton 2011: 105). What specific kinds of motivating reasons qualify is a matter of continuing debate. Other philosophers argue that the victim must go through a certain kind of process that ensures her forgiveness is compatible with self-respect, including, but not limited to, recovering her self-esteem and coming to fully appreciate the nature of the wrongdoing and why it was wrong (Holmgren 1993: 343–344).

More contentious is the claim that the wrongdoer must meet certain conditions if the victim's forgiveness is to have positive moral status. Some argue, for example, that the wrongdoer must apologize, repent, or have a change of heart (Haber 1991; Wilson 1988; see also Griswold 2007: 47–51; Murphy 2003: 36). Two kinds of reasons are commonly given for this requirement. First, some claim that forgiving a wrongdoer who hasn't done these things evinces a failure to take the wrongdoing seriously enough. By forgiving the unrepentant, we in effect condone the wrongdoing (Kolnai 1973: 95–96). Second, forgiving an unapologetic and unrepentant wrongdoer is thought to evince a lack of self-respect. In such cases, the victim will often "underestimate their own worth and fail to take their projects and entitlements seriously enough" (Novitz 1998: 299; see also Murphy 1982: 505; Griswold 2007: 64–65). In response, however, some philosophers have argued that there is nothing necessarily morally untoward about forgiving an unapologetic and unrepentant wrongdoer (Garrard and McNaughton 2002, 2011; Holmgren 1993: 341; Pettigrove 2004, 2012).

Although the consensus of both philosophers and the wider culture has been that forgiveness is a virtue and that forgiving is intrinsically good, not everyone agrees. For some, the value of forgiveness is merely remedial. The victim's attitudes and actions with which forgiveness deals—guilt, resentment, bitterness, rancor, vengefulness, hatred—are, for one reason or another, unbefitting responses in the first place. So forgiveness may be good, but only in the life of someone who has already erred in how she responded to wrongdoing. It has been argued that so-called perfectionists like Plato, Aristotle, the Stoics, and the Epicureans take this approach to the ethics of forgiveness (Griswold 2007: 2–14).[26] Nietzsche, too, can be read as a critic of forgiveness, involving as it does a commitment to a slave morality that valorizes the victims and the weak as they overcome their emotional reactions to having their will to power frustrated by others (Griswold 2007: 15; Blustein 2014: 23–30). Martha Nussbaum (2016) has argued that not only does forgiveness respond to an already normatively problematic attitude (i.e., resentment), it also takes on in its "transactional" form a kind of morally suspect down-ranking: the victim demands apology and humility from the wrongdoer, thereby bringing her low until the victim is ready to move on from her anger. According to John Kekes, "when blaming wrongdoers is reasonable, there is no reason to forgive them; and when

[26] See also Griswold and Konstan (2011).

blaming them is unreasonable, there is nothing to forgive" (2009: 488; see also Kolnai 1973; Zaibert 2009; Hallich 2013). If someone has done nothing blameworthy, then "neither blame nor forgiveness is appropriate" (2009: 501). However, if someone has done something blameworthy, then "blame [of the right kind and degree] is appropriate and forgiveness is not" (2009: 501). Either way, Kekes claims, to forgive would be to do something morally inappropriate.

We have only scratched the surface regarding the norms of forgiveness. For an entire edited collection on this topic, see Fricke (2011). Here is a sampling of some remaining questions:

- Is forgiveness intrinsically or instrumentally valuable? If so, why?
- How can one know whether, in a particular instance, forgiveness is the right thing to do?
- Is forgiveness ever a duty or obligation? Can a wrongdoer ever have a right to be forgiven?
- Is being forgiving a moral virtue? If so, in what does that virtue consist?
- What is the relationship between forgiveness and other alleged virtues, such as love, hope, justice, and generosity?

This Volume

This book contains entirely new chapters on forgiveness by some of the world's leading moral philosophers. Some contributors have been writing about forgiveness for decades. Others have taken the opportunity here to develop their thinking about forgiveness they broached in other work. For some contributors, this is their first time stepping into the forgiveness literature. While all the contributions address core questions about the nature and norms of forgiveness, they also collectively break new ground by raising entirely new questions, offering original proposals and arguments, and making connections to what have until now been treated as separate areas within philosophy.

Three chapters approach questions about the nature and norms of forgiveness by focusing in very different ways on the connection between forgiveness to blame and blaming attitudes that are meant to be renounced or replaced or eliminated in forgiveness. Each offers a nonstandard account of such attitudes, while proposing new ways of thinking about forgiveness.

In "The Forgiven," David Shoemaker argues for a Copernican Revolution in how we theorize about forgiveness. Many philosophers focus on the for-giver and then theorize what it means for a forgiver to overcome or forswear resentment. But there is widespread disagreement about what resentment is. These disagreements ramify when theorists use resentment to tell us about the nature of both blame and its resolution in forgiveness. Shoemaker instead proposes that we start with an account of what it takes to be successfully *forgiven*. This approach, he argues, promises to yield several more determinate conclusions about the enterprise, including about (a) when the withdrawal of blame and forgiveness is appropriate and why; (b) the nature of the hard feelings that paradigm forgiveness withdraws; (c) why judgment is super-fluous to this blaming and forgiving exchange; and (d) why resentment has been the wrong core blaming component to lean on all along. He uses these resources to propose a tidy solution to a famous puzzle about the relation be-tween forgiveness, excusing, and responsibility, explaining why forgiveness is fitting when it is.

In "Fitting Attitudes and Forgiveness," Glen Pettigrove offers an extended reflection on the relationship between wrongdoing, resentment, and forgive-ness, while focusing on the role that the notion of fittingness has played in the debate. Many philosophers hold that the appropriate response to wrong-doing is anger or resentment, an assumption that has been thought to lead to paradox, or at the least a challenge to explain how forgiveness could be justified if it is the foreswearing of an emotion that by assumption is fitting. One way such a claim might be defended would appeal to a fitting attitude account of value. Fitting attitude accounts are built around the intuitive link between certain attitudes or emotions and their corresponding objects: there is a connection between love and the lovable, shame and the shameful, de-light and the delightful. Pettigrove argues that a fitting attitude account of the link between resentment and wrongdoing is more complicated than one might have thought. The complications that emerge, Pettigrove argues, prove illuminating both for our thinking about forgiveness and for our thinking about fittingness, and they offer an intriguing way of meeting the challenge of justifying forgiveness that includes expanding our sights well beyond resentment.

In "Forgiveness as Renunciation of Moral Protest," Derk Pereboom also draws our attention to the notion of blame at issue in theorizing about for-giveness. He begins with an account of blame as moral protest, in stark con-trast to traditional accounts that take anger and related emotions as central to the blame that is relevant to forgiveness. In turn, forgiveness is understood as the renunciation of blame, so understood. In developing this account, Pereboom finds common ground with emotion views that take forgiveness to be the foreswearing of blame, while also accommodating commitments of norm-changing views, since what is foresworn is blame as protest, in particular. Finally, he is able to make room for forgiveness in a world in which no one is a free agent and so no one can be blameworthy in a sense that involves desert, thereby addressing what has been seen to be a significant disadvantage of free will skepticism, namely, that it would be a world where forgiveness would be impossible.

In "Forgiveness and Freedom to Do Otherwise," Ishtiyaque Haji defends the opposite conclusion from Pereboom's and, in a very different way, turns our attention to the largely unexplored conceptual terrain between forgiveness and free will. He argues for a surprising conclusion: forgiveness requires that the forgiven have alternative possibilities—with respect to at least some actions, the forgiven can do otherwise. In developing his argument, Haji appeals to commitments of norm-changing accounts of forgiveness, and in particular to the idea that forgivers change the status of wrongdoers' obligations incurred in virtue of their wrongdoing. If this is correct, and obligations require alternative possibilities, then forgiving presupposes that forgivers have alternative possibilities, at least with respect to the obligations they incur as a result of wrongdoing. Given that Haji takes free agency to be having such alternatives, it follows that our genuinely forgiving entails a rejection of free will skepticism.

In "Forgiving as a Performative Utterance," Richard Swinburne also defends a kind of norm-changing account of forgiveness, but which differs from those to which Haji appeals in some ways, including by being intimately connected to a religious framework. Swinburne contends that while saying "I forgive you" may sometimes constitute a report of a mental state (e.g., that you no longer resent someone's wrong actions), more often, he thinks, it is a performative utterance in the sense that it makes something (other than itself) the case. On his view, performative forgiveness effects the cancellation of a certain kind of debt between persons. The sense of forgiveness as performative utterance, Swinburne claims, is primary and a morally more important kind of forgiveness. Swinburne then argues that the Christian theory of how the life, death, and Resurrection of Jesus made God's forgiveness available to humans can be made sense of according to this analysis of forgiveness.

In "Institutional Apologies and Forgiveness," Angela Smith addresses the thorny issue of institutional apology and forgiveness. Many governments, universities, corporations, and other institutions have issued public apologies for the roles they played in instances of serious historical injustice. These apologies are particularly interesting in the case of wrongs that occurred in the distant past against individuals who are no longer living, as one might have doubts about the conceptual and moral intelligibility of such apologies. What is the point? Smith offers a general account of the nature and function of apologies in ordinary interpersonal contexts, and the role such apologies typically play in laying the groundwork for interpersonal forgiveness and reconciliation. Her account, like Pereboom's, recognizes a central role for the attitude of protest. She then argues that this general account can be extended to make sense of the notion of university apologies for historical wrongdoing and sketches an account of the nature of institutional forgiveness.

Several other chapters take on normative questions about whether forgiveness is necessarily gift-like, and thus always discretionary, whether it is ever prohibited, and whether it is required in general (or at least whether there are always strong pro tanto reasons for forgiving). These chapters start with commitments to emotion theories of one type or another, but they vary greatly in just which emotions and judgments they build into their accounts of forgiveness.

In "*The Sunflower*: Guilt, Forgiveness, and Reconciliation," Eleonore Stump draws upon Simon Wiesenthal's book *The Sunflower: On the Possibility and Limits of Forgiveness* to motivate her reflections on the relationships among guilt, forgiveness, and reconciliation. She argues that while love and forgiveness are morally obligatory after being wronged, reconciliation with the wrongdoer is not. And this is so even in cases of the most egregious wrongs, such as those committed by Nazi soldiers during World War II. At least in cases of very serious wrongdoing, forgiveness and reconciliation can therefore come apart. One can love and forgive one's wrongdoer without thereby flouting any moral obligations by refusing to reconcile with them. Furthermore, Stump argues, contrary to many philosophers, that repentance, reparation, and penance are not necessary for morally appropriate forgiveness. Nor, she claims, are they sufficient for the removal of guilt.

Addressing the very same atrocities, long-time collaborators Eve Garrard and David McNaughton turn their attention in "Forgiving Evil" to the question of whether it is morally *permissible* to forgive people for such evil actions, let alone required. In addressing this normative question, their paper explores both the nature of evil and the nature of forgiveness. Extant theories of evil, they argue, neither preclude nor legitimate forgiveness. Yet, drawing upon their own account of forgiveness as the overcoming of hostile attitudes, Garrard and McNaughton argue that we have reasons of solidarity to forgive evildoers, and hence that it's morally legitimate to do so. This places them in a middle ground of sorts between permissibility and obligation.

In "Forgiveness, Self-Respect, and Humility," Margaret Holmgren also defends the strong conclusion that it is always desirable and appropriate from a moral point of view for a victim who has sufficiently completed the process of addressing the wrong to forgive her offender, regardless of whether the offender repents and regardless of what he has done. She develops a view she has defended in past work, but here she focuses on a pressing problem for it, namely, that a state of unconditional genuine forgiveness can be very difficult to achieve, especially in cases in which the wrong perpetrated against us is serious. To address this difficulty, Holmgren examines some of the virtues that come into play in attaining a state of unconditional genuine forgiveness, specifically on the virtues of self-respect and humility. While these two virtues may seem initially to be opposed to one another, Holmgren argues that when they are properly understood, they are fully compatible with one another. Further, they each have significant roles to play in the process of forgiving one's offender.

In "Forgiveness as a Virtue of Universal Love," Christine Swanton draws on a variety of resources to argue that the virtue of forgiveness is, as Immanuel Kant would put it, a virtue of universal love. This means that the virtue of forgiveness, like other virtues of universal love, enjoins forms of coming close as opposed to the distance-keeping of respect. Swanton then shows how the virtue of forgiveness is to be distinguished from other forms of universal love (such as beneficence) and, appealing to Aristotle's so-called doctrine of the mean, offers a way of thinking about the relationship between the virtue of forgiveness, on the one hand, and processes or individual acts of forgiveness, on the other.

Departing from the strong conclusion that forgiveness is obligatory, while also appealing to Kant, Lucy Allais aims to capture the idea that forgiveness is instead discretionary and gift-like in "Frailty and Forgiveness: Forgiveness for Humans." Here she brings together an account of human frailty and the nature of agency inspired by Kant and an account of the reactive attitudes drawn from P. F. Strawson to resolve a persistent worry about forgiveness, namely, that it is committed to a kind of paradox. The paradox runs as follows: on the one hand, if a wrongdoer is blameworthy, a forgiving attitude toward her is not justified. On the other hand, if a wrongdoer no longer warrants resentment and blame, then forgiveness is simply the appropriate response to take and is in no sense discretionary, praiseworthy, or generous. In short, forgiveness is either unjustified or trivial. Allais, drawing from Kant and Strawson, constructs an account of a change of heart that, when put at the center of forgiveness, avoids the paradox while doing justice to central features of forgiveness and its role.

Finally, in "Forgiveness and Consequences," Richard Arneson sets out to do what, to our knowledge, no philosopher has attempted: explore the norms of forgiveness from an explicitly act-consequentialist normative ethical theory. As should be evident from our survey thus far, most approaches to the norms of forgiveness have been deontological, virtue-theoretic, or at least nonconsequentialist. Arneson defends the commonsense thought that when it comes to the norms of forgiveness, what one should do is act for the best. In addition to defending this act-consequentialist view, Arneson articulates and defends what he calls the "spare account" of forgiveness. Whether the spare account is the right way to think about the nature of forgiveness, argues Arneson, the act-consequentialist will hold that whatever forgiving turns out to be, one should forgive just in case doing so will bring about the best consequences.

References

Adams, Marilyn McCord, 1991, "Forgiveness: A Christian Model," *Faith and Philosophy* 8(3): 277–304.

Allais, Lucy, 2008, "Wiping the Slate Clean: The Heart of Forgiveness," *Philosophy and Public Affairs* 36(1): 33–68.

Amaya, Santiago, 2019, "Forgiveness as Emotional Distancing," *Social Philosophy and Policy* 36(1): 6–26.

Austin, J. L. (1962) 1975, *How to Do Things with Words*, 2nd ed., J. O. Urmson and Marina Sbisá (eds.), Cambridge, MA: Harvard University Press (1st ed.).

Bash, Anthony, 2007, *Forgiveness and Christian Ethics*, Cambridge: Cambridge University Press.

Bash, Anthony, 2015, *Forgiveness: A Theology*, Eugene, OR: Cascade Books.

Baumeister, Roy F., Julie Juola Exline, and Kristin L. Sommer, 1998, "The Victim Role, Grudge Theory, and Two Dimensions of Forgiveness," in *Dimensions of Forgiveness: Psychological Research and Theological Forgiveness*, Everett Worthington, Jr. (ed.), West Conshohocken, PA: Templeton Press, pp. 79–104.

Bell, Macalester, 2008, "Forgiving Someone for Who They Are (and Not Just What They've Done)," *Philosophy and Phenomenological Research* 77(3): 625–658.

Bennett, Christopher, 2018, "The Alteration Thesis: Forgiveness as a Normative Power," *Philosophy & Public Affairs* 46(2): 207–233.

Blustein, Jeffrey M., 2014, *Forgiveness and Remembrance: Remembering Wrongdoing in Personal and Public Life*, New York: Oxford University Press.

Butler, Joseph, 2017, *Fifteen Sermons and Other Writings on Ethics*, David McNaughton (ed.), Oxford: Oxford University Press.

Coates, Justin D., and Neal A. Tognazzini, 2012, *Blame: Its Nature and Norms*, Oxford: Oxford University Press.

Chaplin, Rosalind, 2019, "Taking It Personally: Third-Party Forgiveness, Close Relationships, and the Standing to Forgive," in *Oxford Studies in Normative Ethics*, Mark Timmons (ed.), Vol. 9. New York: Oxford University Press, pp. 73–94.

Darwall, Stephen, 2006, *The Second-Person Standpoint: Morality, Respect, and Accountability*, Cambridge, MA: Harvard University Press.

Enright, Robert D., David L. Eastin, Sandra Golden, Issidoros Sarinopoulos, and Suzanne Freedman, 1992, "Interpersonal Forgiveness within the Helping Profession: An Attempt to Resolve Differences of Opinion," *Counseling and Values* 36(2): 84–103.

Fischer, John Martin, 1994, *The Metaphysics of Free Will*, Oxford: Oxford University Press.

Fischer, John Martin, and Martin Ravizza, 1998, *Responsibility and Control: A Theory of Moral Responsibility*, Cambridge: Cambridge University Press.

Fricke, Christel (ed.), 2011, *The Ethics of Forgiveness*, New York: Routledge.

Garcia, Ernesto V., 2011, "Bishop Butler on Forgiveness and Resentment," *Philosophers' Imprint* 11(10): 1–19.

Garrard, Eve, and David McNaughton, 2002, "In Defence of Unconditional Forgiveness," *Proceedings of the Aristotelian Society* 103(1): 39–60.

Garrard, Eve, and David McNaughton, 2010, *Forgiveness*, Durham, NC: Acumen.

Garrard, Eve, and David McNaughton, 2011, "Conditional Unconditional Forgiveness," in Fricke 2011, pp. 97–106.

Griswold, Charles L., 2007, *Forgiveness: A Philosophical Exploration*, New York: Cambridge University Press.

Griswold, Charles, and David Konstan, eds., 2001, *Ancient Forgiveness: Classical, Judaic, Christian*, Cambridge: Cambridge University Press.

Haber, Joram Graf, 1991, *Forgiveness*, Lanham, MD: Rowman and Littlefield.

Haji, Ishtiyaque, 1998, *Moral Appraisability: Puzzles, Proposals, and Perplexities*, Oxford: Oxford University Press.

Hallich, Oliver, 2013, "Can the Paradox of Forgiveness Be Dissolved?" *Ethical Theory and Moral Practice* 16(5): 999–1017.

Hieronymi, Pamela, 2001, "Articulating an Uncompromising Forgiveness," *Philosophy and Phenomenological Research* 62(3): 529–555.

Holmgren, Margaret R., 1993, "Forgiveness and the Intrinsic Value of Persons," *American Philosophical Quarterly* 30(4): 341–352.

Holmgren, Margaret R., 2012, *Forgiveness and Retribution: Responding to Wrongdoing*, Cambridge: Cambridge University Press.

Horsbrugh, H. J. N., 1974, "Forgiveness," *Canadian Journal of Philosophy* 4(2): 269–282.

Hughes, Paul M., 1993, "What Is Involved in Forgiving?" *Journal of Value Inquiry* 27(3): 331–340.

Kekes, John, 2009, "Blame versus Forgiveness," *The Monist* 92(4): 488–506.

Kolnai, Aurel, 1973–1974, "Forgiveness," *Proceedings of the Aristotelian Society* 74: 91–106.

Lauritzen, Paul, 1987, "Forgiveness: Moral Prerogative or Religious Duty?" *Journal of Religious Ethics* 15(2): 141–154.

Londey, David, 1986, "Can God Forgive Us Our Trespasses?" *Sophia* 25(2): 4–10.

MacLachlan, Alice, 2007, "In Defense of Third-Party Forgiveness," in *The Moral Psychology of Forgiveness*, Kate Norlock (ed.), Lanham, MD: Rowman & Littlefield.

McKenna, Michael, 2012, *Conversation and Responsibility*, Oxford: Oxford University Press.

McKenna, Michael, 2013, "Directed Blame and Conversation," in *Blame: Its Nature and Norms*, Justin Coates and Neal A. Tognazzini (eds.), New York: Oxford University Press, pp. 201–218.

Milam, Per-Erik, 2015, "How Is Self-Forgiveness Possible?" *Pacific Philosophical Quarterly* 96(1): 49–69.

Murphy, Jeffrie G., 1982, "Forgiveness and Resentment," *Midwest Studies in Philosophy* 7: 503–516.

Murphy, Jeffrie G., 2003, *Getting Even: Forgiveness and Its Limits*, New York: Oxford University Press.

Murphy, Jeffrie G., 2012, *Punishment and the Moral Emotions*, New York: Oxford University Press.

Murphy, Jeffrie G., and Jean Hampton, 1988, *Forgiveness and Mercy*, Cambridge: Cambridge University Press.

Neblett, William, 1974, "Forgiveness and Ideals," *Mind* 83(330): 269–275.

Nelkin, Dana Kay, 2013, "Freedom and Forgiveness," in Haji and Caouette 2013, pp. 165–188.

Nelkin, Dana Kay, 2016, "Blame," in *The Routledge Companion to Free Will*, Kevin Timpe, Neil Levy, and Meghan Griffith (eds.), New York: Routledge, pp. 600–611.

Norlock, Kathryn J., 2009, "Why Self-Forgiveness Needs Third-Party Forgiveness," in *Forgiveness: Probing the Boundaries*, David White and Stephen Schulman (eds.), Oxford: Inter-Disciplinary Press, pp. 17–30.

Novitz, David, 1998, "Forgiveness and Self-Respect," *Philosophy and Phenomenological Research* 58(2): 299–315.

Nussbaum, Martha, 2016, *Anger and Forgiveness: Resentment, Generosity, Justice*, New York: Oxford University Press.

O'Shaughnessy, R. J., 1967, "Forgiveness," *Philosophy* 42(162): 336–352.

Pereboom, Derk, 2014, *Free Will, Agency, and Meaning in Life*, Oxford: Oxford University Press.

Pettigrove, Glen, 2004, "The Forgiveness We Speak: The Illocutionary Force of Forgiving," *The Southern Journal of Philosophy* 42(3): 371–392.

Pettigrove, Glen, 2009, "The Standing to Forgive," *The Monist* 92(4): 583–603.

Pettigrove, Glen, 2012, *Forgiveness and Love*, Oxford: Oxford University Press.

Richards, Norvin, 1988, "Forgiveness," *Ethics* 99(1): 77–97.

Russell, Luke, 2016, "Forgiving While Punishing," *Australasian Journal of Philosophy* 94(4): 704–718.

Russell, Paul, 1995, *Freedom and Moral Sentiment. Hume's Way of Naturalizing Responsibility*, Oxford: Oxford University Press.

Smith, Nick, 2008, *I Was Wrong: The Meanings of Apologies*, Cambridge: Cambridge University Press.

Strabbing, Jada Twedt, 2017, "Divine Forgiveness and Reconciliation," *Faith and Philosophy* 34(3): 272–297.

Strawson, P. F., 1962, "Freedom and Resentment," *Proceedings of the British Academy*, 48: 1–25. Reprinted in 2003, *Free Will* (2nd ed.), Gary Watson (ed.), Oxford: Oxford University Press, pp. 72–93.

Stump, Eleonore, 2018, *Atonement*, Oxford: Oxford University Press.

Swinburne, Richard, 1989, *Responsibility and Atonement*, New York: Oxford University Press.

Tosi, Justin, and Brandon Warmke, 2017, "Punishment and Forgiveness," in *Routledge Handbook of Criminal Justice Ethics*, Jonathan Jacobs and Jonathan Jackson (eds.), New York: Routledge, pp. 203–216.

Walker, Margaret Urban, 2013, "Third Parties and the Social Scaffolding of Forgiveness," *Journal of Religious Ethics* 41(3): 495–512.

Wallace, R. Jay, 1994, *Responsibility and the Moral Sentiments*, Cambridge, MA: Harvard University Press.

Warmke, Brandon, 2011, "Is Forgiveness the Deliberate Refusal to Punish?" *Journal of Moral Philosophy* 8(4): 613–620.

Warmke, Brandon, 2013, "Two Arguments Against the Punishment-Forbearance Account of Forgiveness," *Philosophical Studies* 165(3): 915–920.

Warmke, Brandon, 2016a, "The Economic Model of Forgiveness," *Pacific Philosophical Quarterly* 97(4): 570–589.

Warmke, Brandon, 2016b, "The Normative Significance of Forgiveness," *Australasian Journal of Philosophy* 94(4): 687–703.

Warmke, Brandon, 2017, "God's Standing to Forgive," *Faith and Philosophy* 34(4): 381–402.

Warmke, Brandon, forthcoming, "Performative Accounts of Forgiveness," in *Routledge Handbook of Forgiveness*, Robert Enright and Glen Pettigrove (eds.).

Warmke, Brandon, and Michael McKenna, 2013, "Moral Responsibility, Forgiveness, and Conversation," in Haji and Caouette 2013, pp. 189–212.

Wilson, John, 1988, "Why Forgiveness Requires Repentance," *Philosophy* 63(246): 534–535.

Wolterstorff, Nicholas, 2009, "Jesus and Forgiveness," in *Jesus and Philosophy: New Essays*, Paul K. Moser (ed.), Cambridge: Cambridge University Press, pp. 215–223.

Zaibert, Leo, 2009, "The Paradox of Forgiveness," *Journal of Moral Philosophy* 6(3): 365–393.

Zimmerman, Michael, 1988, *An Essay on Moral Responsibility*, Lanham, MD: Rowman and Littlefield.

2

The Forgiven

David Shoemaker

According to most responsibility theorists, for a response to a personal offense to count as *blame*—at least in its paradigm form as directed at and
expressed to an offender—it must include an emotional component, and this
is almost always taken to be resentment.[1] To understand the nature, reach,
and ultimate resolution of blame, then, it has seemed natural to start theorizing by providing an analysis of resentment. The most familiar story about
it goes as follows. Resentment is an angry emotional response to an offender
containing a constitutive judgment, a judgment about the responsibility,
wrongdoing, or threatening character of the offender.[2] Resenting an offender
is appropriate when its constitutive judgment is true. To the extent that you
care about how others treat you, and you care about morality generally, when
someone violates morality's tenets with respect to you, your triggered resentment expresses that caring (see, e.g., Franklin 2013; Wallace 2010: 323–324;
Wallace 2013: 230). This is blame.

Unfortunately, there are numerous conflicting accounts of both the nature of resentment and its function. Start with its nature. Some think of resentment as an essentially *moral* reactive attitude (Wallace), but some do
not (Rawls 1971: sec 73; Strawson 1962). Margaret Holmgren claims that resentment involves a general "feeling of moral anger" that can run the gamut
from "mild righteous anger" to "righteous hatred" (Holmgren 2012: 30).
Eve Garrard and David McNaughton understand resentment as characteristically involving "hostile feelings" (2002: 44), which typically include
one's "wishing harm to someone" who has wronged you and "relishing the
discomfort and pain that he suffers" (Garrard and McNaughton 2010: 23).
But contrast this account with that of Judith Boss: "[R]esentment is not the

[1] It's easier to note the main exceptions than present the long list of theorists advocating such a
view: Sher 2006 and Scanlon 2008.
[2] See, e.g., Wallace 1994; Hieronymi 2001; D'Arms and Jacobson 2003; Darwall 2006; McKenna
2012; and many others.

David Shoemaker, *The Forgiven* In: *Forgiveness and Its Moral Dimensions.* Edited by: Brandon Warmke,
Dana Kay Nelkin, and Michael McKenna, Oxford University Press. © Oxford University Press 2021.
DOI: 10.1093/oso/9780190602147.003.0002

same as vindictiveness or a desire to 'get even' or to retaliate, as many people assume" (Boss 1997: 236). Charles Griswold describes resentment as "a reactive as well as retributive passion that instinctively seeks to exact a due measure of punishment" (2007: 39). Jeffrey Blustein describes resentment as being a member of a class of attitudes that are "feelings of insult" (Blustein 2014: 33). Given all of these different characterizations, it is thus surprising that Holmgren claims in her 2012 work that there is very little disagreement about the nature of resentment![3]

What does resentment do or aim at? Here, too, there is plenty of disagreement. Some take it to be a *protest* (Hieronymi 2001, 2004; Smith 2013; Talbert 2012); others take it to be a kind of *demand* (Darwall 2006; Strawson 2003; Wallace 1994; Walker 2006; Watson 2004; Shoemaker 2007); others take it to be an *invitation to reply* (Macnamara 2013); and still others take it to play a *conversational* role (McKenna 2012). And even within these camps there is little agreement over, for example, what precisely blame protests *against* or what it is a demand *for*.

The numerous disagreements yielded by the front-end investigation of blame's nature and function ramify when the results of these investigations are deployed in theoretical treatments of blame's resolution at the back end of interpersonal exchanges, that is, when people withdraw blame in forgiveness. But if we cannot agree on what resentment's nature or function is, we are going to have even more of a problem agreeing what appropriately dissolves it.

What has gotten us into this mess, I suggest, is that blame theorists have put all of their eggs into the resentment basket on the front end of the blaming exchange.[4] They have assumed that resentment is the paradigmatic blaming attitude, and then they lean on their theoretical treatments of resentment to work out the nature of the rest of the blame-to-forgiveness interpersonal exchange. But as these problems suggest, we cannot squeeze so much out of resentment; indeed, it has been wrung dry. In this chapter, therefore, I outline a fresh approach to these issues by starting at the *back end* of

---

[3] Brandon Warmke (2015) makes this point, too, and I'm grateful to him for drawing my attention to many of these conflicting sources as well as to his article, which in many respects anticipates some of the motivation for the present chapter.

[4] They also occasionally spend time leaning on indignation and guilt, I hasten to add, but these are almost invariably treated as parasitic on—mere targeting variants of—resentment. Resentment is generally thought to be about a victim's second-personal response to someone who has wronged her, indignation is thought of as the third-personal form of resentment, apt on behalf of someone else who has been wronged, and guilt is thought of as the first-personal form of resentment, apt at oneself for having wronged someone else. But resentment is the emotion nearly all theorists start with.

the directed blaming exchange, namely, the point at which one's hard feelings toward someone for what that person did to one (or the attitudes the person expressed to one) are appropriately withdrawn in forgiveness.[5] In particular, I will focus on paradigm instances of what it takes to be appropriately *forgiven*. This approach may reveal fruit we cannot find by leaning on an understanding of resentment at the front end of the blaming exchange, including (a) when the withdrawal of hard feelings and the move to forgiveness are appropriate and why; (b) the nature of the hard feelings that paradigm forgiveness withdraws; (c) why judgments (about wrongdoing, responsibility, and/ or threats, say) are superfluous to this blaming and forgiving exchange; and (d) why resentment has been the wrong paradigm blaming attitude to lean on all along. This is a lot of fruit, so let's get picking.

Giving Up Blame and the Puzzle of Forgiveness

Suppose someone injures you, and you immediately respond to the injurer with "hard feelings" (the phrase I will use to avoid begging any questions about the nature of emotional blame). You might appropriately give up this blaming attitude were you to find out, first, that the injurer was ineligible for blame generally, for example, if he were a bear or a baby, or if he had a severe mental illness. Second, you might aptly give up your hard feelings were you to find out that there was really no *offense* that is properly attributable to the injurer, for example, if he had been justified in injuring you or if what he did was an accident. Our interest, however, is in a third kind of case, in which one gives up blame even though an injurious offense occurred that is properly attributable to an eligible agent (cf. Allais 2008: 7–10).

Why might one give up blame if such an offense occurred? To adopt the terminology of those in the value theory literature, there may be reasons of the wrong kind and reasons of the right kind to do so (see D'Arms and Jacobson 2000). To explain, many universal emotions represent their object

---

[5] In Victoria McGeer's psychologically insightful "Civilizing Blame," we see a glimpse of this sort of argumentative strategy, more generally applied to "what makes our blaming emotions go away" (McGeer 2013: 174). She is less concerned with forgiveness, though, than with excuses and exemptions. Note also that I'm concerned here just with the case of directed second-personal blame and forgiveness, where I blame and forgive you for what you did to me, and not, say, to you for what you did to someone else, or to me for what I did to another. I can allow, therefore, that third-person or first-person blame and forgiveness may involve something other than what I think second-personal blame and forgiveness, in their paradigm forms, involve.

in an evaluative way. Fear, for example, represents its object as posing a threat of some kind, that is, as *fearsome*. Shame represents its object (oneself) as, roughly, falling below some standard (e.g., moral, prudential, aesthetic, genealogical, dermatological, and so on), that is, as *shameful*. Reasons of the "right" kind for having such attitudes stem from the correctness of their representations: a reason of the right kind to fear a rabid dog is that it does pose a threat. Call these "reasons of fit" or "fitting reasons." Reasons of the "wrong" kind for or against such attitudes are just reasons that don't have to do with this representational relationship. So while I may have a reason of fit to fear the rabid dog—it is in fact a threat—I may also have a prudential reason *not* to fear the dog, as perhaps it can smell fear and, if it does so, it will make its threat a reality. These prudential reasons are reasons of the wrong kind. But they are to be assessed alongside reasons of the right kind, and they may turn out to outweigh the latter in a determination of my *all-things-considered* reasons for or against having the attitude in question.

Applying this model to our project, if blaming emotions are among those subject to this treatment, then one might also withdraw them for reasons of the wrong or the right kind. To illustrate the former, one might stop blaming someone because she has already beaten herself up enough for an offense she nevertheless did commit. Or one might withdraw blame because one lacks a certain sort of standing with respect to the blamee: perhaps the offense was none of one's business, or perhaps one has committed a similar offense oneself and so would be a hypocrite in blaming her (see Smith 2007; Scanlon 2008; for criticism, see Bell 2013). These reasons for withdrawal are moral or prudential, so they are not about the accuracy of the blaming emotion's evaluative representation of its object. That is to say, the offending agents may still be fitting targets of emotional blame, even if one is not all-things-considered *justified* in blaming them.

By contrast, reasons of the right kind for withdrawing blaming emotions would be those making reference to the incorrectness of their emotional evaluations. The most familiar account of blame is that it fits responsible and culpable violations of moral requirements.[6] So if, for example, you knowingly and deliberately wrong me, it is fitting for me to have the blaming emotions

---

[6] See the many interesting essays in Coates and Tognazzini 2013, which, while they differ in many other details, are often in agreement on this point. Notice that the account says only that blame would be fitting, which means one only has *a* reason to feel it. There may still be weighty "wrong" kinds of reasons not to feel it, though, including, e.g., that it happened a really long time ago, or in a galaxy far, far away.

toward you, as those emotions ostensibly appraise you as having wronged me. And it is unfitting for me to blame you if you have not responsibly and culpably wronged me (or otherwise transgressed against morality).[7]

This account of blame, however plausible it is, famously gives rise to a puzzle about forgiveness: How could a forgiver aptly withdraw her blame of an offender without *excusing* the offender? (Hieronymi 2001: 530). On its face, to forgive someone for wronging you is to withdraw or foreswear your no-longer-appropriate hard feelings for him while simultaneously maintaining that he is still responsible for wronging you. But if blaming emotions "fit" responsible wrongdoing, then it looks like you can't coherently do both. In other words, how might one appropriately withdraw blaming emotions fitting for someone's culpable moral transgression without also withdrawing the judgment making them fitting, namely, that that person culpably committed a moral transgression?[8]

The basic assumption of this view is that blame responses are constituted by *judgments* about what the offender did (e.g., that the offender wronged one). Blame's fittingness is thus a correctness relation running between one's (emotional) judgments and the world: To the extent that one's judgments are true, the hard feelings partly constituted by those judgments are fitting thereby.[9] Call this view *judgmentalism*.

Judgmentalism ostensibly provides a way out of the forgiveness puzzle. If the fittingness of blame's hard feelings is solely a function of the truth of their

---

[7] Thus advocates of this view like Wallace maintain that "the fact that A has complied with moral requirements in A's interactions with other people provides A with a certain level of normative protection from the emotional reactions that are characteristic of blame" (Wallace 2013: 232).

[8] Why not instead just deny that forgiveness is about fittingness at all? Perhaps when one forgives it is for the "wrong kind of reasons," that is, the appropriateness of one's withdrawal of hard feelings is a function only of moral, prudential, or strategic reasons (even though they would still be fitting), akin to how one might withdraw one's blame of someone because she's already beaten herself up enough. Those who believe in "elective forgiveness" seem to view it this way (see, e.g., Allais 2008). Here is how Wallace puts it: "[I]n forgiving people we express our acknowledgment that they have done something that would warrant resentment and blame, but we *renounce* the responses that we *thus acknowledge to be appropriate* (Wallace 1994: 73; first emphasis in original; second emphasis mine). We can see the difference between this view and mine when thinking about cases in which someone has wronged me and then done everything a person could ever be reasonably expected to do to earn my forgiveness. Suppose I nevertheless withhold my forgiveness, persisting in my hard feelings. On the fittingness account of blame and forgiveness, I'm being irrational. On the "elective" account, I'm (merely?) being an asshole. Both ways of being are obviously criticizable. But only the fittingness view faces the basic puzzle motivating my investigations in the text, so that's the one I'm going to focus on here.

[9] Hieronymi puts it as follows: "An articulate account [of forgiveness] must make use of the fact that emotions are subject to rational revision by articulating the revision in judgment or change in view that allows us to *revise* our resentment while maintaining the judgments that occasioned it" (Hieronymi 2001: 535; emphasis in original).

constitutive judgments, *and there are multiple judgments involved in blame*, then the fittingness of one's blaming emotions could just be a function of some of those judgments and not others, leaving it in principle possible to withdraw some of those judgments but not others in a way that would maintain an "uncompromising forgiveness," which is the stated aim of Pamela Hieronymi's influential (2001) account. On her view, when you commit a moral offense against me, I aptly make many judgments, but the two that matter are these: (a) my judgment that you (responsibly) wronged me; and (b) my judgment that, in wronging me, you have expressed the false claim that I can be treated in the poor way you treated me—that such treatment is acceptable—and this false claim, if unaddressed, remains an ongoing threat to me (Hieronymi 2001: 546).[10]

How do we come to see all of this? By adopting the familiar methodology I laid out at the beginning: "[W]e need to delve more deeply into the attitude of resentment" (Hieronymi 2001: 545), which Hieronymi takes to be the paradigm blaming emotion. She characterizes resentment as an emotional protest fundamentally grounded by my (b)-judgment earlier (Hieronymi 2001: 548), so it is fitting for me to resent you just in case what you've done actually constitutes that ongoing threatening false claim. Consequently, when you genuinely apologize and renounce your deed, and I subsequently forgive you, my resentment no longer fits insofar as your renunciation has wiped out the threatening false claim to which my resentment is a protest, and so it has rendered my resentment's (b)-judgment false. In such a case, "resentment loses its footing" (Hieronymi 2001: 549). Nevertheless, my other judgments about what you did, including my (a)-judgment that you responsibly wronged me, are still true. But insofar as the fittingness of resentment is not fundamentally a function of the truth of the (a)-judgment (i.e., I can judge that you responsibly wronged me without there yet being a reason of fit to resent you), it is possible for me both to maintain that (a)-judgment and coherently forgive you by withdrawing the now-false (b)-judgment and subsequently having my resentment fade away, being no longer rationally grounded.

This is an elegant solution. But we only get to it via the worrisome method I have flagged, namely, by leaning heavily on a judgmentalist characterization of resentment right up front, according to which resentment is an emotional

---

[10] Other judgments include that the offender is a fellow member of the moral responsibility community and that he's worth being upset by (Hieronymi 2001: 530). Cf. Zaragoza 2012 and Warmke 2015.

protest grounded fundamentally in a judgment that some past action continues to make a threatening claim that it's acceptable to treat one in a shabby way (Hieronymi 2001: 546; see also Talbert 2012 and Smith 2013). But given all the other, conflicting accounts of resentment documented earlier, we have good reason to be suspicious of any conclusion about forgiveness that starts with such a controversial premise about the nature of resentment. Might we do better, then, if we start at the opposite end of the blaming exchange?

Withdrawing Hard Feelings

The front-end strategy starts by telling us what paradigm blame consists in (resentment), and then it provides a philosophical characterization of that blaming attitude and its fittingness conditions before showing what that attitude implies about the nature of apt forgiveness and so, finally, what it takes to be appropriately forgiven. The back-end strategy does the opposite: It starts by specifying what it takes to be appropriately forgiven, then it draws from that answer to determine the nature of apt forgiveness, and finally it shows what that account of forgiveness implies about the nature of blame and the core blaming attitudes.

So what does it take to be aptly forgiven? In other words, what must occur in an offending agent that renders unfitting an offended agent's hard feelings (without excusing what the offender did)?

The empirical psychological literature suggests that the degree to which forgiveness may be successfully predicted in offended subjects depends on the degree to which an offender expresses various things, including apologizing, admitting fault, admitting damage done, and offering to make amends (see Schmitt et al. 2004; Zechmeister et al. 2004; and Dill and Darwall 2014: 51). But by far the most significant predictor of forgiveness is an offender's expressed (or perceived as sincere) *remorse* (Darby and Schlenker 1982; Davis and Gold 2011: 392).

So what is remorse? In the psychological literature, there have been several conceptual constructs, but most gravitate toward similar features. Some put it that remorse is the painful feeling people have when they remember or think about a loss, in particular a loss they contributed to (Switzer 1988). Others put it that remorse "entails coming to terms with what one did, realizing that it was wrong, acknowledging the pain it caused others, and desiring to do something different in the future" (Brooks and Reddon 2003: 3). And in the prompts of various psychological experiments on remorse, here is how it has been put in surveys: "I feel really sorry for what I have done. I know how you feel now" (Schmitt et al. 2004: 469).

In the philosophical literature, though, there are surprisingly few accounts of the nature of remorse (exceptions include Thalberg 1963 and Baron 1988). Some seem to think it isn't a unique emotion at all, subsuming it under the far more discussed notions of guilt or shame (or a hybrid of both). Nevertheless, I think there is a distinctive and highly plausible characterization of remorse compatible with the intuitive understanding of it that psychologists have been studying.

The most basic human emotions have a "Triple A" syndrome: affect, appraisal, and action tendency (for summary, see Szigeti 2015). That is to say, pan-cultural emotions (such as anger and fear) consist in a feeling of some type, as well as an evaluative appraisal of their triggering object. But for identification and differentiation purposes, the most important element of this syndrome is the emotion's action tendency (Scarantino 2014: 168–183), which is a state "of readiness to execute a given kind of action," one "defined by . . . [the] . . . end result aimed at" (Frijda 1986: 70; quoted in Scarantino 2014: 169).

Now given this structure, I think the philosophical characterization of remorse articulated by Alan Thomas—one that resonates with the psychological characterizations given earlier—is most plausible: "Remorse, by contrast with either shame or guilt, [is a response to] the destruction of value rather than [to] the infringement of standards of right and wrong" (Thomas 1999: 130). While the affect and appraisal aspects of remorse may feel a bit like they overlap with those of guilt and shame, its action tendency distinguishes it. In cases of interpersonal offenses, guilt's action tendency motivates one to repair the relationship one harmed, right the wrong one caused, and/or compensate the party one hurt.[11] When one is ashamed by what one did, given one's failure with respect to certain expectations or ideals, one is typically moved to hide, either from the gaze of the wronged party or from one's fellow community members. But remorse need involve neither action tendency. What distinguishes it from both guilt and shame is that it tends one toward

---

[11] How, then, might guilt regarding what one did to the dead be fitting if one can no longer right the wrong, repair the relationship, or apologize? Answer: These are just the action *tendencies* of guilt, which are mere motivational impulses. That one can never *do* the thing one is nevertheless motivated to do doesn't render the tendency itself unfitting; indeed, this is why cases of undischarged apology or reparation tear people up inside: it involves a frustrated action tendency.

reflecting on—or often wallowing in—the disvaluable state of affairs that one caused. It moves one to relive the relevant events over and over, bemoaning the loss one caused. But there is also, in its most powerful and pure examples, a sense of impotence to remorse, a sense that *all* one can do now is to reflect on or to wallow in the damage done (Deigh 1996: 49; Thomas 1999).

Furthermore, where the value damaged is a fellow moral creature, one's contemplation of this lost value is typically a function of one's identification with that fellow (cf., Deigh 1996: 50), wherein one feels from the other's perspective what it was like to have suffered the loss of value. Of course, cruel people may be moved to identify with their victims and *delightfully* reflect on what they did to them in a nonremorseful way. So we must make sure to incorporate into our account the *painfulness* involved in this particular ruminative activity. My remorse for something I did to you, then, in its most familiar form, consists in a painful emotional response to my recognition of having caused you an irremediable loss of value, a response which constitutively involves my being moved to reflect on (over and over) what I did from your perspective. If this is what remorse is, then as an appraising emotion, one has a reason of fit to feel it when one has caused such a loss (cf. D'Arms and Jacobson 2000, 2003, 2006).[12]

There's a puzzle left, though: If I felt no pain on actually damaging someone's value at the original time of action (which is usually the case), then why should I feel pain on later imaginatively revisiting what I did? The answer has to be that I am not simply replaying that action in my head as it was experienced by me; that is, the imaginative revisitation is not a mere memory. Rather, I must now be seeing what I did from a different perspective, namely,

---

[12] Many questions surely remain, but I can address only some of them briefly here. First, is remorse fitting for *all and only* such states of affairs? I don't know, although I doubt it. My only aim here is just to give a sufficient condition for the fittingness of what I think is a very familiar characterization of remorse. Second, could remorse of this sort be fitting for losses of value in others that one caused *nonculpably*? It seems to me that the answer is yes: Insofar as remorse's action tendencies are to identify with the victim and to wallow in the loss caused, one's culpability or lack thereof in causing that loss can be irrelevant. Third, I've claimed that sometimes remorse involves the sense that *all* one can do is reflect on the lost value. But if that's true, goes a worry, then feeling both remorse and guilt—whose action tendency involves repairing or compensating for the damage caused—would exhibit a kind of incoherence. This isn't right, though. Guilt and remorse (of this sort) have action tendencies that tug us in different directions, that's surely correct. But as desiring creatures, we should be quite used to that sort of multidirectional tugging. Being moved in two directions isn't incoherent, though. Perhaps, then, the competing emotional *appraisals* are? No. Guilt, say, evaluates what one did as involving a slight to someone else (see Shoemaker 2015a: Ch. 3 for extended defense of this gloss). Remorse evaluates what one did as causing a loss in value to someone else. These evaluations are not in tension either, as slights sometimes just *consist in* losses in value. So there's no incoherence here. (I'm grateful to Michael McKenna and Dana Nelkin for raising versions of these worries.)

the perspective of those who lost the value. In the most familiar cases, this will be the direct victim of my value-damaging ways (although it may sometimes include the victim's friends and family). For me to be remorseful for the loss I caused you, I must take up your perspective and be open to feeling some approximation of how you felt upon being the victim of my bad treatment. The painful feeling of remorse is to a great extent a simulacrum of how you feel about the loss I caused, as from your perspective. In other words, the type of remorse that typically predicts successful forgiveness in interpersonal cases is what I will also call *painful empathic acknowledgment*.[13]

So where do we stand? The empirical literature reveals that by far the best predictor of forgiveness is the offending agent's remorse. I take it that this is a most familiar, resonant phenomenon: We generally take ourselves to have lost a reason (of fit) for hard feelings toward people when they have shown us true remorse.[14] I have given a philosophical characterization of remorse that sharpens the characterization given in the psychological studies, one that makes it a matter of painful empathic acknowledgment. To the extent that this is what's being tracked in the paradigm cases of second-personal forgiveness, we take ourselves to have lost our reason (of fit) to continue having hard feelings toward someone in the face of that agent's painful empathic acknowledgment of the loss in value he or she caused. When these blaming emotions are no longer fitting, then, and in the absence of other considerations (Blustein 2014: 45 ff.), forgiveness seems appropriate.[15]

---

[13] This may, to some, still sound a lot like guilt. There will of course be lots of overlap between the two emotions, as I've already allowed (see previous note). But there are cases of guilt without remorse, and cases of remorse without guilt, and they are distinguished primarily by their action tendencies. Sometimes I may wrong you without causing you any loss of value, as when I trespass on your land. Your confronting me about this may aptly produce guilt, but not remorse: I'm motivated to apologize or repair the relationship, but not wallow in any loss of value I caused, quite simply because I didn't cause any loss of value. Alternatively, I may damage some value in you without wronging you, as when I make a casual remark at a party about how ridiculously silly I think circus performers are, but it hurts your feelings because as it turns out your parents are trapeze artists, even though no reasonable person could have known that about you (you keep that information private). I may be moved, if I find out this information, to think about how that must have hurt, from your perspective, without being motivated to admit fault or compensate for my wronging you, say, *given that I didn't wrong you*. (Thanks to Michael McKenna for raising this issue.)

[14] Blustein 2014 (45), following Walker 2006, argues that aptly continuing to blame someone for something she has done is compatible with aptly forgiving her for having done so, at least on a Scanlonian model where blame consists in relationship modification (and so not necessarily hard feelings). I can, of course, agree with this point as, recall, I'm interested only in the type of blame that *does* involve apt hard feelings, and I take it that Blustein and Walker would agree that those sorts of feelings are incompatible with apt forgiveness.

[15] But is it *really* appropriate? Huge metaethical issues lurk here. One could think that there are objective normative facts about the aptness of forgiveness. Or one might be a subjectivist about these facts. Or one might think these facts are a function of a certain kind of intersubjectivity. Or one might just think there are no such facts. I'm not going anywhere near this dispute here. Rather, my aim is

Remorse and Repudiation

Suppose I have committed an offense against you, but I now feel complete remorse for it; that is, I have, as fully as one could reasonably expect, taken up your emotional perspective on what I did, and so I have come to feel a simulacrum of what you felt when I offended against you. I am painfully ruminating over and mourning the loss of value I caused. Once this occurs and you perceive it, most of us would think you have lost your reason (of fit) for hard feelings toward me—for blaming me—making it (other things equal) appropriate for you to withdraw those feelings and forgive me.

Nevertheless, what I have done fails to meet the conditions of Hieronymi's protest-based account of apt forgiveness: My empathic acknowledgment, in and of itself, is insufficient to make false your key resentful judgment about me, namely, the judgment that I continue to make the threatening false claim that you can be treated poorly. Why not? Empathic acknowledgment simply consists in an *emotional perceptual stance*, that is, my seeing with your emotional lenses on how it (must have) felt for you to be treated in the way I treated you.[16] But how things (descriptively) appear to me emotionally has no direct connection to, or expected effects, on my threatening (prescriptive) judgments about *how you may be treated*; they are just two very different categories of psychic events. A psychic bridge is thus needed to forge the gap between them if we are to save Hieronymi's judgmentalist account.

The most obvious candidate for doing so is what many theorists (including Hieronymi) have in fact appealed to, namely, *repudiation* (O'Shaughnessy 1967; Hieronymi 2001; Bennett 2003; Blustein 2014: 49). Perhaps, then, what I perceive in empathically taking up your perspective are facts about you that thereby *give me reason* to repudiate my threatening judgment toward you, but it's not until I repudiate that judgment that your withdrawal of hard feelings toward me is rendered fitting.

I want to argue that remorse can be perfectly sufficient to render paradigm forgiveness appropriate, even without repudiation, and that repudiation itself is sometimes insufficient for the task. Two types of case illustrate the first

to set forth an extremely familiar form of forgiveness in our interpersonal lives, one that presents itself to us as having a normatively binding status (i.e., we think forgiveness is indeed appropriate). Regardless of one's metaethical leanings, then, one must at least take this phenomenon into account in one's theorizing about "truly" apt forgiveness (or explain it away).

[16] I explain this idea in much greater detail in Shoemaker 2014 and 2015a: 99–100.

point. Consider, to begin, cases in which, while we can allow that the blamed agent did make a threatening false claim via the social meaning of her treatment of someone, her painful empathic acknowledgment alone after the fact nevertheless undercut the *need* for her repudiation by rendering one aspect of its targeted claim unsustainable. Let me explain. What one repudiates is supposed to be one's (ongoing) threatening false judgment that the blaming agent can be treated in the way one did. But that target has two components: a (false) judgment and a threat. These components may be prized apart. One could easily perform an action whose social meaning expressed the judgment without the threat, as in a case of noblesse oblige. Being treated "honorably" and "generously" by someone who takes himself to be superior to you is surely worthy of hard feelings, as it expresses a false judgment about how you may be treated. But this isn't a *threatening* judgment, precisely because it doesn't involve a poor (or insufficiently good) quality of will. A poor quality of will typically consists in, or is expressed via, an attitude like hostility, disdain, or uncaring negligence.

Given that there are two distinct components of the target of Hieronymian repudiation, then, sometimes the sheer disvalue of what one did, when seen by the blamed agent from the perspective of the blaming agent, will be sufficient all by itself to eliminate one of those components, namely, the *threat*. A perceptual stance, as already noted, can't directly undermine a judgment (and vice versa), as perceptual stances and judgments just aren't the kinds of psychic events that engage with one another (see Scanlon 1998: 65). But a perceptual stance *can* directly engage with, and so undercut or bring about, certain attitudes, in particular, certain emotions. Suppose you are promoted over me and I get jealous. When I fully appreciate from your emotional perspective your own insecurities about deserving that promotion, this new perceptual stance may serve to directly dissolve my jealousy of you. Or when you, my nemesis, undergo some tragedy, once I take up your grief-stricken perspective, my hatred for you may directly dissolve (and sympathetic concern may be directly generated in its place). Or, most relevantly, when I feel what it was like for you to have suffered the loss in value I destroyed, my remorse may of itself be sufficient to dissolve my earlier hostility, my threatening quality of will toward you, *even in the absence of my repudiation of the false judgment with which the hostility had been a conjunctive component.*[17]

---

[17] The basic thought that a perceptual stance may alter attitudes in a way that judgments don't or can't is the subject of Shoemaker 2015b.

One might well respond thus: Doesn't my remorse in such cases just *constitute* a repudiation of the threatening quality of will in such cases?[18] I doubt it. That a threatening quality of will becomes unsustainable for someone doesn't yet implicate that person's *repudiation* of the attitude, which to my ear requires active rejection on the agent's part. But readers who remain suspicious should consider the second type of case in which repudiation of a threatening false claim is unnecessary for apt forgiveness where remorse is present.

Suppose I am texting while driving and I run over your dog because of my lack of attention to the road. Once I see the damage I have caused, I am overwhelmed with remorse. I, too, have a dog, and I can pretty fully imagine just what it must be like for you, so I am able to feel a simulacrum of your pain at the loss of value I caused from your perspective. Once again, it looks appropriate for you to abandon hard feelings in favor of forgiveness just as soon as you have witnessed (and believed) my own sincere emotional devastation in light of what I did.[19] It is, after all, obvious that I clearly and truly "get" what I did, which looks to be enough to disarm your blaming appraisal of me, even without my repudiating some false threatening claim. But here's the real reason no repudiation is necessary: In this case, *I didn't even make such a claim.* I hadn't even acknowledged you (or your dog) to begin with, and so I never had an opportunity to make the threatening judgment about you. Indeed, emotionally wrought acknowledgment often gets us to realize that, while someone may have acted *as if* she had made such a claim, she really hadn't; instead, she was just blithely unmindful. But you may aptly forgive her offensive obliviousness while still maintaining that she *was* offensively oblivious (so you do not merely excuse her).[20]

There are lots of cases like this once we realize the wide array of activities and attitudes for which remorse and forgiveness are appropriate (Blustein

---

[18] My thanks to Heidi Giannini for raising a version of this point.

[19] In 2011, Patricia Machin's husband was hit and killed by a careless driver. In a note forgiving the utterly distraught man, she wrote, "However bad it was for me, I realize it was 1,000 times worse for you." From *The Telegraph*, February 20, 2013, http://www.telegraph.co.uk/news/politics/david-cameron/9883398/Humbled-by-the-courage-of-those-who-forgive.html.

[20] An objection: If I obliviously offend against you, and you have hard feelings toward me, but I go on in my fashion without apologizing, etc., then isn't it made obvious that my obliviousness was making a threatening claim after all? No. The threatening claim arises *only in my going on*. Prior to that, however, I was just oblivious; no claim at all was being made (explicitly or implicitly). (Thanks to Heidi Giannini for raising the issue.)

2014: Ch. 1). Suppose that I haven't been sufficiently grateful for your re-peated aid. Perhaps when someone points this out to me, I feel and express my sincere remorse to you, and you forgive me thereby. There was no re-pudiation of a threatening false claim on my part, because merely being insufficiently grateful doesn't seem to involve a *threatening* claim to begin with. Or consider a son who marries someone his mother really can't stand, someone it will break her heart for him to marry. He may well feel remorse for causing his mother heartbreak (in a way rendering her forgiveness of him apt), without repudiating the decision at all, again, because it constituted no threat, and he'd do it all over anyway (see Phillips and Price 1967 for this case). So there are plenty of cases in which remorse without repudiation may fittingly salve a blamer's blame.

We have been investigating what changes on the part of the forgiven agent best explain why the hard feelings directed toward him by a blaming agent may be rendered unfitting. On the Hieronymian resentment- and judgment-based answer, the forgiven agent needs to have repudiated his persistent threatening false claim that the blaming agent can be treated as he was. This repudiation then makes the blamer's constitutive resentful judgment about the offender false, which only then renders resentment unfitting. But re-morse, as we have seen, can—and often does—undermine blame's fittingness all on its own, even in the absence of any repudiation.

Further, now that we have prized apart the two distinct components of the false claim that purportedly needs to be withdrawn (its threat and its false judgment), we can see that repudiation on its own also isn't *sufficient* to make hard feelings unfitting. On the Hieronymian story, a candidate for forgiveness is one who withdraws—repudiates—a false judgment (about how the blamer can be treated). But repudiating that judgment doesn't imply a withdrawal of *hostility* (or a more generally poor quality of will). Someone may fully understand that he can't treat someone a certain way while nevertheless still *wanting* to (and being fully behind that desire). And it's the wanting to—the poor quality of will—that is for many people the proper target of blame, as that's what constitutes the hostile heart of the objectionable threat (see, e.g., Strawson 2003 and the many others who followed in his wake).

Remorse, then, is a better candidate than repudiation for what explains why the hard feelings constituting paradigm blame become unfitting (when excuse and exemption are off the table). So what might we learn from this result?

The Function of Blaming Emotions

Why do we tend to think that an agent's coming to be remorseful is the best reason for dissolving our hard feelings toward that agent? The most straight-forward answer is that the hard feelings have a function, the sustaining conditions of which remorse has undercut.

Of those theorists who are sympathetic to a functional treatment of blame, there is disagreement, as noted at the beginning, over what blame's function *is*. The two leading candidates have been *protest* and *demand*. On the former view, blame protests wrongdoing and/or the offender's threatening judgment that the protester can be treated a certain way. Unfortunately, protest accounts in the literature almost always deploy a repudiation account of what aptly addresses it, and we have already seen reason to worry about repudiation's role in paradigm forgiveness. But there's a further problem here, for regardless of whether we appeal to re-pudiation or remorse as grounding the withdrawal of hard feelings, neither seems to sit well with a protest function for blame. This is because protest often has multiple aims and audiences. Yes, protest often directly targets offenders, but it also is said to be deployed often on behalf of third parties and the protester herself, as its wider aims may include both rallying others to a cause and standing up for oneself (Blustein 2014: Ch. 1; Smith 2013). As a result, it often just won't matter much to protest's continuing aptness whether the offender changes his ways or rejects what he did. The wider aims of protest are forward-looking features that, like many consequen-tialist treatments of blame, may not in the end be closely attached to the offender's actual *offense*. So given that we are looking for what blame does that is aptly dissolved in the face of an offender's remorse, a protest theory will have a hard time fitting the bill.[21]

The painful empathic acknowledgment of remorse does not answer to or engage directly with judgment. Rather, it involves taking up another's emo-tional perceptual stance and coming to see various facts about that person in a particular emotional light. To the extent that remorse most aptly dissolves blame's hard feelings, taking the relevant perceptual stance must effectively undercut blame; that is, it must adequately address blame's function. It most obviously would do so were blame's function to *ask* for it.

---

[21] For many other objections to a protest theory of blame, see Shoemaker and Vargas 2019.

This function is in line with a popular theory, namely, that blame's function is to *demand* something of the blamed agent.[22] There are two serious worries with this theory, though. First, its advocates almost invariably think of blame's core hard feeling as being resentment, but we already know that this concept has been analyzed in such a variety of ways that there could hardly be (and isn't) an agreed-upon subsequent account of what it demands. Second, even if we could settle on one these proposed accounts of blame's demanding function, there seem to be serious problems attached to all heretofore proposed functions.

The story of resentment's purportedly demanding function veers quickly into *Rashomon* territory, for what resentment is said to demand depends on who tells the tale (and some people tell two tales!). On one story, resentment expresses a demand that the offender not violate the moral requirement he violated (e.g., Wallace 1994: 245–246; also see Darwall 2006: 72, 76). On a second, resentment expresses a demand for good will or reasonable regard (Watson 2004: 223). On a third, it expresses a demand for guilt (Darwall 2006: 71, 79, 85–86[23]). And on a fourth, resentment expresses a demand for rectification (Walker 2006: 25–26). So which one is it? It's just not clear, and it's also not clear how we could arbitrate between them.

Of course, one might think that at least *one* of these accounts would be viable. But as Coleen Macnamara has effectively shown, every one of these proposals is actually quite problematic. Regarding the first proposal, if the offender has already violated the terms of morality, what could be the point of demanding from her afterward that she should not have done so? Regarding the second, if the resenter is just demanding that the offender manifest good will or reasonable regard in the future, then it looks like we aren't accounting for resentment's essential *backward*-looking feature, a response to past poor quality of will (Macnamara 2013: 154–155). Regarding the third, if resentment demands "acknowledgment of fault, where this includes both feeling guilt and expressing it via apology and amends" (Macnamara 2013: 150), then it is incoherent as a demand. After all, guilt is an emotion, and emotions are not subject to our will, so it is unintelligible to demand that others feel guilt.[24] And regarding the fourth proposal (that resentment demands rectification),

---

[22] Recall that those advocating a demand-based theory of blame include, among others, Wallace 1994; Strawson 2003; Watson 2004; Darwall 2006; Walker 2006; and Shoemaker 2007.

[23] More precisely, Darwall suggests that resentment is a demand for an acknowledgment of fault *via* guilt. However, it really does seem to be guilt that does the requisite work for him, not the acknowledgment per se. I discuss Macnamara's rejection of this view in a note later.

[24] As Brandon Warmke rightly points out, this last inference seems false, as we make such demands all the time (e.g., "You ought to be ashamed of yourself!"), and they can be perfectly intelligible as

those who defend such a view are most plausibly construed instead as actually advancing a nondemand view, one in which resentment *invites* or *seeks* a certain sort of response (Macnamara 2013: 157–159).

If this is an exhaustive list of resentment's possible demanding object, and each entry is problematic, then it may seem that blame's function cannot be to demand. Perhaps it is instead, as Macnamara thinks, an invitation to respond. This inference would be too quick, though, as Macnamara's list of blame's possible demanding aims is not exhaustive, failing, as it does, to include empathic acknowledgment.[25] But if empathic acknowledgment can appropriately resolve the hard feelings of blame in paradigm cases of forgiveness, then blame could still consist in a demand for what resolves the blame, namely, empathic acknowledgment. Of course, this sort of demand may just amount to the same thing as Macnamara's "invitation to respond." I'm not interested in terminology. All that matters for my purposes is that emotional blame of the familiar sort *requests* (the term I will use from here on out) remorseful empathic acknowledgment, and once the blamed agent responds with that acknowledgment, then blame's request (its demand/invitation/expectation) ought to be withdrawn, for there is no longer any reason for it.

Taking the Resentment out of Blame

I have been speaking all along of the resolution of the *hard feelings* of blame. These have long been presumed basically to consist in resentment (or have resentment as their core). But now I want to show that when we start at the back end of the blaming exchange with the forgiven agent and work our way to the front end, resentment comes to seem like it was the wrong blaming attitude to emphasize all along.

Nearly everyone these days agrees at least on a formal feature of resentment, namely, that it is a "cognitively sharpened" version of *anger*

---

long as we recognize that the set of aptly demanded actions or attitudes isn't governed exclusively by volition. Another governor is evaluative judgment. See Smith 2005.

[25] She does include acknowledgment of fault *via guilt* (Macnamara 2013: 148–156). But her objection to that option, recall, is that guilt is an emotion, and one cannot coherently demand that others feel emotions. Her mistake is thus to attach the acknowledgment option to a demand for guilt. But while guilt very often predictably accompanies acknowledgment, it's not the aim of blame's demand. And demanding acknowledgment of someone is perfectly intelligible insofar as it is a function of taking up the empathic perspective, which *is* subject to our will, at least for all those capable of empathy.

(D'Arms and Jacobson 2003: 143), sharpened by a judgment of some sort.[26] Resentment, then, is just anger *plus* a judgment (that, say, the resented agent made the threatening false claim about the resenter). But as we have seen, the painful empathic acknowledgment that on its own can render forgiveness fitting doesn't directly engage with judgment. Suppose, then, that you resent me, a wrongdoer, and so (constitutively) you judge that I have made the threatening false claim against you. Now suppose, further, that you fittingly come to abandon your resentment solely in light of my empathic acknowledgment of what I did. Insofar as my empathic acknowledgment doesn't engage with resentment's judgmental component, it must have resolved your resentment in virtue of resolving its anger.

Recall that basic emotions have a triple syndrome—felt affect, appraisal, and action tendency—and their identifying and differentiating feature is their action tendency. What, then, is anger's action tendency? Our folk talk of anger is actually ambiguous between emotional syndromes with two distinct action tendencies. The first version is what I will call *goal-frustration anger*, which is, as the label suggests, an angry response to not getting what one wants, where the cause of the frustration can be anything from the weather, to a pothole-filled road, to one's computer, to other people. Babies and bears, as well as normal adult humans, experience this sort of anger. Its action tendency is to try and remove or get around the obstruction, and, in so doing, "to regain control or freedom of action" (Frijda 1986: 88). The second type of anger is a response to *slights*, and it has since Aristotle been thought to have the action tendency for revenge (Aristotle/Roberts 1954: 92/1378a). This very familiar version of anger is what I will call *agential anger* (or sometimes *angry blame* or *blaming anger*, both of which stress the fact that agential anger could be just one type of blame; see Watson 2004; Griswold 2013; Shoemaker 2015a: Ch. 3; Shoemaker 2018; and Shoemaker and Vargas 2019).

Now while the action tendency of agential anger has long been thought to be revenge, I have argued at length elsewhere that revenge is not actually its core unifying action tendency. Yes, specific bouts of anger often contain such an impulse. But the tendency toward revenge is really just the most dramatic method for carrying out the more fundamental action tendency of agential anger, namely, the impulse to *communicate* it.[27] An argument for this view

[26] I say nearly everyone "these days," because I do not think that when Strawson introduced talk of "resentment" into the literature he had in mind an attitude so cognitively sharpened as this. See also Deigh 2011; Griswold 2013 (on "vengeful anger"); and Shoemaker 2015a: 88–89.

[27] Note that even Aristotle claims that the relevant impulse is "to a *conspicuous* revenge for a conspicuous slight" (Aristotle/Roberts 1954: 92/1378a; emphasis mine). I believe that it is the

comes from consideration of pairwise cases, the first in which one's angry revenge for a wrong is delivered without the wronging agent ever knowing that one was its angered source, and the second in which the same revenge is delivered alongside the successful communication that one was its angered source (see Griswold 2013: 87; Shoemaker 2015a: 104–105). Only the latter feels like fully discharged anger.[28] This feeling is widely shared by subjects in several empirical psychological studies. After one such study, Gollwitzer and Denzler note:

> [O]ur findings corroborate the notion that revenge aims at delivering a message between the victim/avenger and the offender, and that revenge is only effective if this message is understood (French 2001). In other words, revenge is not a goal in itself, but rather a means to achieve a higher-order goal. (Gollwitzer and Denzler 2009: 843)

Another argument in favor of the communication model of agential anger draws from the myriad of cases in which one's fully discharged agential anger communicates itself without revenge. Think here of being in a close interpersonal relationship and quietly shutting a door on your hurtful partner, or writing a note detailing the other's wrongdoing, or, in a shaking voice, telling the other that you will no longer be ignored (Shoemaker 2018).

Agential anger's fundamental action tendency is thus, I believe, to communicate itself to the angering party (with or without revenge). But *to what end*? If it were just to let you know that I'm angry, then it's hard to see either why my anger doesn't just dissipate once you understand that message or why your remorse fittingly dissolves it instead.

The answer is somewhat complicated, and unfortunately I lack space to elaborate on it here.[29] But the basic idea should be fairly familiar and resonant: When I communicate my agential anger to you, I'm also conveying lots of other information about myself to you (and to others); that is, I'm

conspicuousness, and not the revenge per se, that is more fundamental. See also Griswold 2013: 87 for brief discussion of what he calls vengeful anger's communicative element.

[28] And communication, to be more than mere expression, requires uptake on the part of the blamed agent. This is another feature I take to be missing in the protest theory of blame.

[29] I have, however, contributed to articulating its details and defense at length elsewhere (see Shoemaker and Vargas 2019).

signaling.[30] What I signal may be conscious or unconscious, intentional or not. The information I convey is mostly about me, including what norms I'm committed to, my competence with respect to the norms you've violated, and, importantly, my willingness to *enforce* those norms (Shoemaker and Vargas 2019). But what does my enforcement consist in? Here's a provocative possibility (one I will elaborate on and defend in the next section): In communicating my agential anger to you in response to the norms you have violated—norms I care about and want to see upheld—I enforce the norms by requesting that you respond with empathic acknowledgment of what you have done. So while anger's action tendency is merely to communicate the anger, its signaled request remains open, and so anger remains fitting to feel, until the blamed agent responds accordingly.

Let us bring together the points in this and the previous sections. Blame's fundamental type of hard feeling, revealed by thinking about forgiven agents in paradigm cases, is agential anger, whose action tendency is to communicate itself to the offending party. This communication signals information about the blaming agent's commitment to enforcing the violated norms, where the enforcement could consist in a request for empathic acknowledgment of what the offender did. This request could appropriately be responded to only by said acknowledgment, which primarily consists in a simpatico (painful) experience of how he made the victim feel, that is, remorse. If this is the right story, then as there are no judgments necessary to any part of this blaming-and-forgiveness exchange, resentment (given that a judgment is its constitutive component) is also not necessary to it.[31]

Empathic Acknowledgment and Normative Equilibrium

But *why* would anger involve a request for acknowledgment?[32] Wouldn't it make more sense to request compensation for the harm caused, or to request that the offender not harm you or anyone anymore, or to request that he

[30] Signaling theory has a long and illuminating history in a wide variety of disciplines. Contemporary defenders of a kind of signaling theory for blaming anger include Nichols 2007 and McGeer 2013.

[31] It's important to note that I am not denying that resentment is very often a blaming response. Rather, I am saying both (a) there are plenty of paradigmatic blaming responses that don't include resentment (as they are instances of mere agential anger), and (b) even when a blaming response does consist in resentment, it is not its constitutive judgmental component that makes it an example of blame; it is rather its (agential) anger component.

[32] Recall that I am using the term "request" as a gloss on demands, expectations, and invitations.

change his harming ways or repair the relationship he impaired? The answer is twofold. First, angry blame aptly targets many types of norm violations beyond just harms or relationship impairments. Regarding the former, I may blame you for trying yet failing to sabotage me, even when your doing so backfired so much that I wound up with a net benefit. Regarding the latter, I may blame a close friend, child, or spouse for something that nevertheless did not impair our relationship one whit, given the strength of its bonds (Wolf 2011; McKenna 2012: 104). Agential anger aptly targets more than just harm and relationship impairment, so it would not make sense for it to be restricted to requesting compensation for harms, future refraining from harming, or relationship repair.

But then why does angry enforcement involve request for acknowledgment instead? To see the answer, recall (or watch!) Dustin Hoffman's character Ratso Rizzo, in *Midnight Cowboy*, crossing a busy New York City street while talking with Jon Voigt's Joe Buck. A taxi comes a bit too near Rizzo, and this is his (and Hoffman's purportedly improvised) classic angry response to the driver as he slams the taxi's hood: "I'm walkin' here! I'm *walkin'* here!" There was no harm caused, no interpersonal relationship impaired,[33] and no interest on Rizzo's part in regulating the blamed agent's future activities. So what was the communicative point of his anger? It issued a request for the driver to *notice* him, a request that he be taken seriously. *I'm* walking here, indeed. But then what Rizzo requested—acknowledgment—was exactly the same thing the driver should have provided *before* their exchange, namely, to have registered the fact of Rizzo's presence. The driver's offense consisted in a failure of acknowledgment. But as such, it makes perfect sense that Rizzo would, in enforcing his default expectation of acknowledgment, request it now.[34]

Or at least this is my proposal about the most familiar cases of blaming anger: Its communication signals a commitment to a set of norms, which includes a commitment to enforcing those norms. Enforcement consists in an explicit request for acknowledgment by offending agents post-offense

---

[33] Scanlon (2008) would retort that the moral relationship the driver and Rizzo bear to one another was impaired, a normative ideal grounded on the fact of their equal standing as rational agents, but this is quite a stretch, and many others have found it quite problematic. See, e.g., Sher 2013.

[34] Perhaps it's a request instead that the driver acknowledge the seriousness of his wrong, rather than a request that the driver acknowledge Rizzo and what he felt? This sort of thing surely occurs, but it won't have the right connection to forgiveness we are seeking, as it's the sort of demand any bystander could make as well, and bystanders don't have standing to forgive. (Thanks to Dana Nelkin for raising the issue.)

precisely because that is what we implicitly request of them pre-offense. Indeed, I will make a very bold claim: This is the only requesting aim of paradigm emotional blame—the familiar second-personal instances involving apt hard feelings where withdrawal of those feelings in forgiveness may also become apt—that seems common to *all* such blameworthy instances of harms and nonharms, relationship impairments and nonimpairments, and between both strangers and intimates. Agential anger requests that one be taken seriously, that one be duly regarded. When you fail to take me sufficiently seriously—by harming me, impairing our relationship, violating my rights, insulting me, being condescending toward me, and so on—I will be disposed to enforce the violated norm by being moved to request, via my communicated anger, that you at least *now* do so.

Of course, while we request acknowledgment both pre- and post-offense, the precise content of the requested acknowledgment differs in each case. Pre-offense, I implicitly request what I request of everyone: that you take me and my ends sufficiently seriously. I *count*, and to the extent that I may be affected by what you do (or by what your attitudes are), your actions or attitudes ought to reflect the fact that you have taken me sufficiently seriously. Post-offense, though, when it is clear that you have not taken me sufficiently seriously, my anger delivers a request that you acknowledge how you made me feel in *not* having properly acknowledged me pre-offense. Those aptly forgiven in paradigm cases are those who have adequately answered this request.

What such acknowledgment achieves most fundamentally and immediately, therefore, seems to be the restoration of a kind of *normative equilibrium* between the blamer and the blamee that was upset by the blamee's (initial and persisting) lack of sufficient acknowledgment. We all expect to count sufficiently in each other's deliberations as we make our way through the world. When someone is walking down the street texting, we expect him to notice and steer clear of us. When trying to work in close quarters on a plane, we expect our chatting neighbors to try and keep their voices down. But when they disregard us in violating these expectations, what this means is that we failed to count (sufficiently) for them. In remorsefully acknowledging us post-offense, therefore, they restore us to (what we take to be) our rightful normative place, recognizing that we have a certain significance after all. Agential anger accomplishes its aim when such acknowledgment occurs, and to the extent that this is the ground for paradigm forgiveness, empathic acknowledgment provides the conditions for anger's apt dissolution.

Resolving the Forgiveness Puzzle without Judgment

We are now, finally, in a position to see how this nonjudgmentalist, emotional, communicative, and requesting account of paradigm blame resolves the puzzle of forgiveness. I can best illuminate the resolution by an analogy with fear, which seems best characterized as an emotional appraisal of some object as a threat (D'Arms and Jacobson 2006) with a distinctive action tendency to get away from the threat (Frijda 1986; Smith and Ellsworth 1987). Suppose that you come across a grizzly bear and this syndrome arises. Your fear is fitting, insofar as the grizzly is a threat. But its constituting a threat to you is relative to your particular circumstances. Once you have successfully escaped its reach, fear appropriately dies away, given that the grizzly no longer constitutes a threat *to you* (you are safe), even though that particular grizzly—and all grizzlies—remains fearsome (i.e., grizzlies merit fear when encountered in the wild). Consequently, to the extent that successful discharge of the action tendency of fear in effect alters the threat status of the feared object relative to you, it renders your fear of that specific object no longer fitting.[35]

Turn, then, to agential anger, which appraises actions or attitudes as slights (my gloss on "insufficient acknowledgment") and whose action tendency is to communicate the anger to the slighter, delivering a request that the slighter empathically acknowledge what he did. By analogy with fear, when the goal of the action tendency has been successfully discharged, one's agential anger is no longer fitting, insofar as the offender's empathic acknowledgment is sufficient to make it the case that *the slight is no more*. This is yet another reason why no repudiation is needed. My slighting you consists in my putting us into normative disequilibrium. We remain in a state of disequilibrium until it is corrected. The sort of empathic acknowledgment rendering forgiveness appropriate restores normative equilibrium, in the way that a successful escape from a threat restores one's safety (and so fittingly calms one's fear). Where there is normative equilibrium, no anger is fitting.[36]

Nevertheless, there *was* normative disequilibrium—a slight—and slighters generally merit anger (they are *angersome*), just as grizzly bears generally

---

[35] These remarks give us another reason to worry about Hieronymi's view of resentment and forgiveness. If the offender's unforgiven offense truly constitutes a persisting threat to me, as Hieronymi claims (Hieronymi 2001: 546), then why isn't the fitting emotional blaming response *fear*, not resentment?

[36] This point is simpatico with the spirit of Warmke 2016.

merit fear (they are *fearsome*). In cases of appropriate empathic acknowledgment, then, the forgiver's anger is no longer fitting in virtue of the forgiver's having successfully gotten what she requested from the offender, but the forgiver can still view what the offender *did* as a slight—he *was* a slighter—and so view the offender as having merit*ed* anger (and so as having been responsible for it). The adherent of my account may thus distinguish excuse- and forgiveness-inducing empathic acknowledgment as follows: the former makes agential anger unfitting in virtue of its revealing that there was no slight; the latter makes agential anger unfitting in virtue of its revealing that what was an ongoing slight *is no more.*[37] While a slighter can never make it the case that he did not slight the victim and so brought about normative disequilibrium with the slighted party, he can at least attempt to restore normative equilibrium between them by heeding agential anger's communicated request and, in so doing, transform an ongoing lack of acknowledgment into the due regard we expect of one another.

Conclusion

My primary aim has been to show how starting at the back end of paradigm blaming-to-forgiveness exchanges—starting with what it takes to be aptly forgiven—can yield genuine theoretical progress. Let us review some of these benefits.

1. Because there is so much disagreement over what resentment is, leaning on it as the core of paradigm blame at the front end of the blaming exchange generates lots of other disagreements about blame (including its function and nature), as well as, ultimately, forgiveness. But if we start with what it takes for someone to be appropriately forgiven, we can get more determinate, univocal answers: Blame (in the most familiar cases) is an emotional communication enforcing one's signaled commitment to the violated norms (among other things) by requesting empathic acknowledgment. Withdrawal of hard feelings and forgiveness are thus apt for those who adequately respond to this request.

---

[37] Cf. Griswold 2013 (96–100) for discussion of what he takes to be three types of fittingness that seem relevant to Aristotle's notion of vengeful anger, although he is mostly focused on discussing the ethics of vengeful anger, which is not my concern.

2. The source of previous problems in theorizing has not merely been the method of starting at the front end of the blaming exchange; in addition, it has been theorists' focus on resentment as the "obvious" paradigm blaming emotion to start with. When we start instead with the forgiven agent, though, the conditions for which are ultimately grounded in empathic acknowledgment (a perceptual stance), we see that judgment may be unnecessary to the entire enterprise. As a result, the core of blame's hard feelings is not necessarily a judgment (about wrongdoing or threatening claims) that might sharpen anger into resentment but the anger in and of itself (in its agential emotional syndrome).

3. Agential anger's action tendency is to communicate itself to the angersome party, and in so doing it delivers a request for empathic acknowledgment. Such a request makes most sense in light of the forgiven agent's previous failure of empathic acknowledgment, a violation of the implicit default expectation of daily interpersonal life. Forgiveness is thus fitting in response to the empathic acknowledgment of the offender in virtue of that acknowledgment having restored the default normative equilibrium between the parties.

4. The puzzle of an "uncompromising" forgiveness is easy to solve on this model: When full empathic acknowledgment has occurred, hard feelings in the form of agential anger no longer fit, as what was a slight no longer exists. One may thus still hold that the offender was responsible for having brought about a persisting slight, even if blame is no longer fitting for him in light of his elimination of that persisting slight.

I realize that these are highly revisionary conclusions. But I just aim to be starting a conversation, and so hopefully people will take these conclusions as what they really are, namely, provocations for more dialogue.[38]

[38] My thanks first and foremost go to the spectacular members of my Spring 2015 seminar on "Agency and Blame" (the seminar that launched five dissertations!) at Tulane University for their help in the germination and early development of this chapter: Nathan Biebel, Eric Brown, Kelly Gaus, Jesse Hill, Cary Krongard, Nick Sars, Nathan Stout, and Dan Tigard. Thanks also to Per Milam and Massimo Renzo for comments on an earlier draft, and thanks to the audience members at the NUSTEP Conference (May 2016) for critical feedback during my presentation of some of this material, especially Heidi Giannini, Pamela Hieronymi, and Nomy Arpaly. Finally, thanks to the editors of this volume for pressing me to think and write about this subject matter for the first time, and then causing me to rethink the project completely with their insightful and tough critical comments on the penultimate draft. I hope I haven't caused them any remorse.

References

Allais, Lucy. 2008. "Dissolving Reactive Attitudes: Forgiving and Understanding." *South African Journal of Philosophy* 27: 1–23.

Aristotle. 1954. *The Rhetoric and the Poetics of Aristotle*. Translated by W. Rhys Roberts. New York: The Modern Library.

Baron, Marcia. 1988. "Remorse and Agent-Regret." *Midwest Studies in Philosophy* 13: 259–281.

Bell, Macalaster. 2013. "The Standing to Blame: A Critique." In Coates and Tognazzini 2013: 263–281.

Bennett, Christopher. 2003. "Personal and Redemptive Forgiveness." *European Journal of Philosophy* 11: 127–144.

Blustein, Jeffrey M. 2014. *Forgiveness and Remembrance*. Oxford: Oxford University Press.

Boss, Judith. 1997. "Throwing Pearls to the Swine: Women, Forgiveness, and the Unrepentant Abuser." In Laurence Bove and Laura D. Kaplan, eds., *Philosophical Perspectives on Power and Domination*. Netherlands: Rodopi Press: 235–248.

Brooks, John H., and Reddon, John R. 2003. "The Two Dimensional Nature of Remorse: An Empirical Inquiry into Internal and External Aspects." *Journal of Offender Rehabilitation* 38: 1–15.

Coates, D. Justin, and Tognazzini, Neal, eds. 2013. *Blame: Its Nature and Norms*. Oxford: Oxford University Press.

Darby, B. W., and Schlenker, B. R. 1982. "Children's Reactions to Apologies." *Journal of Personality and Social Psychology* 43: 742–753.

D'Arms, Justin, and Jacobson, Daniel. 2000. "The Moralistic Fallacy: On the 'Appropriateness' of Emotions." *Philosophical and Phenomenological Research* 61: 65–90.

D'Arms, Justin, and Jacobson, Daniel. 2003. "The Significance of Recalcitrant Emotions (or, Anti-Quasijudgmentalism)." In Anthony Hatzimoysis, ed., *Philosophy and the Emotions*. Cambridge: Cambridge University Press: 127–146.

D'Arms, Justin, and Jacobson, Daniel. 2006. "Anthropocentric Constraints on Human Value." *Oxford Studies in Metaethics* 1: 99–126.

D'Arms, Justin, and Jacobson, Daniel, eds. 2014. *Moral Psychology and Human Agency*. Oxford: Oxford University Press.

Darwall, Stephen. 2006. *The Second-Person Standpoint*. Cambridge, MA: Harvard University Press.

Davis, James R., and Gold, Gregg J. 2011. "An Examination of Emotional Empathy, Attributions of Stability, and the Link between Perceived Remorse and Forgiveness." *Personality and Individual Differences* 50: 392–397.

Deigh, John. 1996. *The Sources of Moral Agency: Essays in Moral Psychology and Freudian Theory*. Cambridge: Cambridge University Press.

Deigh, John. 2011. "Reactive Attitudes Revisited." In Carla Bagnoli, ed., *Morality and the Emotions*. Oxford: Oxford University Press: 197–216.

Dill, Brendan and Darwall, Stephen. 2014. "Moral Psychology as Accountability." In D'Arms and Jacobson 2014, pp. 40–83.

Franklin, Christopher Evan. "Valuing Blame." In Coates and Tognazzini 2013, pp. 207–223.

French, P. A. 2001. *The Virtues of Vengeance*. Kansas: The University Press of Kansas.

Frijda, Nico. 1986. *The Emotions*. Cambridge: Cambridge University Press.

Garrard, Eve, and McNaughton, David. 2002. "In Defense of Unconditional Forgiveness." *Proceedings of the Aristotelian Society* 103: 39–60.

Garrard, Eve, and McNaughton, David. 2010. *Forgiveness*. Durham, UK: Acumen.

Gollwitzer, Mario, and Denzler, Markus. 2009. "What Makes Revenge Sweet: Seeing the Offender Suffer or Delivering a Message?" *Journal of Experimental Social Psychology* 45: 840–844.

Griswold, Charles L. 2007. *Forgiveness: A Philosophical Exploration*. New York: Cambridge University Press.

Griswold, Charles L. 2013. "The Nature and Ethics of Vengeful Anger." *Nomos* 53: 77–124.

Hieronymi, Pamela. 2001. "Articulating an Uncompromising Forgiveness." *Philosophy & Phenomenological Research* 62: 529–555.

Hieronymi, Pamela. 2004. "The Force and Fairness of Blame." *Philosophical Perspectives* 18: 115–148.

Holmgren, Margaret. 2012. *Forgiveness and Retribution: Responding to Wrongdoing*. Cambridge: Cambridge University Press.

Macnamara, Coleen. 2013. "Taking Demands Out of Blame." In Coates and Tognazzini 2013: 141–161.

McGeer, Victoria. 2013. "Civilizing Blame." In Coates and Tognazzini 2013: 162–188.

McKenna, Michael. 2012. *Conversation and Responsibility*. New York: Oxford University Press.

Nichols, Shaun. 2007. "After Compatibilism: A Naturalistic Defense of the Reactive Attitudes." *Philosophical Perspectives* 21: 405–428.

O'Shaughnessy, R. J. 1967. "Forgiveness." *Philosophy* 42: 336–352.

Phillips, D. Z., and Price, H. S. Price. 1967. "Remorse without Repudiation." *Analysis* 28: 18–20.

Rawls, John. 1971. *A Theory of Justice*. Cambridge, MA: The Belknap Press of Harvard University Press.

Scanlon, T. M. 1998. *What We Owe to Each Other*. Cambridge, MA: Belknap Press of Harvard University Press.

Scanlon, T. M. 2008. *Moral Dimensions: Permissibility, Meaning, Blame*. Cambridge, MA: Belknap Press of Harvard University Press.

Scarantino, Andrea. 2014. "The Motivational Theory of Emotions." In D'Arms and Jacobson 2014: 156–185.

Schmitt, M. et al. 2004. "Effects of Objective and Subjective Account Components on Forgiving." *The Journal of Social Psychology* 144: 465–486.

Sher, George. 2006. *In Praise of Blame*. Oxford: Oxford University Press.

Sher, George. 2013. "Wrongdoing and Relationships: The Problem of the Stranger." In Coates and Togazzini 2013: 49–65.

Shoemaker, David. 2007. "Moral Address, Moral Responsibility, and the Boundaries of the Moral Community." *Ethics* 118: 70–108.

Shoemaker, David. 2014. "McKenna's Quality of Will." *Criminal Responsibility and Philosophy*. DOI: 10.1007/s11572-014-9322-5.

Shoemaker, David. 2015a. *Responsibility from the Margins*. Oxford: Oxford University Press.

Shoemaker, David. 2015b. "Ecumenical Attributability." In Randolph Clarke, Michael McKenna, and Angela M. Smith, eds., *The Nature of Moral Responsibility*. Oxford: Oxford University Press: 115–140.

Shoemaker, David. 2018. "You Oughta Know! Defending Angry Blame." In Owen Flanagan and Myisha Cherry, eds., *Anger*. London: Routledge: 67–88.

Shoemaker, David, and Vargas, Manuel. 2019. "Moral Torch Fishing: A Signaling Theory of Blame." *Nous*. https://doi.org/10.1111/nous.12316.

Smith, Angela. 2005. "Responsibility for Attitudes: Activity and Passivity in Mental Life." *Ethics* 115: 236–271.

Smith, Angela. 2007. "On Being Responsible and Holding Responsible." *Journal of Ethics* 11: 465–484.

Smith, Angela. 2013. "Moral Blame and Moral Protest." In Coates and Tognazzini 2013: 27–48.

Smith, Craig A., and Ellsworth, Phoebe C. 1987. "Patterns of Appraisal and Emotion Related to Taking an Exam." *Journal of Personality and Social Psychology* 52: 475–488.

Strawson, P. F. 1962. "Freedom and Resentment." *Proceedings of the British Academy* 48: 1–25. Reprinted in Gary Watson, ed., *Free Will*, 2nd ed. Oxford: Oxford University Press: 72–93 (page numbers in text are from this reprinting).

Switzer, D. K. 1988. "The Remorseful Patient: Perspectives of a Pastoral Counselor." *Psychotherapy Patient* 5: 275–290.

Szigeti, András. 2015. "Sentimentalism and Moral Dilemmas." *Dialectica* 69: 1–22.

Talbert, Matthew. 2012. "Moral Competence, Moral Blame, and Protest." *Journal of Ethics* 16: 89–109.

Thalberg, I. 1963. "Remorse." *Mind* 72: 545–555.

Thomas, Alan. 1999. "Remorse and Reparation: A Philosophical Analysis." In Murray Cox, ed., *Remorse and Reparation*. London: Jessica Kingsley: 127–134.

Walker, Margaret Urban. 2006. *Moral Repair: Reconstructing Moral Relations after Wrongdoing*. Cambridge: Cambridge University Press.

Wallace, R. Jay. 1994. *Responsibility and the Moral Sentiments*. Cambridge, MA: Harvard University Press.

Wallace, R. Jay. 2010. "Hypocrisy, Moral Address, and the Equal Standing of Persons." *Philosophy & Public Affairs* 38: 307–341.

Wallace, R. Jay. 2013. "Rightness and Responsibility." In Coates and Tognazzini 2013: 224–243.

Warmke, Brandon. 2015. "Articulate Forgiveness and Normative Constraints." *Canadian Journal of Philosophy* 45: 490–514.

Warmke, Brandon. 2016. "The Normative Significance of Forgiveness." *Australasian Journal of Philosophy* 94: 1–17.

Watson, Gary. 2004. *Agency and Answerability*. Oxford: Oxford University Press.

Wolf, Susan. 2011. "Blame, Italian Style." In R. Jay Wallace, Rahul Kumar, and Samuel Freeman, eds., *Reasons and Recognition: Essays on the Philosophy of T.M. Scanlon*. New York: Oxford University Press: 332–347.

Zaragoza, Kevin. 2012. "Forgiveness and Standing." *Philosophy and Phenomenological Research* 84: 604–621.

Zechmeister, J. S. et al. 2004. "Don't Apologize Unless You Mean It: A Laboratory Investigation of Forgiveness and Retaliation." *Journal of Social and Clinical Psychology* 23: 532–564.

3

Fitting Attitudes and Forgiveness

Glen Pettigrove

The appropriate response to wrongdoing, many have suggested, is anger or resentment.[1] One way in which such a claim might be defended would appeal to a fitting attitude account of value. Fitting attitude accounts are built around the intuitive link between certain attitudes or emotions and their corresponding objects: There is a connection between love and the lovable, shame and the shameful, delight and the delightful. I shall argue that a fitting attitude account of the link between resentment and wrongdoing is more complicated than one might have thought. The complications that emerge prove illuminating both for our thinking about forgiveness and for our thinking about fittingness.

Forgiveness and Resentment

Jeffrie Murphy, in "Forgiveness and Resentment," asserts that a person ought to resent wrongs that are done to her. The "ought" in question is not an instrumental "ought," as in the judgment that one ought to brush one's teeth before bed in order to avoid cavities. Nor is it the "ought" of etiquette, as in, "One ought to place the salad fork to the left of the plate when setting the table." The "ought" Murphy has in mind is considerably more demanding: "A failure to resent moral injuries done to me is a failure to care about the moral value incarnate in my own person (that I am in Kantian language, an end in

---

[1] One person to have defended this view recently is Amia Srinivasan in an insightful paper (Srinivasan 2018) that was published in the interval between the submission of this chapter and the publication of the collection of which it forms a part. Things I say here overlap with Srinivasan's project, but because this piece was completed before Srinivasan's article appeared, I regret that I did not have an opportunity to engage with her work. The same regret applies to the chapters of Myisha Cherry's and Owen Flanagan's nice collection, *The Moral Psychology of Anger* (Cherry and Flanagan 2017).

Glen Pettigrove, *Fitting Attitudes and Forgiveness* In: *Forgiveness and Its Moral Dimensions*. Edited by: Brandon Warmke, Dana Kay Nelkin, and Michael McKenna, Oxford University Press. © Oxford University Press 2021. DOI: 10.1093/oso/9780190602147.003.0003

myself) and thus a failure to care about the very rules of morality" (Murphy 1988, 18).

If we define forgiveness, as Murphy does, as "the forswearing of resentment" (1988, 15), then a problem arises.[2] If one ought to resent, and forgiveness is the forswearing of resentment, then it looks as though the forgiver is doing something she ought not do. Or at least she appears to be neglecting something she ought to do.

Murphy addresses this problem by adding a crucial qualifier to the forswearing of resentment: "Forgiveness is . . . forswearing resentment on moral grounds" (1988, 24). Provided the moral grounds outweigh, cancel, or supersede the moral grounds for resentment, forgiveness will be permissible. The moral grounds Murphy discusses include the following:

1. He [i.e., the wrongdoer] repented or had a change of heart *or*
2. he meant well (his motives were good) *or*
3. he has suffered enough *or*
4. he has undergone humiliation (perhaps some ritual humiliation, e.g., the apology ritual of "I beg forgiveness") *or*
5. old time's sake (e.g., "He has been a good and loyal friend to me in the past"). (1988, 24)

Murphy argues it is permissible to forgive at least some individuals who satisfy one or more of these conditions. Nevertheless, although forgiveness need not be objectionable, the burden of proof still rests squarely on the shoulders of the would-be forgiver to demonstrate that she has not done something dodgy. In other words, the presumption is that the forgiver is guilty until proven innocent.

Murphy has modified his view in a number of ways since the publication of "Forgiveness and Resentment." In his second book on the topic (Murphy 2003) he made more room for forgiveness and identified a wider range of reasons that might justify it. But as the book's title, *Getting Even: Forgiveness*

---

[2] A number of authors have argued that forgiveness is something other than the foreswearing of resentment. The most common alternative involves expanding the range of emotions forgiveness might overcome. I defend one such view in Pettigrove 2012a. However, for the purposes of this chapter I shall follow Murphy (1988), Hieronymi (2001), and Griswold (2007) in treating forgiveness as involving the overcoming of anger or resentment, since they present the most challenging version of the position I wish to contest. Those who argue that wrongdoing elicits a more expansive range of attitudes or emotions and who define forgiveness in terms of overcoming some of these other emotions are invited to apply the argument that follows, mutatis mutandis, to their preferred range of emotional reactions to wrongdoing.

and Its Limits, and chapter titles like "Two Cheers for Vindictiveness," make clear, the default response to wrongdoing, by his lights, remains (and should remain) anger or resentment. They are the responses transgressions call for. To respond in some other way requires special justification.

Following Murphy's lead, a number of other theorists have defended views that are built around similar assumptions regarding the link between wrongdoing and resentment. For example, Joram Haber (1991, 72) insists that resenting wrongdoing is a key component of a well-functioning "sense of right and wrong." That is because "resentment is the proper response to personal injury and . . . the failure to resent under certain circumstances is indicative of a moral defect" (1991, 70). A self-respecting person who cares about morality "will express this care in the form of resentment when she is the object of moral injury" (1991, 72–73).

Pamela Hieronymi contends that, when we are warranted in judging that we have been unjustly wronged by a responsible member of the moral community, "our first response is, and ought to be, anger and resentment" (Hieronymi 2001, 530). While it is possible for someone to judge that a wrong has been done to her without feeling anger or resentment—perhaps by recognizing that moral rule R governs a certain class of actions C and that action A falls within C and is a violation of R—the person who both recognizes the wrong and feels anger is better situated vis-à-vis the wrong.[3] "To be angry and resentful is to be involved with and committed to these judgments in a way that goes beyond merely assenting to their truth. (I take the difference between merely assenting to these judgments and being angry or resentful to be the same sort of difference as that between agreeing that something is good and wanting it, or agreeing that something is dangerous and fearing it)" (2001, 530).

Charles Griswold (2007, 26 and 39) agrees with Murphy, Haber, and Hieronymi that "it is appropriate . . . to respond with anger when wrongly injured." And like them he defines forgiveness in terms of a reduction in this anger or resentment: "forgiveness requires that resentment for the relevant injury be appropriately moderated and that the agent make a further commitment to work toward a frame of mind in which even that resentment is let go" (2007, 42). However, before it is appropriate to moderate one's

---

[3] "Anger" is often used as a parent term for a whole family of hostile emotions, including irritation, indignation, resentment, hatred, and rage. I shall follow this usage and in subsequent sections refer to "anger" rather than "anger and resentment," since anger so understood includes resentment.

resentment, he argues, a wrongdoer must "qualify for forgiveness" (2007, 59). If she does, then "forgiveness is commendable because it is what the offender is due" (2007, 69). If not, she should not be forgiven, for she is "undeserving of the honor" (2007, 63–64).

Even John Kekes (2009, 489), who objects to views—like Murphy's, Haber's, Hieronymi's, and Griswold's—that try to define forgiveness as the overcoming of resentment, nevertheless insists that evil ought to "be remembered bitterly and resentfully." It is "obscene" to encourage victims of evil to avoid or overcome bitter and resentment-filled remembering. His story is not much different when he turns from evil actions—which he takes to be distinguished by the degree of harm that they cause and their malevo-lent motivation (2009, 490)—to more garden-variety wrongdoing. He argues that it is appropriate for a person to respond to a harm he has suffered with an emotion like "resentment, bitterness, anger, hatred, [or] indignation" that "is roughly proportional to the harm" (2009, 499). Not responding with pro-portional anger to harms one has suffered is suspicious and calls for special explanation.

The list could go on. The so-called paradox of forgiveness, for example, on which a lot of ink has been spilled since Aurel Kolnai's influential Aristotelian Society address, is built around the assumption that we ought to resent wrongdoers.[4] However, the passages cited earlier are sufficient to show that the assumption that resentment or anger is the appropriate response to a wrong that one has suffered is widespread in the philosophical literature. And they indicate the kind of challenge this assumption poses for forgive-ness. The person who forgives is engaging in a practice that is out of step with the appropriate response to wrongdoing, and for that reason her actions de-mand special justification.

Fitting Attitudes

How might one go about defending the assumption that anger or resentment is the appropriate response to wrongdoing? A promising way to motivate these claims is provided by a fitting attitude analysis of value. Fitting attitude accounts come in two sizes. In their broadest, most encompassing form, fit-ting attitude accounts claim that an object, action, or event has value if and

[4] See Kolnai (1973–1974), Johansson (2009), Zaibert (2009), and Hallich (2013).

only if it is the "fitting object of a pro-attitude" (Ewing 1948, 152). How the relevant "pro-attitudes" are described varies somewhat by theorist. David Wiggins (1998, 206) speaks of "approbation"; Franz Brentano (1969, 18) of "love"; W. D. Falk (1986, 117) of "favor," "desire," and "approval"; and A. C. Ewing (1948, 149) of "desire," "liking," "approval," and "admiration" as well as more active responses such as "choice" and "pursuit." Regardless of their preferred parent term for pro-attitudes, it is clear that each of these theorists intends his term(s) to include a wide range of positive affects, attitudes, and action orientations. As Ewing puts it, ""Pro attitude" is intended to cover any favourable attitude to something" (1948, 149). These theorists advance a similar account of disvalue: an object, action, or event has disvalue if and only if it is the fitting object of a con-attitude. Franz Brentano (1969, 18) and Noah Lemos (1994, 12) choose "hate" as the parent term that covers the full range of con-attitudes. But other theorists prefer to work with more fine-grained responses—such as guilt, remorse, shame, resentment, outrage, blame, and anger—to pick out the negative value range (Gibbard 1990, 41–42). What unites these theorists is a shared commitment to defining good and evil, value and disvalue by reference to fitting attitudes on the part of suitably situated observers.

Fitting attitude theories also come in a smaller, more modestly proportioned size. Theorists of this second sort agree that *some* values should be defined via fitting attitudes. They agree, for example, that the irritating should be defined in terms of its connection with irritation, the enviable in terms of its connection with envy, and the funny in terms of its connection with amusement. They wish to account for the pleasurable, the agreeable, the fearsome, the offensive, and the disgusting in similar ways, defining them in relation to attitudes, emotions, and reactions that fit them.[5] But they stop short of trying to define *all* value concepts, properties, or relations in this way.

Fitting attitude theories stand in contrast to robust realist accounts of value (Jacobson 2011). The robust realist takes the goodness of good news and the excellence of personal excellence to exist independently of our valuing attitudes. Some robust realist accounts resemble fitting attitude accounts by giving emotions a central role. When in the presence of valuable properties, joy and pride are explained as the natural response of the clear-eyed observer. Such emotions may even be the means by which we become aware of these value properties.[6] But the goodness or badness of these things in

---

[5] See Johnston (2001) and D'Arms and Jacobson (2000b).
[6] See Zagzebski (2004) and Pelser (2014).

no way depends upon our responses. Fitting attitude theorists, on the other hand, think value depends upon valuers in some way, so that if there had never been and would never be any valuers, there would be no value.

Fitting attitude theories also stand in contrast to dispositionalist accounts of value; however, the contrast is not as sharp as the one between fitting attitude theories and robust realism. A dispositionalist view of value claims that for an object to have value X is for it to be such that ordinary people in standard conditions respond to it X-ly. For example, "a dispositionalist view of value understands funniness . . . in terms of whatever amuses normal humans in standard conditions" (Jacobson 2011). Similarly, the fearsome will be whatever provokes fear, the shameful what evokes shame, the horrific what elicits horror, and the irritating what causes irritation among standard perceivers in standard conditions. Both the dispositionalist and the fitting attitude theorist take concepts like the funny, fearsome, shameful, and irritating, to be response-dependent concepts.[7] Mark Johnston suggests these value concepts are like color concepts, insofar as they depend upon qualities of both the object and the perceiver. In the case of color, our perceptions of the redness of an apple depend upon the ways in which different wavelengths of light are reflected from the apple's surface. However, the apple's reflectance profile by itself is not sufficient for the concept of redness. REDNESS also depends upon the cone structure of the human eye. Were there no eyes that processed light in the way ours do, then even though there would still be apples with the same reflectance profile, we would have no reason to formulate the concept of redness, no opportunity to become aware of it, and no way of knowing when or whether it applied to any of them. Our concept of the apple's redness depends upon both its reflectance profile and the phenomenal qualities we experience when the reflected light is processed by the cones of the human eye. Johnston argues that something similar applies in the case of value concepts like being awesome, irritating, shameful, or funny.

What distinguishes a fitting attitude theory from a dispositionalist theory is that the former leaves room for the possibility that the normal response could be mistaken. A fitting attitude theory of value is concerned not with whether it is normal but whether it is fitting to value something in one way or another. An action, attitude, or object has valuable property X, the fitting

---

[7] Johnston introduces response-dependent concepts in (1989, 145). In more recent work (Johnston 2001) it becomes clear that he does not think a response-dependent account is limited to making claims about concepts. There can also be response-dependent properties that correspond to our response-dependent concepts.

attitude theorist contends, if it is fitting to value it X-ly. For example, a person is admirable if it is fitting to admire her, an action is shameful if it is fitting to feel ashamed of it, etc. (Jacobson 2011).

One reason to prefer a fitting attitude theory over a dispositionalist one is that it leaves room for moral reformers to challenge widely shared attitudes. For instance, a century ago standard perceivers in standard conditions responded to mixed-race, mixed-caste, and same-sex romantic relationships with indignation. Standard perceivers whose adult children were part of such a relationship found it deeply shaming. A fitting attitude theory has space built into it to accommodate criticism of such norms. A second reason for preferring a fitting attitude theory is that it presents itself as a normative theory, rather than a descriptive one. As Daniel Jacobson (2011) observes, "To call something funny is in some way to endorse amusement at it, not to report or predict it."

Thus, fitting attitude theories are distinguished by (a) their attempt to explain at least some value notions in terms of fitting attitudes[8] and (b) their commitment to response dependence (Jacobson 2011). Within these parameters, however, there is still a lot of scope for disagreement. Some fitting attitude theorists think that there can be both response-dependent concepts and response-dependent properties. That is, they not only think the *concepts* RED and LOVABLE depend upon our responses, but they also think the *properties* of being red or being lovable depend upon our responses. Such theorists are realists about value properties, even though they endorse response dependence and are thereby distinguished from the robust realists discussed earlier. Others, like Allan Gibbard who champions an expressivist account of ethics, are happy with response-dependent concepts but do not think we can take the further step to posit "real" properties that correspond to these concepts.

Both realist and expressivist fitting attitude theorists have the resources to make sense of the kinds of remarks that Murphy, Hieronymi, Griswold, and others have made about the link between anger and the judgment that I have been wronged. According to each, being angry is the fitting response to undeserved injury at the hands of another agent. Furthermore, the wrongness

---

[8] That is to say they attempt to explain (some set of) axiological concepts in terms of deontic concepts. As Wlodek Rabinowicz (2013) puts it, "value is explicated in terms of the stance that *ought* to be taken toward the object."

or disvalue of the injury is partly constituted by people having this response when they observe or suffer such injuries.

Fitting attitude accounts have a number of attractive features. They capture something intuitive about our valuing attitudes. Joy is a fitting response to good news, whereas sadness is a fitting response to bad news. Something would be amiss if you responded to good news with sadness or bad news with joy. Similarly, shame is a fitting response to personal failure and pride to personal excellence. A person who responded to personal failure with pride or to personal excellence with shame would have her wires crossed. Indeed, it would be hard for us to make sense out of her experience at all. And within fitting attitude theories these emotional or attitudinal responses are not just along for the ride. They are in the driver's seat, making the valuing omnibus go.

The Wrong Kinds of Reasons for Forgiving?

According to fitting attitude theories, the judgment that X is good is the judgment that one ought (or has reason) to respond to it with a pro-attitude. However, not all situations in which one ought (or has reason) to have a pro-attitude toward X are situations in which X is good. To illustrate, imagine that both W and X come from a culture in which arranged marriages are common and, although they have not met, their parents have arranged their betrothal. Knowing that their future life together will be better (happier, more harmonious) if they have pro-attitudes toward one another like love and respect, W and X each recognize that they ought to love one another. But insofar as they do not yet know each other, neither of them is in a position to judge that the other is good (lovable, worthy of respect). In this case the pro-attitudes they ought to have (because it would be advantageous for them to do so) are not fitting. Or, to be more precise, they do not fit what they know of their betrothed. In such a situation, W's reasons are what Wlodek Rabinowicz and Toni Ronnow-Rasmussen (2004) have called "the wrong kind of reasons" for loving X.

What distinguishes the right kinds of reasons from the wrong kinds has been the subject of much debate. Some, like Derek Parfit (2001), have suggested that what distinguishes W's reasons from reasons of the right kind for loving X is that reasons of the right kind are provided by the *object* of the valuing attitude (X), whereas W's reasons are given by facts about being in the *state* of loving X. The value of being in the state of loving X gives W a reason to *want to love* X, but it does not give her a reason *to love* X (Gibbard 1990, 37; Pillar 2001, 204–205). The problem with W's loving X in this case is that the reasons W has for loving X "have to do with the value of that attitude itself and not with the value of the object" (Rabinowicz and Ronnow-Rasmussen 2004, 402; cp. Hieronymi 2005).

Distinguishing between properties of the object and properties of the attitude and using that as a tool for separating reasons of the right kind from reasons of the wrong kind looks promising. However, Rabinowicz and Ronnow-Rasmussen have drawn attention to a possible problem with this strategy. For every object-property P, there is a corresponding attitude-property, P′, which is "the property of being such that its object has (or would have) property P. Thus, to each object-given reason corresponds an attitude-given reason, and vice versa" (Rabinowicz and Ronnow-Rasmussen 2004, 406). To return to our example, X has the property of being such that if he were loved by W, then X's and W's life together would be better. This is a property of the object rather than a property of the attitude, but it is still the wrong kind of reason for loving X.

To address this worry, Gerald Lang, Sven Danielsson, and Jonas Olson have suggested that what distinguishes the right kind of reasons from the wrong kind is that "reasons of the right kind are not provided by the consequences of taking up the relevant attitude" (Danielsson and Olson 2007, 513). Insofar as W's reasons for loving or respecting X have to do with the beneficial consequences of loving or respecting him, they are reasons of the wrong kind to value him in either of these ways or to see him as possessing the corresponding value properties of being lovable or respectable (Lang 2004, 484). As Lars Samuelsson (2013, 389) puts it, "if we take a thing to have value, we should not have to enter into *any* consideration regarding what will *follow* if we respond to it (in the way that we take to correspond to its value) in order to find out whether we have *some* reason to respond to it in that way."

Regardless of which account one thinks accurately distinguishes the wrong kinds of reasons from the right ones, a number of the reasons that have been offered for forgiving appear to be reasons of the wrong kind. For example, in *Forgiveness and Love* I suggested the following considerations could provide suitable reasons for forgiving:

Ella might forgive David because doing so will improve Ella's own psychological health. . . . Madison may forgive David because it was her mother's dying wish that she restore the family peace. And Tristan may forgive David because he wants to impress his girlfriend, who thinks anger is a sign of weakness. . . . A fourth reason may be the forgiver's realization that her resentment will do neither her nor the person at whom it is directed any good. . . . A fifth reason may derive from the value of the forgiver's relationship with the forgiven. . . . Finally, a person may choose to forgive simply because she thinks it will bring the one forgiven more joy than he would otherwise have. (Pettigrove 2012a, 147–149)

Similarly, Stephen Ingram (2013) highlights "the prudential value of forgiveness." Because our acquisition of knowledge depends on standing in congenial relationships both with particular individuals and with the wider epistemic community, by maintaining stable and congenial epistemic relations forgiving is conducive to our epistemic welfare. Forgiveness enables former wrongdoers to set aside worries about future punitive demands being made by their former victims and enables those victims to lay aside the prosecution of past offences in order to move on with life and attend to other matters. Thus, forgiving can free both the wrongdoer and the wronged to pursue future goods. In short, he argues, "forgiving, and being disposed to forgive, tends to contribute to one's well-being" (Ingram 2013, 1070).

Comparable reasons feature in much of the therapeutic literature on forgiveness. For example, in *Forgiveness Is a Choice*, Robert Enright lists eight categories of reasons to forgive, most of which are concerned with the benefits of forgiving:

1. You forgive to quiet your angry feelings.
2. Forgiveness changes destructive thoughts into quieter, more healthy thoughts.
3. As you forgive, you want to act more civilly toward the one who hurt you.
4. Forgiveness of one person helps you interact better with others.
5. Forgiveness can improve your relationship with the one who hurt you.
6. Your forgiveness actually can help the one who hurt you to see his or her unfairness and to take steps to stop it. Your forgiving can enhance the character of the one who hurt you.
7. You forgive because God asks you to do so. You forgive as an act of love toward God.

8. Forgiveness, as an act of kindness and love toward the one who hurt you, is a moral good regardless of how the other is responding to you. Loving others, while protecting yourself from harm, is a morally good thing to do.[9]

Fred Luskin (2002), likewise, focuses on the benefits of forgiving for oneself and for one's friends and family. Forgiveness promises emotional benefits for the forgiver: "People who are taught to forgive become less angry, more hopeful, less depressed, less anxious, less stressed, more confident, and they learn to like themselves more" (Luskin 2002, 78). It promises physical benefits as well: forgiveness is correlated with lower blood pressure, less frequent short-term physical complaints, and fewer chronic illnesses (79–80). It promises agential benefits: Forgiveness enables the forgiver to regain her agency by putting the past behind her, rather than continuing to be a victim who is held hostage by the past actions of another (75). And it promises moral and relational benefits: Forgiving reduces the likelihood that we will take the wounds we have suffered in past relationships and reproduce them in present and future ones, and it can inspire others who are struggling with anger, resentment, or bitterness by showing them it is possible to heal (74).

The problem with the reasons Enright, Ingram, Luskin, and I discuss, a fitting attitude theorist might urge, is that they are reasons *to want* to have a forgiving attitude rather than reasons *to have* a forgiving attitude. Or they are reasons given by the consequences of forgiving, rather than reasons given by the value of the person being forgiven. Some of the reasons that have been put forward in support of anger also seem to be reasons of the wrong kind. For example, Joseph Butler (1726, 70) argues that wrongdoers pose a threat to us, which gives us a reason to defend ourselves and anger is part of that defense.[10] However, the reasons put forward by Murphy, Hieronymi, and Griswold are reasons of the right kind.[11] Hieronymi, like Butler, presents anger or resentment as a way of responding to a threat, but she does not construe it as a form of self-defense. Rather, she takes resentment to be a form of protest that marks an action as an instance of wrongdoing (Hieronymi 2001,

[9] Enright 2001, 45–46. A number of the people whose stories are collected in Arnold (2008) echo the reasons Enright outlines.

[10] See also Murphy 2003, 19–20.

[11] Most of them are, at any rate. Murphy's example of forgiving for old time's sake is harder to cash out in terms of the right kinds of reasons, unless remembering our past relationship is thought to provide a more accurate perspective on the wrongdoer's character or motivation than would be provided by the transgression alone.

546–547). As such, it is the value/truth-tracking aspect of resentment that has center stage. Murphy (1988, 18) and Griswold (2013, 78–79) take anger to be an expression of self-respect or self-esteem and its absence to be indicative of a lack of such. And Murphy (2003, 19) and Hieronymi (2001, 530) take anger to track violations of the moral order. Anger registers this violation from the vantage of someone who has respect for morality and its demands. Turning to forgiveness, the fact that the wrongdoer meant well, or has repented and made amends, would be a reason for adopting an attitude other than anger or resentment. The wrongdoer has different value properties than he previously had (or would otherwise have had if his intentions had been different) and a different valuing orientation is fitting (Griswold 2013, 85).

The Fitting Should and the Moral Should

There are a number of ways in which one might respond to the claim that anger is the fitting attitude to wrongdoing and that one should not forgive for the reasons Enright, Luskin, Ingram, and I have offered because they are of the wrong kind. I shall begin with the most irenic and then move on to consider responses that part ways with fitting attitude accounts more dramatically.

Let us assume that a virtuous agent responds to objects, actions, and events as they should. If the *should* in question is the *should* associated with fitting attitudes, then in many (perhaps most) situations where an agent has been wronged, she should feel a number of different attitudes.[12] Because the action is wrong and she is its victim, Griswold, Hieronymi, Murphy, and company contend that anger or resentment is the fitting response. However, if she sees the action as a cry for help from someone who feels as though he has run out of other options, then the fitting attitude may be compassion. If the action is performed by someone she greatly admired and this action reflects a deep character flaw, then the fitting response might be sadness or disappointment. If she realizes that the action is just like something she did to someone last week, she may feel chagrin.[13] If the wrongdoer is someone for whose

---

[12] In subsequent work Murphy has conceded at least part of this point, granting that resentment need not be "the *only* fitting response to being wronged." Even so, he remains "suspicious" of "those who do not resent being wronged" (Murphy 2012, 224–225).

[13] This example presupposes that "the virtuous person" can be distinguished from "the perfectly virtuous person," since the latter would not have done something about which she might feel chagrin. Those who take the virtuous to be perfectly virtuous are invited to lengthen the period of time to something longer than a week. On the assumption that even the perfectly virtuous were not always

education she is responsible, then the fitting attitude might be excitement at the teaching opportunity the action affords. If the transgression is the action of an all-too-human being whom she loves, then the fitting response may be to carry on loving him as before. And if there is reason to believe that there is some likelihood the transgressor will eventually come to see the error of his ways and change his behavior, then the fitting response may be to hope for the realization of that possibility.

Note that, unlike the reasons offered in the third section, each of these considerations is focused on the object of the attitude, not on the state of having the attitude. They are focused on the transgressor or transgression, not on the consequences of adopting a particular attitude toward them. They do not get their purchase on the victim's attitudes by redirecting her attention to something else, like her own future mental health or her mother's dying wish. Each of them involves focusing on different aspects of the transgressor or transgression, seeing this moment against distinct, albeit overlapping, backdrops.

Recognizing the multiplicity of attitudes that fit the situation poses a challenge for those who wish to blaze a trail from a fitting attitude theory to the assertions about anger quoted in the first section. A human agent cannot feel all of the aforementioned attitudes at the same time. Even emotions like anger and sadness, which have often been lumped together as "negative emotions," are distinct enough that it is not possible to feel certain types of anger and sadness at the same time. They express themselves in different facial configurations (Ekman and Oster 1979). They are correlated with differences in skin conductance and blood pressure (Cacioppo et al. 2000). They prime different (and opposing) ways of processing information and making predictions (Keltner, Ellsworth, and Edwards 1993). They also involve distinct phenomenologies. Even when they attend to the same object, they construe that object differently. Sadness focuses on insufficient levels of value in the situation, whether in absolute terms or relative to what was hoped or expected. Anger focuses on the thwarting of desire, typically against the backdrop of what one thinks was deserved. Sadness involves a desire that things be better than they are; anger a desire that its object suffer harm of some sort. Most forms of sadness involve a stepping back, a withdrawal,

---

perfectly virtuous, there will be some point prior to reaching perfection at which they will have done some action they now regret. So, for example, the ideally virtuous might realize that the wrong action is just like something she did to someone when she was the wrongdoer's age, in which case a fitting response might be regret or chagrin.

whereas anger characteristically involves an aggressive stepping forward, encouraging confrontation with the object of one's anger. The upshot is that one cannot be in the physiological and phenomenological state of feeling many forms of anger and sadness at the same time. This is not to deny that one can *be* sad (i.e., have the dispositional emotion of sadness) while one is feeling angry (i.e., experiencing the occurrent emotion of anger) or vice versa (more on this in a moment). Nor is it to deny that one can readily move from one occurrent emotion to the other and back again. It is merely to say that the occurrent emotions of anger and sadness are unhappy bedfellows, each of which tends to crowd the other out.

When we turn our attention to some of the other attitudes that might fit a situation, the incompatibility is still more pronounced. Anger and chagrin are even less compatible than anger and sadness, which is one of the reasons why helping an angry person see that she has acted in ways that are similar to what has provoked her anger is often an effective way of defusing a conflict situation. The same is true of anger and hope, as well as anger and compassion. Anger focuses on something with negative value, while hope focuses on something with positive value. Anger desires its object to suffer harm, while compassion longs to alleviate suffering. The focal objects, characteristic desires, action tendencies, and defining affects of these emotions not only differ from one another, but many of them are at odds with one another. If ought implies can, then it is not the case that the virtuous agent should feel all of the attitudes that fit the situation, because she is not able to do so.

Defenders of the claim that the proper response to wrongdoing is anger have three rejoinders available to them at this point. First, so far the argument has only shown that it is not the case that the virtuous agent should feel every attitude that fits the situation *simultaneously*. However, even if she cannot feel every fitting attitude at the same time, it might still be possible for her to feel them *in sequence*. Perhaps she can begin with anger and then move to sadness, or compassion, etc., working her way through them like the stages of grief.

The sequential view is certainly more attractive than the simultaneous one; however, as a general strategy for handling the multiplicity of fitting attitudes, it still comes up short. Given the speed with which we move through the landscape of valuable objects, actions, and events, it is not possible for finite agents to experience all of the attitudes that fit all of the valuable things we encounter. With a few major events—like the loss of a loved one—we might have the opportunity to remain in the moment, as it were, and sequentially work our way through each of the attitudes that fit. But we can only do so by ignoring other features of the situations around us. Most events on most days will pass us by without our having registered more than a fraction of the attitudes that fit them. And we will not have the luxury of the time needed to make up the difference.

Even if we can surmount that difficulty, the sequential solution will not support the position of those who think that anger is not only called for when one is the victim of wrongful harm but should persist until the wrongdoer has apologized and made amends (à la Griswold). If the virtuous agent is to work through the attitudes that fit a situation in sequence, and anger or resentment is incompatible with some of those other attitudes—at least in the sense of making it difficult to feel them fittingly—then it follows that the virtuous agent is not obliged to continue feeling anger or resentment toward an as yet unreformed wrongdoer. Even if anger were compatible with each of the other fitting attitudes, there would be limitations on how many of the relevant attitudes could be experienced at once. Given this limitation, in order to move through each of the fitting attitudes in sequence, one would have to set aside some fitting attitudes in order to make space for others. So the theorist who insists that the virtuous victim should feel anger and should continue doing so will need something other than the sequential view in order to motivate his position.

The second rejoinder would begin with the observation that the discussion so far has focused on occurrent emotions. However, it seems unlikely that Hieronymi, Murphy, and Griswold are only talking about occurrent emotions. They are not claiming that one should continuously feel angry from the time of the transgression to the time of its correction. What they mean by being angry includes dispositional as well as occurrent anger.[14] And, as noted earlier, it is possible for dispositional anger to coexist alongside occurrent sadness, and vice versa. Perhaps the same is true of the other fitting emotional responses we have been considering.

While this rejoinder looks more promising than the last one, it suffers from some of the same problems. Dispositional anger alone is not going to be enough to capture what Griswold, Hieronymi, Murphy, and others mean when they claim that we ought to respond to wrongdoing with anger. A disposition to anger that never made itself felt would look more like the sublimated anger that Murphy considers unhealthy than it would like the self-respect

[14] I am grateful to Brandon Warmke for encouraging me to say more on this front.

preserving emotion he has in view. Mere dispositional anger would not satisfy the fitting attitude theorist, either. Fitting attitude theorists routinely
liken fitting responses to perceptual experiences. Having the disposition to
perceive an object when it is in one's visual field is different than perceiving it.
For an agent to perceive the value in a particular action, agent, object, or situation X, she will need to feel the relevant attitudes in response to X; that is,
she will need to experience the occurrent emotions of anger, sadness, compassion, and the like. At this point, the problems of the last few paragraphs re-
assert themselves: There will be limits on the number of occurrent emotions
a human being can experience either simultaneously or sequentially. There
will also be limits on the kinds of dispositional emotions that can coexist.
While it is possible for dispositional anger to coexist with dispositional compassion when they take different objects (so that one is angry at X and com-
passionately disposed toward Y), problems emerge when they take the same
object. Were our emotions perfectly rational, then it would not be possible
for them to coexist, since one favors an increase and the other a decrease in
X's suffering. As it stands, human emotions are not perfectly rational, so it is
possible for us to have conflicting dispositional emotions. However, the virtuous agent will be committed to resolving such conflicts when they occur
and reducing the likelihood of their reoccurrence.

A third option would be to develop a *hierarchical* account. Within such an
account there would be a hierarchy among the fitting attitudes, so that if two
of them conflict, one takes priority over the other. The theorist who thinks
the virtuous victim should feel anger rather than, say, compassion or disappointment could give anger a privileged place within the hierarchy. However,
she would then owe us an explanation of why anger takes priority over other
fitting responses.

The authors cited in the first section offer three reasons for feeling anger
that might be marched out in support of giving it such priority: (1) anger
reflects an accurate perception of one's own worthiness of respect, (2) it
expresses respect for morality, and (3) it deters future transgressors. As noted
earlier, the last of these reasons is of the "wrong kind." It is built around the
consequences of adopting the attitude, rather than on properties of the object of the attitude. Since it is in the same basket as the reasons offered by
Enright, Luskin, Ingram, and me that were discussed in the third section,
we can set it to one side. With regard to reasons 1 and 2, it is not clear why
the forms of respect they identify command more immediate attention than
the values highlighted by disappointment, hope, compassion, or love. One

might try to dismiss the teacher's excitement by insisting that moral concerns outweigh pedagogical ones. But one cannot shrug off the disappointment, hope, compassion, and love mentioned earlier, since each of them is built around moral concerns as well. However, let us assume, for the sake of argument, that the values reflected in respect for oneself and for morality override other values that might be present in the situation. Whether respect for oneself and for morality speak decisively in favor of anger will then depend upon whether it is possible for agents with attitudinal stances other than anger to perceive accurately their own worthiness of respect and to express their respect for morality. The answer to this question appears straightforwardly to be, Yes. Widely acknowledged exemplars in Hindu, Jewish, Buddhist, and Christian traditions have worked to root out anger from their field of emotional responses. This does not appear to have undermined either their self-respect or their respect for morality. Nor has it kept them from judging that certain actions are wrong or from being motivated to prevent or correct such actions (Pettigrove and Tanaka 2014).

The options we have considered thus far all assume that the "should" in the assumption "a virtuous agent responds to objects, actions, and events as they should" is the should of fittingness. Another possibility is that it is not a fitting should but a moral should. Many theorists who are sympathetic to fitting attitude accounts of value, including Mark Johnston, Justin D'Arms, and Daniel Jacobson, have defended it as a plausible theory of (at least some) value, but they have suggested that other factors might also need to be taken into account before we can determine what a person morally ought to do. A joke might be clever and unexpected, and amusement might be a fitting response. At the same time the joke might also be cruel, and as a result, it might be morally objectionable not only to tell it but also to be amused by it (D'Arms and Jacobson 2000a). Those who insist that the virtuous victim should feel anger (and continue feeling it) and who wish to pursue this route would owe us two stories. The first would explain the relationship between fitting attitudes and the moral should. The second would build on that foundation in order to show that anger is the moral response.

Depending on how one defines the moral should, there may be yet another step required for the argument to work. Some theorists take the moral should to be identical to the all-things-considered should; it picks out what one ought to do once all relevant factors have been taken into account. Others, however, take the moral should to apply only to what we owe to others. If the moral should is defined in this narrower fashion, then there will be a further step to explain how one goes from the moral to the all-things-considered should. The should of fittingness is an epistemic should. It is concerned with the accuracy of a person's perception of value. This epistemic should will need to be factored in alongside the pragmatic should, which is concerned with effective means to achieve a desired or valuable end. The ethical should, which might be concerned with the pursuit of self-perfecting ideals, will also need to be taken into account. There may be others, as well, such as the should of etiquette and the should of law. All of these shoulds—epistemic, moral, pragmatic, ethical, social, legal—are relevant to determining the all-things-considered should. So those who insist that the appropriate response to being wronged is anger will need to explain how the should of fitting anger, when combined with these other shoulds, prevails in the determination of the all-things-considered should.[15]

I have argued that the attempt to support claims made by Murphy, Hieronymi, Griswold, and others that anger is *the* appropriate response to being wronged by grounding them in a fitting attitude theory of value is more difficult than one might think. There are many attitudes that might fit the same situation and we cannot feel them all, whether simultaneously or in sequence. There is also a question of how one moves from the fitting should to the moral or all-things-considered should. The case becomes even more challenging when one revisits the issue we set aside a minute ago regarding the wrong kinds of reasons (WKRs).

The WKR problem was used in the third section to help motivate the claim that Murphy and company's reasons for forgiving were superior to Enright's, Ingram's, Luskin's, and mine and to reinforce the claim that in the absence of reasons like Murphy's, the appropriate response was anger. However, we observed earlier that Butler and Murphy highlight anger's importance as a form of self-defense, which is an appeal to the wrong kind of reason. What is more, their dependence on WKRs is not limited to reasons offered for anger. It also applies to the reasons on which they will depend in a number of contexts in which they deem forgiveness fitting. For example, Griswold

---

[15] Some value theorists may wish to treat the legal, social, pragmatic, and ethical as domains of fittingness that call for different characteristic responses. That is to say, they might wish to reduce all of the relations described here to relations between different types of fitting attitude. Such theorists will still need to account for these different kinds of attitudes and the relations between them, so the issues described in this paragraph will still need to be addressed. However, they will address the relationship between the dictates of personal ideals and those of pragmatism, for example, not in a separate step beyond the dictates of fittingness, but rather as a step along the way from the should of fittingness to the all-things-considered should.

(2007) argues that a wrongdoer who has expressed contrition and attempted to make amends is "due" forgiveness (51, 62, and 69). In some cases such forgiveness will be a natural and immediate response to the offender's contrition. However, in the case of serious wrongs, the kinds of reasons Enright, Ingram, Luskin, and I put forward may be psychologically required in order to forgive. This will not only be true in cases of what Alisa Carse and Lynne Tirrell (2010, 45) have called "grave, world-shattering wrongs," like those of the Hutu who participated in the genocide of Tutsi in Rwanda.[16] It will also be true of those who have been victims of more mundane misdeeds. The victim who suffered years of bullying at school may have trouble seeing even a repentant bully without experiencing anger. There may not be any direct, immediate route from the recognition of a changed state of affairs to the experience of a changed state of emotion. In many cases the only chance she will have of giving the contrite offender his "due" will be indirect, by attending to the kinds of reasons Enright, Luskin, and other therapists have highlighted.

If all parties to the discussion appeal to factors that would count as the WKRs, it is difficult to use their status as WKRs as grounds for dismissing some of the reasons on offer but not others. Of course, one might attempt to do so by drawing a distinction between different sorts of reasons that have been lumped together as reasons of the wrong kind. The cases that have featured most prominently in the WKR literature have been cases in which there is a conflict between pragmatic reasons and epistemic ones when, for example, a demon threatens to punish us unless we admire him (Rabinowicz and Ronnow-Rasmussen 2004, 407; see also Gibbard 1990, 37). In such cases, it would be advantageous to believe something false. Similarly, in the marriage case discussed earlier, it would be beneficial for W to believe X possesses qualities that would make him lovable, but she lacks the evidence to support such beliefs. However, unlike the reasons offered in each of these cases, the reasons Enright, Ingram, Luskin, and I advanced in favor of forgiving do not involve coming to believe anything false. Thus, the reasons for forgiving that were discussed in the third section are not ruled out by the most prominent distinction drawn in the current discussion.

Moreover, the fitting attitude account that would make anger the way in which we perceive the disvalue of a wrongful act fails to square with the temporal nature of many of our emotional experiences. It is natural to feel differently about an action or event after the passage of time than we did in the

---

[16] Griswold might deem such agents and their actions "unforgivable."

heat of the moment. This is true for a range of emotions both positive and negative. But this does not mean that we will assess the value of the action or event differently. At forty, the insults we endured at fourteen are unlikely to provoke our anger, but we are still likely to hold fixed our judgment that it was wrong for the insulter to say what he did. So even if—contra the argument offered earlier—anger were required in order to recognize an action as wrong, there is no reason to think forgiving remains illicit after the passage of time.

Pro Tanto Reasons for Anger?

Where does the argument of the last section leave the claim that our response to being wronged "is, and ought to be, anger and resentment" (Hieronymi 2001, 530)? One might try to accommodate the preceding discussion by acknowledging that a number of other readily available reasons can override the reason to feel angry, so it does not make sense to presume the forgiver is guilty until proven innocent. Nevertheless, it might be urged, wrongdoing still gives us a pro tanto reason—a reason to that extent—to be angry.[17] Evaluating this claim would require settling a number of heated debates regarding the nature of reasons, which is more than can be undertaken in the remainder of this chapter. However, it is worth identifying some of the factors that would contribute to its evaluation.

The first factor concerns the strength of pro tanto reasons. A strong conception of pro tanto reasons would hold that once we have been presented with such a reason we must comply with it. The only way in which not complying is justified is if that reason is overridden by others. A weak conception would hold that a pro tanto reason is sufficient—in the absence of other reasons—to *commend* (re)acting in a certain way, but it need not be sufficient to *compel* (re)acting in that way on pain of irrationality. It will be easier to make the case for the claim that being wronged gives us a pro tanto reason to be angry if we are working with a weak conception of pro tanto reasons than if we adopt a strong conception. On a weak conception, it would make sense for someone to respond to being wronged with anger—it would, in this sense, be fitting—but there would be nothing wrong if the person did not. This would not give us anything as forceful as "one ought to be angry." But it

---

[17] I am grateful to Dana Nelkin for encouraging me to address this issue.

would give anger at least some normative status. On a strong conception, not getting angry would only make sense if there were some other reason that overrode it. But even here, if there were numerous reasons that were readily available in most contexts and sufficient to override anger, then the claim that wrongdoing gives us a pro tanto reason to be angry might still be defensible. Within such a framework, saying anger is a fitting response to wrongdoing might be a way of picking out the fact that wrongdoing gives us a pro tanto reason to feel angry, but whether we have an all-things-considered reason or a moral reason to feel angry will depend upon how this pro tanto reason relates to the other reasons we have.

The second factor concerns the nature of anger. Murphy (1988, 18) claims that anger is important because it expresses a recognition of one's own value and a commitment to the rules of morality. However, as we have already seen, a number of emotions can express these same commitments. Hope that the wrongdoer will reform her ways and not reoffend can be an expression of these commitments. So can compassion, disappointment, and love. What distinguishes anger from these other responses? The most common answer is the one presupposed in the preceding discussion, namely, anger's desire that its object suffer.[18] If that is correct, then whether or not there is a pro tanto reason to be angry will depend on whether there is a pro tanto reason to desire another's suffering. This raises two further questions: (1) Is this the right account of what distinguishes anger from other emotions? (2) Are there certain kinds of actions that are so morally objectionable that we cannot have even a pro tanto reason to do them?

Regarding the first question, as previously noted, anger comes in many forms, including irritation, indignation, resentment, hatred, and rage. Do they all involve the desire that their object suffer? Resentment, hatred, and rage clearly do. What about irritation and indignation? The question is not whether they *can* involve such a desire but whether they *must*. It seems clear that irritation need not. It is chiefly concerned that the irritant go away, but that departure need not involve harm. Indignation is a harder case. Often the indignant want the object of their indignation to be punished, which characteristically involves suffering of some description. But in some cases it would seem more accurate to describe what they want in terms not of the wrongdoer suffering but rather in terms of her not benefitting from the transgression. They do not want the wrongdoer to get ahead as a result of her wrong.

---

[18] See Roberts 2003, 204; Pettigrove and Tanaka 2014, 275; and Nussbaum 2016, 5.

This may be coupled with a desire that the wrongdoer acknowledge her wrong for what it was, but this is not desired because they think the acknowledgment would be painful. If this is right, then, in at least some instances, the normative status of anger need not be contingent on the normative status of desiring another's suffering.

Regarding the second question, a number of people contend that what might have been a reason in some contexts can be neutralized by other factors that take priority. The fact that an action would bring me pleasure would in most contexts provide me with a reason to do it. But what if the action is cruel? John McDowell (1998, 17) argues, "To embrace a specific conception of eudemonia is to see the relevant reasons for acting, on occasions when they coexist with considerations that on their own would be reasons for acting otherwise, as, not overriding, but silencing those other considerations—as bringing it about that, in the circumstances, they are not reasons at all." On such a view, if it turns out that being angry is inconsistent with the standards of virtue, then being wronged would not provide even a pro tanto reason to be angry. So addressing the question of whether we have a pro tanto reason to be angry when we are wronged will require deciding whether reasons can be nullified (as opposed to overridden).

The last factor I will discuss has to do with the agent. Wrongdoing gives us a pro tanto reason to reject and resist it. Some agents have other emotional and behavioral resources besides anger that equip them to reject the kind of wrongful treatment to which they have been subjected and resist similar wrongs in the future. Other agents will lack these resources. For agents of the former type, wrongdoing might not even provide a pro tanto reason for anger. But agents of the latter type might very well have a pro tanto reason for anger that is derived from the pro tanto reason to reject wrongdoing.

Conclusion

I have argued that the attempt to motivate views like those outlined in the first section by appealing to the distinction between right and wrong kinds of reasons does not work. Most moral theorists working out the norms that apply in the aftermath of wrongdoing will have cause to appeal to reasons of both kinds. And the attempt to use a fitting attitude theory of value to justify the claim that anger is the appropriate response to being wronged likewise runs into difficulties. The argument, if correct, puts a wider range of reasons to forgive back on the table. It also undermines many of the assumptions that made forgiveness look questionable in the first place. Along the way the discussion has highlighted some of the challenges facing anyone who wishes to move from a modest fitting attitude account to a more encompassing moral account of what one should do.

It is worth adding one final observation. Murphy's, Butler's, and Hieronymi's discussion of threats draws attention to another attitude besides anger that fits many cases in which one has been the victim of wrongdoing, namely, fear. Understanding this fear is crucial for understanding the anger that many transgressions provoke. The fear that I could be treated like this and might be again plays an enormous emotional role in a person's readiness to forgive. We can see this most clearly in cases where that fear is quickly eliminated because the threat of future harm is completely neutralized. Often in such cases the accompanying anger also rapidly dissipates. We also see it in those cases where overcoming anger is most difficult, where vulnerability and fear are still most salient. So if one were really interested in providing a complete fitting attitude account of the aftermath of wrongdoing, one would need to give considerable attention to fear. It is interesting that philosophers have not given fear anything like the same attention they have given anger in such situations.[19] No one has argued that one ought to persist in being fearful and perhaps even nurture one's fear until the wrongdoer repents and makes amends. And while we might acknowledge both fear's accuracy and its utility in many conflict situations, this does not pose an objection to those who seek to develop a virtue (namely, courage) that might lead to a reduction in their fear. Furthermore, it is widely assumed to be a characteristic of courage that it can help a person overcome her fear without blinding her to the dangers she faces. If these assumptions are correct, then it recommends the possibility of a comparable virtue with respect to anger that enables one to overcome one's anger (a) even when anger remains fitting and (b) without blinding one to the qualities of the person, action, or situation such anger might fit.[20]

---

[19] My discussion of vulnerability (Pettigrove 2012b) and Nussbaum's of helplessness (Nussbaum 2016) invite readers to consider the relevance of fear to forgiveness, but we only scratch the surface.

[20] I am grateful to Marinus Ferreira, Dana Nelkin, Christine Swanton, and Brandon Warmke for helpful feedback on earlier drafts of this chapter.

References

Arnold, Johann Christoph. 2008. *Why Forgive?* Walden, NY: Plough Publishing House.

Brentano, Franz. 1969. *The Origin of Our Knowledge of Right and Wrong.* Roderick Chisholm and Elizabeth Schneewind, trans. Abingdon, UK: Routledge and Kegan Paul.

Butler, Joseph. (1726) 2017. "Upon Resentment." In *Joseph Butler: Fifteen Sermons and Other Writings on Ethics.* David McNaughton, ed., 68–74. Oxford: Oxford University Press.

Cacioppo, John, Gary Berntson, Jeff Larsen, Kirsten Poehlmann, and Tiffany Ito. 2000. "The Psychophysiology of Emotion." In *Handbook of Emotions*, 2nd ed. M. Lewis and J. M. Haviland-Jones, eds., 173–191. New York: Guilford Press.

Carse, Alisa, and Lynne Tirrell. 2010. "Forgiving Grave Wrongs." In *Forgiveness in Perspective*, Christopher Allers and Marieke Smit, eds., 43–65. Amsterdam: Rodopi.

Cherry, Myisha, and Owen Flanagan. 2017. *The Moral Psychology of Anger.* Lanham, MD: Rowman and Littlefield.

D'Arms, Justin, and Daniel Jacobson. 2000a. "The Moralistic Fallacy: On the "Appropriateness" of Emotions." *Philosophy and Phenomenological Research* 61: 65–90.

D'Arms, Justin, and Daniel Jacobson. 2000b. "Sentiment and Value." *Ethics* 110: 722–748.

Danielsson, Sven, and Jonas Olson. 2007. "Brentano and the Buck-Passers." *Mind* 116: 511–522.

Ekman, Paul, and Harriet Oster. 1979. "Facial Expressions of Emotion." *Annual Review of Psychology* 30: 527–554.

Enright, Robert. 2001. *Forgiveness Is a Choice.* Washington, DC: American Psychological Association.

Ewing, A. C. 1948. *The Definition of Good.* Abingdon, UK: Routledge and Kegan Paul.

Falk, W. D. 1986. *Ought, Reasons, and Morality.* Ithaca, NY: Cornell University Press.

Gibbard, Allan. 1990. *Wise Choices, Apt Feelings.* Cambridge, MA: Harvard University Press.

Griswold, Charles. 2007. *Forgiveness: A Philosophical Exploration.* Cambridge: Cambridge University Press.

Griswold, Charles. 2013. "The Nature and Ethics of Vengeful Anger." In *Passions and Emotions (Nomos 53)*, James Fleming, ed., 77–124. New York: NYU Press.

Haber, Joram. 1991. *Forgiveness: A Philosophical Study.* Lanham, MD: Rowman and Littlefield.

Hallich, Oliver. 2013. "Can the Paradox of Forgiveness Be Dissolved?" *Ethical Theory and Moral Practice* 16: 999–1017.

Hieronymi, Pamela. 2001. "Articulating an Uncompromising Forgiveness." *Philosophy and Phenomenological Research* 62: 529–555.

Hieronymi, Pamela. 2005. "The Wrong Kind of Reason." *The Journal of Philosophy* 102: 437–457.

Ingram, Stephen. 2013. "The Prudential Value of Forgiveness" *Philosophia* 41: 1069–1078.

Jacobson, Daniel. 2011. "Fitting Attitude Theories of Value." *Stanford Encyclopedia of Philosophy*, Edward Zalta, ed. (http://plato.stanford.edu/archives/spr2011/entries/fitting-attitude-theories).

Johansson, Ingvar. 2009. "A Little Treatise of Forgiveness and Human Nature." *The Monist* 92: 537–555.

Johnston, Mark. 1989. "Dispositional Theories of Value." *Aristotelian Society Supplement* 63: 139–174.

Johnston, Mark. 2001. "The Authority of Affect." *Philosophy and Phenomenological Research* 63: 181–214.

Kekes, John. 2009. "Blame versus Forgiveness." *The Monist* 92: 488–506.

Keltner, Dacher, Phoebe Ellsworth, and Kari Edwards. 1993. "Beyond Simple Pessimism: Effects of Sadness and Anger on Social Perception." *Journal of Personality and Social Psychology* 64: 740–752.

Kolnai, Aurel. 1973–1974. "Forgiveness." *Proceedings of the Aristotelian Society* 74: 91–106.

Lang, Gerald. 2008. "The Right Kind of Solution to the Wrong Kind of Reason Problem." *Utilitas* 20: 472–489.

Lemos, Noah. 1994. *Intrinsic Value: Concept and Warrant*. Cambridge: Cambridge University Press.

Luskin, Fred. 2002. *Forgive for Good*. New York: Harper Collins.

McDowell, John. 1998. "The Role of *Eudaimonia* in Aristotle's Ethics." *Mind, Value, and Reality*. Cambridge, MA: Harvard University Press.

Murphy, Jeffrie. 1988. "Forgiveness and Resentment." In *Forgiveness and Mercy*, Jeffrie Murphy and Jean Hampton, eds., 14–34. Cambridge: Cambridge University Press.

Murphy, Jeffrie. 2003. *Getting Even: Forgiveness and Its Limits*. New York: Oxford University Press.

Murphy, Jeffrie. 2012. *Punishment and the Moral Emotions* New York: Oxford University Press.

Nussbaum, Martha. 2016. *Anger and Forgiveness*. New York: Oxford University Press.

Parfit, Derek. 2001. "Rationality and Reasons." In *Exploring Practical Philosophy: From Action to Values*, Dan Egonsson, Jonas Josefsson, Björn Petersson, and Toni Ronnow-Rasmussen, eds., 17–39. Farnham, UK: Ashgate.

Pelser, Adam. 2014. "Emotion, Evaluative Perception, and Epistemic Justification." In *Emotion and Value*, Sabine Roeser and Cain Todd, eds., 107–123. Oxford: Oxford University Press.

Pettigrove, Glen. 2012a. *Forgiveness and Love*. Oxford: Oxford University Press.

Pettigrove, Glen. 2012b. "Forgiveness without God?" *Journal of Religious Ethics* 40: 518–544.

Pettigrove, Glen, and Koji Tanaka. 2014. "Anger and Moral Judgment." *Australasian Journal of Philosophy* 92: 269–286.

Pillar, Christian. 2001. "Normative Practical Reasoning." *Aristotelian Society Supplementary Volume* 75: 195–216.

Rabinowicz, Wlodek. 2013. "Value, Fitting-Attitude Account of." In *The International Encyclopedia of Ethics*, Hugh LaFollette, ed., 1–9. Oxford: Blackwell.

Rabinowicz, Wlodek, and Toni Ronnow-Rasmussen. 2004. "The Strike of the Demon: On Fitting Pro-Attitudes and Value." *Ethics* 114: 391–423.

Roberts, Robert. 2003. *Emotions*. Cambridge: Cambridge University Press.

Samuelsson, L. 2013. "The Right Version of the 'Right Kind of Solution to the Wrong Kind of Reason Problem.'" *Utilitas* 24: 383–404.

Srinivasan, Amia. 2018. "The Aptness of Anger." *Journal of Political Philosophy* 26: 123–144.

Wiggins, David. 1998. "A Sensible Subjectivism." In *Needs, Values, Truth*, 3rd ed., 185–214. Oxford: Oxford University Press.

Zagzebski, Linda. 2004. *Divine Motivation Theory*. Cambridge: Cambridge University Press.

Zaibert, Leo. 2009. "The Paradox of Forgiveness." *Journal of Moral Philosophy* 6: 365–393.

4

Forgiveness as Renunciation
of Moral Protest

Derk Pereboom

Introduction

On the standard view, when we forgive, we overcome or renounce future blaming responses to an agent in virtue of what the forgiver understands to be, and is in fact, an immoral action he has performed. Crucially, on the standard view the blaming response is understood as essentially involving a reactive attitude and its expression. In the central case in which the forgiver has been wronged by the party being forgiven, this reactive attitude is moral resentment, that is, anger with an agent due to a wrong he has done to oneself. When someone other than the forgiver has been wronged by the one being forgiven, the attitude is indignation, anger with an agent because of a wrong he has done to a third party. Such a position was developed by Joseph Butler (1749/1900), and in more recent times endorsed by P. F. Strawson (1962), Jeffrie Murphy (1982), and Jay Wallace (1994). Wallace (1994: 72), for example, claims that "in forgiving people we express our acknowledgment that they have done something that would warrant resentment and blame, but we renounce the responses that we thus acknowledge to be appropriate."

The standard view has in recent times been subjected to challenge. Eve Garrard and David McNaughton (2003), Dana Nelkin (2008, 2011: 44–50), and Brandon Warmke and Michael McKenna (2013) contend that in cases in which the forgiver is the wronged party, forgiveness need not involve an overcoming of resentment. In Nelkin's view, someone might not feel resentment in the first place and still forgive; one might, for instance, correctly perceive that one has been wronged, but not feel resentment, and then forgive the transgressor. The defender of the standard view may respond by arguing that in such cases, resentment was nonetheless appropriate, and believed to be so by the wronged party, while the forgiver renounces future resentment

Derk Pereboom, *Forgiveness as Renunciation of Moral Protest* In: *Forgiveness and Its Moral Dimensions*. Edited by: Brandon Warmke, Dana Kay Nelkin, and Michael McKenna, Oxford University Press. © Oxford University Press 2021. DOI: 10.1093/oso/9780190602147.003.0004

or its expression on her part. This route may well not be available to free will skeptics such as myself, who are concerned that resenting a wrongdoer is never appropriate due to resentment's presupposing that the wrongdoer basically deserves to be its target (Pereboom 2001, 2014), or due to resentment's commitment to a retributive desire (Honderich 1988, cf., Nussbaum 2016).[1] One possibility is that the renounced blaming responses need not be attitudes such as resentment and indignation, contested by free will skeptics (Pereboom 2014: 189–190), and I will now develop this claim. At the same time, even for the free will skeptic, if, despite her general rejection of its appropriateness of resentment, she nonetheless resents, forgiveness on her part would still involve her renouncing it and its expressions.

Separating Blameworthiness from the Appropriateness of Anger

Forgiveness requires that the wrongdoer was in fact morally responsible (in some sense) for his wrongdoing, thus blameworthy for his wrongdoing, and is believed to be blameworthy by the forgiver. This belief would have to be retained by the forgiver, on the pain of giving up a false belief. Hence it mustn't be the belief that the wrongdoer was blameworthy that the forgiver renounces. Rather, it must be attitudes and expressions of those attitudes that are justified in virtue of the wrongdoer's being blameworthy. Again, these attitudes are often specified to be reactive attitudes such as resentment and indignation. But perhaps this is a mistake. There may be cases of blameworthiness in which such attitudes are suboptimal, and even cases in which they are inappropriate. If so, supposing that wrongdoing in such cases can be forgiven, renouncing resentment and its expressions will not be required for forgiveness.

On one reading of P. F. Strawson's (1962) "Freedom and Resentment," blameworthiness is a response-dependent notion, according to which it's a particular emotional, attitudinal response that makes an action blameworthy; the blameworthy just is whatever occasions or perhaps merits such

---

[1] I've endorsed the cognitivist position on which having a reactive attitude such as resentment or indignation essentially involves as a component a belief that its target basically deserves to be blamed for an action (Pereboom 2001, 2014; cf. Wallace 1994; Nussbaum 2016). On this conception, it would be doxastically irrational for a free will skeptic to have such an attitude; she also believes that no agent ever basically deserves to be blamed, and thus she would have conflicting beliefs. Still, being angry and expressing anger may yet sometimes be practically rational.

a response. The response specified by Strawson in the case of a wrong done by another is one's moral resentment or indignation, both of which qualify as anger toward the other in virtue of his having done wrong.

David Shoemaker (2017) recently develops and defends such a Strawsonian account:

> **Fitting Response-Dependence about the Blameworthy:** The blameworthy (in the realm of accountability) just is whatever merits anger (the angerworthy); that is, someone is blameworthy (and so accountable) for X if and only if, and in virtue of the fact that, she merits anger for X.

Shoemaker contends that what unifies all of the properties that make anger appropriate is just that they merit anger, and this is what makes the account truly a response-dependent one. He argues that this is analogous with response dependence about the funny; what unifies all of the properties that make the amusement response appropriate is just that they merit this response. Most of his discussion defends his specific notion of response dependence, and not the selected type of response: anger.

As Shoemaker points out, there is a response-independent account that also features anger, but as a response which is independent of the property in which blameworthiness consists, while anger is made appropriate in virtue of that property:

> **Response-Independence about the Blameworthy:** The blameworthy consists in a property (or properties) of agents that makes anger at them appropriate, a property (or properties) whose value-making is ultimately independent of our angry responses. Anger at someone for X is appropriate if and only if, and in virtue of the fact that, she is antecedently blameworthy (and so accountable) for X. What makes her blameworthy is thus ultimately response-independent. (Fischer and Ravizza 1998; Brink and Nelkin 2013)

In this view, blameworthiness is not essentially dependent on the response of anger. But anger is the property chosen to fix the reference of the term "blameworthy." The blameworthy consists in properties that in fact actually merit anger, even if blameworthiness doesn't just consist in whatever merits anger.

Here I raise two concerns about the choice of anger in each of these accounts (Pereboom 2019). First, there are cases of blameworthiness that are plausibly not cases of angerworthiness. Athena is a parent, and her kids misbehave in minor, common, predictable ways; they squabble, fail to clean their rooms, and text their friends when they should be sleeping. Some parents respond with anger, but she doesn't, and instead responds from the sense of a duty to correct and educate, combined with care, but not with anger. The anger response is plausibly optional, and in many such cases seems in fact inappropriate. Basil is a teacher, and in every class at least some students misbehave in minor ways; they come unprepared not having done the assigned reading, talk about non-class-related matters in distracting ways, or surf the Internet instead of participating and paying attention. Suppose they're blameworthy. Basil responds with protest but not with anger. The anger response again seems optional, and here very plausibly inappropriate. In each of these cases, the angry response stands to be counterproductive and to undermine Basil's effectiveness and the respect students have for him. Evidence for the inappropriateness of anger in these kinds of cases is that parents and teachers who show anger in such cases are routinely criticized for being inappropriate.

One possible fix is to claim that the misbehavior in these cases is nevertheless pro tanto angerworthy, and that's enough to make it blameworthy. In reply, extending a point Victor Tadros (2016: 119) makes against Michael Moore's (1998) view about alleged pro tanto duties to criminalize, it's questionable that a response is pro tanto justified if the response is almost never appropriate, which in these cases the angry response would seem to be (Pereboom 2019).

The second concern is that anger has a strong tendency to distort judgments of blameworthiness, and that it's dubious that to be blameworthy is to be worthy of a reactive attitude that systematically distorts judgments of blameworthiness. Surveys conducted by Mark Alicke and his associates indicate that subjects who spontaneously evaluate agents' behavior unfavorably are apt to exaggerate their causal control and any evidence that might favor it while deemphasizing counterevidence (Alicke, Davis, and Pezzo 1994; Alicke 2000; Alicke, Rose, and Bloom 2012). Alicke calls this tendency *blame validation*. In the last several decades, impressive experimental evidence that blaming behavior is widely subject to problems of these kinds has been mounting (e.g., Nadelhoffer 2006).

There is reason to believe that it's the blame that accompanies anger that leads to these problems (Duggan, forthcoming). Psychological research indicates that anger, once activated, degrades subsequent reasoning processes in various ways (e.g., Lerner et al. 1998; Goldberg et al. 1999; Litvak et al. 2010). Anger increases tendencies to overlook mitigating details before attributing blame, to perceive ambiguous behavior as hostile, to rely on stereotypes, concerning, for example, ethnicity in assigning blame, and to discount the role of uncontrollable factors when attributing causality and punitiveness in response to witnessing mistakes made by others. Anger makes us slower to associate positive traits than negative traits with an out-group. Julie Goldberg and her associates (1999) find in one of their studies that when the retributive desire to harm is not satisfied, anger "activate[s] an indiscriminate tendency to punish others in unrelated situations without regard for whether their actions were intentional."

Strawson (1962) draws our attention to the attitudes appropriate upon wrongdoing within interpersonal relationships of mutual regard, such as intimate relationships and friendships, which has had the effect of participants in the debate focusing on attitudes attendant upon serious wrongdoing in such relationships. Reactive attitudes, involving moral anger, as expressions of blame might be particularly salient in these contexts. But much wrongdoing takes place outside such relationships, in parental relationships, and in relationships between teachers and students, as in the examples of Athena and Basil. One might respond by arguing that these are not paradigm cases, since they are not relationships of mutual regard. But consider relationships between faculty members or relationships between administrators and faculty. Nonmajor but significant wrongdoing in such relationships is frequent and to be expected. For example, university faculty are partial to their close colleagues and political allies when it comes to hiring and perks, and in many cases the resulting advocacy is wrong. Suppose Chloe is a university administrator and often faces these sorts of issues with faculty in her purview. Imagine she responds not with anger, but calmly with arguments that invoke the wider considerations. In such cases, angry responses typically reduce one's effectiveness and tend to cause false judgments which in turn motivate defective solutions.

These observations call for a general characterization of blameworthiness that does not highlight anger. Together with several others, I propose moral protest as the key notion. This, in turn, motivates an alternative conception of forgiveness, first proposed by Pamela Hieronymi (2001), according to which forgiving someone for doing wrong involves renunciation of the stance of moral protest against him for performing the action in question (Pereboom 2014: 189–190). In what follows, I develop and defend a version of this view.

Blame as Moral Protest

Pamela Hieronymi (2001), Matt Talbert (2012), Angela Smith (2013), and, in effect, Michael McKenna (2012) have proposed that blame should be understood as moral protest, and I follow their lead. Hieronymi (2001) connects moral protest and the reactive attitudes (as do the others just mentioned); for her, moral protest is a reactive attitude such as resentment. I maintain that moral protest need not involve resentment or indignation. When Athena, Basil, and Chloe protest the behavior at issue, they are morally concerned, but not resentful or indignant. I think of moral protest as a disposition, in the central case, to engage in confrontational verbal protest against an agent for having performed an action that the protester perceives to be morally wrong. Moral protest may be accompanied by emotions such as concern, disappointment, or sorrow; while it may be conjoined with a reactive attitude such as resentment or indignation, it need not be.

I've endorsed the following version of a moral protest view of blame (Pereboom 2017):

> **Moral Protest Account of Blame:** For B to blame A is for B to issue a moral protest against A for immoral conduct that B attributes (however accurately) to A.

The immoral conduct will typically be an immoral action, but there are cases in which the action considered separately from the reasons for which it's performed is not wrong, but the reasons make the overall conduct wrong (e.g., Haji 1998; Hanser 2005). Sometimes blame is misplaced, since no wrongful actions have been performed, but the protest can still count as blame. This may happen when B believes A to have acted wrongly but the belief is false, perhaps due to misinformation or improper consideration of evidence. This can also happen when B does not believe that A acted wrongly but nonetheless represents A as having acted wrongly, as in cases of false accusation motivated by rivalry. It's often the case that blame functions, as in Hieronymi's proposal, as a moral protest against an agent for a past action that persists as a present threat, and I agree that this is one highly important objective for blame. But not all blame has this point, as when we blame the dead, or blame someone who is alive but lacks a persisting disposition to act badly—someone, for instance, who has already undergone moral reform. In such cases protest can yet have the function of explicitly noting immoral behavior in order to encourage moral improvement on the part of an audience. In the example of the already-reformed wrongdoer, blame might still function as a step in the process of reconciliation.

An objection to the protest account of blame is that while unexpressed blame is possible, the idea of unexpressed protest is not even coherent, and hence blame cannot be accounted for in terms of protest. The concern is that protest is essentially communicative, and unexpressed protest is not communicative. Eugene Chislenko (2019) has recently provided a response, citing the distinction Coleen Macnamara draws between the activity of communicating—of which mental states kept private are not instances—and the idea of a communicative entity (Macnamara 2015b: 217). An unsent e-mail, even though it does not actually perform the function of communicating, has the function of evoking uptake of representational content in a recipient (Macnamara 2015a: 548). An unsent e-mail is thus communicative in nature; and similarly, unexpressed protest is communicative in nature. For a case in point, an unsent email might be an unexpressed message of protest. Chislenko says, "We can even say, as [Angela] Smith does of blame, that the email 'expresses protest, and . . . seeks some kind of moral reply' (2013: 39), even when the email is unsent" (Chislenko 2019). We can add that the email can express protest even if its author never intends to send it; and similarly, someone who privately blames may never intend to communicate it.

In accord with the protest account of blame, I propose the following amended version of Shoemaker's response-dependent view about the blameworthy:

> **Fitting Response-Dependence about the Blameworthy:** The blameworthy (in the realm of accountability) just is whatever merits moral protest (the protestworthy); that is, someone is blameworthy (and so accountable) for X if and only if, and in virtue of the fact that, she merits moral protest for X.

This account has a response-independent correlate, which also invokes moral protestworthiness but claims that there are properties that make wrongdoing protestworthy that are independent of our protest responses, while appropriate moral protest can serve to fix properties which "blameworthiness" picks out:

> **Fitting Protest-Response-Independence about the Blameworthy:** The blameworthy (in the realm of accountability) consists in a property (or

properties) of agents that makes morally protesting their wrongdoing appropriate, a property (or properties) whose value-making is ultimately independent of our responses of moral protest.

What are these properties? I've argued (2014: 134–135; 2017) that there is a largely forward-looking conception of blameworthiness, which aims at goods such as moral formation of character, reconciliation in relationships, retention of integrity of a victim, and protection from harm. Blame as moral protest can be understood as having these forward-looking components, together with a minimal backward-looking element: that the agent knowingly acted wrongly is part of what makes the protest appropriate. In accord with a broad consensus, it's the agent's responsiveness to reasons that's engaged in central cases of blaming, since blaming confronts its target with moral reasons. Thus, these properties would include the agent's knowingly having acted wrongly, her being reasons responsive, and her being disposed to moral protest's realizing the forward-looking aims.

Following Shoemaker, in these formulations I've retained the idea that the notion to be characterized is blameworthiness in the realm of accountability. If accountability requires the appropriateness of resentment and indignation, I would then want to reject accountability and advocate for answerability instead (as I do in Pereboom 2014: 131–138). But does blameworthiness in the realm of accountability essentially involve confrontation by such reactive attitudes? Shoemaker thinks so, but here is a lean characterization of accountability he himself provides:

> To be accountable for something is to be liable to being appropriately *held* to account for it, which is to be eligible for a range of fitting responsibility responses with a built-in confrontational element. (Shoemaker 2015: 87)

However, like anger, moral protest is essentially confrontational. But I'm fine with my proposal not counting as a view about accountability; this is likely a verbal issue.

Forgiveness as Renunciation of Moral Protest

If in many cases of personal wrongdoing, moral anger is not optimal or even appropriate, forgiveness should not generally be taken to be renunciation of moral anger and its expressions. In specific cases in which it is appropriate, forgiveness may involve its renunciation. But in cases of wrongdoing in which the angry response is not optimal and one does not in fact respond with anger but rather with concern, one's forgiveness cannot plausibly consist in the renunciation of moral anger and its expressions. This leaves it open that forgiveness involves the renunciation of whatever negative attitudes and their expressions are appropriate, where such attitudes differ across cases. This I accept, but let's explore the possibility that forgiveness nevertheless has a simple unified essence. Hieronymi suggests that forgiveness essentially involves the renunciation of moral protest. While she thinks of protest as involving resentment, at least in central cases, this connection can be denied, which I do. Even if resentment generally involves protest (cf. Hampton, in Murphy and Hampton 1988),[2] it's possible for moral protest not to involve any sort of moral anger, or even a belief in its appropriateness.

Imagine a friend has wronged you in some way a number of times by acting inconsiderately, and you find yourself resolved to end your relationship with him. You engage in a moral conversation with him, protesting against him for the wrong he has done and for the threat that his disposition to act in this way poses. In response, he is contrite, assumes a firm disapproving stance toward that disposition, and commits himself to full elimination. You might now withdraw your protest and agree to continue the relationship on a better footing. In Hieronymi's conception, forgiveness is such a withdrawal of a protest to a threat upon acknowledgment of the offender's change of heart:

If I ask for forgiveness, I am not asking you to understand why I did the deed, from my point of view. (I may no longer fully understand that myself. In any case, if I am properly repentant I surely don't recommend that point of view.) To ask you to understand things from my point of view is to hope for an excuse, not to ask for forgiveness. Nor, when I ask for forgiveness, am I asking for your pity or compassion in response to the pain of my remorse. Nor am I asking you simply to acknowledge the fact of my repentance and reform. I am instead asking you to believe me when I say that I no longer

---

[2] Jean Hampton writes: "[r]esentment is a kind of anger which protests the demeaning treatment to one who could and should have known better, and this protest is frequently linked to verbal rebuke, reprimand or complaint direct at the insulter" (Murphy and Hampton 1988: 55).

see what I did to you as acceptable, to recognize and so ratify my change of heart. (Hieronymi 2001: 554)

Even if forgiveness sometimes involves the renunciation of resentment, and sometimes the renunciation of a different emotional attitude, I contend that in every case it involves renunciation of morally protesting against the wrongdoer for having committed the specific wrong at issue. This renunciation involves one's acquiring a belief that such protest on one's own part is no longer appropriate, and a commitment to acting on this belief. This renunciation is compatible with the forgiver never having actually protested the wrong, since in renouncing moral protest one renounces potential and not only actual protest.

Here is a case of Per-Erik Milam's (2021 that serves to illustrate this proposal:

Infidelity. David cheats on his partner, Donna. At first he thinks it's no big deal, but he begins to feel more and more ashamed of his behaviour and guilty about betraying her trust. David recognizes what his remorse is telling him and he recommits himself, in his own mind, to being a faithful partner. Shortly thereafter he admits to Donna what he did, apologizes to her, and assures her that it won't happen again, explaining how guilty and ashamed he feels and how much he values their relationship. Donna is understandably upset and, at first, does not know what to do. Eventually though she comes to believe that David is sincere in his remorse and apology, that he is trustworthy, and that they can still have a healthy and fulfilling relationship together. Donna overcomes her blame and tells David that she forgives him.

One might ask what Donna's forgiveness consists in. In my view, it's Donna's believing that moral protest on her part against David for what he has done is no longer appropriate, and being committed to acting on this belief. We can imagine that Donna has never actually protested the action. Nevertheless, she can still renounce future moral protest against David for his infidelity. If Donna does say at some future time, "You are such a jerk for being unfaithful; I can't believe that you did this!" it seems clear that she hasn't forgiven him.

In the case of Basil, the teacher, suppose one day, Emma, a student for whom he has high hopes, for the first time in the course is not paying attention to class proceedings and is surfing the Internet instead. Protest is appropriate even if anger is not, and forgiveness, as the renunciation of further moral protest, may be granted upon contrition and apology. Basil may say to Emma: "Your surfing the Internet is distracting to other students, and it would be best for you to pay attention instead" without being angry but with moral concern for her and from a sense of duty for seeing to her education and moral formation. Suppose Emma expresses contrition and apologizes, and her subsequent behavior in the class indicates, to Basil, a change of heart. If at that point he nevertheless calls her aside to say: "You were wrong to surf the Internet that day; it distracts other students, and you should have been paying attention," it would be clear that he hadn't yet responded to her contrition with forgiveness. Suppose instead that in response to Emma's contrition Basil renounces appropriateness of this sort of protest on his part. This would be a case of forgiveness with renunciation of moral protest but without renunciation of resentment. However, if resentment were appropriate—suppose that free will skepticism is false and resentment was appropriate upon discovery of unfaithfulness in an intimate relationship—forgiveness upon contrition and apology would involve renunciation of further moral protest, even if it would also involve renunciation of resentment. Thus, I propose, renunciation of moral protest can qualify as the essence of forgiveness.

Forgiveness might involve an occurrent belief that morally protesting a wrongdoer's having performed an action is no longer appropriate, together with an overt verbal communication to the wrongdoer that she has been forgiven. But in some cases the belief that protest was appropriate may be merely dispositional and not occurrent, and the indication to the wrongdoer that she has been forgiven might be understated—evident, for example, only in subtle changes in the forgiver's behavior and expression. What is ruled out upon having forgiven is overt verbal moral protest against the agent for having performed the act in question, and also a continuing dispositional but uncommunicated stance of moral protest. Some overt specifications of wrongdoing don't count as protest. In cataloguing instances in which a forgiver has been wronged in the past, she might cite a wrongdoing she has forgiven in a way that doesn't count as moral protest against the wrongdoer. But she might cite the wrongdoing in such a way as to indicate that she hasn't forgiven, and this would be the case if how she expresses it is indicative of a stance of protest against the wrongdoer for having acted as he did.

Renunciation of Moral Protest Must Be
for the Right Reason

Moral protest might come to be regarded as inappropriate for various reasons. One is that the putative wrongdoer has a valid excuse. One might initially think that it is legitimate to protest against the fellow subway passenger for stepping on your foot, but then come to realize that this was neither intentional nor negligent, but that he inadvertently stepped on your foot due to being pushed by another passenger. Here one renounces moral protest, but this is not a case of forgiveness. More generally, renouncing protest due to recognition of an excuse is not forgiveness (cf. Nelkin 2013).

Suppose a senior colleague is a conversation dominator; in an average one-on-one conversation, through the mastery of various techniques, such as not breathing between changes of topic, your colleague manages 90% air time. You've protested against him for this behavior in the past, but to no avail, and you've come to believe the condition is unalterable, except perhaps by neural intervention, which you believe is on balance morally inadvisable in this case. You then come to renounce the appropriateness of moral protest, but specifically because you have come to believe the condition is conventionally unalterable. This is again not a case of forgiveness, even though it involves the renunciation of moral protest. Renunciation of protest due to regarding behavior as incorrigible does not count as forgiveness. Milam (2019) would classify this as a case of *letting go*, not of forgiveness, and I agree.

Imagine that a friend has certain habits that result in behavior that is morally wrong but only in a minor way; being somewhat too angry at bad drivers, being mildly noncharitable toward rival philosophers, or insufficiently restraining irritability when tired. One might renounce moral protest in such cases because the moral offenses are too minor, and even if there's a chance of the protest being effective, you think it's not worth the disruption of one's relationships to achieve the result. Here again one renounces moral protest, but without forgiveness. This is plausibly also a case of letting go.

Central cases of forgiveness involve the renunciation of moral protest in response to contrition on the part of the wrongdoer, or as Milam (2019) puts it, in response to perceived change of heart on the part of the wrongdoer. Perhaps the wronged party *should*, at least pro tanto, forgive upon recognition of contrition, since not forgiving in such circumstances fails to respond to sufficient reason to forgive. Contrition can be manifested through apology, but sometimes through other verbal and behavioral expressions.

Milam argues that other sorts of reasons to cease to engage in blaming are not reasons to forgive. We might renounce moral protest because the offender had good intentions (Murphy and Hampton 1988), or because the threat incipient in the offence has been neutralized (Hieronymi 2001), or out of solidarity (Garrard and McNaughton 2003), but these are not cases of forgiveness. Are there any cases of forgiveness that aren't responses to contrition, change of heart? Nelkin (in correspondence) suggests that we sometimes forgive a wrongdoer just because we believe he has suffered enough, even if he hasn't undergone a change of heart. But perhaps this is also a case of letting go and not of forgiveness.

One might suggest instead that forgiveness is essentially relationship focused; perhaps what it is to forgive is to cease to regard the wrong done as a reason to weaken or dissolve a relationship. This feature can be seen as retracting blame in the sense Scanlon characterizes it (Scanlon 2009: 128). My forgiving someone who has wronged me would involve my initially having judged that what he did showed something about his attitude toward me that impairs his relationship with me, but in response to his repentance, my no longer taking this relationship to be modified in a way that this judgment of impaired relations justifies as appropriate. The judgment of impaired relations is withdrawn because I take him to have given up the attitude toward me that impairs our relationship. A concern for Scanlon's view, pressed by Susan Wolf (2011), is that relationships are often resilient to and not impaired by blameworthiness of a minor sort. Routine and expected wrongdoing, such as a spouse's snappy irritability when tired, or a child's not cleaning his room, may not be relationship impairing (Pereboom 2017). Such wrongdoing might still might be forgiven--by renunciation of protest against the wrongdoer, and so forgiveness is not essentially relationship restoring.

Forgiveness, the Standard View, and Norm Changing

Problems noted for the standard view, notably that forgiveness does not require renunciation of actual resentment or other initially appropriate negative reactive attitudes, have motivated development of an alternative conception by philosophers such as Brandon Warmke and Dana Nelkin: the norm-changing view. In Nelkin's conception, it is sufficient for forgiving that one choose to release an offender from certain obligations generated by his offence, whether or not one continues resenting or blaming him (Nelkin 2013). On her view, blameworthy action generates an obligation on the part of the wrongdoer to apologize or make amends, and for the wronged party to forgive the wrongdoer is to release him from this obligation. Warmke (2016) argues that forgiveness changes the normative significance of the offence from one which warrants various negative responses to a state where at least some of these responses are no longer justified. In his view, in forgiving, a victim releases the wrongdoer from certain personal obligations to do these things, and the victim can release the wrongdoer only from those obligations over which the victim has normative authority. The victim may tell the wrongdoer that he does not need to keep apologizing and that no further restitution or penance is expected. In Warmke's view, in forgiving, the victim releases the wrongdoer from certain obligations but also gives up certain rights to blame, and thus norms for both wrongdoer and wrongdoer are changed. On such a conception, forgiveness resembles norm-changing actions such as debt forgiveness or waiving a promise (Twambley 1976; Nelkin 2013; Warmke 2016).

Warmke further maintains that, generally speaking, paradigmatic cases of forgiveness involve both psychological changes and a certain kind of communicative, norm-changing act that is motivated and rationalized by those psychological changes. I endorse Warmke's general conception. I want to emphasize that altering the norms between victim and offender is not itself sufficient for forgiveness. In my view, the change of norms that partially constitutes forgiveness would have to be brought about by a change of attitude in the forgiver, and this change of attitude is the core element of forgiveness. This core element always involves a renunciation of moral protest, and it will sometimes involve the renunciation of anger. That this is the core element of forgiveness can be seen by examining central cases of forgiveness. In the case of serious interpersonal wrongdoing, as in the *Infidelity* example, forgiveness is a response to a wrongdoer's change of heart expressed in apology and offering to make amends. Imagine that in this case the amends consist in David's making a sincere commitment to spending less time away from Donna and engaging in activities that stand to renew the relationship. But then it's implausible that Donna's forgiveness would consist in Donna releasing David from the obligation to apologize and to make these amends. David has already apologized, and in the normative case, the apology is ongoing in the sense that it's not retracted. One might imagine Donna asking for the apology to be made again; that might be consistent with her forgiveness if what she wants is for the apology not to be retracted. The amends are an on-going project, and releasing David from the obligation to make these amends is not a requirement of forgiveness in this case. True, asking him to make yet further amends might well be at odds with forgiveness. But we can now see that the core element of her forgiveness is her renunciation of protest, and perhaps anger. Donna's protest: "You are such a jerk for being unfaithful; I can't believe that you did this!" would clearly indicate that she hasn't forgiven him.

Warmke (2016) contends that the overcoming of resentment can't have the norm-changing function that he specifies:

> How could giving up my resentment towards someone else have an effect not only on how I am morally permitted to treat that someone, but also on how that person is morally obliged to treat me? I see no way of linking my overcoming of resentment to the inappropriateness of, say, asking for apologies or engaging in other forms of overt blame. Nor can I see how my overcoming resentment would release you from certain personal obligations to, say, apologize to me or offer me restitution. (Warmke 2016: 692)

He is right that my mere *overcoming* of resentment can't affect how I am obligated to treat the wrongdoer. But my *renunciation* of resentment, since it involves a moral commitment I make, can have this function, and similarly renunciation of moral protest. But, as Warmke plausibly contends, releasing the wrongdoer from obligations such as further amends cannot be private; it must be communicated to the wrongdoer. So as Milam (2020) points out, it is not enough to *intend* to release the offender from his obligation because one might still fail to carry through or abandon the intention. Richard Swinburne's conception satisfies this constraint; he argues that "forgiving is a performative act—achieved perhaps by saying solemnly 'I forgive you,' or perhaps by saying 'That's all right,' or maybe by just a smile" (Swinburne 1989: 85). In Warmke's view, forgiving is a declarative act, but he emphasizes that it must feature an appropriate rational and motivational mesh between the act and mental states. The forgiver must, for instance, intend to forgive by means of the words he uses. Here the importance of the forgiver's mental state of renunciation of a stance such as resentment or protest can be highlighted. Suppose I'm self-deceived in my belief that I no longer resent you for maligning me, and that my attempt to renounce the stance of moral protest is a failure. Then I am mistaken when I say, "I forgive you"; I say the words, but I don't forgive. Some norms may have changed by my having said what I did, but forgiveness hasn't occurred. A pronouncement of forgiveness thus has content that can be falsified by the nature of one's attitudinal stance.

Donna's forgiving David features the belief that he was blameworthy for his wrongdoing, and on a moral protest view of blameworthiness this entails that his action was protestworthy. Donna has renounced moral protest on her own part against David for his infidelity, but this is consistent with others appropriately not renouncing their moral protest against David for this wrongdoing, in particular if he has not manifested his contrition to them. Imagine David has been unfaithful with someone in the purview of his professional responsibility. In forgiving, Donna does not renounce moral protest on the part of relevant figures in his profession; Warmke (2016) makes this point. Donna might see continued moral protest on the part of those figures as appropriate, but in view of the apologies and amends David has made to her, renounce moral protest on her own part.

Summary

My proposal for an account of forgiveness, like Warmke's (2016), combines elements of both the standard and the norm-changing views. Forgiveness need not be preceded by actual resentment, or indeed any actual angry emotion. Rather, the forgiver, by virtue of regarding the wrongdoer as blameworthy for a past wrongdoing, regards moral protest against him for this specific wrongdoing as having been appropriate. In forgiving, she renounces such moral protest on her own part going forward, both the psychological stance and its expressions. This renunciation is constitutively norm changing, first of all because it involves moral protest on her part changing from being appropriate to being inappropriate. Other alterations in norms may accompany this change: earlier the wronged party legitimately demanded apology and amends, while when she forgives, the request for new apologies and additional amends become inappropriate.[3]

---

[3] Thanks to Brandon Warmke, Dana Nelkin, and Michael McKenna for valuable comments and discussion.

References

Alicke, M. D. 2000. "Culpable Control and the Psychology of Blame." *Psychology Bulletin* 126: 556–574.

Alicke, Mark. D., T. L. Davis, and M. V. Pezzo. 1994. "A Posteriori Adjustment of a Priori Decision Criteria." *Social Cognition* 8: 286–305.

Alicke, Mark., D. Rose, and D. Bloom. 2012. "Causation, Norm Violation and Culpable Control." *Journal of Philosophy* 106: 587–612.

Brink, David, and Dana Nelkin. 2013. "Fairness and the Architecture of Responsibility." In *Oxford Studies in Agency and Responsibility*, vol. 1., edited by David Shoemaker, 31–54. New York: Oxford University Press.

Butler, Joseph. 1900. *The Works of Bishop Butler*. London: Macmillan.

Chislenko, Eugene. 2019. "Blame and Protest." *The Journal of Ethics* 23: 163–181.

Duggan, Austin. forthcoming. "A Genealogy of Retributive Intuitions."

Fischer, John M., and Mark Ravizza. 1998. *Responsibility and Control*. Cambridge: Cambridge University Press.

Garrard, Eve, and David McNaughton. 2003. "In Defence of Unconditional Forgiveness." *Proceedings of the Aristotelian Society* 100: 39–60.

Goldberg, Julie, J. Lerner, and P. Tetlock. 1999. "Rage and Reason: The Psychology of the Intuitive Prosecutor." *European Journal of Social Psychology* 29: 781–795.

Haji, Ishtiyaque. 1998. *Moral Accountability*. New York: Oxford University Press.

Hanser, Matthew. 2005. "Permissibility and Practical Inference." *Ethics* 115: 443–470.

Hieronymi, Pamela. 2001. "Articulating an Uncompromising Forgiveness." *Philosophy and Phenomenological Research* 62: 529–554.

Honderich, Ted. 1988. *A Theory of Determinism*. Oxford: Oxford University Press.

Lerner, Jennifer S., Julie H. Goldberg, and Philip E. Tetlock. 1998. "Sober Second Thought: The Effects of Accountability, Anger, and Authoritarianism on Attributions of Responsibility." *Personality and Social Psychology Bulletin* 24, no. 6: 563–574.

Litvak, Paul M., Jennifer S. Lerner, Larissa Z. Tiedens, and Katherine Shonk. 2010. "Fuel in the Fire: How Anger Impacts Judgment and Decision-Making." In *International Handbook of Anger*, edited by Michael Potegal, Gerhard Stemmler, and Charles Spielberger, 287–310. New York: Springer.

Macnamara, Coleen. 2015a. "Reactive Attitudes as Communicative Entities." *Philosophy and Phenomenological Research* 90: 546–569.

Macnamara, Coleen. 2015b. "Blame, Communication, and Morally Responsible Agency." In *The Nature of Moral Responsibility: New Essays*, edited by Randolph Clarke, Michael McKenna, and Angela M. Smith, 211–235. New York: Oxford University Press.

McKenna, Michael. 2012. *Conversation and Responsibility*. New York: Oxford University Press.

Milam, Per-Erik. 2019. "Reasons to Forgive." *Analysis* 79, no. 2: 242–251.

Milam, Per-Erik. 2020. "Forgiveness." In *The Oxford Handbook of Moral Responsibility*, edited by Dana K. Nelkin and Derk Pereboom. Oxford: Oxford University Press.

Moore, Michael. 1998. *Placing Blame*. Oxford: Oxford University Press.

Murphy, Jeffrie. 1982. "Forgiveness and Resentment." *Midwest Studies in Philosophy* 7, no. 1: 503–516.

Murphy, Jeffrie, and Jean Hampton. 1988. *Forgiveness and Mercy*. Cambridge: Cambridge University Press.

Nadelhoffer, Thomas. 2006. "Bad Acts, Blameworthy Agents, and Intentional Action." *Philosophical Explorations* 9: 203–220.

Nelkin, Dana. 2008. "Responsibility and Rational Abilities: Defending an Asymmetrical View." *Pacific Philosophical Quarterly* 89: 497–515.

Nelkin, Dana. 2011. *Making Sense of Freedom and Responsibility*. Oxford: Oxford University Press.

Nelkin, Dana K. 2013. "Freedom and Forgiveness." In *Free Will and Moral Responsibility*, edited by Ishtiyaque Haji and Justin Caouette. Newcastle: Cambridge Scholars Press.

Nussbaum, Martha. 2016. *Anger and Forgiveness*. Oxford: Oxford University Press.

Pereboom, Derk. 2001. *Living without Free Will*. Cambridge: Cambridge University Press.

Pereboom, Derk. 2014. *Free Will, Agency, and Meaning in Life*. Oxford: Oxford University Press.

Pereboom, Derk. 2017. "Responsibility, Regret, and Protest." In *Oxford Studies in Agency and Responsibility*, vol. 4., edited by D. Shoemaker, 121–140. New York: Oxford University Press.

Pereboom, Derk. 2019. "Free Will Skepticism and Prevention of Crime." In *Free Will Skepticism in Law and Society*, edited by Gregg Caruso, Elizabeth Shaw, and Derk Pereboom, 99–115. Cambridge: Cambridge University Press.

Scanlon, Thomas M. 2009. *Moral Dimensions*. Cambridge: Harvard University Press.

Shoemaker, D. 2015. *Responsibility from the Margins*. Oxford: Oxford University Press.

Shoemaker, D. 2017. "Response-Dependent Responsibility." *The Philosophical Review* 126: 481–527.

Smith, Angela. 2013. "Moral Blame and Moral Protest." In *Blame: Its Nature and Norms*, edited by N. Tognazzini and J. Coates, 27–48. New York: Oxford University Press.

Strawson, Peter. F. 1962. "Freedom and Resentment." *Proceedings of the British Academy* 48: 187–211.

Swinburne, Richard. 1989. *Responsibility and Atonement*. Oxford: Clarendon Press.

Tadros, Victor. 2016. *Wrongs and Crimes*. Oxford: Oxford University Press.

Talbert, Matthew. 2012. "Moral Competence, Moral Blame, and Protest." *Journal of Ethics* 16: 89–101.

Twambley, P. 1976. "Forgiveness." *Analysis* 36, no. 2: 84–90.

Wallace, R. Jay. 1994. *Responsibility and the Moral Sentiments*. Cambridge, MA: Harvard University Press.

Warmke, Brandon. 2016. "The Normative Significance of Forgiveness." *Australasian Journal of Philosophy* 94, no. 4: 687–703.

Warmke, Brandon, and Michael McKenna. 2013. "Moral Responsibility, Forgiveness, and Conversation." In *Free Will and Moral Responsibility*, edited by Ishtiyaque Haji and Justin Caouette, 189–212. Newcastle upon Tyne: Cambridge Scholars Press.

Wolf, Susan. 2011. "Blame, Italian Style." In *Reasons and Recognition: Essays on the Philosophy of T. M. Scanlon*, edited by R. Jay Wallace, Rahul Kumar, and Samuel Freeman, 332–347. New York: Oxford University Press.

5

Forgiveness and Freedom to Do Otherwise

Ishtiyaque Haji

Preamble

Let's say that one has free will with respect to an action if and only if one can both perform it and refrain from performing it. It may be thought that the following propositions inform a relatively straightforward approach to whether forgiveness and free will are inextricably associated. (1) It is uncontroversial that one can duly be forgiven for something only if one is to blame for this thing. (2) However, although this is more controversial, Frankfurt examples show that blameworthiness does *not* require that one have alternative possibilities (Frankfurt 1969).[1] Hence, there is no interesting connection between forgiveness and free will unless (3) there are *other* reasons to believe that forgiveness has crucial ties to free will.

Arguably, (3) is true. To explain, in addition to presupposing blameworthiness, it is commonly thought that forgiveness also presupposes moral impermissibility. One can properly be forgiven for something only if it is impermissible for one to do this thing. This is the putative *impermissibility presupposition* of forgiveness. Some people are more cautious. Skeptical of anyone's ever being able to advance an analysis of forgiveness, they claim that paradigmatic instances of forgiveness presuppose impermissibility.[2] If this is so, it is easy to unearth a clear-cut connection between forgiveness and freedom to do otherwise. For impermissibility entails avoidability: Since "impermissible" is equivalent to "ought not"—principle *Equivalence*—if it is impermissible for one to do something, then one ought not to do it. Since "ought not" implies "can" refrain from (and "ought" implies "can")—principle *OIC*—if one ought not to do something, then one can refrain from

---

[1] Insightful papers on Frankfurt examples are to be found in Widerker and McKenna 2003.

[2] See, for example, Warmke and McKenna 2013, pp. 197–198. In a footnote (2013, p. 210, n. 5), Warmke and McKenna caution that they do not want to commit to the claim that forgiveness entails impermissibility.

Ishtiyaque Haji, *Forgiveness and Freedom to Do Otherwise* In: *Forgiveness and Its Moral Dimensions*. Edited by:
Brandon Warmke, Dana Kay Nelkin, and Michael McKenna, Oxford University Press. © Oxford University Press 2021.
DOI: 10.1093/oso/9780190602147.003.0005

doing it. Hence, if it is impermissible for one to do something, then one can refrain from doing it. But as forgiveness (or prime cases of it) presupposes impermissibility, it follows that forgiveness (or central cases of it) cannot be divorced from at least freedom to do otherwise. Assessing this argument, which putatively links forgiveness with alternative possibilities, sets the stage for this chapter.

In what follows, first I argue that Frankfurt examples go a long way toward showing that the impermissibility presupposition of forgiveness (or paradigm instances of forgiveness) is mistaken. Indeed, it seems that forgiveness does not even presuppose that the forgiven believe that it is impermissible for her to do (or fail to do) whatever it is for which she is forgiven. Focusing, then, on the alleged impermissibility presupposition of forgiveness to unearth an essential connection between forgiveness and freedom to do otherwise appears to be wide off the mark.

Second, I motivate the view that forgiveness, in virtue of presupposing blameworthiness, is essentially connected to prima facie obligation, which, in turn, *is* necessarily associated with free will. But this route to exposing a nontrivial link between forgiveness and free will saddles us with a dilemma: Either reject one or more of what appear to be plausible principles that establish conceptual connections among forgiveness, blameworthiness, and prima facie obligation, or renounce Frankfurt examples. I comment on each horn and my preference to reject the first.

Why Forgiveness Does Not Presuppose Impermissibility

Typical Frankfurt examples, frequently called upon to cast suspicion on the principle of alternate possibilities—persons are morally responsible for having done something only if they could have done otherwise—may be partitioned into two stages. In stage 1, Mary ridicules her friend, Ben, for questionable reasons. Assume that in this stage, she could have refrained from deriding Ben, and it is both impermissible for her to deride him and she is blameworthy for doing so. In stage 2 (which may be thought of as a "rerun" of stage 1), a counterfactual intervener, who fails to show his hand, would have forced Mary to ridicule Ben had she displayed an involuntary sign that she was about to refrain. But Mary acts no differently in this stage than she does in the former. It looks like she is blameworthy for her relevant behavior in stage 2, even though she could not have done otherwise. If we accept the argument in the first section for the conclusion that impermissibility entails avoidability, then contrary to what one may believe, although it is impermissible for Mary to ridicule Ben in stage 1, it is not impermissible for her to do so in stage 2.[3]

Revert now to the impermissibility presupposition of forgiveness. It may be formulated more perspicuously in this way: Just as resentment may be misplaced because, for instance, the recipient of this reactive attitude is not blameworthy for the germane bit of behavior, so forgiveness may be misplaced or not well-founded. Confining attention to "proprietary" forgiveness, the proposal is that

> F1: If at time, t, T brings about state of affairs, A, at time t^* (where t^* may be identical to or later than t), and S forgives T for bringing about A, then at t it is impermissible for T to bring about A at t^*.[4]

F1 has many partisans. For example, Derk Pereboom proposes that forgiveness presupposes not only that the forgiven is deserving of blame but that she has done wrong, and the forgiver is willing to cease to regard the wrong done to him as a reason to weaken or dissolve the relationship with the forgiven (1995, p. 40). Similarly, Jeffrie Murphy claims that forgiveness "essentially involves an attempt to overcome resentment," and resentment—and thus forgiveness—is directed toward responsible wrongdoing (Murphy and Hampton 1988, p. 20). Murphy adds that "if forgiveness and resentment are to have an arena it must be where such wrongdoing remains intact—i.e., neither excused nor justified" (p. 20). Jean Hampton also agrees that forgiving someone presupposes that the action to be forgiven was wrong (Murphy and Hampton 1988, pp. 40, 54–55). Pamela Hieronymi ventures, like Murphy, that forgiveness is the overcoming of resentment, the overcoming must be sensitive to reasons in the form of a change in judgment, but this change not include retraction of the view that the forgiver has been significantly wronged by a responsible agent (2001, p. 546). Dana Nelkin theorizes that forgiveness entails releasing the forgiven from a certain sort of obligation incurred as a result of committing some wrong against one (2013, p. 175).

---

[3] Nelkin argues (e.g., in 2011) that even in stage 2, the agent has alternatives. I reply in Haji 2014 and 2016.

[4] I assume that "ought" statements are agent and time indexed in this way: As of t, S ought (or it is impermissible or permissible for S) to do A at t^*. For simplicity, I will sometimes suppress one or both of the temporal indices in "ought" statements.

Margaret Holmgren claims that "forgiveness rather than resentment is the morally appropriate attitude for the victim who has sufficiently completed the process of addressing the wrong" (2014, p. 173). Lucy Allais proposes that "the possibility of forgiveness comes into play precisely in relation to unexcused, unjustified, unacceptable wrongdoing, which warrants resentment (or, more generally, negative appraisal evaluations)" (2014, p. 41).[5]

However, the Frankfurt example featuring Mary and Ben undermines F1. Suppose Ben gets wind of Mary's untoward behavior (in stage 2). He finds it in his heart to forgive her. Without good reason to believe otherwise, it appears that there is nothing suspect about this instance of forgiveness. The presence of the counterfactual intervener (perhaps together with his mind-reading gismo if he uses one) ensures that Mary could not have done other than ridicule Ben in stage 2, and so renders it true that it is *not* impermissible for Mary to ridicule Ben. But the intervener's presence does nothing, it appears, to call into question Ben's forgiving Mary for behavior that turns out not to be impermissible for Mary. Mary would have acted no differently in stage 2 in the intervener's absence, and we may assume that with the passage of time, Ben would still have forgiven Mary for mocking him. Notice, furthermore, that (without the intervener in stage 2) this is a *typical* sort of scenario involving forgiveness. We may conclude that forgiveness does not presuppose impermissibility.

According to the ledger account of moral responsibility, to be morally responsible is to be such that one's moral standing or record as a person is affected by some episode in, or aspect of, one's life. Unlike a rival Strawsonian account, which conceptualizes responsibility as susceptibility to certain reactive attitudes, the ledger account identifies responsibility with that in virtue of which one is susceptible to such attitudes (M. Zimmerman 1988, pp. 38–39; 2002, p. 555; Haji 1998.) On this account, when a person is praiseworthy, her moral standing has been enhanced in virtue of some episode in her life; when blameworthy, her moral standing has been diminished. Metaphorically speaking, when blameworthy, a negative mark has been entered into her appropriate moral ledger. The ledger account has it that it is because one's moral standing has been diminished that one is a suitable candidate for reactive attitudes such as resentment and indignation. This account aligns felicitously with the view that judgments of moral responsibility are "agent focused" in

---

[5] See also Holmgren 1993; Hughes 1993; Murphy 2003; and Allais 2008. Perhaps these authors might be using "wrong" or "wrongdoing" loosely, simply to denote the kind of conduct that makes one a candidate for forgiveness. I thank Brandon Warmke for this suggestion.

this way: when a person is blameworthy for an action, she takes this action to be morally impermissible for her. In one variation of the ledger view, she performs this action while believing that she is doing wrong. When a person is praiseworthy for an action, she does what she is deserving of praise for doing while believing that she is doing right. Suppose you freely did what you thought was impermissible even if it was not in fact impermissible. Since you *willingly* did what from your perspective *was* impermissible for you, you are complicit; you are blameworthy for what you did. You were ready to, and did in fact, taint or dirty your hands. We may assume that as Mary satisfies this sort of belief condition in stage 2, she is blameworthy for ridiculing Ben even though it was not impermissible for her to ridicule him.

Leaning toward such a view of blameworthiness (and praiseworthiness), it is not unreasonable to divorce forgiveness from impermissibility per se and associate it instead with believing that one is doing something impermissible. The guiding thought is that since forgiveness entails blameworthiness, and blameworthiness entails belief in impermissibility, forgiveness presupposes belief that one is doing something impermissible:

F2: If at, *t*, *T* brings about state of affairs, *A*, at *t* *, and *S* forgives *T* for bringing about *A*, then *T* takes it to be that at *t* it is morally impermissible for *T* to bring about *A* at *t**.

Assuming forgiveness presupposes blameworthiness, the consequent of F2 derives from the following principle of blameworthiness:

Blame-1: *T* is blameworthy for doing *A* only if *T* believes that it is impermissible for *T* to do *A*.
Blame-1 suffers from the problem that *T* might not believe that doing *A* is impermissible but nonetheless be (indirectly) blameworthy for doing *A* due to being blameworthy for the ignorance of wrongdoing from which *T* does A. Accepting this, I've been inclined toward *Blame-2* (which I've advanced in a number of places):
Blame-2: *T* is blameworthy for doing *A* only if *T* nonculpably believes that it is impermissible for *T* to do *A*.

But as Michael Zimmerman has emphasized in correspondence, *Blame-2* still does not encapsulate what I want precisely because *T* might not believe that doing *A* is impermissible and yet still be blameworthy for doing

A. Suppose *T* believes that it's permissible for her to do *T* on the advice of an acquaintance she does not trust. Assume, then, that *T* does not believe that doing *A* is impermissible, and *A*-s. *T* may still be blameworthy for doing *A* because she is blameworthy for not believing that it's impermissible for her to do *A*. I need something along the lines of this:

> *Blame-3*: *T* is morally blameworthy for doing *A* only if either *T* believes that doing *A* is impermissible or *T* is blameworthy for failing to believe that doing *A* is impermissible.

Blame-3 still might not be quite right, though, since it fails to distinguish between acting *in* and acting *from* ignorance. There is reason to think that ignorance excuses only if one acts from ignorance, and not merely in ignorance. Suppose it is wrong for you to do *A*. You believe, however, that it is permissible for you to do *A*, and when you do *A*, you act on the basis of this false belief. Assume that you are, indeed, blameworthy for not having the belief that it's impermissible for you to do *A*, and had you had this belief, you would not have had the belief that it is permissible for you to do *A*, and, moreover, you would not then have done *A*. In this case, we can say that you act *in* ignorance. Your *A*-ing issues from ignorance, but it seems that you are still to blame for *A*-ing. In a slight variation of this case, suppose, again, that you're culpable for failing to have the belief that it's wrong for you to do *A*, you have the false belief that doing *A* is permissible for you, but when you do *A* you don't act on the basis of this belief. It's true that you do *A* *while* having this belief but imagine that you do *A* on the basis of the true belief that it's prudentially best for you to do *A*. I'm drawn to the view that in this variation you act *from* ignorance. Although there is a sense in which your act issues from ignorance, you are not blameworthy for this act. However precisely the distinction between acting in and from ignorance is to be analyzed, these remarks yield:

> *Blame-4*: *T* is morally blameworthy for doing *A* only if either *T* believes that doing *A* is impermissible or *T* is blameworthy for failing to believe that doing *A* is impermissible, and if *T*'s *A*-ing issues from ignorance, *T* acts in ignorance.

Reverting to F2 (roughly, the proposal that if *S* forgives *T* for something *A*, then *T* takes *A* to have been morally impermissible for *T*), merely to simplify the discussion, take the consequent of F2 to derive from *Blame-4*. Although

I won't modify the consequent to reflect the pertinent qualifications, assume that these qualifications are suppressed.

Even if F2 is understood to incorporate these qualifications, it is still mistaken. One may forgive someone for doing something that it is permissibly suboptimal for one to do. To be more precise, the forgiven need not take herself to have done anything impermissible because she did something that it was permissibly suboptimal for her to do, still be blameworthy for doing this thing, and is forgiven for having done this thing. To elaborate, Paul McNamara, among others, has proposed that our ordinary moral conceptual scheme allows for the notions of permissibly doing the least one can do, and permissibly doing more than one has to do (2008, 2011). If this is so, it is possible to have a range of *ranked* permissible options, some such options being better than others. According to McNamara, a range of acceptable alternatives yields ranked permissible options, with two extreme poles—the best of the permissible alternatives (the permissibly "maximum") and the least of those (with the prospect of doing more than the least of those or permissibly less than the best of those). Call the value in terms of which alternatives are ranked *deontic value*. Now consider this example.

Embellished Contact: Suppose I can fulfill the obligation to contact you in these ways: putting in a personal appearance at your store ($w1$); phoning you ($w2$); writing you ($w3$); or scribbling a message on your store window ($w4$). Suppose that my other obligations make me too busy permissibly to do any two of these things; doing one of them precludes me permissibly from doing any of the others (but doing each is permissible). Finally, imagine that $w1$ is the best of these four options, and in the progression from $w1$ to $w4$, the deontic value of each decreases so that $w4$ is relatively worst; morally, I put in a better performance if I visit than if I phone, write, or scribble a message. Lest one think these rankings arbitrary, we may add some more details. I'm a store owner, too, and you and I are friendly rivals. I'm a few blocks away from you, and during early afternoons when customers are sparse, I can close the store for a bit to attend other concerns, such as zipping over to the bank, post office, and so on. To nurture our growing friendship, it would be better to put in a personal appearance than to phone you. Writing a note is acceptable but too impersonal; it is something neither one of us would do. Finally, scribbling a message on your store window would cause you some trouble; you would have to clean up the window, and so forth.

Suppose I'm aware of these relative rankings. Intuitively, at least, if I deliberately scribble, knowing that it would hardly have taken much for me to do significantly better—I could have sauntered over in the afternoon—I'm blameworthy (to a moderate degree) for scribbling. Similarly, if I deliberately write, aware that I could have done better by putting in a personal appearance, I am blameworthy even if only to a small degree for writing: I act in light of the belief that I have done something that it is, for lack of better expression, "morally amiss" for me to do.

Suberogatory acts are the roughly symmetric flip sides of supererogatory ones. McNamara (e.g., 2011, p. 231) proposes that an act is suberogatory for S if and only if it is optional for S to do (that is, it is neither obligatory for S to do it nor obligatory for S to refrain from doing it), it is blameworthy for S to do, it is not praiseworthy for S to omit, and it is precluded by the maximum S can do.[6] Since any suberogatory act is incompatible with doing the maximum one can do, and one is blameworthy for such an act, one can be blameworthy for doing what it is permissibly suboptimal for one to do.

Furthermore, once again there would be nothing untoward about my forgiving you for failing to put in a personal appearance. Forgiveness would also be apt with other instances of suberogation or permissible suboptimality. The two lovers who want to cuddle may forgive you for taking the only bench seat that's unoccupied on the bus, or Jack may forgive the business persons who linger a bit too long at the fashionable bistro when they are well aware of the pressing demand for their table. Even if, then, one is skeptical of Frankfurt examples, instances of forgiveness in which one is forgiven for a permissibly suboptimal act show that both F1 and F2 are defective.

Suppose that the relevant condition of forgiveness should be modified yet again to the following.

F2*: If at, t, T brings about state of affairs, A, at t *, and S forgives T for bringing about A, then T takes it to be that at t it is morally amiss for T to bring about A at t^*.

However, it is difficult to assess F2* without an analysis of moral amissness. In particular, without the analysis, it is unclear whether one can infer from F2*, in conjunction with other premises, that forgiveness is essentially associated with free will.[7]

---

[6] See also, e.g., Mellema 1991 and Driver 1992.
[7] See Haji 2016 for more on moral amissness.

Forgiveness and Obligation

One may endeavor to forge such an association by exploiting an alleged link between forgiveness and obligation. The general pattern of argument to be explored is this: (1) Forgiveness is essentially tied to obligation. (2) In turn, obligation is essentially tied to free will. Hence, forgiveness is essentially tied to free will. Beginning with (1), how do we conceptualize the crucial link, if there is one, between forgiveness and obligation?

In one of her recent and insightful discussions on forgiveness, Dana Nelkin writes:

> [F]orgiveness is constituted (at least in part) by a special kind of release from a special kind of obligation the offender has to the victim. In typical cases, the obligation might be fulfilled by apology, sincere remorse, penance or related phenomena. In forgiving, one ceases to hold the offense against the offender, and this in turn means releasing them from a special kind of personal obligation incurred as the result of committing the wrong against one. (2013, p. 175)

On personal obligations, Warmke remarks:

> The obligations are personal because the wrongdoer can be released only from those obligations over which the victim has normative authority. For example, a wrongdoer might have obligations to apologize or make amends due to reasons having to do with etiquette, the law, or one's personal moral commitments. The victim does not have the normative standing to release the wrongdoer from these obligations. But it still makes perfect sense for a victim to tell the wrongdoer, "Look, as far as our relationship is concerned, you are forgiven: you don't need to keep apologizing and I do not expect further restitution or penance." (2016b, p. 4)

Nelkin speaks of releasing the offender from a special kind of obligation. What is this special obligation? Nelkin explains:

> People owe each other a variety of things for all kinds of reasons. We incur obligations all the time on the basis of voluntary actions for which we are not blameworthy. But when we wrongfully and culpably harm others, we incur at least two sorts of obligations: the obligation to make restitution for

the loss or harm suffered (if we stole a bicycle, then we owe a bicycle or as close to the equivalent as we can provide), and the obligation to somehow make up for or in some way address the wrong itself. (2013, pp. 176–177)

In this passage, Nelkin emphasizes putative obligations of the *forgiven*. Attention to these obligations suggests one way in which forgiveness is supposedly tied to obligation:

F3: If at t, T brings about state of affairs, A, at t^*, and S forgives T for bringing about A, then (1) at t it is impermissible for T to bring about A at t^*, and (2) at some time after t but prior to the time at which S forgives T for bringing about A, T has an obligation—T ought—to make restitution and ought to address the wrong.

F3 includes clause (2) because it may be thought that the forgiver "releases" the forgiven from the germane obligation, and when one is released from an obligation, one no longer has this obligation.[8]

F3 is consonant with the so-called debt release, or, as Warmke says, "economic model" of forgiveness. Richard Swinburne proposes that when one wrongs another, one is in "somewhat like the legal situation of a debtor who owes money. The wrong needs righting. There is an obligation [on the part of the forgiven] to do something like repaying" (1989, p. 74). Warmke characterizes the economic model—a model that elucidates the *practice* of forgiveness—as having three primary constituents:

M1. The moral debt-incurring event (e.g. Julia's deceiving Otto).
M2. The state of being morally obligated (e.g. Julia's now being in moral debt to Otto).
M3. The moral debt-forgiving event (e.g. Otto's releasing Julia from an obligation to apologize and make reparations, and Otto's giving up his right to censure, make moral demands, ask for apologies, etc.). (2016a, p. 4)

M3 suggests another way in which forgiveness and obligation are associated. The attention, this time around, is on the presumed obligations of the *forgiver* and not the forgiven. According to Warmke:

---

[8] I leave unanalyzed the concept of *one's releasing another from an obligation*.

[I]n paradigmatic cases of forgiveness, forgiving alters the norms of interaction for both the victim and the wrongdoer in certain characteristic ways: the victim relinquishes certain rights or permissions and the wrongdoer is released from certain personal obligations. (2016b, p. 16)

Warmke theorizes that forgiving alters the norms of interaction between victim and wrongdoer insofar as "forgiving affects the operative standards governing how the victim and wrongdoer are morally obliged or permitted to regard and treat one another" (2016b, p. 2). As a victim of "interpersonal wrongdoing" (2016, p. 2), the forgiver:

inherit[s] certain sorts of rights or permissions—namely, the right or permission to blame the wrongdoer in certain ways. Some of these blaming-rights are shared by others in the moral community: rights to censure or denounce, for example, are often held by third parties. Other blaming-rights are usually unique to the victim—such as the right to request an apology or demand restitution, or the right to alter the terms of that specific relationship in certain ways (such as to withdraw from weekly lunches). When a victim forgives his wrongdoer, he relinquishes at least some of these rights. (2016b, p. 2)

Warmke mentions other rights. He says that upon "declaring the wrongdoer forgiven, one relinquishes . . . the rights to demand apology, request restitution, and so on" (2016b, p. 13). These rights appear to be or are akin to claim rights. Claim rights are rights that one person (or any entity that is the subject of such rights) holds against another person or persons (or "right bearers" if things other than persons can be such bearers). Such rights, it seems, are associated with morally deontic obligations owed to agents in this way:

Correlativity: S has a claim right against another, T, that T perform some act if and only if T has a moral obligation owed to S to perform that act.[9]

It seems plausible that if the forgiver has a right against the forgiven that she (the forgiven) apologize, then the forgiven has a moral obligation owed to the

---

[9] I expand on obligations being owed to persons later.

forgiver to apologize. The simple moral is that in virtue of the forgiver's having these sorts of rights, forgiveness once again implicates moral obligation.

In addition, Warmke emphasizes that "some previously permissible modes of treating the wrongdoer become impermissible upon forgiving" (2016b, p. 4. See also p. 12). But then we have another link between forgiveness and obligation: If forgiveness is (among other things) an alteration of the norms of interaction—forgiveness alters how the forgiver and forgiven are obligated or permitted to regard or treat one another—then upon forgiving, the forgiver *ought not* to treat the forgiven in various ways. So we have:

F3*: If at t, S forgives T for bringing about A, then at t or at some time after t, S ought not to treat T in certain ways. (For example, S ought not to engage in various sorts of blaming behavior.)

If F3 and F3* bring to light vital connections between forgiveness (or paradigm instances of it) and obligation, then forgiveness is also tied to freedom to do otherwise and, indeed, to free will. This is because just as "impermissibility" entails avoidability, so does obligation. I have argued for this view elsewhere (e.g., Haji 2012, 2016). Here, I simply summarize one consideration in its favor.

As a preliminary remark, just as moral responsibility presupposes freedom or control, so does moral obligation. The "ought" implies "can" principle captures one element of the basic sort of control that obligation requires: If one ought to do something, one has the ability and opportunity to do it. Barring special reason to believe otherwise, if obligation requires freedom or control, so do permissibility and impermissibility.

Restricting attention to impermissibility, here is a line of reasoning in support of the view that "impermissibility" entails "can." (We have already seen that "impermissibility" entails "can refrain from.") As a point of departure, I begin with a powerful analysis of the concept of obligation.

MO-1: A person, S, morally ought, as of t, to see to the occurrence of a state of affairs, p, if and only if there is a world, w, accessible to S at t in which S brings about p, and it is not the case that S refrains from bringing about p in any accessible world as deontically good as or better than w. (see, e.g., Feldman 1986, p. 37; Zimmerman 1996, pp. 26–27; Haji 2016, ch. 2)

MO-1 has it that the obligatory is the deontically best. The axiological issue of just what is deontically best is of no significance for this discussion. Some may identify what is so best, for example, with what is intrinsically best, others with maximal compliance with God's commands, and so forth. If worlds are accessible to you in which you do something, and no better worlds are accessible to you in which you refrain from doing this thing, then according to *MO-1*, you ought to do this thing. More intuitively, and simplifying somewhat, if *MO-1* is true, as of some time, you morally ought to perform an act—an act is *morally obligatory* for you—if and only if you can do it, and it occurs in all the best worlds accessible to you at this time. In all your best life histories, you perform this act at the relevant time. As of some time, it is morally permissible for you to perform an act if and only if you can do it and it occurs in some of the best worlds accessible to you at this time. And as of some time, it is impermissible for you to perform an act if and only if you can do it and it does not occur in any of the best worlds accessible to you at this time. According to *MO-1*, on each occasion, one ought to do the best one can. *MO-1* validates both "ought" implies "can" and "permissibility" implies "can"; if *MO-1* is true, these principles are true, too.

Consider, next, this other principle:

Impermissible/Permissible Possibility: If, at *t*, it is impermissible for *S* to do *A* at *t*, then, at *t S* can do something else, such as refraining from doing *A*, which it is permissible for *S* to do at *t*.

I find this principle plausible. Indeed, I think a logically stronger principle is true, too:

Impermissible/Obligation Possibility: If, at *t*, it is impermissible for *S* to do *A* at *t*, then, at *t S* can do something else, such as refraining from doing *A*, which it is obligatory for *S* to do at *t*.

Suppose you've made a promise, and it's impermissible for you not to keep it; that is, it is impermissible for you to break it. Then it seems plausible that you ought to keep it. Keeping the promise precludes you from breaking it, and breaking it precludes you from keeping it. We can generalize: If, at some time, *t*, it is impermissible for you to do something, *A*, at *t*, then, at *t*, you ought to do something, *C* (such as refraining from doing *A*), that is incompatible with your doing *A*—*C* precludes you from doing *A*—and doing, *A*, in turn, precludes you from doing C. But then it follows immediately that if it is impermissible for you to do something, then there is something else that it is obligatory (and, hence, permissible) for you to do.

Assume, now (for *reductio*), that one denies that "impermissible" implies "can." However, one endorses the view that "ought" and "permissible" each implies "can" perhaps because one finds *MO-1*—the principle that one ought to do the best one can—endearing. In addition, include among these "starting assumptions" the assumption that there are no genuine conflicts of obligation (*MO-1* rules out such conflicts). Imagine a situation in which, as of *t*, you cannot do some heinous deed, A, at *t*. You are fast asleep at *t*, and you cannot then intentionally do A, and you cannot then intentionally refrain from doing A. Given the starting assumptions, at *t*, it is neither (directly) obligatory nor (directly) permissible for you to do A at *t*, although it may be that at *t*, it is (directly) impermissible for you to do A at *t*.[10] Given the starting assumptions, at *t*, it is neither obligatory nor permissible for you to do A at *t*, although it may be that at *t*, it is impermissible for you to do A at *t*. But then both principles *Impermissible/Permissible Possibility* and *Impermissible/Obligation Possibility* are violated. Although (let's suppose), at *t*, it is impermissible for you to do A at *t*, it is false that, at *t*, you can do something else that it is obligatory or permissible for you to do then.

If "impermissible" implies "can," then the following argument confirms that "ought" implies "can refrain from": If one ought not to do something, then it is impermissible for one to do it. If it is impermissible for one to do something, then one can do it. Therefore, if one ought not to do something, then one can do it. But it is also true that if one ought not to do something, one can refrain from doing it. Hence, if one ought to do something, then one has free will concerning it; one can do it and one can refrain from doing it.

We may conclude that obligation, permissibility, and impermissibility require alternatives.[11] Briefly put, obligation requires dual control, the ability to perform and to refrain from performing an action.

---

[10] If you have an indirect obligation to do something, you have this obligation in virtue of having an obligation to do something else. You have a direct obligation to do something if and only if this obligation is not indirect. Similarly, we may distinguish between direct and indirect permissibility and impermissibility, too. Direct obligation (permissibility and impermissibility) is restricted to intentional actions; not so with indirect obligation. See, for example, Zimmerman 2006, p. 602, and Haji 2012, p. 30.

[11] Here, I take no stance on whether the alternatives are "weak" alternatives that one can have even if determinism is true or "strong" alternatives that determinism rules out. Suppose, at *t*, you intentionally refrain from doing A at *t* in possible world *w*. You have at *t* a strong alternative to do something else, such as A, if and only if there is some other possible world with the same past right up to *t* as *w*, and the same laws, in which at *t* you do A. It is widely presumed that determinism rules out

Reverting, now, to F3, F3 entails that if S forgives T for something A, then T ought, as of some appropriate time, to make restitution. But if T ought, at this time, to make restitution, then it is true both that, as of this time, T can make and T can refrain from making restitution.[12] We would then be able to conclude that forgiveness presupposes the existence of free will.

However, F3 is suspect. Suppose T has unjustifiedly derided S and is blameworthy for doing so. T is about to die very shortly after this unhappy incident and is aware of his impending death. In the time he has left prior to his demise, T can either address the wrong or make peace with his son, but he cannot do both. It is possible that as of a certain time—the only time he has left—there is a world accessible to him in which he makes amends, and there is no better world (or there are no better worlds) accessible to him in which he fails to make amends. Then he ought to make amends. It is then false that if S forgives T for deriding her, T ought to address the pertinent wrong. So F3 is problematic. Nevertheless, this principle points to some other condition concerning not obligation but blameworthiness that may be promising. I will address this principle in the fifth section.

Reconsider F3*: If at t, S forgives T for bringing about A, then at t or some time after t, S ought not (i.e., it is impermissible for S) to treat T in various ways. F3* suffers from the same sort of defect as F3. What you ought to do as of a certain time depends on which worlds are accessible to you as of this time. The best world (or worlds) accessible to S as of the relevant time may well be a world (or worlds) in which S does treat T in various ways in which S would not normally treat T after having forgiven T. In addition, as "ought not" implies "can," there is this additional worry. Suppose S has forgiven T at t0 and now, at a later time t, refrains from engaging in a particular bit of blaming behavior, B. Assume that if F3* is true, then it is impermissible at t0 and at t for S to do B. A counterfactual intervener, however, sees to it that S cannot at t0 or at any other time after t0, do B. Then it is false that it is impermissible at t0 (or at any later time) for S to do B. Thus, F3* is not true. This same sort of concern afflicts F3 as well.

anyone's having alternatives of this sort. The alternative, *had you wanted to, you would at t have done A*, is weak; it's an alternative you can have even if determinism is true.

[12] One might prefer the following: *Forgiveness/Obligation* entails that if S forgives T for something A, then T ought to have made restitution. But if T ought to have made restitution, then it is true both that T could have made, and T could have refrained from making restitution.

A Way Out?

Warmke, like McKenna, stresses that he is concerned with *paradigmatic* cases of forgiveness. He writes:

> Embedded in our practices of forgiving is the default assumption that for- giving typically results in the alteration of certain kinds of norms. But I do think that there are cases of forgiveness that do not alter norms in these characteristic ways. Forgiveness is a diverse and diffuse practice, admitting of a multitude of modes or ways of forgiving. But any account of the para- digmatic cases of forgiveness should at least have the resources to explain [relevant norm alterations]. (2016, p. 5, note omitted)

Someone might object that cases involving counterfactual interveners are not paradigmatic cases of forgiveness; these fall outside the boundaries of typical scenarios. Similarly, cases in which the forgiven is about to die shortly after having been forgiven are atypical. So one shouldn't rely on such cases to undermine principles such as F3 and F3* because these are limited to or ad- dress *typical* cases.

One sort of worry with this kind of objection, at least when it is "test examples" involving counterfactual interveners that are the objects of crit- icism, is that the interveners do *not* intervene. The key characters—the forgiven or the forgiver—act in just the way in which they would have had the intervener not been present. This should give us reason to resist the view that that such test examples fail to call into question the pertinent principles. A second sort of worry concerns philosophical methodology: It is received philosophical practice to test principles, such as F1, F2, F3, and F3*, by attempting to construct counterexamples against them. It strikes me as improper to evade these counterexamples *merely* by the ex- pedient that the principles are true of only paradigmatic cases. Finally, there is another sort of concern. Suppose one argues that paradigmatic instances of forgiveness all display feature *f*, but there are genuine cases of forgiveness without *f*. All these other genuine cases have features that they share with the paradigmatic cases, but they don't have *f*. Maybe *f* is intricately associated with free will. If someone were to ask me whether forgiveness has anything *essential* to do with *f* or free will, my response would be a confident "no."

Blameworthiness, Forgiveness, and Prima Facie Obligation

Whereas it is controversial whether forgiveness presupposes impermissibility, it is not contentious that forgiveness presupposes blameworthiness: S forgives T for doing something A only if T is blameworthy for doing A. Regarding her account of forgiveness, Nelkin says:

> The model I have developed . . . retains the idea, suggested in Strawson's paper, that forgiveness is rightly counted as a reactive attitude. When one forgives an offense, one is committed to the proposition that the offender acted freely and was responsible for the offense. (Nelkin 2013, p. 183)

Similarly, Warmke and McKenna emphasize that "directed forgiveness presumes that the person forgiven is indeed blameworthy, and that the forgiver had blamed the person previously, or at least held her morally responsible and blameworthy" (Warmke and McKenna 2013, p. 205). In an independent paper, Warmke remarks that forgiveness "does not change the fact that one did something for which one is guilty and is liable to punishment by the appropriate moral, civil or even divine authorities" (2016b, p. 13).

Since there is this highly plausible connection between forgiveness and blameworthiness, and, presumably, this connection is conceptual, it may be thought that there is a fairly easy route to the conclusion that forgiveness entails that the forgiven have some alternative possibilities. For (1a) if one is forgiven for performing an action, A, then one is blameworthy for doing A; (2a) if one is blameworthy for doing A, then it is impermissible for one to do A; (3a) if it is impermissible for one to do A, then both one can do and one can refrain from doing A; hence, (4a) if one is forgiven for performing an action, A, then both one can do and one can refrain from doing A.

However, this argument is not sound because (2a), the principle that blameworthiness requires impermissibility, is mistaken (see, e.g., Zimmerman 1988, 1997, 2008; Haji 1998, 2002, 2012, 2016). Again, I won't dwell on this principle here save for the following. First, if one is convinced that in stage 2, Mary is blameworthy for deriding Ben even though she could not have done otherwise, then one should reject (2a) because Ben is blameworthy for doing something that it is not impermissible for him to do. Second, if one can be blameworthy for something that it is permissibly suboptimal for one to do, then, again, one should reject the view that blameworthiness requires impermissibility.

In the remainder of this chapter, I uncover another possible path to the conclusion that forgiveness entails freedom to do otherwise. Imagine that T has done something, A, which involves S. I'll say little about the sense of "involves" here with the exception that T's A-ing is in some way associated with S. Suppose T is blameworthy for doing A. The principle to be examined is that T has a *prima facie* (as opposed to an *overall*) *obligation* to make amends or to address his morally amiss behavior that involves S. Let's start with this preliminary point. One can have a moral obligation to some persons but not to others. I may promise Tim's mother but not his father that I will attend her son's graduation ceremony. In virtue of promising, I have an obligation to Tim's mother—in this sense I "owe" her but not the father—an obligation to attend. Some obligations are not owed. One may have an obligation to do some voluntary work, but this obligation may not be owed to anyone. Similarly, one may have a prima facie obligation that is owed to some agent. We may reform the principle to be scrutinized in this way: If T's A-ing involves S, and T is blameworthy for A-ing, then T has a *prima facie obligation* that T owes to S to make amends or to address his morally amiss behavior that involves S.[13]

David Ross (1930) spoke explicitly of the prima facie duties of reparation. If someone has previously "injured" some other person, and can now perform an act that would serve to make up for that injury, then she has a prima facie duty to do so. The fact that the act would "repair" a past injury provides a moral reason for doing such an act. I'm using "injury" broadly. The past injury may be a past wrongdoing. I may have done wrong in gratuitously insulting Ted. Hence, I may incur a prima facie obligation to apologize to him. Even if not a past wrong, the "injury" may be something that was morally amiss; it may for instance, have been a suberogatory act. Roughly, again, an act is suberogatory for an agent if it is a permissible act that is worse than at least some of its permissible alternatives, it is optional, the agent is blameworthy for doing it, and the agent is not praiseworthy for refraining from doing it. Or the "injury" may even have been something that it was overall

---

[13] Maybe this is Nelkin's view; perhaps she accepts this principle and takes the relevant obligations to be prima facie. Regarding the forgiver, Warmke claims that "some previously permissible modes of treating the wrongdoer become *prima facie* impermissible upon forgiving because one gives up certain kinds of rights to blame *qua* victim of the wrongdoing" (2016a, p. 6). He also claims that before being forgiven, the wrongdoer may have a prima facie obligation to apologize or to make some kind of restitution (2016a, p. 7).

obligatory for one to do. One may have done something on the basis of the nonculpable belief that it was impermissible for one to do it when it was actually obligatory for one to do it. Taking note of the diagnosis that turned out to be mistaken, Doc injected the patient—his old adversary—with medicine A on the basis of the nonculpable belief that giving A would kill the patient; all the evidence supported his belief that he would be doing something impermissible in giving A. However, giving A *facilitated* recovery—unbeknown to him it was in fact obligatory for Doc to give A when he did. I propose (at least initially) that Doc's giving A on the basis of the nonculpable belief that he was doing something impermissible in giving A is an "injury." In another example, Sam believes he is disclosing to others something that he (falsely) believes Salima had revealed to him in strict confidence. But he is simply misremembering. If he spills the beans on the basis of the nonculpable belief that in so doing, he is doing something that it is impermissible for him to do, his supposedly breaking trust is an "injury." In virtue of what he takes to be violating confidence, it appears that he has a prima facie obligation to make amends or to address in some appropriate way this seemingly impermissible behavior. Generalizing, the following principle is reasonable:

Injury: If S does something, A, which involves T, and S does A while nonculpably believing or on the basis of the nonculpable belief that it is impermissible or morally amiss (as, for instance, when it is suberogatory for S to do A) for S to do A, then S's doing A is an injury.

As should be clear by now, I also believe this principle is credible:

Injury/Reparation: If S does something, A, which involves T, and S's doing A is an injury, then S has a prima facie duty of reparation that S owes to T; for example, S has a prima facie duty to apologize to T, make amends, or to address this injury.

If one has done something that is an injury, when does one incur the prima facie duty of reparation? A temporally strict view says that one incurs it as of the time one commits the act that is the injury. A temporally lax rival says that one may incur the prima facie obligation at this or some later time. The temporally lax view is to be preferred to the temporally strict one because it may turn out that at the time one performs an act that is or is presumed to be an injury, one may be unable to do whatever one would be called upon to do if one were to have the duty of reparation. For example, if, at t, I've gratuitously insulted Ted, I will not have a prima facie obligation at t to make reparation (then or a bit later) by apologizing because it may be that at t (or shortly after) I cannot for whatever reason apologize. This, however, does not preclude me from having a prima facie obligation I owe to Ted at some other time when I *can* make reparation or apologize.

I now advance one more principle (or sort of principle) that I have long defended:

> *Blameworthiness*: If S is blameworthy for doing A, then (1) S believes that it is impermissible or morally amiss (as, for instance, when it is suberogatory for S to do A) for S to do A or (taking into account the qualifications introduced in *Blame-3*), (2) S is blameworthy for failing to believe that doing A is impermissible.[14]

Collecting results, from *Blameworthiness* and *Injury*, we may infer that if S does something, A, which involves T, and S is blameworthy for doing A, then S's doing A is an injury. This result in conjunction with *Injury/Reparation* yields the following principle:

> *PFO/Blameworthiness*: If S is blameworthy for doing A, and S's A-ing involves T, then S has a prima facie duty of reparation that S owes to T; for example, S has a prima facie obligation to apologize to T, make amends, or to address the injury.

Needless to say, immediate shortcomings in the line of reasoning that culminates in this principle include not having analyses of *moral amissness* or *prima facie duty*.[15]

In addition, the following principles are also plausible:

> *PF-OIC*: If T prima facie ought to do A, then T can do A; and if T prima facie ought not to do A, then T can refrain from doing A.
>
> *PF-Equivalence*: It is prima facie impermissible for T to do A if and only if T prima facie ought not to do A.
>
> *PF-IOC*: If it is prima facie impermissible for T to do A, then T can do A.

---

[14] I omit refinements not essential for formulating and assessing the relevant principle in question (principle *PFO/Blameworthiness*) to be introduced shortly.

[15] Zimmerman develops an analysis of something's being a prima facie duty in his 1996, ch. 5.

Concerning the first and third of these principles, if "ought" implies "can," I see no reason to deny that "prima facie ought" does not imply "can," too. Similarly, if "impermissible" implies "can," so does "prima facie impermissible." This trio of principles entails that there is a requirement of alternative possibilities for prima facie obligation: If S prima facie ought to do A, then S can do, and S can refrain from doing, A.

We now have all the ingredients in place to sketch an argument for the thesis that there is a nontrivial connection between forgiveness and free will:

1. If S forgives T for doing A, then T is blameworthy for doing A.
2. If T is blameworthy for doing A, and T's A-ing involves S, then T has a prima facie obligation that T owes to S to make amends to S (or to address his morally amiss behavior).
3. If T has a prima facie obligation that T owes to S to make amends to S, then T can make and T can refrain from making amends to S.
Hence, (4), if S forgives T for doing A (and T's A-ing involves S), then T can make and T can refrain from making amends to S.

To evaluate this line of reasoning, introduce slight changes in Stage 2 of the Frankfurt example featuring Mary, Ben, and the counterfactual intervener. (Call the resulting case "*Test*.") At t Mary ridicules Ben on the basis of the nonculpable belief that it is impermissible for her to do so. She cannot do anything other than ridicule Ben at t. Furthermore, she never makes reparation for this deed—for instance, she never apologizes—and she could not have made reparation for it because of a perpetually present counterfactual intervener who would have prevented Mary from apologizing if she had revealed any sign that she was about to apologize. As *PFO/Blameworthiness* is unsatisfied—there is no time at which Mary has a prima facie obligation to apologize—she is not blameworthy for ridiculing Ben. But surely something has gone very wrong here, or so one may think. If Mary is blameworthy for ridiculing Ben in a standard Frankfurt example with a nonperpetual counterfactual intervener, why should she not be just as blameworthy if she acts no differently when the counterfactual intervener is ever present? In brief, we're enmeshed in a dilemma. On the one hand, the plausible principles *Injury*, *Injury/Reparation*, and *Blameworthiness*, from which we derive *PFO/Blameworthiness*, generate the result that in *Test* Mary is *not* blameworthy for ridiculing Ben. Again, if S is blameworthy for doing A, and S's A-ing involves *T*, then *S* has a prima facie duty of reparation that *S* owes to *T*. Hence, if Mary is blameworthy for ridiculing Ben in *Test*, she has a prima facie duty of reparation that she owes to Ben. But since she cannot do otherwise than ridicule Ben in *Test*, and having a prima facie duty of reparation requires that she could have done otherwise, she has no such duty. So it follows that she is not blameworthy for ridiculing Ben in *Test*. On the other hand, *Test*, a Frankfurt example with an ever-present counterfactual intervener, strongly suggests that Mary *is* blameworthy for ridiculing Ben. Roughly, she is blameworthy because she behaves no differently than she would have if there were no intervener monitoring at every time her every move. Therefore, either one or more of the plausible principles from which *PFO/Blameworthiness* derives ought to be rejected, or we ought to jettison Frankfurt examples.

It's not transparent to me what way to go, although I lean toward rejecting the first horn. If we agree with one of the alleged lessons of Frankfurt example *Test*—Mary is blameworthy despite there being no time at which she has a prima facie obligation to make reparation—which one of the three implicated principles do we reject? As I accept (or, minimally, find highly sensible) *Blameworthiness* and *Injury/Reparation*, the only option is to renounce *Injury*. In favor of giving up *Injury*, perhaps some may urge that if *S* does something, *A*, which involves *T*, and *S* does *A* while nonculpably believing or on the basis of the nonculpable belief that it is impermissible or morally amiss for *S* to do *A*, then *S*'s doing *A* is *not* an injury but something *S* takes or should take to be an injury. If *S* has wronged *T* in or by doing *A*, then *S*'s doing *A* *is* an injury (as Ross would presumably agree). If, however, *S* does something *B*, which involves *T*, and *S* does *B* while nonculpably believing or on the basis of the nonculpable belief that it is impermissible or morally amiss for *S* to do *B*, but it is in fact obligatory (or permissibly suboptimal) for *S* to do *B*, then *S*'s doing *B* is no injury at all. Roughly, the idea is that just as there is a distinction between what is obligatory and what one may believe to be obligatory, so there is a distinction between an injury and what one may take to be an injury. Avoid this confusion and the troublesome dilemma dissolves or may be evaded. My hesitation with this proposed rejection of *Injury* has to do with what I find to be the absorbing thought that just as there is something to "repair" or "make up for" with a past wrongdoing, so there is something to repair or make up for with, for instance, freely doing something one nonculpably takes to be wrong. In Stage 2 of *Test*, we may safely assume that from her point of view (though not in fact) Mary has done wrong. She takes herself to be doing deliberate wrong in ridiculing Ben. The strong ties of friendship between Ben and Mary both speak to Ben's being the victim of—being "injured" by—Mary's behavior, and, hence, there surely being something that calls for Mary's making reparation, and Mary's being an apt candidate for forgiveness on the part of Ben. True friendship or moral conscientiousness demands a fitting reaction from Mary, and this demand very strongly suggests that an injury of sorts has befallen Ben.

Alternatively, one may attempt to argue in this way. *PFO/Blameworthiness* says: If *S* is blameworthy for doing *A*, and *S*'s *A*-ing involves *T*, then *S* has a prima facie duty of reparation that *S* owes to *T*; for example, *S* has a prima facie obligation to apologize to *T*, make amends, or address the injury. Reflecting on the objection I previously presented against principle F3, presumably, whether, as of some time, one of your options is a prima facie obligation for you depends on what, as of that time, your *other* options are. Suppose, at *t*, you do *A* (at *t*), your *A*-ing involves Tim, and you are blameworthy for doing *A* at *t*. Whether at some time t^* (t^* may be identical to *t* or a time later than *t*) you have a prima facie obligation to, say, apologize to Tim depends, again, on the alternatives you have at t^*. It seems as though there may be cases in which apologizing (or doing anything else that qualifies as making reparations) may be prima facie *impermissible* even though you may be blameworthy for the relevant deed. Hence, *PFO/Blameworthiness* is not true. If *PFO/Blameworthiness* is false, at least one of *Injury, Injury/ Reparation*, and *Blameworthiness* is false. Finally, if *Injury/Reparation* and *Blameworthiness* are beyond reproach, the culprit is *Injury*. Again, however, the rub is that *Injury* seems tenable.

Rejecting the other horn—in effect, rejecting Frankfurt examples—is unattractive (or at least unattractive to me), although I agree that these examples are not uncontroversial. In particular it is hard to see why, if one finds "prior sign" Frankfurt examples with the usual nonperpetual counterfactual intervener effective—if one takes the customary examples to support the view that blameworthiness does not require alternative possibilities—one should find problematic Frankfurt examples with ever-present counterfactual interveners ineffective. In either version of such a case, Mary (presumably) freely and intentionally does something that from her point of view is wrong; she nonculpably believes that she has wronged Ben. Why is she not blameworthy in either?

Concluding Remarks

I have advanced an admittedly controversial argument for the thesis that for-giveness requires that the forgiven have alternative possibilities—with respect to at least some actions, the forgiven can do otherwise. Even if one is inclined to accept this argument—as we have seen, there is reason to believe that this argument is suspect—there is the further issue of whether these alternatives are strong incompatibilist alternatives in that given exactly the same past and the laws, the agent could have done otherwise, or weak alternatives that de-terminism does not preclude. Presumably, some libertarians will favor the former, and if forgiveness is indeed nonproprietary in the absence of the forgiven's having some (pertinent) strong alternatives, and furthermore, if determinism effaces strong alternatives, then determinism undermines for-giveness. Committed compatibilists will, of course, disagree. They will in-sist that if forgiveness presupposes our being able to do otherwise at least regarding the apt actions of concern—actions that are putative prima facie obligations of making reparation owed to others—forgiveness remains in-tact even if determinism is true because the alternatives at issue are weak alternatives.

Semicompatibilists with respect to moral responsibility affirm that even if determinism undermines freedom to do otherwise, it does not undermine moral responsibility because responsibility does not require *such* freedom (Fischer and Ravizza 1998, p. 53). Here, it does not matter whether the alternatives are strong or weak. Conceive of semicompatibilists concerning forgiveness as claiming that determinism leaves forgiveness unscathed de-spite its being the case (if it is the case) that determinism expunges freedom to do otherwise. The pertinent argument in the next to last section of this chapter, if sound, supports the view that semicompatibilism concerning for-giveness is untenable.[16]

[16] Very many thanks, indeed, to Michael McKenna and Brandon Warmke for their insightful comments and suggestions on earlier drafts. This chapter was completed during my tenure of a Social Sciences and Humanities Research Council of Canada (SSHRC) grant. I am most grateful to this granting agency for its support.

References

Allais, Lucy. 2008. "Wiping the Slate Clean: The Heart of Forgiveness." *Philosophy and Public Affairs* 36: 33–68.

Allais, Lucy. 2014. "Freedom and Forgiveness." In *Oxford Studies in Agency and Responsibility, Volume 2*. Oxford: Oxford University Press, 33–63.Driver, Julia. 1992. "The Suberogatory." *Australasian Journal of Philosophy* 70: 286–295.

Feldman, Fred. 1986. *Doing the Best We Can*. Dordrecht: D. Reidel.

Fischer, John M., and M. Ravizza. 1998. *Responsibility and Control: A Theory of Moral Responsibility*. Cambridge: Cambridge University Press.

Frankfurt, Harry. 1969. "Alternate Possibilities and Moral Responsibility." *The Journal of Philosophy* 66: 829–839.Haji, Ishtiyaque. 1998. *Moral Appraisability: Puzzles, Proposals, and Perplexities*. New York: Oxford University Press.

Haji, Ishtiyaque. 2002. *Deontic Morality and Control*. Cambridge: Cambridge University Press.

Haji, Ishtiyaque. 2012. *Reason's Debt to Freedom: Normative Appraisals, Reasons, and Free Will*. New York: Oxford University Press.

Haji, Ishtiyaque. 2014. "Blameworthiness and Alternate Possibilities." *The Journal of Value Inquiry* 48: 603–621.

Haji, Ishtiyaque. 2016. *Luck's Mischief: Obligation and Blameworthiness on a Thread*. New York: Oxford University Press.

Hieronymi, Pamela. 2001. "Articulating an Uncompromising Forgiveness." *Philosophy and Phenomenological Research* 62: 529–555.

Holmgren, Margaret R. 2014. "A Moral Assessment of Strawson's Retributive Reactive Attitudes." In David Shoemaker and Neal Tognazzni, eds., *Oxford Studies in Agency and Responsibility, Volume 2*. Oxford: Oxford University Press, 165–186.

Holmgren, Margaret R. 1993. "Forgiveness and the Intrinsic Value of Persons." *American Philosophical Quarterly* 30: 341–351.

Hughes, P. M. 1993. "What Is Involved in Forgiving?" *Journal of Value Inquiry* 27: 331–340.

McNamara, Paul. 2008. "Praise, Blame, Obligation, and Beyond: Toward a Framework for the Classical Conception of Supererogation and Kin." In Ron van der Meyden and Leendert van der Torre, eds., *Deontic Logic in Computer Science*. Berlin: Springer Verlag, 233–247.

McNamara, Paul. 2011. "Supererogation, inside and out: Toward an Adequate Scheme for Common-Sense Morality." In Mark Timmons, ed., *Oxford Studies in Normative Ethics, Volume 1*. New York: Oxford University Press, 202–235.

Mellema, Gregory. 1991. *Beyond the Call of Duty: Supererogation, Obligation, and Offence*. Albany: State University of New York Press.

Murphy, Jeffrie. 2003. *Getting Even: Forgiveness and Its Limits*. New York: Oxford University Press.

Murphy, Jeffrie, and J. Hampton. 1988. *Forgiveness and Mercy*. New York: Cambridge University Press.

Nelkin, Dana K. 2011. *Making Sense of Freedom and Responsibility*. New York: Oxford University Press.

Nelkin, Dana. "Freedom and Forgiveness." 2013. In Ishtiyaque Haji and Justin Caouette, eds., *Free Will and Moral Responsibility*. Newcastle upon Tyne: Cambridge Scholars Publishing, 165–188.

Pereboom, Derk. 1995. "*Determinism* al Dente." *Nous* 29: 21–45.

Ross, William David. 1930. *The Right and the Good*. Oxford: Clarendon Press.

Warmke, Brandon. 2016a. "The Economic Model of Forgiveness." *Pacific Philosophical Quarterly* 94: 687–703.

Warmke, Brandon. 2016b. "The Normative Significance of Forgiveness." *Australasian Journal of Philosophy* 94: 1–17.

Warmke, Brandon, and Michael McKenna. 2013. "Moral Responsibility, Forgiveness, and Conversation." In Ishtiyaque Haji and Justin Caouette, eds., *Free Will and Moral Responsibility*. Newcastle upon Tyne: Cambridge Scholars Publishing, 189–212.

Widerker, David, and Michael McKenna. 2003. *Freedom, Responsibility, and Agency: Essays on the Importance of Alternative Possibilities*. Aldershot, UK: Ashgate Press.

Zimmerman, Michael. 1988. *An Essay on Moral Responsibility*. Totowa, NJ: Rowman & Littlefield.

Zimmerman, Michael J. 1996. *The Concept of Moral Obligation*. Cambridge: Cambridge University Press.

Zimmerman, Michael J. 1997. "A Plea for Accuses." *American Philosophical Quarterly* 34: 229–243.

Zimmerman, Michael J. 2002. "Taking Luck Seriously." *The Journal of Philosophy* 99: 553–576.

Zimmerman, Michael J. 2006. "Moral Luck: A Partial Map." *Canadian Journal of Philosophy* 36: 585–608.

Zimmerman, Michael J. 2008. *Living with Uncertainty*. Cambridge: Cambridge University Press.

6

Forgiving as a Performative Utterance

Richard Swinburne

Forgiving as No Longer Resenting

When a person says "I forgive" someone, that may sometimes constitute a report of a mental state; the person reports that he no longer resents someone's wrong actions. But more often, I believe, it is a performative utterance in the sense that necessarily it makes something (other than itself) the case and does not merely report something. In this chapter, I shall be concerned mainly with forgiving as a performative utterance, which I believe to be the primary and morally more important kind of forgiveness. In the second section, I analyze the nature of such forgiveness; in the third, I argue that the utterances of Jesus, as reported in the Gospels, about interhuman forgiveness, fit this analysis; and in the final section, I argue that the account in the New Testament Letter to the Hebrews and in one later Christian theory of how the life, death, and Resurrection of Jesus made God's forgiveness available to humans also fits this analysis.

But I begin with a brief assessment of the nature and appropriateness of forgiving as the mental state of no longer resenting the wrong action of someone who has wronged you. This sense is the only one recognized by Joseph Butler and some modern authors, and by Buddhists. For Holmgren (2012, 39), to forgive someone is to adopt an attitude of not resenting the wrong which someone has done, but instead maintaining toward that person an attitude of "respect, compassion, and real goodwill," which it is good to hold toward all humans. Garrard and McNaughton (2003, 44) likewise think of the desirable good of unconditional forgiveness as overcoming not only resentment but any other hostile feelings such as anger and hatred. For Griswold (2007, 42) one forgives someone if one is less resentful than one was and is trying to abolish resentment altogether. For Stump (2016, 156 n.16, and 2018, 438 n.17; see also her 2018 passim), forgiveness is what real love of someone who has wronged you amounts to. While all these authors consider that

Richard Swinburne, *Forgiving as a Performative Utterance* In: *Forgiveness and Its Moral Dimensions*. Edited by: Brandon Warmke, Dana Kay Nelkin, and Michael McKenna, Oxford University Press. © Oxford University Press 2021. DOI: 10.1093/oso/9780190602147.003.0006

forgiveness in their sense is always a good, Butler (1902, 467) considers that a moderate amount of resentment at the wrongdoer is proper ("resentment is not inconsistent with good will"), but we have a duty to curb it and not to take revenge, and fulfilling this duty is what forgiveness consists in. Other writers also—for example, Murphy (2003, ch. 2)—have urged that a certain amount of resentment is proper since our moral judgments (e.g., that A did wrong) should be backed by emotion, as such emotion involves respect for the moral order.

Garrard and McNaughton (2003, 53–59) ground the goodness of forgiveness (in their sense) in our solidarity with other humans in our weakness and proneness to wrongdoing. Here I share Holmgren's (2012, 96) objection that "shared dreadful propensities are not and cannot be a basis for respect. Respect is an attitude that recognises and responds to something of value." Butler sees the obligation to forgive humans as arising simply from a human "being a sensible creature; that is, capable of happiness or misery" (1902, 467); but surely an attitude will only count as an attitude of "forgiveness" if it is an attitude toward a wrongdoer, and being a wrongdoer involves having moral beliefs and the capacity to act on them. One cannot (in a literal sense) "forgive" an animal. Hence Holmgren (2012, 137–140) grounds the value of forgiveness (in her sense) on the equal moral worth of all humans in such features as their ability to experience happiness or misery, to make moral choices, and to live meaningful lives. I am happy to endorse her view that we should maintain the attitude of respect to all humans which she commends, while allowing the propriety of some resentment at them for their wrongdoing. While Holmgren and Garrard and McNaughton regard this kind of unconditional forgiveness as supererogatory, Stump (2016, 157) regards it "on traditional Christian ethical views" (which she holds) and finds in Aquinas (Stump 2018, 82) as always obligatory (since "the absence of love is morally blameworthy"), and Griswold (2007, 67) regards it as "blameworthy" not to forgive "under certain circumstances," constituted by the wrongdoer making himself worthy of forgiveness. But, for reasons which I shall develop later with respect to forgiveness in what I regard as its primary sense, it seems implausible to think that by hurting the victim and even making what I will call full "atonement," the wrongdoer imposes on him an obligation—to forgive. Also, as Griswold recognizes, since emotions are not fully or sometimes at all under our control, any obligation must be at most an obligation to try to forgive. For Holmgren (2012, 43–45) (and I suspect for most of the other writers discussed earlier) the main point of saying to the wrongdoer "I forgive you" is to convey the information that the speaker does not resent the wrongdoer, that is, to assure the wrongdoer that that forgiving attitude is her attitude.

Forgiving as Performative

In supposing that forgiveness as a mental state of non-resentment is the only important kind of forgiveness, these authors seem to me to ignore the significance of what I consider to be certain important metaethical truths. The first of these is that there is a distinction between actions which are obligatory and actions which are supererogatorily good. The second truth is that doing what is wrong, that is what is obligatory not to do, or not doing what is obligatory to do, is always to wrong some other person(s) (or other sentient beings). The third truth is that doing wrong makes the agent guilty and so—if the agent believed that he was doing wrong—blameworthy. Only given these truths does it begin to become plausible that—as I am going to claim—(necessarily) the wrongdoer's guilt can be removed by the joint actions of the wrongdoer in making (what I will call) atonement, and of the victim in forgiving. Forgiving consists in saying "I forgive you" or some less solemn words, such as "that's alright," or perhaps even by a nonverbal action, such as a smile, which in the context means "I forgive you." When saying "I forgive you" (or uttering some less solemn words) necessarily (together with the wrongdoer's action) has an effect on the wrongdoer's moral condition, it must constitute a performative utterance.

I do not see the need these days to argue for the distinction between the supererogatory and the obligatory; and most of the authors mentioned earlier would accept it. But it is important to note how obligations arise. Positive obligations arise from commitments by one's actions or from benefits received. The commitments may be explicit, as when we make a promise; or implicit, as, when we beget children, we become obliged to nurture and educate them. The benefits received include the benefits of life, nurture, and education, which we receive from parents and others, and the benefits of friendship and company. There are also positive obligations to other humans (and maybe animals) who are close to us and in great need to help to satisfy their needs; but it is very unclear where the border lies between those close to us in great need whom we are obliged to help and those not close to us or those whose need is not great, whom it would be merely supererogatory to help. Negative obligations are simply obligations not to deprive anyone of anything which belongs to them—their life, their faculties, their property, their reputation, or their respect. The second truth follows from these being the ways in which obligations arise. We have obligations to those to whom we have made commitments, those from whom we have received benefits, and to those close to us in great need, to do certain things, and to all beings not to deprive them of anything that belongs to them; and a failure to fulfil those obligations wrongs those people. The third truth seems intuitively correct to many people, and I am going to assume it in my subsequent discussion. It is Holmgren's denial (in connection with her views about punishment) that the worth of a person is damaged by his or her doing wrong actions, and so her denial of my third truth which leads to her failure to recognize the performative sense of "forgive."[1] For if there is no guilt to be removed, forgiveness cannot make a difference to the moral status of the wrongdoer.

The third truth does, however, depend on certain metaphysical claims: that persons continue to exist over periods of time and that personal identity is not a matter of degree (any future person is either totally the same as, or totally different from, any past person), and that persons have free will of a certain important kind. Those philosophers who do not accept one or other of these metaphysical claims are unlikely to recognize my third truth. Holmgren holds (2012, 147)—surely correctly—that her "paradigm of forgiveness" is compatible with a reductionist theory of personal identity and with Christine Korsgaard's Kantian compatibilist theory of moral responsibility. Yet a reductionist conception which (2012, 146) "holds that the self is not some metaphysical entity that exists beyond the body, brain and series of mental and physical events" does naturally lead to a view that personal identity is a matter of degree; and so that a later person can only be partly the same as an earlier person, and so less responsible for the wrongdoing of the earlier person who had the "same body." And a compatibilist theory of moral responsibility having the consequence that guilt can belong to a person in virtue of their actions caused ultimately by forces beyond their control does naturally lead to the view that their actions do not make the serious difference to their moral worth that a libertarian theory can suppose.[2] It is, I assume,

---

[1] Holmgren assumes (2012, 12) that "all persons have equal intrinsic worth and moral status" and so rejects "the claim that moral worth is based on moral merit." Of course, no one wishes to deny that wrongdoers have, in virtue of still being moral agents, very considerable moral worth; but she denies that they have any less moral worth in virtue of having done wrong, and that involves a denial that they suffer from a guilt which constitutes a stain on their nature.

[2] For justification of the claims of the last two sentences, see Swinburne (2013, 214–227).

because Buddhism rejects the notion of any continuing self, and also holds the doctrine of karma, that our destiny depends solely on the choices of those earlier persons, our "earlier selves," who—though not identical with us—are causally connected to us—that it does not recognize forgiveness of the performative utterance kind. For, since your guilt could only be possessed by a continuing you, neither your repentance nor forgiveness by your victim could help to remove guilt for a past action which—to speak strictly—would not be your past action. The present "you" has no guilt to be removed. And anyway, given the doctrine of karma, the actions of anyone apart from your "earlier self," including the action of forgiving you, can make no difference to the state of your "later self." Since there is no guilt to be removed, forgiveness could not remove it.[3]

So on the assumption that my three metaethical "truths" are indeed truths, how can guilt be removed, in particular by forgiveness? Many recent writers have given accounts of forgiveness which have been derived from reflection on different human situations described in detail, leading to moral intuitions about whether forgiveness can be given in these situations and by whom, and when it would be effective in removing guilt. There is no doubt that many of these intuitions are those which many morally sensitive persons have. But these intuitions are often in conflict with each other; and if we are to make progress, we need to check whether our moral intuitions about forgiveness fit with our moral intuitions about obligation, blame, guilt, punishment, merit, reparation, justice, mercy, repentance, praise, and reward. That I try to do in my own account of the performative sense of "forgive," which I will now re-present.[4]

A wrongs B by taking away from B what belongs to B (or what A believes to belong to B), or not giving to B what A owes (that is, has an obligation

---

[3] Eckel (1997, 132) mentions the practice of monks of Theravada Buddhism to confess at twice-a-month ceremonies the occasions on which they have broken the monastic code. He quotes a recent account of this code which "makes it clear that the purpose of confession is not to wipe away guilt or to eliminate the effects of bad action." Confession is useful, however, according to this account, "to strengthen one's resolve to refrain from such behaviour in the future, and to reassure other bhikkhus that one is still serious about the training." Humphreys (1951, 123–124) quotes Amanda Coomaraswany, writing, "The Karmic law . . . asserts that this direction [of our life] cannot be altered suddenly by the forgiveness of our sins, but must be changed by our own efforts."

[4] The account of my own views (as opposed to my responses to the views of others) which I give in this and subsequent sections is almost entirely the same as that put forward in Swinburne (1989), especially chapters 5 and 10. My view of a paradigm use of forgiving as a performative utterance is developed in Warmke (2016). For reasons of space, my account in the present chapter discusses only its application to paradigm cases where one individual can forgive another individual. I do not discuss its application to groups forgiving or being forgiven, or its application to cases where either the victim or the wrongdoer is dead.

to give) (or believes that he owes) to B. What A takes away or does not give may be a piece of property, or it may be life, service, respect, and so on. If A wrongs B, A acquires guilt—objective guilt, if A takes away what does belong to B or does not give to B what A owes; subjective guilt if A takes away what A believes belongs to B (and so is wrong to take) or does not give what he or she believes that he or she owes to B. The guilt is greatest if it is both subjective and objective, less if it is merely subjective, and very much less if it is merely objective. Objective guilt is simply a bad condition; subjective guilt is a stain on the soul, caused by the agent intentionally doing wrong, making him or her blameworthy.

By A's action of wronging B, A acquires an obligation to make the world as far as is possible a world in which A had not done that wrong. I will call this A's obligation to make atonement to B. A cannot, of course, bring it about that the past act did not occur. But he can now restore what he stole or hand over what he ought to have handed over earlier. If he has stolen B's watch, he can return it; if he has damaged B's reputation by a false accusation, he can tell others that the accusation was false, and thereby restore B's reputation. If it is not possible to restore a stolen item, A has an obligation to replace it by a similar item or an item chosen by B which B would reasonably consider to be of equivalent value to him—subject to a qualification to which I shall come shortly. But A will have caused damage, not merely by the immediate effects of his action, but by the fact that A caused those effects. All that A can do about that is to distance himself from the act, by expressing regret for having done it, resolving not to do similar actions in the future, and showing the regret to be genuine by giving B more than the equivalent of what he took from B—what I will call a "penance." If A believed his action to be wrong, A's regret must take the form of repentance for the intention. In summary, by his wrongdoing, A acquires an obligation to make atonement, which has four parts—regret, apology, reparation, and penance—although in the case of less severe unintentional wrongdoing, no penance is needed. (In future, unless I specify that the wrongdoer did not believe his action to be wrong, I shall assume that he did so believe it, and so that his regret must take the form of repentance.) Sometimes when wrongdoers are not able to make adequate reparation (and penance), others can help them to do so. If your son intentionally breaks the neighbor's window and does not have the money for it to be repaired, you may give him the money; but it is he who must arrange for the repair, show repentance, and make apology.

Forgiving in the performative sense consists in deeming the wrongdoer's atonement sufficient, and thereby it involves a promise. One who promises creates an obligation to do or not do some future act; she does not merely report something which would be so whether or not the report was made. The promise which B makes by forgiving A is, I suggest, a promise to treat A insofar as is possible as someone who has not wronged B by her past action. In making atonement, A is handing over something to B, something owed and so not a "gift." By forgiving A, B gives something back. B undertakes to treat A insofar as is possible as if she had not wronged B by her past act. B does not undertake to assume that the past act as described in nonmoral terms did not happen. If, for example, A has broken B's vase, B in forgiving him does not undertake to assume that B did not break the vase. Consequently, even if B has forgiven A for some act, it may still be permissible for B to take precautions against the possibility of A committing a similar act in the future. If A has stolen money from B's wallet which he left in public view, B may in the future keep his wallet hidden. What B does undertake is not to "hold it against A" that he did this; and so B undertakes not to blame A for what has happened—for to blame someone is to describe him or her as subjectively guilty—and to try not to feel resentment at A. (Feelings not being fully under our immediate control, all that someone can do about his or her feelings is to try to control them.) When A has made some atonement, and B has forgiven A and thereby deemed the atonement sufficient, A no longer has any obligation arising from his wrongdoing. So together A and B have done all that can be done to make the world a world in which A had not done that wrong; and that latter state, I suggest, constitutes the removal of A's guilt.

While only someone wronged by the wrongdoer has the status to forgive him, there are indirect victims (wronged to a lesser extent) as well as direct victims of wrongdoing. If A hurts B directly (e.g., by running her over when driving a car dangerously), and so wrongs B, A also wrongs (to a lesser degree) those who have helped to make B the kind of person she is— the parents, teachers, and friends who have formed B and given her the capacity which (temporarily or permanently) she can no longer exercise. And A has also wronged those who formed A, by misusing the abilities which they have given him. Parents often need to forgive their own children for "letting them down," as well as to forgive those who hurt their children. A wrongs these close indirect victims, not only (or primarily) because he has caused them grief or anger, but because A has hurt B, and that is an indirect wrong to them, whether or not they feel it. Writers who have developed this point claim that in order for others to be indirect victims of wrongdoing, there must be a "social context" (Pettigrove 2012, ch. 2) in which this identification with the victim makes sense, and I suggest that it is the involvement of the others in the formation of victim or wrongdoer which provides that context.

What is not possible, despite frequent contemporary use of the phrase, is—in the sense in which I am using the word "forgive"—to "forgive oneself"; and that is because wronging someone creates a debt which there is an obligation on the wrongdoer to pay, and one cannot have a debt to oneself. Griswold (2007, 61) criticizes the debt analogy on the grounds that "when X wrongs Y, she does not borrow and is not loaned something. She forcibly takes something from Y without her consent. By contrast, the taking on of a debt is consented to by the lender, who is (as she thinks) benefited thereby." Now certainly not all cases of becoming indebted are cases of wronging someone and so becoming guilty; but what I am claiming is that all cases of becoming guilty are cases of acquiring a debt. It is like giving yourself an unauthorized bank loan, by "withdrawing" money from your bank account which you don't have in it, rather than receiving an authorized bank loan.[5] While allowing that forgiving is an appropriate response to repentant apology, Griswold (2007, 62) strangely claims that "the logic of forgiveness does not require compensation and reparation; but this is perfectly compatible with the view that *justice* requires them"; but compensation may be "offered for its symbolic or expressive value." But A could not possibly be repentant for having stolen B's watch if he refused to return the watch. For A to repent is to recognize that he has done wrong and to distance himself insofar as this is possible from the wrong act; that must include removing its consequences, and so taking steps to return the watch. Of course, B may then say that A can keep the watch, but that would be a new act. When it is not possible to remove the consequences—when the watch has been destroyed or the harm is of a kind that cannot be undone—A must do the nearest thing to removing the consequences. This means offering to B reparation of equivalent value to B, subject to the qualification to which I will come shortly. Again, B may waive the need for that, but that would be a further act.

I argued earlier that obligations arise from commitments in one's actions, from benefits received, or from great needs of those close to us. I now argue from that that there is as such no general obligation to forgive even those

---

[5] On the appropriateness of the debt analogy, see Warmke (2014).

who do make full atonement.[6] (I write "as such" because, when A wrongs B, B may have an obligation to forgive A arising from another source—e.g., B may have promised C that he will forgive A if A makes atonement or even without requiring more than repentance and apology. This includes the case—see the next section—where C is God, who gives us forgiveness on condition that we forgive others.) When A hurts B, B has not thereby made any commitments. When A makes due reparation, A has merely restored the status quo, and B has not received a net benefit. Maybe wrongdoers have a great need to have their guilt removed; but I shall be arguing shortly that there is another way, even though a more demanding way, by which, if the victim does not forgive the wrongdoer, this can often be secured. Hence I find it implausible to suppose that by hurting B and then making atonement, A can put B under an obligation to do something—that is, to forgive A. It is, however, normally good to forgive, supererogatorily good, for the simple reason that forgiveness is giving a gift to someone in need (though not great need), and it is good for the wrongdoer if the victim is the agent of the removal of his or her guilt, and thereby promises to treat the wrongdoer as one who has not wronged the victim. Generosity is normally good. In some cases, however, it may be good to delay the forgiveness in order to ensure that the atonement is genuine—for example, that A's apology was backed by genuine repentance, which could be shown by, among other ways, A not doing any similar wrongful acts for a while.

In a "Wild West" situation, that is, a situation before the existence of societies with laws, judges, and police forces, if A steals some item from B, and A does not voluntarily make atonement, B surely has the right to take it back without asking A's permission, and to take also some extra thing in compensation for the trouble involved in taking back the stolen item. If the item has been destroyed or is not the sort of thing which can be returned, B surely has the right to take something of greater value, greater so as to include compensation both for the loss of the original item and for the trouble involved in getting compensation. "Compensation" is thus the equivalent of

---

[6] For the contrary view that at least in some cases, especially when full atonement has been made, there is an obligation on the victim to forgive, see Nelkin (2013, 161) and Griswold (2007, 67). But if it were the case, that under certain conditions, the victim has an obligation to forgive the wrongdoer, then, I think that it follows analytically—contrary to Griswold (2007, 67) and Nelkin (2013, 161)—that the wrongdoer has "a right" to be forgiven; although, as they both insist, it is compatible with the view that the wrongdoer is not "entitled to demand" the fulfilment of the obligation. I argue later that there is just possibly one kind of case where there is an obligation on the victim to forgive, and that is where the wrongdoer tries very hard but is unable to make full atonement and so the victim alone can remove his guilt.

the "reparation" and "penance" involved in the wrongdoer making atone-ment. Now suppose the harm done is physical damage to B, say A has put out B's eye, it might then seem to follow that B has the right to put out A's eye—"an eye for an eye, and a tooth for a tooth"—and to cause further harm to B. Or suppose A kills B, and thus deprives B's family of B. Then B's family would seem to have the right to kill A, and perhaps also injure some rela-tive of A. These conclusions follow unless there is a superior conflicting ob-ligation, such as that it is always wrong to kill or physically mutilate anyone, unless by doing so you can cause a similar good state. In my view the con-flicting obligation is the one just stated; those who accept that there is some superior conflicting obligation may acknowledge only a more limited one, for example one forbidding bodily mutilation but allowing killing even when it causes no subsequent good. But given a superior obligation not to muti-late except when by doing so you can cause a similar good state, then even if A has put out B's eye, B does not have the right to put out A's eye—unless (for example) A's eye can be transplanted and put into B's eye socket and made to function there. And given a superior obligation not to kill unless by doing so you can cause a similar good state, then even if A has killed B, B's family does not have the right to kill A unless (for example) by doing so they can prevent A killing others. In these cases clearly B or B's family has the right to take compensation from A, but there are plausible moral limits to the way in which "equivalent" or "greater" compensation can be construed. In such cases B or B's family has the right to take very considerable compensation of a different kind, for example money or property or many years of compulsory service. I wrote earlier with respect to voluntary atonement that if it is not possible to restore a stolen item, A has an obligation to replace it by a similar item or an item chosen by B which B would reasonably consider to be of sim-ilar value to him, subject to a qualification. We can see from these plausible limits to the kind of compensation which can be taken involuntarily, the kind of qualification on the reparation and penance that can be required from a victim: that the victim cannot require from the wrongdoer his life or a phys-ical mutilation, unless the wrongdoer suffering these things is the means to a similar benefit for someone else.

Few humans today live in a Wild West situation; we belong to nation states which have courts of law to determine (for most serious kinds of wrong-doing) who has wronged whom, and of what kind the compensation should be, and police to enforce the decisions of law courts. In accepting member-ship of nation states, which we almost all do—albeit implicitly, we hand over to the law courts our right to take back our own stolen property or compensation for it. Law courts determine on our behalf the kind of compensation to which we are entitled; and insofar as it consists of elements other than restitution (in a literal sense) of stolen property or property of equivalent value, it is called punishment. And law courts have the right (within limits laid down by laws issued by the governing authority of the nation state) to determine the nature and amount of the punishment on grounds additional to retributive ones—for example, on the utilitarian grounds of preventing similar crimes by the wrongdoer, deterring others from committing similar crimes, and reforming the wrongdoer. But the wrongdoer still owes repentance and apology to the victim, and the victim alone can forgive him. Courts of law often—for utilitarian reasons—take into account in determining the punishment any repentance shown and apology offered by the wrongdoer. It is, of course, good for all of us that (for most kinds of wrongdoing) we do hand over the right to determine the amount of compensation and punishment due, and the duty to extract the compensation and administer the punishment. But the consequent separation between the victim who has the right to forgive and the judges who have the right to extract the equivalent of reparation and penance means that the victim's decision to forgive can be independent of the amount of reparation and penance determined by judges and whether or not it has been extracted.

It is important to clarify the relation between the victim's right to compensation and the state's duty to punish the wrongdoer. By his wrongdoing, the wrongdoer has given the victim the right to compensation which (subject to such superior obligations as I mentioned) he (or the state on his behalf) may take in the form of harm to the wrongdoer. The wrongdoer "deserves" to be punished in the sense that he has lost some of his normal rights. But it doesn't follow that it is always bad if he is not punished. My argument suggests that at least in some cases the state has the right to impose the death penalty for murder—for example, when the wrongdoer is likely to kill again—but I endorse the normal Western European view that, barring quite exceptional circumstances, it would be bad to do so, despite the financial cost of life imprisonment, for the utilitarian reasons of the benefit to the wrongdoer of life, the risk of a mistaken conviction, and the effect of the practice of capital punishment in brutalizing society. And similar reasons, albeit less strong ones, count also against the use by the state of corporal punishment (beating). The state does not, however, in modern Western societies take over responsibility for dealing with the consequences of all serious wrongdoing (for example, marital infidelity) and does not take over responsibility for dealing with the consequences of most lesser wrongs (for example, insults).

Just as no one has any obligation to forgive, so no one has any obligation to treat the wrongdoer who does not repent as one who has wronged them. The victim could simply ignore the wrongdoing and continue to have exactly the same relations as before with the wrongdoer. But, I suggest, in the case of serious intentional wrongdoing, it would be bad to do so. To use again the example which I used in Swinburne (1989), suppose that I have murdered your dearly loved wife; you know this, but for some reason I am beyond the power of the law. Being a modern and charitable person, you decide to overlook my offence. "The past is the past," you say; "what is the point of nursing a grievance? The party we are both going to attend will go with more of a swing if we forget about this little incident." But, of course, that attitude of yours trivializes human life, your love for your wife, and the importance of right action. And it involves you failing to treat me seriously, to take seriously my attitude toward you expressed in my action. Thereby it trivializes human relationships, for it supposes that good human relations can exist when we do not take each other seriously. We could describe this as a situation where you have "forgiven me," but it was bad to do so; but I suggest that it is more natural to count it as a situation when you have condoned, not forgiven, my act. (By "condoned" the act, I mean "treated the act as too trivial to need forgiveness.") We should count an act of no longer treating the wrongdoer as one who has wronged you as an act of "forgiving," only if it is a response to at least some repentance and apology on the part of the wrongdoer. It is, of course, appropriate to treat wrongdoing which is really trivial as trivial—that is, to condone it.

The victim has no obligation to insist on reparation and penance before forgiving the wrongdoer; as with any obligation, the one to whom the obligation is owed can waive the obligation. But while one may forgive someone without insisting on reparation (let alone, penance), it is sometimes good (in a situation where the law is not involved) if the victim insists on some reparation. It is good for the wrongdoer that he himself should take responsibility for what he has done, and so try to make reparation. But it is up to the victim to determine how much reparation (up to a maximum proportional to the wrong done) to demand before he gives forgiveness. If he insists on reparation, the victim can only—except when the law takes on the responsibility to exact reparation—give conditional forgiveness in advance of the reparation being paid. When the state has taken on the responsibility for imposing reparation and so punishment, and determined its amount by law, judges have an obligation to impose punishment within the bounds allowed by law. For the victim not to insist on some or any reparation is to show mercy, and likewise for judges to impose no punishment (if the law allows this) or to impose a lesser punishment within the range allowed by the law, is also to show mercy.

When the victim has forgiven the wrongdoer, the victim's guilt is wiped away. But suppose the wrongdoer repents sincerely, and apologies profusely, gives (or has taken from him by judges) full reparation and penance, and the victim still refuses to forgive, does the wrongdoer's guilt remain? I suggest that under those circumstances the wrongdoer's guilt disappears, since the wrongdoer has done all that is required on his part to make the world as far as is possible a world in which he had not done that wrong. His moral condition is as far as possible such as it would be if he had not done the wrong—even if the world is not as far as possible such as it would be if the wrong had not been done. In that circumstance, the victim no longer has the right to blame the wrongdoer. We speak of a wrongdoer having "atoned for his wrong-doing," quite apart from whether the victim has forgiven him. But the victim has the ability to remove the wrongdoer's guilt long before the wrongdoer has made full atonement; and he has the right to refuse to do that. The victim has the right not to be the agent of the removal of the wrongdoer's guilt. But if the wrongdoer is not able to make proper atonement, or—though able—does not do so, only the victim's forgiveness can remove the guilt. While, as I wrote earlier, I find it implausible to suppose that normally by wronging a victim and then seeking forgiveness, the wrongdoer can put the victim under an obligation to do a new act—of forgiving him—there is an issue of whether, when the wrongdoer is unable to make proper atonement after trying for a long time to do so, the victim then has an obligation to forgive. On that, I find my own intuitions unclear. But undoubtedly it would be a very good thing for the victim to forgive the wrongdoer in this situation. And even if the wrong-doer has removed his guilt by making full atonement, it is still good for the victim to forgive him, because only if the victim forgives the wrongdoer (and so himself undertakes no longer to regard the wrongdoer as someone who has wronged him and so no longer "holds it against" the wrongdoer that he did the wrong) will both parties have done what they can to make the world be as far as possible a world in which the wrong was not done. Only then would the world be as far as it is possible for anyone to make it thus, a world in which the wrong was not done.

The Teaching of Jesus on Forgiveness

Such is my account of the nature of forgiveness in the "performative utterance" sense, which fits—I claim—naturally with other moral concepts. It is sometimes claimed that the Greeks did not have this concept; they were often reconciled with their enemies or agreed to overlook the wrongdoing of others, but they did not forgive them. (See, for example, Konstan 2010, chs. 2 and 3.)[7] It is, however, very widely agreed that the concept of forgiveness plays a crucial role in the Judeo-Christian tradition; and I endorse the view that the importance of forgiveness is central to the teaching of Jesus, as set out in the Gospels. This has been denied by Konstan on the grounds that the teaching of Jesus and the subsequent Christian church is primarily concerned with God's forgiveness of human sins, not with forgiveness by one human of the wrongdoing of another human. However, contrary to Konstan, it seems to me that the teaching of Jesus contains all the elements involved in interhuman forgiveness which I have been describing.[8] The "Lord's prayer" (Matthew 6:9–13 and Luke 11:2–4) was clearly the only prayer taught by Jesus to be learned by rote by his disciples. The prayer asks God the Father to "forgive" (ἀφεῖναι) our "sins" (ἁμαρτίαι) (in Luke's version) or our debts (ὀφειλήματα) (in Matthew's version) just as we forgive everyone indebted (ὀφείλοντι) to us. The same word—ἀφεῖναι—is used for what we ask God to do to us, as we claim to do to other humans. For some people to use one word and other people to use a different word in a prayer learned by rote suggests that they thought that the difference in words made little difference to the meaning, and so that a "sin" was a "debt." That same word, ἀφεῖναι, is used elsewhere in the New Testament for what God does for us if we repent (μετανοεῖν). And we are told to forgive those who sin (ἁμαρτεῖν) against us seven times in one day (Luke 17:4) or "seventy times seven" (Matthew 18:22) each time they sin; and the qualification "if [the sinner] repents" is added in two separate verses of the Lukan version (Luke 17:3 and 4). Matthew's version of the Lord's Prayer is followed by Jesus's instruction that if you forgive the faults (παραπτώματα) of humans, your Father will forgive you, but if you do not forgive other humans, your Father will not forgive you. The parallel

---

[7] See Carter (2018) for detailed justification of the claim that Aristotle had a full concept of forgiveness.

[8] For fuller analysis of what I understand as Christ's view of the nature of the forgiveness and the conditions under which God will forgive us, see Swinburne (2019). Quotations from the Bible in this chapter are taken from the translation in the New Revised Standard Version.

between God forgiving us and us forgiving others is made very clearly explicit, when sin is treated as a debt. And this is reemphasized in the parable of the two debtors (Mathew 18:23–35), A who owed his Lord an enormous sum, and B who owed A a small sum. At A's pleading the Lord forgave A his debts, but despite B's pleading A refused to forgive B his small debt. The parable ends with the Lord retracting his forgiveness of A; the next verse is "So will my heavenly Father do to every one of you, if you do not forgive your brother from your hearts."

These passages make it very clear that humans wrong each other as well as God, that wronging involves incurring a debt which has to repaid, and that the victim may choose to forgive or not forgive. Humans would not need to pray to God to forgive them if God would do so automatically; and God's forgiveness is not unconditional. The condition for us to receive forgiveness from God for our much greater wrongs against God without God insisting on compensation (except—see the final section—that provided by God himself) is that we should forgive other humans for their much smaller wrongs against us. It is also a natural interpretation of these passages that God will not forgive unless we repent, for to ask for forgiveness is to acknowledge having done wrong and so to repent. The Gospel which the disciples were told to preach to the world was one of "repentance for the forgiveness of sins" (Luke 24:47).

The passages cited against this natural interpretation of the Gospels include the response of Jesus to scribes' exclamatory question "who can forgive sins but God alone?" that he "The Son of Man" "has authority on earth to forgive sins" (Mark 2:1–12); and the prayer of Jesus from the Cross about his executioners, "Father, forgive them for they know not what they do" (Luke 23:34). The response of Jesus to the scribes might seem to suggest that forgiving sins is the prerogative of God and those to whom he gives special authority to do this. But, when one human A wrongs another human B, he also wrongs those who have made A and B the kind of people they are. Hence—since God is the total cause of the existence of A and B and of all those who have nurtured A and B having the power to do—all sins against humans are also sins against God. Further, some sins are sins only against God, for example, sins of blasphemy and failure to worship. So God (or his appointed deputy) is the major victim of our wrongdoing, and only he (or his deputy) can forgive those wrongs. In purporting to forgive the paralyzed man, Jesus was not acting as the direct human victim; for the paralyzed man had, as far as we know, no previous interaction with the human Jesus. He was purporting, to exercise God's right to forgive sins against God, and it was to that that the scribes were objecting, not to the possibility of humans forgiving other humans.

The prayer of Jesus from the cross for his executioners—"Father, forgive them for they do not know not what they are doing" (Luke 23:34)—might seem to imply that God can forgive without the wrongdoer needing to acknowledge his wrongdoing. But there is no need to understand it in that way. Perhaps, because there is no obvious other word in contemporary Greek for "condone," Jesus is asking the Father to condone the wrongdoing of the executioners for the reason that their sins were unintentional, and so their guilt is merely objective. So I stand by my view that the Gospels picture Jesus as expounding the doctrine that forgiveness in return for atonement has the same form when the victim is human, as when the victim is God, given that we bear in mind that God is always at least the indirect victim of all wrongdoing. Contemporary English usage is such that it seems odd to call wronging a human "sinning" against him, and we may wish to call wronging a person "sinning" against him only when that person wronged is God; but sinning is always wrongdoing, and it is the logic of wrongdoing and its consequences that I have been exploring.

How Jesus Made God's Forgiveness Available

It is a central Christian doctrine that forgiveness from God is available to us only through the life, death, and Resurrection of Jesus Christ. There have been various different theories in the history of Christian thought of how the life, death, and Resurrection of Jesus provided the atonement for our sins which made that forgiveness available to us. (See, for example, Swinburne 1989, chapter 10.) But the one which fits best with my account in this chapter of the nature of forgiveness is Anselm's "satisfaction" theory as improved by Aquinas. "Satisfaction" is Anselm's word which Aquinas adopts, for what I have called "reparation and penance." Aquinas acknowledged (3a.48. 2 ad1) that "the one who sins must repent and confess" but "satisfaction consists in an exterior act, for which one can make us of instruments, among which friends are included"; and Aquinas is saying that the wrongdoer (a human) can present to the victim (God) reparation and penance made by a friend, that is, Jesus Christ. (Going forward, when speaking of "reparation," I include also "penance.") I noted earlier that when wrongdoers are not able to make adequate reparation, others can provide the reparation for them; but it is the wrongdoers who must offer the reparation to the victim, repent, and apologize. We humans wrong God so often. As I commented earlier, when we hurt our fellow humans, we wrong God in two ways—first, because God made and sustains in existence those fellow humans, and, second, because God made and sustains in existence us wrongdoers who have misused the powers which God gave us; and we also wrong God in not interacting with him adequately in prayer and worship, seeking to discover and to execute his will for us. Yet we owe God so much anyway that it would be difficult for us to make adequate reparation, which anyway we have often have little inclination to do. We need someone else to provide the reparation for us to offer to God. It is up to the victim, in this case God, to determine (within reason) what would constitute adequate reparation; and one perfect human life (especially if it is a voluntarily offered life of a divine person who is also human) would surely not be too small a reparation. So a generous God might well himself live a perfect human life under the most difficult circumstances under which many humans live which we could offer back to him, saying "Please accept, instead of the life which we ought to have lived, this perfect human life." A perfect human life lived under the most difficult circumstances under which humans live might well end in a painful death, of a kind wrongly judged by others to be shameful.

God could, of course, have forgiven us in response to our repentance and apology, without requiring the reparation which we are unable ourselves to provide. But it is good for wrongdoers to take responsibility for their serious wrongdoing, and they do that to a limited extent if they have to offer to God such a serious sacrificial offering. Various passages in the New Testament assert that forgiveness is available through the death and Resurrection of Jesus Christ, whom other passages and subsequent Christian tradition identify as God himself, God the Son, whose life was offered to God the Father on our behalf. Some theologians seem to have thought of the reparation made by Christ merely as his death. But Christ did not commit suicide (and in my view, it would have been wrong for him to have done so). What was important about his death was that it was the result of a series of events which led to his involuntary death, brought about by his free actions of living a perfect life under the difficult circumstances when telling the truth is likely to lead to a cruel involuntary death. It was this life leading to his cruel involuntary death which constituted the reparation for our sins; and his subsequent Resurrection which constituted God the Father's acceptance of that reparation.

This account of how Christ made an atonement coincides with the account in terms of sacrifice given in the Letter to the Hebrews, the one book of the New Testament which discusses the mechanism of the Atonement at any length. The letter regards Christ's death as an effective sacrifice which achieved what the sacrifices in the Jewish temple could not achieve. "The blood of Christ" constituted a sacrifice "without blemish" (Hebrews 9:14) to "bear the sins of many" (9:28). It was offered only once, and that was all that was needed—"He entered once for all into the Holy Place, not with the blood of goats and calves, but with his own blood, thus obtaining eternal redemption" (9:12). In the most primitive way of thinking about sacrifice lying behind (the far more sophisticated) Old Testament thought, a sacrifice is the giving of something valuable to God who consumes it by inhaling the smoke, and often gives back some of it to be consumed by the worshippers (who eat some of the flesh of the sacrificed animal). (See Pedersen 1959, 299–375, esp. 359.) The sacrifice of Christ is then Jesus Christ, the Incarnate God the Son, giving to God the Father the most valuable thing he has—his human life, a perfect life of service to God and humans in difficult circumstances, leading to its being taken from him by his crucifixion. In order for the sacrifice to be successful (that is, for God to accept the sacrifice), Christ "entered into heaven itself, now to appear in the presence of God on our behalf" (Hebrews 9:24); and the letter also alludes to what the writer must regard as our evidence of Christ's exaltation, that God "brought [him] back from the dead . . . by the blood of the eternal covenant" (13:20).

I have written that Christ "provided" an atonement and pointed out that the benefits of sacrifice are available only to those who associate themselves with it. And clearly Christians have always claimed that Christ's act makes no difference to us if we do not in some way appropriate it for ourselves. (Christ is "the source of salvation to all who obey him"—Hebrews 5:9.) We can say to God, "Please accept instead of the life which I ought to have led the perfect life of Christ as my reparation." Thereby we join our repentance and apology with the reparation which Christ provides. The ceremony of entry into the Christian church is baptism. The Nicene creed echoes various New Testament texts in affirming belief in "one baptism" (that is, a nonrepeatable ceremony) "for the forgiveness of sins." The answer of Peter to the crowd who heard his Pentecost sermon and asked "What should we do?" was "Repent and be baptized every one of you in the name of Jesus Christ so that your sins may be forgiven" (Acts 2: 37–38).[9] The

---

[9] In discussing the paradigm case of the forgiveness of sins in adult baptism, I pass over its application to infant baptism, and to the forgiveness of "original sin." I discuss "original sin" in Swinburne (1989, 137–147, 157, 161).

association of Christ's death with the forgiveness of human sins, established by baptism is renewed at each Eucharist when, St Paul claims, "as often as you eat this bread and drink this cup, you proclaim the Lord's death until he comes" (I Corinthians 11:26). In Matthew's account of the Last Supper, Jesus describes the wine of the Eucharist as "my blood of the covenant for the forgiveness of sins" (Matthew 26:28). So various New Testament texts claim, as does later theological tradition, that God forgives us in response to us asking for that forgiveness by associating ourselves with Christ's sacrifice in seeking baptism and offering the eucharist. He utters that forgiveness by providing baptism and holy communion. But these paradigm ways in which we seek and he provides forgiveness do not rule out other ways in which this might happen.

References

Aquinas, St Thomas. 1963 (Latin c. 1274). *Summa Theologiae*. Blackfriars translation. New York: McGraw Hill.

Butler, Joseph. 1902 (originally published 1729). *The Analogy of Religion*. Edition containing his Sermons at the Rolls Chapel. "Sermon 9: On the Forgiveness of Injuries." London: George Bell and Sons.

Carter, J. 2018. "Aristotle and the Problem of Forgiveness." *American Catholic Philosophical Quarterly* 92 (1): 49–71.

Eckel, M. D. 1997. "A Buddhist Approach to Repentance." In A. Etzoni and D. E. Carney (eds.), *Repentance: A Comparative Perspective*. Lanham, MD: Rowan and Littlefield.

Garrard, E., and McNaughton, D. 2003. "In Defence of Unconditional Forgiveness." *Proceedings of the Aristotelian Society* 103: 339–360.

Griswold C. 2007. *Forgiveness* Cambridge: Cambridge University Press.

Holmgren, M. 2012. *Forgiveness and Retribution*. Cambridge: Cambridge University Press.

Humphreys, C. 1951. *Buddhism*. London: Penguin Books.

Konstan, D. 2010. *Before Forgiveness*. Cambridge: Cambridge University Press.

Murphy, J. G. 2003. *Getting Even*. Oxford: Oxford University Press.

Nelkin, D. 2013. "Freedom and Forgiveness." In Ishtiyaque Haji and Justin Caoette (eds.), *Free Will and Moral Responsibility*. Newcastle upon Tyne: Cambridge Scholars Press, pp. 148–170.

Pedersen, J. 1959. *Israel, Its Life and Culture*. Rev. ed. Oxford: Oxford University Press.

Pettigrove, G. 2012. *Forgiveness and Love*. Oxford: Oxford University Press.

Stump, E. 2016. "Love and Forgiveness: Swinburne on Atonement." In M. Bergmann and J. E. Brower (eds.), *Reason and Faith*. Oxford: Oxford University Press, pp. 148–170.

Stump, E. 2018. *Atonement*. Oxford: Oxford University Press.

Swinburne, R. 1989. *Responsibility and Atonement*. Oxford: Oxford University Press.

Swinburne, R. 2013. *Mind, Brain, and Free Will*. Oxford: Oxford University Press.

Swinburne, R. 2019. "Stump on Forgiveness." *Faith and Philosophy*.

Warmke, B. 2014. "The Economic Model of Forgiveness." *Pacific Philosophical Quarterly*.

Warmke, B. 2016. "The Normative Significance of Forgiveness." *Australasian Journal of Philosophy* 94: 687–703.

7

Institutional Apologies and Forgiveness

Angela M. Smith

Introduction

Recently, many governments, universities, corporations, and other institutions have issued public apologies for the roles they played in serious instances of historical injustice.[1] These apologies are particularly interesting in the case of wrongs that occurred in the distant past against individuals who are no longer living. When both the original perpetrators of these wrongs and their original victims are no longer living, one might have doubts about the conceptual and moral intelligibility of such apologies. What is the point, one might ask, of one group of people apologizing on behalf of another group of people to a third group of people for wrongs that were done to a fourth group of people?

My aim in this chapter is to try to answer this question, by examining the logic of such institutional apologies and their relation to questions of institutional blame and institutional forgiveness. I will focus, in particular, on whether it makes sense for American colleges and universities to offer apologies for their historical involvement with the practice of chattel slavery.[2] In the aftermath of Brown University's groundbreaking report on its own ties to slavery and the transatlantic slave trade in 2006,[3] as well as Craig Steven Wilder's widely discussed 2013 book *Ebony and Ivy: Race, Slavery, and the*

---

[1] For a helpful summary and discussion of the wave of institutional apologies in the 1990s, see Robert Weyeneth, "The Power of Apology and the Process of Historical Reconciliation," *The Public Historian* 23:3 (2001): 9–38. See also the essays in the volume *The Age of Apology: Facing Up to the Past*, edited by Mark Gibney, Rhoda E. Howard-Hassmann, Jean-Marc Coicaud, and Niklaus Steiner (Philadelphia: University of Pennsylvania Press, 2009).

[2] Max Clarke and Gary Alan Fine provide a very helpful exploration of how this question was addressed at two universities, Brown University and the University of Alabama, in "'A' is for Apology: Collegiate Discourses of Remembrance—The Cases of Brown University and the University of Alabama," *History and Memory* 22:1 (2010): 81–112.

[3] "Slavery and Justice: Report of the Brown University Steering Committee on Slavery and Justice." The full report can be found online at https://www.brown.edu/Research/Slavery_Justice/documents/SlaveryAndJustice.pdf

Angela M. Smith, *Institutional Apologies and Forgiveness* In: *Forgiveness and Its Moral Dimensions*. Edited by: Brandon Warmke, Dana Kay Nelkin, and Michael McKenna, Oxford University Press. © Oxford University Press 2021. DOI: 10.1093/oso/9780190602147.003.0007

Troubled History of America's Universities,[4] dozens of American colleges and universities have launched initiatives to uncover, acknowledge, and come to terms with their past involvement with slavery. While many of these institutions have offered official statements of "regret" for this history, few have offered official apologies for their past wrongdoing. I will argue that this reluctance to use the language of apology is misguided, and that institutions of higher learning are especially well placed to lay the groundwork for institutional forgiveness and reconciliation through sincere statements of apology.

My strategy will be as follows. I will begin by offering a general account of the nature and function of apologies in ordinary interpersonal contexts, and the role such apologies typically play in laying the groundwork for interpersonal forgiveness and reconciliation. I will then consider whether this general account can be extended to make sense of the notion of university apologies for historical wrongdoing. There are various grounds upon which one might resist this extension: first, one might deny that universities are "moral agents" that are capable of acknowledging and accepting moral responsibility for past wrongdoing; second, one might deny that universities are blameworthy for their past involvement with these unjust practices; third, one might deny that universities are capable of expressing attitudes such as remorse and repentance; fourth, one might question the power of university apologies; and finally, one might doubt whether there are proper "addressees" of such apologies who can (in principle) offer forgiveness for these wrongs. I will argue that none of these objections ultimately stands up to critical scrutiny, and that universities have compelling moral reasons to apologize for their involvement with the practice of chattel slavery. Finally, in the fourth section I will sketch an account of the nature of institutional forgiveness, and I will show how properly executed university apologies can lay the groundwork for forgiveness on the part of those wronged by these institutions' past injustices.

Apology and Forgiveness in Interpersonal Relationships

Before turning to the case of institutional apologies for historical wrongdoing, it would be helpful to examine the role that apologies play in ordinary

---

[4] Craig Steven Wilder, *Ebony and Ivy: Race, Slavery, and the Troubled History of America's Universities* (New York: Bloomsbury Press, 2013).

interpersonal relationships. I am interested, in particular, in what Trudy Govier and Wilhelm Verwoerd call "moral apologies," which involve an expression of sincere remorse for moral wrongdoing and typically imply a request for forgiveness and reconciliation.[5] These sorts of apologies should be distinguished from what we might call "polite apologies," which are appropriate when we commit minor transgressions against others that do not pose a serious challenge either to the moral status of the other person or to our continuing relationship—for example, "I'm sorry for being late (forgetting the milk, stepping on your foot, falling asleep in the movie)." Unlike moral apologies, polite apologies do not usually embody a request for forgiveness so much as a request for pardon. (In a healthy relationship, one should not need to beg forgiveness for forgetting the milk.[6]) This is not, however, to say that these polite apologies are unimportant. For they serve the important function of *forestalling* possible breaches in our relationships with others, insofar as they make clear that one takes the other person seriously and recognizes that one has acted in a way to which the other person could reasonably object.

Moral apologies, however, might be understood as attempts not to forestall but rather to *repair* breaches in relationships that have already arisen. They are appropriate in cases where one has committed a serious moral wrong that has jeopardized one or more of one's relationships with others. A sincere apology to another conveys a number of things. First, it conveys that one *recognizes* and *accepts* that one has acted in a way that is wrong and morally disrespectful of the other, and that one has thereby caused harm both to the other person and to the relationship itself. It is important that one correctly identify the specific wrong one has done and why it was morally disrespectful and injurious to the other. "I'm sorry if I've hurt you" is an unsatisfying apology, for it does not identify the ground of the moral injury, and thus leaves it unclear whether one understands why the other is rationally *justified* in feeling hurt. Second, a sincere apology conveys that one accepts *moral responsibility* for this wrong and for the harm it has caused. While it

[5] Trudy Govier and Wilhelm Verwoerd, "The Promise and Pitfalls of Apology," *Journal of Social Philosophy* 33:1 (2002): 67–82, 67. I say "typically" imply, because in the case of some very serious wrongdoings, one might recognize that forgiveness is "more than one could ask for." In such cases, we often make clear along with our apology that we have no expectation of forgiveness. I am grateful to Michael McKenna and Brandon Warmke for helpful discussion on this point.

[6] "That's okay," "don't worry about it," and similar expressions are the most natural responses to such apologies, and it would be somewhat jarring to be told that we have been "forgiven" for such minor transgressions.

is tempting to dilute apologies with excuses or justifications, or with morally distancing language (e.g., "mistakes were made"), a sincere apology is morally nonevasive. It acknowledges that one was the responsible agent of a serious moral wrong, and that one did not have an excuse or justification for doing what one did. Third, a sincere apology conveys that one *disavows* and *repudiates* the disrespectful moral claim about the other's moral status implicit in the original act of wrongdoing. It is important not only to *identify* the specific wrong one has done but also to make clear that one finds the *message* conveyed by one's wrongful act completely morally unacceptable. "You did not deserve to be treated that way, and it was outrageous for me to act as if you did." Fourth, a sincere apology conveys that one feels sincere remorse and guilt for both the wrong done and for the harm it has caused. Many apologies fail because it is unclear whether the wrongdoer really feels remorse for what she has done.[7] Someone who says, "Look, I said I was *sorry*, okay? Can't we just move on?" seems to care more about closing the books on her misdeed than about conveying her genuine sorrow for what she has done to the victim. Finally, a sincere apology conveys that one is prepared to do what is necessary to atone for the wrong one has done. Often this involves acknowledging that forgiveness and reconciliation are too much to expect, but that one is committed to taking steps to regain the victim's trust and goodwill. When all goes well, a sincere expression of apology, backed up by credible reparative efforts, can lay the groundwork for forgiveness and for the reestablishment of a relationship between the victim and the offender.

How, exactly, does a sincere apology lay the groundwork for forgiveness? And how should we understand the nature of "forgiveness" in the interpersonal context? Like many writers on this topic, I think it is helpful to begin with the commonly held view that forgiveness involves the forgoing of resentment.[8] But I agree with Pamela Hieronymi that not just any "forgoing" of resentment will count as an instance of forgiveness.[9] After all, I might forgo

---

[7] Such apologies "fail" in the sense that they do not properly lay the groundwork for forgiveness, as discussed later.

[8] This view was often attributed to Bishop Joseph Butler in his *Fifteen Sermons Preached at Rolls Chapel*, edited by Samuel Halifax (New York: Carter, 1846). As Brandon Warmke has reminded me, however, many recent writers on forgiveness have resisted this interpretation, arguing persuasively that Butler thinks forgiveness is quite compatible with resentment (and it is what prevents resentment from turning into revenge). For my purposes, however, it is still worth starting with the commonly held view.

[9] Pamela Hieronymi, "Articulating an Uncompromising Forgiveness," *Philosophy and Phenomenological Research* 62:3 (2001): 529–555. For what it is worth, I am not sure that the action in question must be "wrong" in the sense of *morally impermissible*; it might simply be deeply morally objectionable (or "suberogatory"), and therefore blameworthy but not wrong. I don't think

my resentment by convincing myself that you just don't matter and are not worth being upset by, or that I really deserved to be treated in this way, or that what you did to me wasn't really that objectionable after all. In such cases, I would not be *forgiving* you, but rather writing you off, or condoning your action, or excusing it as unimportant. Genuine forgiveness, however, seems to require something much more difficult: a revision of judgment and attitude toward an offender whom one regards as morally responsible for committing a significant moral wrong against one's person without sufficient excuse or justification. As Hieronymi puts it, forgiveness requires one to hold in place three interrelated judgments: "(1) The act in question was wrong; it was a serious offense worthy of moral attention. (2) The wrongdoer is a legitimate member of the moral community who can be expected not to do such things. As such, she is someone to be held responsible and she is worth being upset by. (3) You, as the one wronged, ought not to be wronged. This sort of treatment is an offense to your person."[10] Hieronymi goes on to note that when these three judgments are warranted, anger and resentment are rationally justified. These responses can be understood as forms of "protest": "In resentment the victim protests the trespass, affirming both its wrongfulness and the moral significance of both herself and the offender."[11] So what forgiveness requires, then, is the simultaneous acceptance of these three judgments together with a commitment to relinquishing the attitudes of protest they rationally warrant. Sincere apology can give the victim moral reasons to relinquish these attitudes of protest insofar as it shows that the offender herself now joins with the victim in affirming the wrongfulness of the offender's action and the moral significance of both herself and her victim. The offender and the victim can now move forward with a shared understanding of what happened and why it was so hurtful to the victim and injurious to the relationship. When things go well, this can also provide a basis for the repair and re-establishment of the breached relationship, though the relationship after such a breach will likely be different than it was before (in the same way that a patched pair of jeans will be different from the original).[12]

---

anything important in the account turns on this issue (and one could substitute "blameworthiness" for "wrongfulness" throughout). I am grateful for Michael McKenna for urging me to clarify my position on this point.

[10] Ibid., 530.

[11] Ibid.

[12] And just as patched jeans can end up looking even *better* than the original item, a relationship repaired after a serious moral breach can end up being even stronger because of the moral effort involved in the process of reconciliation. But this need not always be the case, and some relationships

I believe Hieronymi's account captures very well the nature of genuine forgiveness, and gives a plausible account of why sincere apologies play such an important role in laying the groundwork for both forgiveness and moral reconciliation. I would only add that serious wrongdoing of the sort addressed by moral apologies might also give rise to (and rationally justify) attitudes other than resentment—such as hurt feelings, sadness, and disappointment—and might also make appropriate other changes to one's attitudes, intentions, and expectations toward the offender. For example, one may no longer trust the offender, may no longer intend to confide in or help her, and may no longer take pleasure in her company or wish her well.[13] These, too, in my view, may be understood as forms of "blame" that embody moral protest.[14] A sincere apology, backed up by credible efforts at atonement, can lay the groundwork for a revision in these attitudes, expectations, and intentions as well. A victim who rationally revises these attitudes, expectations, and intentions in response to sincere expressions of apology can also be said to "forgive" the offender.

With this understanding of the nature of moral apology and the nature of forgiveness on the table, we can now turn to the question of whether these responses make sense in the case of universities coming to terms with their historical involvement in the wrong of chattel slavery. Though there is widespread agreement that it is important for universities to make this history known, and several universities have chosen to acknowledge it with "regret," most universities have declined to offer official apologies for their involvement with slavery.[15] In the next section, I will consider some of the reasons one might think that apology is inappropriate in this case, and I will argue

may be so damaged by the moral wrongdoing that repair and reconciliation is not possible (even if forgiveness is).

[13] Here I am in broad agreement with T. M. Scanlon's more expansive account of the nature of blame, defended in *Moral Dimensions: Permissibility, Meaning, Blame* (Cambridge, MA: Harvard University Press, 2008).

[14] I defend this claim in "Moral Blame and Moral Protest," in Justin Coates and Neal Tognazzini, eds., *Blame: Its Nature and Norms* (New York: Oxford University Press, 2013): 27–48.

[15] To my knowledge, the University of Alabama is the only university that has issued an official apology for its historical ties to chattel slavery, and this apology was adopted and issued by its faculty senate (not by its president or board of trustees). For a helpful discussion of the process leading up to this apology and its meaning, see Alfred Brophy, "The University and the Slaves: Apology and Its Meaning," in *The Age of Apology: Facing Up to the Past*, 109–119. Several other universities have issued official statements of "regret" for their past involvement with slavery, including Brown University, Washington and Lee University, the University of Virginia, the University of Maryland, and Emory University. The College of William and Mary passed a resolution that "acknowledges" past injustices, but quite explicitly does not express "regret." See http://www.wm.edu/sites/lemonproject/about/resolution/index.php

that they are not compelling. In the final section, I will suggest that such apologies can lay the groundwork for something recognizable as forgiveness on the part of those who have been wronged by these historical injustices.

Institutional Apologies for Historical Wrongdoing

In 2003, President Ruth Simmons of Brown University appointed a Steering Committee on Slavery and Justice to investigate and issue a public report on that university's historical relationship to slavery and the transatlantic slave trade. This unprecedented three-year investigation resulted in a 107-page report documenting the university's relationship to slavery and examining how other institutions and societies have dealt with legacies of gross injustice. The report concluded with seven recommendations, which ranged from "acknowledging publicly the participation of Brown's founders and benefactors in the institution of slavery" to "memorializing" this history through "a living site of memory, inviting fresh discovery without provoking paralysis or shame," to expanding opportunities both at Brown and in the local Providence community for those "disadvantaged by the legacies of slavery and the slave trade."[16] In discussing the university's official response to this report in February of 2007, President Simmons acknowledged that an apology was an "implicit recommendation" of the committee report, but said that she intentionally excluded an apology because it "seemed like a dollop of whipped cream on a very serious and extensive process." She went on to say that "In drafting the response, I found it hardest to get my head and heart around that notion. I found it strange to even contemplate how one would do that."[17]

A number of other university presidents have made similar remarks about the strangeness or inappropriateness of offering apologies for these historical wrongs, opting instead for official statements of "acknowledgement" and "regret." For example, in the spring of 2014, a number of black law students at Washington and Lee University demanded that the university offer an official apology for its participation in chattel slavery and a denunciation of Robert E. Lee's participation in slavery. In responding to this demand, university

[16] See "Slavery and Justice," 83–87.

[17] See Michael Skocpol, "Simmons Explains to BUCC Why U. Won't Apologize for Slavery," *The Brown Daily Herald*, March 14, 2007. Accessed online at http://www.browndailyherald.com/2007/03/14/simmons-explains-to-bucc-why-u-wont-apologize-for-slavery/

president Ken Ruscio acknowledged what he termed "a regrettable chapter of our history" and agreed that this is a chapter "we must confront and try to understand." But he deliberately avoided the language of apology. In an NPR interview with Melissa Block, he explained his reasoning in this way: "I'm in a position where I represent the university and I am stating what I believe to be something the university ought to acknowledge and ought to acknowledge with regret. It is a part of our history that we wish were different, but it wasn't."[18] When pressed, however, he agreed that this was not an apology per se.[19] Emory's President James Wagner went even further in explaining his own opposition to issuing an official university apology: "It would seem inappropriate," he said, "and some might say disingenuous to try to issue a kind of apology that would impose our values, today's values, on earlier colleagues and try to put words in the mouths of the deceased." At the same time, he said, the trustees and others at the university came to the conclusion that "we could look back and say that we really regret" these ties to slavery, and that it was therefore appropriate to "make a statement of institutional regret."[20]

I want to begin by considering some of the philosophical reasons so many university representatives may be reluctant to use the language of apology in referring to their institutions' historical ties to slavery.[21] If we take the case of interpersonal apology and forgiveness as our paradigm, it might

[18] See "Washington and Lee Confronts the Weight of Its History," NPR All Things Considered, July 10, 2014. Accessed online at http://www.npr.org/2014/07/10/330496157/washington-and-lee-confronts-the-weight-of-its-history

[19] Though I will go on to criticize President Ruscio's refusal to use the language of apology in what follows, I want to make clear that he took several other important and meaningful steps at the university as a response to these students' concerns. Thus some of the necessary "reparative work," which in my view should accompany a sincere apology, is already well under way.

[20] See Scott Jaschik, "Emory's 'Regret' for Slavery Ties," Inside Higher Ed, January 25, 2011. Accessed online at https://www.insidehighered.com/news/2011/01/25/emory_expresses_regret_for_its_ties_to_slavery. Emory's official statement of "regret" states that "Emory acknowledges its entwinement with the institution of slavery throughout the college's early history. Emory regrets both this undeniable wrong and the university's decades of delay in acknowledging slavery's harmful legacy. As Emory University looks forward, it seeks the wisdom always to discern what is right and the courage to abide by its mission of using knowledge to serve humanity."

[21] I will set aside one reason that may, as a matter of actual fact, be motivating at least some of this reluctance. Some university representatives might be worried that an official statement of apology would open the university up to legal demands for reparations. (Thanks to Frances Kamm for raising this possibility.) Though there is no legal precedent for this worry (and some important case law establishing that apologies do *not* automatically grant a legal entitlement to compensation), it is possible that the fear of this possibility has led some universities to avoid using the language of apology. This strikes me as a morally repugnant reason for refusing to apologize for historical wrongdoing, not to mention a philosophically uninteresting one; so I will not consider it in what follows. I am grateful to Nico Cornell for helpful discussion of this issue. For a helpful critical discussion of a recent Supreme Court case establishing that the US apology for overthrowing the native government of Hawaii does not create any substantive changes to the government's legal rights and obligations, see Nico Cornell, "Hawaii Apology Resolution," Harvard Law Review 123:153 (2009): 302–312.

seem that universities lack certain features that are necessary for intelligibly *issuing* moral apologies, and that they also cannot be appropriate *recipients* of moral forgiveness. In what follows, I will try to respond to these concerns. Universities, I will argue, should be understood as *temporally extended institutional moral agents* that are capable of entering into robust moral relationships with individual moral agents. As such, they both can and should issue moral apologies when they engage in serious moral wrongdoing, and they are also intelligible recipients of forgiveness on the part of those they have wronged.

Objection 1: Institutions Are Not "Moral Agents" That Are Capable of Acknowledging and Accepting Moral Responsibility for Past Wrongdoing

The first, and most obvious, reason why present-day university representatives may be reluctant to issue apologies for their institutions' historical involvement with chattel slavery is that this would seem to involve apologizing for wrongs committed by *other* people, in another time. When President Simmons said she "found it strange to even contemplate" how one would issue an apology of this sort, it may be that she found it conceptually incoherent to offer an apology for wrongs that neither she, nor any present-day university officials, actually committed. While we may *regret* the decisions made by past representatives of an institution, to *apologize* for them would seem to imply that we bear some *culpability* for them. But just as we do not expect children to apologize for the sins of their fathers, we should not expect current members of institutions to apologize for the sins of their prior members.

There are actually two distinct, and important, objections embodied in this line of thought, which are worth identifying and treating separately.[22] The first objection is that institutions, as such, cannot bear moral responsibility for wrongdoing. While individual *members* of institutions, such as presidents, CEOs, or board members, may bear moral responsibility for wrongdoing, it is a mistake to think that an *institution* can be morally responsible or commit a moral wrong. The second objection is that, even if it makes sense to think that an institution can bear moral responsibility for

---

[22] I am grateful to Brandon Warmke for urging me to distinguish these issues.

wrongdoing, it is a mistake to think that a present-day institution can bear moral responsibility for wrongs committed by that institution in the past.

In order to respond to the first objection, we need to spend some time looking carefully at the relations officials bear to the institutions of which they are a part and at whether it makes sense to talk of "institutional moral responsibility" as something distinct from individual moral responsibility. The first thing to note is that by an "institution" I am referring to a particular type of collective agent: one that persists over time and that retains its identity through continuous changes of membership.[23] Examples of "institutions" in the sense I have in mind include corporations, churches, clubs, sports teams, state and national governments, and universities. Corporations such as Brooks Brothers and sports teams like the Chicago Cubs have existed for well over one hundred years, and the Catholic Church has maintained a recognizable identity for centuries. Collective agents of this sort operate through their members, but they have procedures in place that allow for the formation and implementation of collective intentions, and they are characterized by shared beliefs, goals, and values. This is what allows us to distinguish "institutions" from mere mobs, or from other groups of individuals who may have something in common but who cannot be said to act on collective intentions (e.g., racial or ethnic groups, sports fans, red heads).[24]

Institutions, as I understand them, then, are functionally defined, temporally extended entities whose continued existence does not depend upon the continued mortal existence of their individual representatives. An institution like Washington and Lee University, for example, is not to be identified with its *existing* administration, Board of Trustees, and faculty. Rather, these individuals are simply the current occupiers of roles and positions that are themselves definitive of the institution as a persisting entity through time. These roles, and the procedures for making institutional decisions, are specified in the university's charter and related institutional documents. The occupiers of these roles, moreover, share an understanding of the institution's central

[23] In this I follow Phillip Pettit, "Responsibility Incorporated," *Ethics* 117:1 (2007): 171–201, 172. Cf. Kay Mathieson, "We're All in This Together: Responsibility of Collective Agents and Their Members," *Midwest Studies in Philosophy* 30 (2006): 240–255, 241.

[24] See Mathieson, "We're All in This Together," 246–248, Chandran Kukathas, "Responsibility for Past Injustice: How to Shift the Burden," *Politics, Philosophy, and Economics* 2:2 (2003): 165–190, 181, and Peter French, "The Corporation as a Moral Person," *American Philosophical Quarterly* 16:3 (1979): 207–215, 211–212. Of course, there will inevitably be some vagueness about which collections of individuals count as "institutional agents" in the relevant sense, but this question is beyond the scope of this chapter. I hope it will be granted that colleges and universities clearly count as "institutional agents" in the relevant sense.

mission, values, and goals, and their decision-making is guided by this understanding. As Kay Mathieson puts it, members of institutions reason from "the first person plural perspective"—they "reason, intend, and act from the perspective of the social group of which [they are] a member."[25] While there may well be disagreement among individual members of an institution about what action to take in a given situation, insofar as that decision emerges from a legitimate institutional decision-making process, it is appropriate to attribute that decision *to the institution itself*, and not merely to its individual members. (Indeed, in some cases, the institutional decision may not reflect the preference of *any* individual member, and yet still be the legitimate decision that emerges from this institutional decision-making process.[26])

If this is correct, then it is appropriate to attribute certain decisions and actions "to the institution itself," and not simply to its individual members. When those decisions lead to wrongful actions, it can be said that the *institution* is morally responsible for engaging in moral wrongdoing. While it is true that institutions are made up of individual members who must exercise their moral judgment in coming to institutional decisions, those decisions are made collectively in light of shared values and goals, and in conformity with institutional processes for the formation of collective intentions. This is not to say that the individuals involved are not *also* morally responsible for their own individual role in this decision-making process; it is simply to say that the collective decision that emerges does not belong to any single member, but to the institution itself. If that decision leads to wrongful action, we can say that the institution is morally responsible for that wrongdoing.

This brings us, however, to the second objection articulated earlier. Even if one accepts the claim that institutions can bear moral responsibility for wrongdoing, one might still be skeptical of the claim that a present-day institution can be morally responsible for the wrongdoing committed by that same institution in the distant past. After all, even if we cannot simply reduce institutional moral responsibility to individual moral responsibility, it is still the case that institutional responsibility *depends upon* the decision-making of its individual members. Given that none of the present-day members of an institution like Washington and Lee were alive at the time this university made the decision to participate in the system of chattel slavery, it may again

---

[25] Mathieson, "We're All in This Together," 246.
[26] For an in-depth discussion of how this may happen, see Pettit, "Responsibility Incorporated," 181–184.

seem odd to expect present-day members to apologize for the institution's past wrongdoing.

This is one of the most frequently heard objections to the idea of institutional apologies for historical wrongdoing, one that is often voiced in debates over whether state and national governments ought to apologize for historical injustices. For example, in explaining his own opposition to a U.S. Senate resolution of apology for failing to enact anti-lynching legislation during the first half of the twentieth century, Mississippi Senator Thad Cochran noted, "I'm not in the business of apologizing for what someone else did or didn't do. I deplore and regret that lynching occurred and that those committing them weren't punished. But I'm not culpable."[27] And former Australian Prime Minister John Howard has steadfastly defended his own refusal to offer an apology to Indigenous Australians for the Australian government's policy of forcibly removing and resettling Indigenous children between 1910 and 1970 by stating, "I have never been willing to embrace a formal national apology, because I do not believe the current generation can accept responsibility for the deeds of earlier generations. And there's always been a fundamental unwillingness to accept, in this debate, the difference between an expression of sorrow and an assumption of responsibility."[28]

The basic idea behind this objection seems to be that the moral responsibility of institutions, while perhaps distinct from the moral responsibility of its members, is always indexed to a specific collection of individuals—that is, to those individuals who were members of the institution at the time a particular decision was made. On such a view, the US Senate in 2017 is, in fact, *a different institution* from the US Senate in 2016 (not to mention from the US Senate in 1964, or 1864), and therefore bears no moral responsibility for any actions these previous Senates may have taken. Given that it consists of a different collection of Senators, it makes no sense to

[27] As quoted by William Raspberry in his Op-Ed, "A 'Sorry' Excuse from Cochran" in the *Washington Post* on June 20, 2005. Accessed online at http://www.washingtonpost.com/wp-dyn/content/article/2005/06/19/AR2005061900701.html. As Raspberry notes in his article, Cochran did, however, cosponsor bills apologizing for the government's treatment of Native Americans and for the World War II internment of Japanese Americans, acts for which Cochran also could not have been "personally culpable."

[28] As quoted in Coral Dow, "Sorry: The Unfinished Business of Bringing Them Home Report," Australian Parliamentary Library, Social Policy Section, April 4, 2008, accessed at http://www.aph.gov.au/About_Parliament/Parliamentary_Departments/Parliamentary_Library/pubs/BN/0708/BringingThemHomeReport#_ftn6. Howard reiterated this stance in a speech at Harvard University in 2008. See Anne Davies, "Nothing to Say Sorry for: Howard," *The Sydney Morning Herald*, March 12, 2008, accessed at http://www.smh.com.au/news/national/nothing-to-say-sorry-for-howard/2008/03/11/1205125911444.html

ask the 2017 Senate to apologize for actions taken by any of these previous Senates. This would, again, be like asking an individual today to apologize for the wrongs of her great-great-grandfather. While she might well *regret* those wrongs, it would be inappropriate, at best, to expect her to *apologize* for them.

In my view, such a position reflects a profound misunderstanding of the nature of institutions and of the relation between these institutions and their individual representatives. The reason we can talk meaningfully about both the triumphs and the failures over long stretches of time of "The US Senate" or "The Catholic Church" or "Harvard University" is precisely because we *do not* think institutions change every time their individual membership changes. Present-day members are simply the current occupiers of institutional roles that have existed for centuries or more, and they generally see themselves as links in an intergenerational chain that extends far into the past and (they hope) well into the future.[29] *All* universities, for example, celebrate their historical achievements and take great pride in them. This would make no sense, however, if the identity of that institution changed each time its membership changed.

More concretely, this view about the relation between the current occupiers of institutional roles and their previous occupants would wreak havoc upon many of our most basic intuitions about institutional responsibility. For it seems clear that when official representatives of an institution take action on behalf of that institution, they can incur obligations or debts for the institution that may fall to future representatives to fulfill. If the trustees of Washington and Lee sign a thirty-year loan, for example, that contract does not become null and void once the last signing trustee has passed away.[30] The obligations generated by previous representatives of the University continue to apply, unless and until current representatives go through proper procedures to nullify those obligations. In fact, it would be quite interesting to apply Senator Cochrane's reasoning about institutional apologies to the case of institutional obligations: "I'm not in the business of fulfilling contracts

---

[29] For a poignant statement of the way in which current university officials see themselves as belonging to an "intergenerational contract" with both the past and the future, see Ken Ruscio's 2016 Alumni Address "A Timeless Trust" at https://www.wlu.edu/presidents-office/about-president-ruscio/speeches/a-timeless-trust

[30] David Boonin uses a similar example in his own argument in defense of the claim that the United States may owe reparations for slavery. See David Boonin, *Should Race Matter?* (Cambridge: Cambridge University Press, 2011): Chapters 1–2. For similar arguments, see Michael Murphy, "Apology, Recognition, and Reconciliation," *Human Rights Review* 12 (2011): 47–69, 60, and Kukathas, "Responsibility for Past Injustice," 182.

someone else did or didn't make. I deplore and regret that previous Senators entered into these contractual commitments, but I am not responsible for fulfilling them." I take it no one would find this sort of reasoning remotely plausible in the case of institutional contractual commitments; I think we should find the parallel form of reasoning about institutional apologies for historical wrongdoing equally suspect.

For these reasons, I believe it is perfectly appropriate for current university officials to apologize for wrongs committed by past university representatives operating in their official capacity (that is, for the *university's* past wrongdoing). The university officials at what was then Washington College who made the decision to accept the enslaved people bequeathed to the school by a local landowner in 1826, to use their labor, and to lease and eventually sell most of these enslaved people for profit were acting in their official capacity as university representatives. Their decisions were guided by their understanding of the mission of the university and their assessment of what would be in the *university's* best interests, not by their own personal goals or reasons. While there may well have been disagreement among individual trustees about what should be done with these enslaved people, it can be assumed that each member was attempting to reason consistently with his understanding of the institution's mission, values, and goals. The outcome of this process of collective deliberation was a decision to participate in the system of chattel slavery. In that sense, these were wrongs committed *by the university itself*, for these actions issued from a legitimate decision-making procedure definitive of the institution understood as a collective agent. The institution that made this decision, moreover, is still in existence, and current university officials consciously conceive of themselves as carrying on with a mission and set of values that can be traced back to its founders in the mid-eighteenth century. For this reason, I think the analogy to the sins of our fathers (or to our great-great-grandfathers) is quite misleading. A multigenerational family is not a collective agent in the same sense, as it does not have functionally defined roles and procedures for decision-making over time, nor does it typically have a self-identified mission or set of values. That is what makes it odd to think that I may owe an apology for wrongs committed by my distant ancestors. But it is entirely appropriate to expect current representatives of Washington and Lee, *acting in their official capacity*, to apologize for, and not merely to regret, wrongs committed by prior university representatives *acting in their official capacity*. It is important to make clear that these are not personal apologies for personal wrongs, but institutional apologies for institutional wrongs.[31] The intelligibility of such apologies requires us to understand universities as temporally extended collective agents with a distinctive identity and set of values, agents that are capable of entering into contracts, and engaging in forms of moral wrongdoing, that may well generate institutional obligations for future representatives to fulfill.

Objection 2: Institutions Are Not *Blameworthy* for Their Ties to Slavery

This brings me, however, to a second reason why current university officials may be reluctant to apologize for wrongs committed by the university in the past. Even if one grants that the official actions of past representatives of Washington and Lee should be understood as actions done *by the university itself*, and therefore as actions for which *the university* is morally responsible; and even if one grants that those past actions were *wrong*, one might still think that these past representatives, and thus the university itself, had an *excuse* for their wrongdoing that undermines blameworthiness. For example, one might think these representatives were nonculpably morally ignorant of the wrongness of their actions in accepting, using, and selling enslaved people. If that were the case, then it might seem that the appropriate response to such past wrongdoing would not be *apology* but *regret*: regret that, due to their nonculpable moral ignorance, official representatives of Washington and Lee engaged in actions that they did not (and perhaps could not) realize at the time were morally wrong.

This moral idea, or something like it, seems to be lurking in the background of some of the statements made by university presidents explaining their decisions not to offer institutional apologies. President Ruscio, for example, refers repeatedly to "the complexity of history" and of the need to take this complexity into account when judging those who came before us.[32] And

---

[31] While Thad Cochran is correct that he is not *personally* culpable for the failure of past Senators to pass anti-lynching legislation, the Senate, understood as a collective agent, is *institutionally* culpable for this. As an elected official of this intergenerational institution, he has standing, together with his current colleagues, to offer an institutional apology for this past wrong. See Kukathas, "Responsibility for Past Injustice," 190fn.48 and Govier and Verwoerd, "The Promise and Pitfalls of Apology," 76.

[32] In his essay "Judging Patron Saints," *Inside Higher Ed*, January 26, 2012, he writes: "We know, or should know, that our own history is complicated. We would appreciate it if those judging us in the future would respect that. We owe the same courtesy to those who came before us." Accessed online at https://www.insidehighered.com/views/2012/01/26/essay-how-university-responded-criticism-one-its-heroes

Emory President James Wagner seems to be gesturing at a similar idea when he says it would be "inappropriate and some might say disingenuous to try to issue a kind of apology that would impose our values, today's values, on earlier colleagues and try to put words in the mouths of the deceased."

It is true that moral apologies of the sort we are considering are appropriate only when one is morally responsible *and* morally blameworthy for serious moral wrongdoing. Those who have a valid excuse for what they did are not blameworthy for their actions: they may still owe their victims expressions of regret for any harm their actions may have caused, but excuses typically block the claim that these actions embody a disrespectful moral claim about their victims' moral status. Since it is precisely this disrespectful moral claim that is the target of resentment and other forms of protest on the part of victims, there is no need for moral apology when such a disrespectful claim is absent.

One question, then, is whether the fact that slavery was a widely accepted practice at the time should lead us to regard those university officials who accepted, sold, and used enslaved people as having an excuse that renders their actions nonblameworthy. Does the sheer pervasiveness of this practice support the claim that their actions did not, in fact, embody a disrespectful moral claim about the moral status of these persons? One might argue that those who engaged in this practice did not see these enslaved people as fully human, and thus could not have regarded them as having a moral status that *could* be disrespected. Just as we would not say that a farmer buying, selling, or using a horse manifests a disrespectful moral claim about the moral status of his farm animal, so, too, one might think, we should not say that a university official buying, selling, or using an enslaved individual in the early nineteenth century manifested a disrespectful moral claim about the moral status of this individual. If, because of the cultural context, these officials were nonculpably morally ignorant of the fact that these enslaved individuals were *human beings*, and therefore deserving of basic forms of moral respect, then perhaps we cannot say that their treatment of these individuals expressed a disrespectful moral claim about their moral status.

There are three significant problems with this alleged excuse, however. First of all, there was never a moment during the history of slavery in the United States that there was any doubt that enslaved individuals were human beings. It is sheer nonsense to suggest that anyone could genuinely have viewed these people as mere animals, like horses, pigs, and donkeys. Indeed, the elaborate laws that were passed to explicitly deny the rights of enslaved people to own property, to read and to write, and to marry and form families, among other things, attest to the fact that slave-owners knew full well that they were dealing with human beings who had recognizable human interests in such things as personal security, education and personal advancement, and the formation of stable social ties.[33] If anyone *really* believed they were mere animals, such laws would have been just as absurd as laws forbidding the education, property ownership, or marriage of donkeys.

Second, enslaved people can and did actively *protest* their treatment, and slave-owners were well aware of this fact. This is why they also passed laws forbidding the assembly and congregation of slaves, for it was understood that such gatherings would make possible organized forms of protest that could pose a serious threat to slave-owners' continued supremacy. Once again, the felt need to pass laws explicitly *forbidding* activities that were allowed to other human beings actually *reinforces* the claim that slave-owners knew full well that they were treating a certain class of human beings as having a lesser moral status than others.

These first two points attempt to refute the claim that slave-owners might have been nonculpably morally ignorant of the fact that slaves were human beings, and therefore deserving of basic moral respect. But, in fact, it's not clear whether it even matters how slave-owners conceived of their own actions. For the real question is whether their *victims* had reason to respond to their treatment with attitudes and dispositions of moral protest.[34] This is the third and most important problem with the excuse analysis given earlier. Does the fact that slavery was a widely accepted practice in the seventeenth and eighteenth centuries *in any way* undermine the moral claim that enslaved people had at the time not to be treated in this way? For if we are to say that the university officials who accepted, sold, and used enslaved people were not *blameworthy* for such treatment, then it seems we must *also* say that their victims were not justified in responding to this treatment with attitudes

---

[33] For a shocking compendium of these laws, which makes perfectly clear that slaves *were* understood to be human beings that had to be affirmatively *stripped* of the usual rights of persons, see William Goodell (1792–1878), *The American Slave Code in Theory and Practice: Its Distinctive Features Shown by Its Statutes, Judicial Decisions, and Illustrative Facts* at http://quod.lib.umich.edu/cgi/t/text/text-idx?c=moa;idno=ABJ5059

[34] In his unpublished paper "Doing What You Think Is Right," Matthew Talbert argues that what matters for determining moral blameworthiness is not the moral perspective of the potential target of praise and blame, but rather *our* perspective as moral judges and whether we think the wrongdoer's action reflected an "objectionable quality of will." By reflecting on whether we think the victims of slavery had any reason to protest their treatment, I think it becomes clear that that treatment involved an "objectionable quality of will" on the part of slave-owners.

and dispositions of moral protest. We must say that these victims should have recognized that these officials had a valid excuse for treating them as pieces of property, and that they therefore should not have felt resentment or indignation about such treatment. But I see no reason to say this, and no reason to privilege the perspective of these university officials in determining whether their actions were, in fact, "protest-worthy." While it may be true that it is easier for us to *see* the moral blameworthiness of these actions from our present-day perspective, this does not change the fact that the official actions of the university embodied deeply disrespectful claims about the moral status of these victims. For this reason, I think it is mistake to excuse these actions as the "regrettable," but nonculpable, consequence of culturally induced moral ignorance.

Objection 3: Institutions Cannot Express Remorse

A third reason why university officials may be reluctant to apologize for historical wrongdoing is the sense that sincere apologies require feelings of remorse, and institutions are not capable of having or expressing such feelings. Only *individuals* can feel moral emotions such as guilt or remorse; institutions, understood as "temporally extended collective agents," are at best artificial persons who may be said to "act" but surely cannot be said to "feel."

In responding to this objection, we must return to the point that institutions are collective agents that *operate through* their members. Individual moral agents make up the "collective" that constitutes an institution, even if the membership of that collective changes continuously over time. Qua member of an institution, there is nothing unintelligible about feeling remorse for past actions done by the institution of which one is a part.

Even if there is nothing "unintelligible" about feeling remorse for the past actions of one's institution, however, one might still worry that such feelings are quite rare. If so, those official representatives who are asked to apologize on behalf of their institutions for historical wrongdoing might feel that they are being asked to engage in an insincere or inauthentic speech act: they are being asked to apologize for something for which they personally feel no real guilt or remorse.[35] For this reason, it might seem morally preferable

---

[35] I am grateful to Michael McKenna for pushing me to say more about this objection.

for institutions to issue statements of "regret" rather than "apology," which would not require their representatives to feign or imply the existence of feelings they do not actually possess.

There is surely something right about this objection, and it helps to explain why so many institutional apologies are viewed with profound cynicism and distrust. This skepticism is particularly common in the case of apologies issued by representatives of for-profit business corporations: we simply don't believe that there is any genuine remorse underlying many of these apologies; thus, we view such apologies as calculated and insincere. Part of the problem in these cases is that we typically do not view corporate representatives as *personally* identified with the mission and values of their institutions, and thus we doubt whether they really feel any personal remorse (qua member) for their institutions' wrongdoing. They are just "doing their job," as it were.

Things are different, I believe, when the apology is issued by a representative of a nonprofit organization with a distinctive moral mission, such as a university president or a church leader. We assume that the individuals occupying these positions are personally invested in the mission and values of their institutions, and thus have reason to feel personal remorse (qua member) when it is discovered that these institutions have engaged in serious wrongdoing (whether in the present or in the past). This assumption is reinforced when we consider that most of these representatives take personal pride (qua member) in both the past and present achievements of their institutions, and feel other sorts of "reactive attitudes" (qua member) when their institutions are either benefitted or harmed (e.g., gratitude when they receive a healthy bequest, and indignation when their institution is criticized in the media). It would be quite odd for institutional representatives to experience this full suite of reactive attitudes yet to deny the appropriateness of guilt and remorse in response to their institutions' past or present failures.

Having said that, it should also be acknowledged that the expression of emotion is probably less important in the case of institutional apologies than in the case of personal apologies. As Govier and Verwoerd point out, what matters most in the case of institutional apologies is the forthright acknowledgment of moral wrongdoing and the affirmation of the human dignity and legitimate feelings of those who were wronged.[36] A sincere and heartfelt affirmation of this sort is surely not too much to expect of university

---

[36] Govier and Verwoerd, "The Promise and Pitfalls of Apology," 74.

representatives apologizing for their institutions' participation in the wrong of chattel slavery.

Objection 4: Expressions of Institutional Regret Are More Powerful Than Expressions of Institutional Apology

A fourth reason why university officials might favor expressions of institutional regret over expressions of institutional apology is the sense that the former embodies a more powerful statement than the latter about the institution's commitment to avoiding wrongdoing in the future.[37] It's easy to say "I'm sorry," after all, and one can say such things without reflecting deeply about what might have led one to act wrongly in the first place, and about how one might avoid similar wrongdoing in the future.[38] An expression of sincere regret, by contrast, implies that one wishes one had acted differently in the past, which implies that one is committed to acting differently in the future. In that sense, an expression of institutional regret might be seen as a more powerful signal of a university's present and future commitment to moral behavior than an expression of institutional apology.

The first thing that needs to be acknowledged in responding to this objection is that both the language of apology and the language of regret can be used in stronger and weaker senses. What I earlier called "polite apologies" are, indeed, "easy" and do not seem to imply much of anything about the issuer's future commitments. But "moral apology," as I defined it earlier, is much more robust, as it implies an acknowledgment of responsibility and blameworthiness for wrongdoing, a recognition of why one's action was morally disrespectful, an expression of sincere remorse, the disavowal and repudiation of the disrespectful moral claim implicit in one's action, and a commitment to taking steps to repair the damage one's action has caused. A sincere moral apology, then, actually implies regret: after all, when one feels genuine remorse for a past action, this implies that one wishes one had acted differently. In that sense, a moral apology captures all of the positive features of regret identified in the earlier objection.

---

[37] I am grateful to Marc Conner for raising this objection.
[38] Perhaps this is the sentiment underlying Ruth Simmons's claim that an apology "seemed like a dollop of whipped cream on a very serious and extensive process."

The problem is that an expression of regret, standing on its own *outside the context of a moral apology*, does not capture all of the positive features of a moral apology. In fact, the language of "regret" is often used when one wants to *avoid* the implications of a moral apology.[39] It allows one to morally distance oneself from uncomfortable realties, by obscuring questions about moral agency, moral responsibility, and moral culpability. We can regret *that* certain things happened, and wish *that* they had been different, without implying anything about our own moral responsibility or culpability for the "regrettable" state of affairs. President Ruscio's acknowledgment that slavery was a "regrettable chapter of our history," a part of our past that "we wish were different, but wasn't" illustrates precisely the sort of distancing I have in mind. This is not a statement of regret *for* a wrongful institutional action, but a statement *that* a certain chapter of Washington and Lee's history is "regrettable." A state of affairs, such as a chapter in a university's history, can be "regrettable" even if there is no agent who can or should *regret* (active verb) its role in bringing about that state of affairs. Simply acknowledging, as a university representative, that a chapter in the university's history is "regrettable" is very different from regretting *on behalf of the university* that the institution engaged in wrongful action in the past. Similarly, we can wish that certain states of affairs had been different without implying that we bear any moral responsibility for the existence of that state of affairs.

Even in cases where we express regret *for* doing something wrong (rather than regret *that* something bad happened), the language of regret leaves ambiguous the *grounds* upon which one wishes one had acted differently. I may regret that I engaged in wrongdoing for reasons that have absolutely nothing to do with the claims of those wronged by my actions. For example, I may regret it because it gave me a bad reputation, or because I got into trouble for it, or because I fell short of my own ideals, not because I recognize that I have treated others in morally unjustifiable ways. An expression of regret, therefore, is morally ambiguous in a way that an expression of apology is not.

When universities use the language of regret *rather than* apology, then, they run the risk of sending unclear messages about their understanding

---

[39] As Robert Weyeneth notes, "Expressing *regret* about a past deed is seldom viewed as equivalent to an apology. Even though an apology can be defined as an expression of regret for a wrong, the apology has a crucial second component: the recognition that one has been in the wrong. The coupling of remorse with recognition of one's responsibility distinguishes the apology from simple regret, and it can make expressions of regret seem less heartfelt than outright apologies." See Weyeneth, "The Power of Apology and the Process of Historical Reconciliation," 17.

of their own moral agency, moral responsibility, and moral culpability for their participation in the wrong of chattel slavery. An expression of apology, by contrast, would make crystal clear three morally important facts: First, that the institution recognizes and acknowledges its past wrongful behavior, including the harms it has caused to its victims; second, that it regards itself as both morally responsible and morally blameworthy for this wrongdoing, and that it disavows the morally disrespectful claims about the victims' moral status reflected in its past behavior; and third, that it is committed to taking steps to try to repair the damage it has done not only to the direct victims of its wrongdoing, but to all those affected by the terrible legacy of slavery. By apologizing, rather than simply expressing "regret," the university would make clear to communities still affected by this terrible legacy that it is affirmatively committed to repairing the relationship to these communities that was breached by its earlier actions.

Objection 5: There Is No One to Whom to Address Institutional Apologies for Historical Wrongdoing

This brings me, however, to the final set of reasons why university officials might doubt the intelligibility of institutional apologies for historical wrongdoing. First, one might wonder *to whom* these apologies are appropriately addressed. Given that the victims of these injustices are long dead, it might seem that an apology at this point is idle or irrelevant. Second, and for similar reasons, one might wonder whether anyone today has standing to *accept* an institution's apology and to *forgive* it for its past wrongdoing. Given that one of the implicit aims of apology is to lay the groundwork for the possibility of forgiveness by, and reconciliation with, the victims of one's wrongdoing, the fact that these victims are no longer living seems to undermine the rationale for these expressions of institutional apology.

In responding to this objection, we might first note that institutions that were involved in serious instances of historical wrongdoing bear a special relationship not only to their immediate victims but also to anyone today who has been affected by the legacy of this wrongdoing.[40] In the case of

---

[40] As Michael Murphy notes, "Given that past injustice is intergenerational in its effects, apology should be viewed as intergenerational in its moral outreach." See Murphy, "Apology, Recognition, and Reconciliation," 54. This point is also emphasized in Scanlon, *Moral Dimensions*, 146–147.

universities with historical ties to slavery, this includes not only the direct descendants of those individuals the university wronged by its participation in chattel slavery but also anyone who still has reason to feel threatened by the disrespectful moral claim implicit in these historical injustices. Universities with historical ties to slavery are "on record" as saying that it is acceptable to treat a certain class of people—namely, people of African descent—as slaves who can be bought, sold, and used by the institution for its own purposes. While no university today would ever endorse such an outrageous claim, and most have taken affirmative steps to demonstrate their complete and utter repudiation of it, it remains true that these institutions once stood for this repugnant proposition. It is particularly damaging that institutions of higher learning, arguably representing the most advanced thinking of the day, should have been involved in these unjust practices. By their actions, they gave intellectual and moral justification for the view that white Europeans were racially superior to, and had a moral right to dominate and enslave, African people. As Craig Steven Wilder notes, "The academy never stood apart from American slavery—in fact, it stood beside church and state as the third pillar of a civilization built on bondage."[41]

Given the prestige and the influence these institutions of higher learning exerted at the time and continue to exert in society today, it should be clear how the disrespectful moral message implicit in their actions could have injurious effects that extend well beyond those directly affected by their wrongdoing. Insofar as this disrespectful message has never been explicitly disavowed through a sincere institutional apology, African Americans today have reason to continue to distrust these institutions and to feel aggrieved by these earlier injustices. While it is clear that these universities no longer endorse slavery or legalized segregation, their refusal to accept responsibility and blameworthiness for their past actions raises a question about these institutions' current commitment to racial equality and justice. This helps to explain why there have been persistent calls for institutional apologies on college and university campuses over the last few years. An institutional apology, addressed both to the original victims and to those today who continue to be affected by the legacy of slavery, would be far from idle or irrelevant. Indeed, such apologies could go a long way toward laying the groundwork for responses of forgiveness on the part of those wronged by these historical injustices.

[41] Wilder, Ebony and Ivy, 11.

The Nature of Institutional Forgiveness

Just as there are puzzles about the intelligibility of institutional apologies, however, there are puzzles about the intelligibility of forgiveness of institutions. What could it mean to forgive an institution for its past wrongdoing? Does that notion even make sense?

While it can seem odd in the abstract to talk of forgiveness of institutions, the notion becomes much less mysterious when we think again about what is involved in the case of interpersonal forgiveness. Recall that for Hieronymi, the essence of interpersonal forgiveness consists in relinquishing or overcoming one's attitude of *protest* toward a morally responsible wrongdoer who has committed a serious moral wrong, without excuse or justification, against oneself (i.e., against a morally considerable person who deserved not to be treated in that way). Strictly speaking, one's protest is directed toward *the disrespectful moral claim* implicit in the wrongdoer's treatment of one. In the absence of a sincere apology on the part of the wrongdoer, one has no reason to think that the wrongdoer disavows this disrespectful moral claim, and thus no reason to relinquish one's attitudes of protest toward that wrongdoer. But when a wrongdoer *does* sincerely apologize, and takes steps to demonstrate that she both recognizes and disavows the false moral claim implicit in her earlier conduct, there are rational grounds for relinquishing these attitudes. Since you and the wrongdoer are now united in your rejection of her earlier disrespectful treatment, protest-laden attitudes of resentment, anger, disappointment, and distrust may rationally give way to a stance of forgiveness on your part.

There is no reason, in principle, why we cannot understand institutional forgiveness in exactly the same way.[42] As we have seen, institutional agents, like individual agents, can be morally responsible and morally blameworthy for serious moral wrongdoing. Through their actions, they can communicate disrespectful moral claims about the moral status of those they wrong, and it is rational and appropriate for those who are subject to this disrespectful treatment to protest such claims through attitudes like resentment, anger, disappointment, and distrust. Victims of institutional wrongs, like victims

---

[42] Here I depart from Charles Griswold, who argues that what I am calling institutional forgiveness (and he calls "political forgiveness") is fundamentally different from interpersonal forgiveness, on the grounds that only the latter can be understood as a matter of overcoming resentment toward a wrongdoer. See *Forgiveness: A Philosophical Exploration* (Cambridge: Cambridge University Press, 2007), Chapter 4. As I argue later, I believe institutions can be the object of resentment, and of related attitudes embodying moral protest.

of interpersonal wrongs, might modify their dispositions, intentions, and expectations toward the institutional wrongdoer in a number of other ways as well. For example, they may withdraw their support from these institutions, may cease to identify with them or to celebrate their successes, and may become cynical and wary about these institutions' motives and intentions.[43] This is particularly true in the case of institutions that profess to be committed to ethical values, such as universities, religious institutions, and non-profit social organizations. When institutional agents of these sorts engage in moral wrongdoing, victims can feel particularly betrayed and morally let down by such treatment, and this can lead to a resentful revision in victims' attitudes of trust toward, and identification with, these institutional agents.[44] As in the interpersonal case, a sincere institutional moral apology, one that makes clear that the institution remorsefully acknowledges moral responsibility and moral culpability for its wrongdoing, and that it recognizes and disavows the false moral claim implicit in its wrongful behavior, can give these victims reason to relinquish their attitudes of moral protest. The institution now *stands with them* in condemning the disrespectful moral message implicit in its earlier actions and seeks to demonstrate that it is now worthy of renewed trust and goodwill. Of course, an apology alone will rarely be sufficient to warrant a change in attitude on the part of these victims. But when an apology is combined with other sincere efforts at atonement, including efforts of commemoration and memorialization, victims of institutional wrongdoing may see sufficient reason to relinquish their attitudes of moral protest and to adopt a stance of institutional forgiveness.[45]

In the case of universities with historical ties to chattel slavery, it seems clear that many (current and potential) students, faculty, and alumni of color at these institutions continue to regard these past injustices as making a disrespectful moral claim in the present that warrants explicit institutional disavowal. I suspect that many of the protests we have seen at universities around the country over the last few years reflect a growing sense that these

[43] Ta-Nehisi Coates captures well the many different forms such protest against unjust institutions can take—from outright rage, to cynical rejection, to aching disappointment—in his powerful memoir, *Between the World and Me* (New York: Random House, 2015).

[44] For a helpful exploration of the connection between institutional apologies and (often unsuccessful) efforts to restore warranted trust, see Alice MacLachlan, "Trust Me, I'm Sorry: The Paradox of Public Apology," *The Monist* 98 (2015): 441–456.

[45] For an insightful examination of the importance of commemoration and memorialization in response to instances of historical injustice, see Jeffrey M. Blustein, *Forgiveness and Remembrance: Remembering Wrongdoing in Personal and Public Life* (New York: Oxford University Press, 2014).

institutions of higher learning have not fully owned up to their moral complicity in these historical injustices, which in turn raises questions about their present commitment to values of racial equality and racial justice. While more and more universities are acknowledging these past injustices, and expressing "regret" for them, the refusal to accept full moral responsibility and culpability for these institutional wrongs gives the appearance of moral evasiveness. This appearance is only reinforced when these same universities happily take moral credit for institutional achievements in the distant past, embracing these earlier achievements as essential elements of their (timeless) institutional identity. It is not surprising, then, that people of color should continue to view these universities with attitudes of resentment, cynicism, skepticism, and distrust. A sincere moral apology on the part of these institutions would be an important first step in laying the groundwork for a warranted revision in these attitudes and, over time, to the adoption of other attitudes—such as (renewed) trust, identification, and good will—that can reasonably be taken to be a manifestation of institutional forgiveness.[46]

[46] An earlier version of this chapter was presented at a conference celebrating the philosophy and teaching of T. M. Scanlon at Harvard University in April 2016. I am grateful to all of the conference participants for their helpful comments and suggestions. I also received very helpful feedback from the audience members at the University of Richmond, where I presented this chapter in October 2016. Thanks also to Sandra Reiter for many productive conversations about the topic of this chapter, and to both Michael McKenna and Brandon Warmke for extremely helpful written feedback. Work on this chapter was generously supported by a 2015 Summer Lenfest grant from Washington and Lee University.

8

The Sunflower

Guilt, Forgiveness, and Reconciliation

Eleonore Stump

Introduction

There is by now a large literature on the nature of guilt and forgiveness. On what might be considered a standard account, it is often thought that the remedy for guilt is forgiveness and that repentance and the making of amends on the part of a wrongdoer are both necessary and sufficient for morally appropriate forgiveness.[1] The making of amends is generally considered to have two parts, namely, reasonable reparation of any damage done by the wrongdoer, and then also something extra, some penance, that compensates for the injustice in the wrongdoing. On this view, forgiveness is the forswearing of resentment. But the wronged person should not forswear resentment and forgive the wrongdoer without the wrongdoer's repentance and making amends. If, however, the wrongdoer has repented and made amends, then the wronged person ought to forswear resentment and forgive the wrongdoer. And if the wronged person does forgive the wrongdoer, then the wrongdoer is relieved of his guilt. Finally, since his guilt is removed, nothing stands in the way of the wronged person's reconciliation with the wrongdoer and the wrongdoer's restoration to his ordinary place in human community.

---

[1] A fairly standard and representative account can be found in Charles Griswold, *Forgiveness. A Philosophical Exploration* (Cambridge: Cambridge University Press, 2007). Excellent thoughtful discussions are given in Martha Nussbaum, *Anger and Forgiveness. Resentment, Generosity, Justice* (Oxford: Oxford University Press, 2016), Linda Radzik, *Making Amends. Atonement in Morality, Law, and Politics* (Oxford: Oxford University Press, 2009), and Margaret Urban Walker, *Moral Repair. Reconstructing Moral Relations after Wrongdoing* (Cambridge: Cambridge University Press, 2006). A classic account of differing positions in dialogue is given in Jean Hampton and Jeffrie Murphy, *Forgiveness and Mercy* (Cambridge: Cambridge University Press, 1988)

Eleonore Stump, The Sunflower In: *Forgiveness and Its Moral Dimensions*. Edited by: Brandon Warmke, Dana Kay Nelkin, and Michael McKenna, Oxford University Press. © Oxford University Press 2021.
DOI: 10.1093/oso/9780190602147.003.0008

So, for example, Richard Swinburne supposes that there is an ordinary process that is required for the removal of guilt consequent on wrongdoing. Swinburne takes this process to consist at least in repentance, and usually also in reparation and penance.[2] As Swinburne uses the term, penance is something which a wrongdoer gives to a person he has wronged and which is in addition to the reparation by which the wrongdoer tries to undo the damage he has done.[3] And so, Swinburne says,

> An agent's guilt is removed when his repentance, reparation, apology, and penance find their response in the victim's forgiveness.[4]

On Swinburne's sort of view, a wronged person should require repentance and making amends on the part of the wrongdoer before granting the wrongdoer his forgiveness. But these things on the part of the wrongdoer are sufficient for the moral appropriateness of forgiveness, and forgiveness removes the guilt of the wrongdoer. For this reason, forgiveness reconciles the wrongdoer with those alienated from him by his wrongdoing and also restores him to the status in community that he had before his wrongdoing. On this way of thinking about the matter, at least for serious wrongdoing, the wrongdoer's repentance, reparation, and penance are necessary and sufficient both for the moral appropriateness of forgiveness of the wrongdoer and for reconciliation with him.

As has been pointed out by others, however, there are many problems with this standard account. To begin with, a wronged person Jerome may feel reactive emotions other than resentment. He may instead feel contempt or alienation or fear with regard to a person Paula who has wronged him.[5] And the claim that the ability of a wronged person Jerome to forgive a wrongdoer Paula depends on Paula's first making amends has counterintuitive consequences. It implies, for example, the unpalatable view that the father

---

[2] Richard Swinburne, *Responsibility and Atonement* (Oxford: Oxford University Press, 1989), p. 81.
[3] Forgiveness of the sort that removes guilt is not possible without such atonement, according to Swinburne, although in some limited circumstances it is possible for the victim of wrongdoing to forgive the wrongdoer without requiring reparation and penance in addition to repentance and apology (Swinburne 1989, p. 85).
[4] Swinburne 1989, p. 85. Swinburne adds that it is "within the victim's power . . . to determine, within limits, just how much atonement is necessary before he is prepared to give the forgiveness which will eliminate guilt" (p. 86). But when sufficient atonement has been made, then, on Swinburne's view, the victim should forswear resentment against the wrongdoer and be willing to be reconciled with him.
[5] See Radzik 2009 for nuanced discussion of the reactive attitudes of victims of wrongdoing.

in the parable of the prodigal son should have waited till his son had made amends before he forgave his son. It also implies that no one can forgive the dead. And it implies that a wronged person Jerome is hostage to the good will of the person Paula who wronged him before he can reach the relative psychic peace of forgiveness.[6] Finally, insofar as forgiveness seems a response to something in the past and reconciliation is an attitude toward a relationship in the future, it seems clear that forgiveness and reconciliation can come apart. Jerome might forgive Paula but be too traumatized by her wrong against him to reconcile with her, for example.[7]

In this connection, consider Simon Wiesenthal's book *The Sunflower: On the Possibility and Limits of Forgiveness*.[8] In that book, Wiesenthal tells the story of a dying German soldier who was guilty of horrendous evil against Jewish men, women, and children, but who desperately wanted forgiveness from and reconciliation with at least one Jew before his death. Wiesenthal, then a prisoner in Auschwitz, was brought to hear the German soldier's story and his pleas for forgiveness. In the story as Wiesenthal presents it, it seems that the German soldier was completely and genuinely repentant. Because he was dying, there was little he could do to make amends; but his broken-heartedness over his evil and his self-excoriating confession of it to Wiesenthal was as much reparation and penance as was possible for him. In the circumstances, in remarkably admirable ways, while the dying soldier was making his confession, Wiesenthal dealt humanely with him. But when the soldier's confession was finally complete, Wiesenthal got up and left him without a word. As Wiesenthal understands his own reaction to the soldier, he did not grant the dying man the forgiveness he longed for.

In *The Sunflower*, Wiesenthal presents reflections on this story by numerous thinkers, many of them noted scholars or eminent religious authorities in differing traditions. He invites these thinkers to consider what they would have done if they had been in Wiesenthal's shoes; he asks them whether they would have forgiven that soldier. Their responses are noteworthy for the highly divergent intuitions they express.

A number of respondents claim with conviction that the repentant dying soldier should be forgiven. So, for example, the influential former president of Notre Dame, Theodore Hesburgh, C.S.C, says,

---

[6] See Nussbaum 2016 for discussion of this problem with the standard account of forgiveness.

[7] See Radzik 2009 for a good account of this dissociation between forgiveness and reconciliation.

[8] Simon Wiesenthal, *The Sunflower: On the Possibility and Limits of Forgiveness* (New York: Schocken Books, 1960).

My whole instinct is to forgive. . . . Of course, the sin here is monumental. It is still finite and God's mercy is infinite. If asked to forgive, by anyone for anything, I would forgive because God would forgive.[9]

The Nobel Prize–winning Anglican bishop Desmond Tutu says,

I have been overwhelmed by the depth of depravity and evil that has been exposed by the amnesty process of the Truth and Reconciliation Commission appointed to deal with the gross human rights violations that happened in our apartheid past. . . . There is also another side—the story of the victims, the survivors who were made to suffer so grievously, yet despite this are ready to forgive. This magnanimity, this nobility of spirit is quite breathtakingly unbelievable. I have often felt I should say, "Let us take off our shoes," because at this moment we were standing on holy ground. So, what would I have done [if I had been in Wiesenthal's place]? . . . Many claim to follow the Jewish rabbi who, when he was crucified, said, "Father, forgive them for they know not what they do . . ." It is clear that if we look only to retributive justice, then we could just as well close up shop. . . . Without forgiveness, there is no future.[10]

But other equally thoughtful respondents report that they share the reaction Wiesenthal had at the time of the soldier's confession. In their view, the soldier's evil was great enough to destroy forever his chance for morally appropriate forgiveness. As they see it, by his monstrous acts, the soldier cut himself off permanently from any reconciliation with others or restoration into ordinary human society. And this evaluation of the soldier would not be altered, in their view, even if he had lived to do some severe penance, even if it were possible for there to be reparation and penance for the unspeakable harm that he had done. For these respondents, the soldier should not be forgiven. On their view, there is no way the soldier's guilt can be removed; there is no morally appropriate reconciliation possible with the soldier, and there is no way the soldier can be restored to any acceptable place within the human community.

So, for example, the highly revered Jewish rabbi Abraham Joshua Heschel says,

---

[9] Wiesenthal 1960, p. 169.
[10] Wiesenthal 1960, pp. 266–268.

No one can forgive crimes committed against other people. It is therefore preposterous to assume that anybody alive can extend forgiveness for the suffering of any one of the six million people who perished.[11]

His daughter, Susannah Heschel, a noted scholar in her own right, shares this view and adds,

I would have done exactly as Simon Wiesenthal did. . . . My father, Rabbi Abraham Joshua Heschel, wrote that "the blood of the innocent cries forever." Should that blood cease to cry, humanity would cease to be. . . . Rather than asking for forgiveness, the descendants of the Nazis should continue to hear the cries of Jewish blood, and thereby preserve their own humanity.[12]

Harry Wu, who has received many honors for his work exposing the horrors of slave labor camps in China, where he himself was imprisoned for many years, shares these intuitions about the unacceptability of forgiveness for great moral evil. He says,

Reading Simon Wiesenthal's autobiographical story brought back a flood of memories about my own experience in China's prison labor camps. . . . During my nineteen years in prison, I often experienced harsh treatment at the hands of guards and prison officials. I was beaten and degraded, and to this day I suffer injuries from the abuses I suffered. . . .[T]he society that the Communists founded was designed to drain any remnants of humanity out of a person. Like Mr. Wiesenthal, I would not have forgiven the Nazi soldier on his deathbed.[13]

On the view of people such as these, it is not the case that repentance, reparation, and penance are sufficient for morally appropriate forgiveness or that these things together with forgiveness are sufficient to remove guilt. Reconciliation may be denied and guilt may remain even where there is repentance with whatever reparation and penance is possible.

In this chapter, I want to consider the standard account of guilt and forgiveness represented by Swinburne's position and the conflicting views about forgiveness on the part of the respondents in *The Sunflower*.

[11] Wiesenthal 1960, p. 271.
[12] Wiesenthal 1960, pp. 172–173.
[13] Wiesenthal 1960, pp. 271–274.

In what follows, I will briefly summarize the account of love and forgiveness I have given elsewhere.[14] On that account, love is always morally obligatory,[15] and so is forgiveness. Consequently, the view that repentance and making amends are necessary for forgiveness should be rejected. For these reasons, it seems to me that those respondents in *The Sunflower* convinced that forgiveness should be denied the dying German soldier are mistaken. In this regard, I side with Desmond Tutu and the others who strongly support the view that forgiveness should be extended to anyone, no matter what evil he has done.

Nonetheless, I will also argue in support of the vehement negative reactions of respondents such as Heschel. In my view, the attitude of those who reject any kind of reconciliation with the dying German soldier is based on intuitions that must also be taken seriously. I will try to show that these respondents are right to suppose that, in some cases of grave evil, repentance and making amends are not sufficient for the removal of guilt, and that reconciliation may be morally impermissible, whatever the case as regards forgiveness.

Consequently, on the account I will defend in this chapter, contra Swinburne and others, repentance, reparation, and penance are not necessary for morally appropriate forgiveness. And, also contra Swinburne and others, for very serious wrongdoing, repentance, reparation, and penance are not sufficient for the removal of guilt. And if they are not sufficient for the removal of guilt, then they are not sufficient for morally appropriate reconciliation either, not even for reconciliation with a person who is forgiven. On the view I will argue for, unlike forgiveness, reconciliation and the removal of guilt cannot be unilateral and unconditional. For the removal of guilt and reconciliation with a wrongdoer, something is required from the wrongdoer; and if the wrongdoer cannot give what is needed to remove his guilt, then reconciliation may be morally unavailable. At least in cases of very serious wrongdoing, forgiveness and reconciliation can therefore come apart. So, contrary to a view such as Swinburne's, guilt may remain even after forgiveness.

---

[14] *Wandering in Darkness: Narrative and the Problem of Suffering* (Oxford: Oxford University Press, 2010).

[15] This claim also implies that love is under voluntary control. In the account of love I give later, love is constituted by two mutually governing desires. Consequently, it is an implication of this claim about love that some desires are also under voluntary control. Not all desires are, of course. Aquinas distinguishes between desires that stem from the sensory appetite, closely tied to the senses, and desires that stem from the rational appetite, closely tied to reason. The latter desires are under voluntary control in one way or another. The desires of love are of the latter sort. For more discussion of this point about desire and voluntary control, see my *Aquinas* (New York: Routledge, 2003), Chapter 9. I am grateful to Michael McKenna for calling my attention to the need to make this point explicit.

The account I will argue for later, then, helps to explain the divergent reactions of the respondents in *The Sunflower*. Those who feel strongly that the soldier should be forgiven are right. And yet those opposed to forgiving the soldier are also right, at least insofar as they are conflating forgiveness and reconciliation. What these respondents are in effect rejecting is the idea that the soldier's repentance and penitential confession are sufficient to remove his guilt. That is why they refuse any reconciliation with him. But their view is compatible with the convictions of those in favor of forgiving the soldier, because for very serious evil, even with forgiveness granted, repentance, reparation, and penance can fail to be sufficient for the removal of guilt.

The Case of John Newton

It helps in thinking about these issues to have in mind a historical case of serious moral wrongdoing in which there is not only grave evil but also exemplary repentance, reparation, and penance. So consider the case of John Newton. On three different occasions, when Newton was still a young man, he was the captain of a slave ship; and, on those three ships alone, he was responsible for transporting many Africans. The conditions on the ships were unspeakable. A large percentage of the Africans transported died during the voyage. Their suffering was heartbreaking, but the suffering of those who survived was worse. They were sold into harsh slavery, and their descendants were born into it.

A lengthy religious conversion changed Newton's life dramatically. First, he left the life of a seaman; then he got a theological education; and eventually he was ordained as an Anglican priest. Gradually, he took on an increasingly influential role in the cultural and religious life of England. Somewhere in the course of this conversion, Newton became horrified at what he had done in the slave trade; he became stricken at the suffering he had helped to bring about.

In his fervent repentance, Newton worked hard, in formal and informal ways, to help bring about the abolition of the slave trade in England. Among other things, he wrote a pamphlet *Thoughts upon the Slave Trade* in which he presented in great detail to public view the horrible suffering he had visited on the Africans on his ships, and he spared himself no humiliation in revealing what he had done. On the contrary, he held himself up to public shock and revulsion for his actions as a slave trader. Newton's pamphlet was widely read, and it made a great difference to the debate in Parliament over the slave trade.

Newton lived long enough to see his efforts victorious. The Slave Trade Act, which abolished the slave trade in England, was passed in 1807; and Newton died shortly after it passed. Newton's efforts at ending the slave trade were his reparation and penance. In his efforts for abolition, and in his public excoriation of himself in his pamphlet, Newton did what he could to make reparation and do penance for the evil of his slave trading.

What should one say about Newton? Is it so much as morally acceptable to forgive him? Were his repentance, reparation, and penance sufficient for the removal of his guilt? Were they sufficient for his reconciliation with the Africans transported on his ships? Were they sufficient to restore him to a place in the human community from which his morally evil actions would otherwise have excluded him?

In what follows, I will argue that forgiveness is not only morally permissible in such a case; rather, like love, it is morally obligatory. However, by themselves alone, even repentance, reparation, and penance may not be sufficient for the removal of guilt, for reconciliation with those harmed by grave wrongdoing, and for restoration to human community.

Love and Forgiveness

To think about forgiveness, it helps to begin with a brief discussion of the nature of love. Although many contemporary philosophers have presented varying accounts of the nature of love, the best account I know is that of Thomas Aquinas.[16] For Aquinas,[17] love requires two interconnected desires:[18]

---

[16] I have argued for this comparative claim in "Love, by All Accounts," *Proceedings and Addresses of The American Philosophical Association* 80, no. 2 (November 2006): 25–43.

[17] Aquinas uses four words for love; in Latin, they are *"amor," "dilectio," "amicitia,"* and *"caritas."* (Cf. ST I-II q.26 a.3.) The first of these is love in its most generic sense, which is included in all the other kinds; for Aquinas, even a rock falling from a higher to a lower place can be said to have love for the place to which it falls, in this generic sense of "love." (Cf. ST I-II q.26 a.1.) The second, *"dilectio,"* emphasizes the element of voluntariness in the love of rational persons; and the third, *"amicitia,"* picks out the dispositions of love in friendship. But, for Aquinas, the fourth, *"caritas,"* is the word for love in its real or complete sense. Since Aquinas privileges *caritas* in this way, I will focus on *caritas* in explaining his account of love, although I understand his views of *caritas* in light of what he says about the more generic *amor*.

[18]. See, e.g., ST II-II q.25, a.3.

(1) the desire for the good of the beloved,[19]

and

(2) the desire for union[20] with the beloved.[21]

Aquinas recognizes different kinds and degrees of love between persons.[22] For example, he thinks that it is possible to desire the good for humanity in general and also to desire some sort of union with all humanity—say, in the shared beatific vision of heaven;[23] and so, on Aquinas's account of love, a person can have an impartial love of all human beings. But Aquinas also supposes that some loves are and ought to be greater than others;[24] a person ought to love all human beings, but not equally. She should love some people more than others in virtue of having certain relationships with them which ought to make her love for them greater than her love for humanity in general.

Certain things are also worth noting with regard to the desires of love.

[19] Cf. ST I-II q.26 a.4, where Aquinas says that to love is to will good to someone. Cf. also ST I-II q.28 a.4, where Aquinas explains the zeal or intensity of love in terms of the strength of a lover's desire for the good of the beloved.

[20] By "union" in this connection, I mean being at one with another, where, clearly, the kind of one-ness brought about by two or more human beings is a function of what elements of life and psyche they are sharing. A mother shares some parts of herself and her life with her newborn; musically gifted friends composing an opera together share other parts of themselves with each other. Union comes in degrees at least in part because a human being, and a human life, is a composite; and it is possible to share some parts of this composite without sharing others. That is why it is possible to desire union with humanity as a whole: one can desire that all human beings be at one with each other, so that war, injustice, and all oppressive inequality cease.

[21] Cf., e.g., ST I-II q.26 a.2 ad 2, and q.28 a.1 s.c., where Aquinas quotes approvingly Dionysius's line that love is the unitive force. Cf. also ST I-II q.66 a.6, where Aquinas explains the superiority of charity to the other virtues by saying that every lover is drawn by desire to union with the beloved, and ST I-II q.70 a.3, where Aquinas explains the connection between joy and love by saying that every lover rejoices at being united with the beloved. For an interesting recent attempt to defend a position that has some resemblance to Aquinas's, see Robert Adams, "Pure Love," *Journal of Religious Ethics* 8 (1980): 83–99. Adams says: "It is a striking fact that while benevolence (the desire for another person's well-being) and *Eros*, as a desire for relationship with another person, seem to be quite distinct desires, we use a single name, "love" or "*Agape*," for an attitude that includes both of them, at least in typical cases" (p. 97).

[22] There are many other details of Aquinas's account of love that are important but that cannot be explored in passing here. For a fuller treatment, see my *Wandering in Darkness: Narrative and the Problem of Suffering* (Oxford: Oxford University Press, 2010), Chapter 5.

[23] If there is a relationship between persons in which it is not appropriate for one person to desire the good for and union with the other, then the relationship is not a relationship of love. Insofar as it is possible to have a general love of humankind, however, then there is no connection between persons which is not also in effect a relationship for which some species of love is appropriate and therefore also obligatory. For some discussion of the claim that obligations and rights are not correlative, see my "God's Obligations," in *Philosophical Perspectives* 6, James Tomberlin (ed.) (Atascadero, CA: Ridgeview, 1992), pp. 475–492.

[24] ST II-II q.26 a.6–12.

To begin with the second desire of love, whatever exactly the union is which is desired in love on Aquinas's account, the desire for it is not equivalent to the desire to be in the company of the beloved.[25] Other philosophers have remarked that one can love a person without desiring to be in that person's company,[26] and being in someone's company is obviously not equivalent to being united to her. It is manifestly possible to be in the company of someone when one is alienated from her, rather than united to her. So desiring union with a person might not include a desire to be in that person's company, at least not now, as that person currently is.

With regard to the first desire of love, the goodness in question is not to be identified with moral goodness only. It is goodness in the broader sense that encompasses beauty, elegance or efficiency, and metaphysical as well as moral goodness.[27] Furthermore, because Aquinas holds that there is an objective standard of goodness, the measure of value for the goodness at issue in love is also objective.[28] On this account of love, then, the good of the beloved has to be understood as that which truly is in the interest of the beloved and which truly does conduce to the beloved's flourishing.

This account of love has significant implications as regards the nature of forgiveness.[29] That is because, whatever exactly is required for forgiveness,[30] it must involve some species of love for the person in need of forgiveness. A person who refuses to forgive someone who has hurt her or been unjust to her is not loving toward the offender, and a person who does forgive someone who has treated her badly also manifests love of one degree or another toward him. It is not part of my purpose in this chapter to try to define forgiveness.[31]

[25] For Aquinas's views on the nature of this union, cf., e.g., ST I-II q.28 a.1, where real union is described as a matter of presence between lover and beloved.

[26] David Velleman, "Love as a Moral Emotion," *Ethics* 109 (1999), p. 353.

[27] The two desires of any love are therefore included under the more general heading of the desire for goodness, as Aquinas understands it. For detailed discussion of Aquinas's views of goodness, understood in this broad sense, see my *Aquinas* (New York: Routledge, 2003), Chapter 2.

[28] The claim that the good desired for the beloved is an objective good therefore results from Aquinas's analysis of the nature of love together with his metaethics. It is not itself implied by Aquinas's analysis of love. I am grateful to Ish Haji for calling my attention to the need to make this point clear.

[29] For more detailed discussion of forgiveness in connection with Aquinas's account of love, see Stump (2010), Chapter 5.

[30] A good recent review of the literature can be found in Griswold 2014. The differences between the account I give and Griswold's are sketched here. My account of forgiveness is not incompatible with the standard account of forgiveness as the forswearing of resentment, but it encompasses also forgiveness as including the desire for union with a wrongdoer.

[31] In fact, although on my view love is necessary and sufficient for morally appropriate forgiveness, it is not the case that forgiveness is nothing but love or that forgiveness reduces to love. Analogously, being risible is necessary and sufficient for being human—anything that is risible is human and nothing that is not risible is human—but being human is not reducible to being risible. Risibility

But whatever else a person's forgiveness may be, it must include a kind of love of someone who has harmed her or committed an injustice against her.

Since love emerges from the interaction of two desires, for the good of the beloved and for union with him, the absence of either desire is sufficient to undermine love. To the extent to which love is implicated in forgiveness, the absence of either desire undermines forgiveness, too. A person who lacks either desire with respect to someone who has wronged him is not forgiving of the wrongdoer.

So, contrary to the standard account focused on the forswearing of resentment, failure to forgive can find expression not only in resentment but also in a rejection of the desire for union with the wrongdoer. On the account of love I am adopting here, a person Paula forgives a person Jerome who has treated her badly only if she desires the good for Jerome and union with Jerome even in the face of his bad treatment of her. If Paula lacks either desire of love where Jerome is concerned, she does not forgive Jerome.

It is important to see that, on this account of love, it is possible for Paula to forgive Jerome unilaterally, without repentance on Jerome's part, because it is up to Paula alone whether she desires the good for Jerome and union with him. [32]

However, *the way* in which the desires of love are fulfilled, or whether they are fulfilled at all, will depend crucially on the condition of the wrongdoer being forgiven. When in forgiveness Paula forms the two *desires* of love for Jerome, the nature of the appropriate *fulfillment* of those desires has to be a function of Jerome's state. Whether Paula can and should have any continued companionship of any kind with Jerome, and the character and extent of such company, depends on Jerome's state. If Jerome poses a serious threat to Paula's having what is good for her, then Paula's staying with Jerome or

---

picks out human beings by an accident which is had by all and only human beings, but the nature of human beings is not nothing but risibility. Because it is not part of my purposes here to define forgiveness, I leave to one side what else might need to be added to love for a definition of forgiveness. I am grateful to Michael Rea for calling my attention to the need to make this point explicit.

[32] Someone might suppose that these things are not up to Paula simply because a desire for these things is not in Paula's voluntary control. But, in this connection, consider the desire to be vegetarian. Clearly, there are two ways to think about this desire. First, there is a desire for vegetarian food that consists in a kind of bodily inclining toward food that is not meat. This is the kind of desire found in a person who really hates eating meat and likes eating vegetables. But this is not the only kind of desire for vegetarian food that there is. There is also the kind of desire for vegetarian food found in a person who loves eating meat and does not care much for vegetables but who is determined to be vegetarian out of ethical considerations. The first kind of desire is not under direct voluntary control, but the second kind clearly is. I am grateful to Michael McKenna for helping me appreciate that this point should be made explicit.

otherwise allowing Jerome to harm her enables Jerome to violate the desires of love for her. But his failure at loving her is not good for Jerome. So Paula is not loving Jerome in letting him harm her or treat her unjustly; rather, she is violating the desires of love with regard to Jerome in being an enabler of his wrongdoing against her.[33]

On this account of love and forgiveness, then, it is possible for Paula to count as forgiving Jerome even if she seeks punishment for him, if punishment is for his good and she desires it as his good. As far as that goes, Paula can also count as forgiving Jerome if she continues to blame him, provided that her blaming is an outgrowth of her real and sincere desire for his good and for union with him. This account of love and forgiveness has these implications because, on this account, a person can forgive unilaterally, as she can love unrequitedly. But the desires of love in forgiveness, like the desires of love generally, are inefficacious by themselves to bring about what they desire. A person who forgives, like a person who loves, has to be responsive to the person who is the object of her desires; and so she cannot have what she wants, in love or forgiveness, just by wanting it. Paula's *desire* for the good for Jerome cannot be fulfilled if, in self-destructive impulses, Jerome refuses the good offered him. And Paula's *desire* for union with Jerome cannot result in any kind of union with him as long as his state of character and current condition keep her from being close to him.

Finally, love is obligatory,[34] in the sense that, for any person, the absence of love is morally blameworthy, and the presence of love is necessary for moral

---

[33] It might appear that Aquinas's account of love succumbs to the same problems as those that seem to some people to afflict an ethics of care. If the value of loving others or caring for others is the fundamental ethical value, then it is not easy to explain why it is morally acceptable to withhold care for others in the interests of pursuing one's own projects. And yet if there is no morally acceptable way of doing so, caring, or loving, can become deeply destructive, dreadfully unjust, with regard to the one doing the caring or loving. So, for example, Virginia Woolf describes the "angel in the house" who loved others totally, who cared for them completely, in this way:

> she never had a mind or a wish of her own, but preferred to sympathize always with the minds and wishes of others. . . I did my best to kill her. My excuse, if I were to be had up in a court of law, would be that I acted in self-defence. Had I not killed her she would have killed me. (From "Professions for Women," quoted in Jean Hampton, "Feminist Contractarianism," in *A Mind of One's Own. Feminist Essays on Reason and Objectivity*, ed. Louis Anthony and Charlotte Witt [Boulder, CO: Westview Press, 1993], 231.)

In my view, considerations similar to those showing that Paula is not loving Jerome in enabling him to harm her apply also to the case in which Paula allows herself to be harmed by myriad others. She is not loving others in allowing them to hurt her, even if the harm done to her takes the actions of a whole group to accomplish.

[34] To say that it is obligatory is not to say that anyone has a right to be loved. On this view, rights and obligations are not correlative.

good or excellence.[35] Given the connection between love and forgiveness, it
follows that forgiveness is also obligatory in the same way and to the same
extent.[36] It does *not* follow that any given person Jerome has a right to forgiveness from any person Paula whom he has wronged. On this account of
love and forgiveness (as also on many contemporary accounts), rights and
obligations are not correlative.[37] Paula can have an obligation with regard to
Jerome even if Jerome does not have a correlative right with regard to Paula.
So even though Jerome has no right to Paula's forgiveness, Paula would be
subject to appropriate moral censure if she refused to forgive Jerome. In
refusing to forgive him, Paula would be unloving toward him; and in being
unloving, Paula would be worthy of moral disapprobation.

Consequently, on this account of love and forgiveness, Swinburne and
others are mistaken in supposing that repentance and making amends are
necessary for morally appropriate forgiveness. Nothing on the part of the
wrongdoer is necessary for forgiveness of him.

For these reasons, forgiveness even of the German soldier in the story in
The Sunflower is obligatory, and it would still be obligatory even if the soldier had not repented. It does not follow, however, that Wiesenthal's behavior
with respect to the soldier should have been otherwise.

To begin with, contrary to Wiesenthal's own self-evaluation, nothing
about Wiesenthal's behavior implies that Wiesenthal failed to forgive the soldier. On the view of love and forgiveness given here, forgiveness is a matter
of desiring what is good—really, objectively good—for a wrongdoer and
desiring union with him, not in the sense of joining him but in the sense of

---

[35] For more discussion of this claim, see my "The Non-Aristotelian Character of Aquinas's
Ethics: Aquinas on the Passions," *Faith and Philosophy* 28, no. 1 (2011): 29–43.

[36] This account has the apparently counterintuitive result that one person Paula can accrue an obligation to a stranger Jerome to love him in virtue of his engaging in wrongdoing against Paula. That
is, on this account, if Jerome is a stranger to Paula but succeeds in robbing her of her pension funds,
then Paula gains an obligation of love with regard to Jerome that she did not have before his theft of
her funds. I appreciate that this result sounds counterintuitive, but a little reflection will show that it
is sadly true nonetheless. When Jerome steals from Paula, he thereby establishes a relationship with
Paula whether she likes it or not, because after his theft there is a connection between them that there
was not before. That connection establishes a relation in which some things are possible that were not
possible before, most notably that Paula can now forgive or fail to forgive Jerome, something not possible for her before he harmed her. I am grateful to Michael McKenna for calling to my attention the
need to make this point explicit.

[37] I have argued for this claim at length in "God's Obligations," in *Philosophical Perspectives* 6, ed.
James Tomberlin (Atascadero, CA: Ridgeview Publishing, 1992), pp. 475–492. To see the point here,
consider, by way of analogy that if Paula were a very rich tourist traveling in a very poor country, she
would be obligated to give some of her money away for charitable purposes in that country if she
were solicited to do so; if she refused all such solicitations, she would be subject to appropriate moral
censure. But it would not be the case that any particular recipient of her donations would have a right
to her money.

being at one with him. These *desires* are what is morally obligatory, and not their fulfillment. And nothing in Wiesenthal's story indicates that Wiesenthal lacked these desires.[38] On the contrary, the details of his dealings with the soldier suggest a humanity and compassion for the dying man grounded in such desires.

Nonetheless, as I will try to show in what follows, even if it were true, contrary to Wiesenthal's own self-assessment, that he did forgive the soldier, nothing about that forgiveness implies that Wiesenthal should have said anything to the soldier to give the soldier what the soldier so badly wanted, namely, a sense of restoration to ordinary human society. Nor does it imply that Wiesenthal should have been willing to be reconciled with the soldier. As I will argue, in cases of grave evil, forgiveness, even with the wrongdoer's repentance and his making what amends he can, may not be sufficient for the removal of guilt or for the moral permissibility of reconciliation. Silently leaving the soldier may have been all that was morally permissible for Wiesenthal to do, as many of the respondents in *The Sunflower* so fervently maintain.

The Problems of Guilt

It helps in this connection to consider the problems that guilt produces for a perpetrator of serious wrongdoing, and Newton's case is helpful here.

When Newton was in his slave-trading years, one problem for him lay in defective states of his psyche. In that period of his life, Newton thought that slave trading was morally acceptable, and he wanted to engage in it. So the first problem for a guilty person lies in himself, in his morally wrong states of intellect and will and the corrupt habits from which they stem or to which they contribute.

Furthermore, these defects of intellect and will do not exhaust the problem in Newton, however important they are. There are also other psychic defects, more subtle but not less damaging to Newton.

For example, there is memory. The very memory of having engaged in a great evil that caused cruel suffering to others diminishes something morally

---

[38] Or, to put the point more carefully, that he lacked them whole-heartedly. It is possible to be internally divided, so that one both desires and rejects the same thing. For more detailed discussion of such divisions in the will, see Stump 2010, Chapters 6 and 7.

good in the wrongdoer's psyche, too. By staying in memory, the evil a person such as Newton did remains part of Newton's present. His remembering his slave trading is not itself an evil act, but there is something morally lamentable about the continued presence of his evil acts in his memory nonetheless. That may be one reason why people who have done monstrous evil find their memories an affliction.

Then there are the empathic capacities. Most people cannot simulate the mind of a person who commits a morally horrific act; and we give expression to that incapacity by saying "I can't imagine how a person could do something like that!" But the perpetrator himself does understand what it feels like to do an evil of that sort and, what is worse, what it feels like to *want* to do an evil of that sort.

The Major in charge of Rudolph Hess at the Nuremberg trials said of Hess,

> I believe by the nature of his make-up, which reflects cruelty, bestiality, deceit, conceit, arrogance, and a yellow streak, that he has lost his soul and has willingly permitted himself to become plastic in the hands of a more powerful and compelling personality.[39]

One might say that, in addition to the defects in intellect and will of a wrongdoer such as Hess, there is a kind of moral elasticity in his psyche. The hard barrier—the "I can't!"—that ordinarily decent people have in their psyches against grotesque evil is missing in the perpetrators of great evil; and the elasticity or flabbiness of psyche, as the Major at Nuremberg characterized it, that is consequent on such evil can remain even if, unlike Hess, the wrongdoer repents.

Because they are not moral defects in the will, these psychological relics of moral wrongdoing in memory and the empathic capacities are not by themselves culpable or worthy of punishment; but there is something morally regrettable about them all the same. [40] As the comments of the Major at

---

[39] Richard Overy, *Interrogations: The Nazi Elite in Allied Hands, 1945* (New York: Viking Press, 2001), p. 401.

[40] Not everything that is morally deplorable is also culpable. That is at least in part because it is possible for a person to be in a morally bad condition without being responsible for being in that condition and therefore worthy of blame for it. A man in an isolated area of Mongolia in the time of the Great Khan might have been completely persuaded that wife beating in certain circumstances was obligatory for him. When he beat his wife in those circumstances, his psychic state would have been morally deplorable. But most people would hesitate to consider him culpable or worthy of punishment for that act, because we would suppose that he is not responsible for his morally bad psychic condition.

Nuremberg illustrate, people react with revulsion to such palpable elements in the psyche of a perpetrator of evil, even if they no longer have any serious concerns that the perpetrator could continue his evil actions.

So defects of psyche in intellect, will, memory, and the empathic capacities are the first problem for a person guilty of serious wrongdoing. The second problem lies in the world, in the effects of the wrongs done. The suffering of the human beings Newton kidnapped and enslaved was horrible, and he was responsible for it. Just restoring Newton's intellect and will to the state and condition of a morally good person, through repentance, for example, leaves unaddressed the suffering he caused. And even if there are no particular victims for a person's wrongdoing, as when someone simply wastes inherited great wealth in trivial pursuits and fails to contribute to society as he might have done, there remains for him the problem that the world is worse than it might have been because of what he did or failed to do.

This second problem can itself be subdivided into two further problems. First, there is the actual harm that a wrongdoer did, by his action or his omission, so that in one sense or another the world is worse because of him. And then there is the injustice of his acting as he did.

It seems clear that harm and injustice can come apart. A person Jerome can do harm without doing an injustice to another, but he can also do an injustice without doing harm. Suppose, for example, that a mother and her young child have been assigned seats some distance apart on a long flight but that they could sit together if Jerome would trade seats with one of them; and suppose also that Jerome could do so at no cost of any kind to himself, not even the inconvenience of moving his possessions. It is clear that the mother has no right to Jerome's seat, and so Jerome does not do her an injustice if he refuses to trade seats with her. But he has done her some harm, since he has made it more difficult for her to sit with her child and so to care for the needs of her child during the flight.[41] However, Jerome can do someone an

---

[41] Actions of this sort, which harm but do no injustice, are like actions in the category that some philosophers have called "the subrogatory": those actions that an agent is not obligated to do but that he is blamed for not doing. Aquinas would not accept this particular way of describing such actions, since for him rights and obligations can come apart. That is, for Aquinas, it is possible for an agent Jerome to be obligated to treat another person Paula in a certain way, even though Paula has no right to be treated in this way. Aquinas's discussion of the alms deeds makes this point clear. The alms deeds are obligatory from Aquinas's point of view; but Jerome's being obligated to give away some of his money to others does not mean that any of those others has a right to Jerome's money. For some recent discussion of these and related issues, see, for example, Julia Driver, "Appraisability, Attributability, and Moral Agency," in *The Nature of Moral Responsibility*, ed. Randolph Clarke, Michael McKenna, and Angela Smith (Oxford: Oxford University Press, 2015), pp. 157–174.

injustice without doing her any harm. Suppose that Jerome utters malicious gossip about Paula to her friend Julia; and suppose that Julia is certain that the gossip is false and that Jerome knows it is false. The result is that, by his action, Jerome lowers himself, not Paula, in Julia's eyes. In this case, Jerome has done Paula an injustice, but he has not harmed her.

In most cases, of course, harm and injustice go together, as they do in Newton's slave trading; but it is helpful to see that they can be disassociated, because seeing their separability helps illuminate the fact that, typically, a wrongdoer such as Newton has two different problems as regards the effects of his wrongdoing on the world. There is the harm he has caused, but there is also the injustice he has done. Just fixing the harm he has caused is generally not enough to fix the injustice. That is why, in addition to reparation, penance is often required for the removal of guilt. Penance helps to make amends for the injustice, as reparation helps to make amends for the harm caused.

The consequence of both the first and the second problem of guilt have the further effect of altering the wrongdoer's relations with others in his society, or, as in the case of the dying German soldier, with the whole human community. The state of the wrongdoer's psyche and the facts about the damage and injustice he has done can leave others angry at him or alienated from him. The victims of his wrongdoing may resent or reject him, and others who learn of his wrongdoing may share those attitudes even if they were not themselves harmed by his wrongdoing. They might nonetheless hate him or turn away from him as someone with whom they refuse to associate, because of what he is and what he has done.

These, then, are the major problems of guilt. On accounts such as Swinburne's, repentance, reparation, penance, and forgiveness are supposed to be sufficient to remedy guilt. Can they in fact resolve these problems of guilt?

The Role of Repentance, Reparation, and Penance in the Removal of Guilt

It is clear that repentance alone can remove some of the defects introduced in the wrongdoer by his morally wrong actions. So, for example, after his repentance, Newton lost the morally wrong states of intellect and will he had during his slave-trading years, and he replaced them with the states of intellect and will of a morally decent person as regards slave trading. We might also safely suppose that his repentance was fervent enough so that even his dispositions were altered: the corrupt dispositions characteristic of a slave trader were lost and replaced by morally good dispositions. At once, or perhaps more slowly over a period of time during his conversion, the defects in Newton's intellect and will, including the morally corrupt dispositions that were the deplorable consequences of his execrable actions, were healed. Through repentance, then, with respect to slave trading, Newton's intellect and will became like those of the abolitionists in his society.

At least in cases of grave moral wrongdoing, repentance alone cannot repair the damage the wrongdoer did or restore the wrongdoer to the place in community he had before his wrongdoing; but reparation and penance help in this connection. For ease of reference, I will refer to reparation and penance together as "making amends" or "satisfaction."[42] The word "satisfaction" comes from the Latin term "*satisfacere*," and the etymology of the Latin term comes from "*satis*" (enough) plus "*facere*" (to do). To make satisfaction by reparation (with regard to the damage one has done) and by penance (with regard to the injustice one has done) is to do what one can and by this means to make amends.

Satisfaction cannot undo the harm done in the original wrongdoing. Newton could not take away the sufferings of the Africans who had been transported on his ships and had lived to become slaves; he could not restore to life those who had died. But in giving himself to the cause of the abolition of the slave trade, a repentant Newton did what he could.

After his conversion, Newton joined forces with the English abolitionist William Wilberforce and others to alter public opinion about the slave trade. By the time Newton died, he was not only friends with these abolitionists, he was in fact held in honor by them. And it is not hard to see why. In Newton's passionate efforts on behalf of the abolition of the slave trade, he tried to make reparation for what he had done as a slave trader. And his pamphlet, which made public revelation of those actions of his of which he was most ashamed, was his penance.

Together these things constituted Newton's satisfaction; and his satisfaction was successful in making him a different man from the man he had been, even from the man he was when he first repented. His repentance for his slave trading healed the psychic defects in his intellect and will, and his

---

[42] In what follows, I will not distinguish between making amends and making satisfaction; and I will use the terms interchangeably.

work of satisfaction tried to undo the damage and the injustice for which he had been responsible. In consequence, it also altered his relationships with others. When Wilberforce was friends with Newton at the time the Slave Trade Act passed, Wilberforce was friends not just with a repentant slave trader; he was friends with a powerful enemy of the slave trade.

The Limits of Repentance and Satisfaction

Repentance and satisfaction, such as that engaged in by Newton, have a useful purpose insofar as they alter both the wrongdoer and the things in the world damaged by his wrongdoing.[43] Certainly, Newton is highly commendable for the way in which he tried to make amends. But contrary to what the reflections earlier about repentance and satisfaction might lead one to suppose, repentance and the attempts at satisfaction on the part of a person such as Newton are not sufficient to remedy the whole problem of guilt.

Consider, to begin with, Newton's relations with others alienated from him because of his slave trading. Newton's repentance and satisfaction are not sufficient to restore these relationships of Newton's to the condition they had or would have had before his wrongdoing.

Someone might object here that the relationship between a wrongdoer and those wronged by him *should* be healed even by the wrongdoer's repentance alone. When the wrongdoer repents, then, as far as his past morally wrong action goes, he has the beliefs and desires of a morally decent person. And so, someone might suppose, others should adopt toward the wrongdoer the same attitudes they would have had toward the wrongdoer before the wrongdoer's bad acts, that is, the same attitudes they would take toward any morally decent person.

But this objection rests on the mistaken assumption that a relationship is not affected by the past states of the persons in it, that only their present condition, the condition marked by the wrongdoer's repentance and satisfaction, is relevant to the relationship. In fact, however, for those who knew his history, Newton's past lives on in memory.

---

[43] In this section of this chapter, I am significantly altering the position I argued for in an earlier paper, "Personal Relations and Moral Residue," in *History of the Human Sciences: Theorizing from the Holocaust: What Is to Be Learned?*, Paul Roth and Mark S. Peacock (eds.), 17, no. 2/3 (August 2004), pp. 33–57. I stand by the arguments of that paper, but they now seem to me not sufficient to establish the conclusion. What else is needed, as I indicate in the conclusion of this chapter, is a well-worked-out theory of atonement.

As far as that goes, it lives on in Newton's memory, too. Newton wrote about his slave trading past,

> I hope it will always be a subject of humiliating reflection to me, that I was once an active instrument in a business at which my heart now shudders.[44]

No doubt, Newton did well to shudder at what he had done on the sea in the slave ships. But if it is always a subject of shuddering for Newton, then it is hard to see that his repentance and satisfaction are sufficient to undo all the morally lamentable effects on his psyche wrought by his slave trading. Something that would have been wholesome and healthy in Newton is diminished and replaced by shuddering in virtue of this memory of his past acts.

Furthermore, it is hard not to share Newton's view that he must never forget these acts. There would be something terrible about his forgetting the evil of his participation in the slave trade. In fact, it is not unreasonable to suppose that there is a duty to remember wrongdoing if the wrongdoing is serious enough.[45]

Thus, Newton's repentance and satisfaction may heal his intellect and will, but they cannot erase the past evil from his memory or remove the correlative elasticity from his empathic capacities either. And the same point holds for others stricken at the story of his acts in the slave trade.

Arguing for something like this conclusion, in the context of a thought experiment about an imaginary friend who has wronged him, Jeffrey Blustein says,

> The question is whether, having forgiven the wrongdoer, some sort of reorientation in how I related to him [before he wronged me] may be justified and appropriate. The answer, I believe, is yes. Forgiveness does not necessarily wipe the slate clean, and this means in part that it does not necessarily restore the relationship to its prior state, emotionally or behaviorally. . . . Forgiving another person doesn't mean that the relationship with him or her has been fully repaired or that they have been reconciled.[46]

---

[44] See John Newton, *Thoughts upon the African Slave Trade*.

[45] See, for example, Jeffrey M. Blustein, *Forgiveness and Remembrance* (Oxford: Oxford University Press, 2014).

[46] Blustein 2014, pp. 45–46.

One reason Blustein gives for this conclusion has to do precisely with memory. He says,

> Forgiveness . . . does not necessarily erase the wronged party's memory of having been wronged.[47]

On the contrary, Blustein holds,

> The wronged party may continue to have emotional memories of being wronged and be disposed to remember the wrong with negative emotions, even after she has forgiven her wrongdoer. These memories, while they may not impede forgiveness, can nevertheless signify that she continues to disvalue how she was mistreated and by whom. . . . [T]he norms for how one should feel about past wrongdoing do not proscribe continuing to disvalue it in one's memories after the wrongdoer is forgiven.[48]

And this seems right. Neither Newton nor any others should forget that Newton had been a slave trader; and no one should fail to continue to be horrified by his slave trading—or, as Blustein puts the point, no one should give up disvaluing it.

If Newton's repentance and satisfaction are not enough to remove the problems of guilt for Newton in his psyche and in his relationships with others, are they nonetheless sufficient to remove his guilt as regards the damage and injustice he did? Satisfaction is a matter of doing what one can and so doing *enough*. And Newton is exemplary in having done all he could, so that on this score it seems that he did enough and more. Consequently, it seems that, in this respect at any rate, his guilt is removed, so that his relationships with others can be restored and he can be reconciled with his victims.

But this optimistic view is not right either, is it? Satisfaction such as Newton's is enough *if* it is considered relative to Newton, that is, relative to what Newton could do. But this is no reason to think that it is enough relative to the victims. How could anything Newton did be enough for those who had suffered from his slave trading? How did his work of satisfaction help those who had suffered or died on his slave ships, or whose children suffered

---

in virtue of having been born into slavery? Nothing in Newton's subsequent efforts to abolish the slave trade in England altered the terrible suffering of those who died on his ships and the even worse suffering of those who lived to be slaves and to see their children enslaved as well. Nothing in what Newton did as satisfaction could make up to *them* the suffering Newton's evil caused them.

One can think of this insoluble difficulty for a perpetrator of serious evil as an analog to a problem much discussed with regard to the problem of evil.

On some proposed theodicies or defenses, the benefit supposedly justifying God in allowing the suffering of some particular person goes to humankind as a whole, and not to the sufferer in particular. But, as objectors to such accounts point out, this seems not to solve the objection to God's existence raised by the problem of evil, but only to move it. How could an omnipotent, omniscient, perfectly good God allow one human being to suffer for some benefit that goes only to the species as a whole? Surely, goodness requires that any putative benefit justifying someone in allowing suffering that he could readily prevent ought to go primarily to the sufferer.

By parity of reasoning, if the satisfaction Newton made constituted a benefit for all those who might have been victimized after 1807, when the slave trade was abolished through his efforts, then the benefit does not go primarily to those afflicted by him in his slave-trading years. But if all people, or all people of his time and society, are benefited by Newton's satisfaction, then it seems that those Africans who suffered from his slave trading suffered for the sake of a benefit that went to everyone. In what sense, then, has Newton done anything to amend *their* suffering in particular? And if there is no acceptable answer to this question, as it seems clear that there is not, then in what sense does Newton's satisfaction remove his guilt with respect to those he enslaved and transported?

Consequently, why should the victims of his wrongdoing, or anyone else horrified at his actions, think his repentance and satisfaction are sufficient to remove Newton's guilt or to restore Newton to the place he would have had in the human community before his slave trading?

Conclusion

Although forgiveness, like love, is obligatory, even for unrepentant wrongdoers, reconciliation does not follow simply from forgiveness. In fact, for perpetrators of grave evil, even their fervent repentance and self-sacrificial satisfaction may not be enough for reconciliation. So it can be obligatory to forgive and nonetheless not morally permissible to be reconciled with a wrongdoer, even when that wrongdoer has repented and made satisfaction.

A relationship is an ongoing interaction among persons, and it is dependent on the characteristics of all the persons in the relationship. If, because of his past acts, a perpetrator of evil is not now the person he was, then others affected by him or aware of his past evil appropriately treat him as if he now were that earlier, innocent person. That is because they cannot unilaterally reform the relationship they had or might have had with him when he was a different person from the person he now is. Consequently, if a person's moral wrongdoing is a great enough evil, it can obstruct or obviate morally appropriate reconciliation with him even if he is genuinely and wholeheartedly repentant. Repentance and satisfaction can make a wrongdoer a different person from the person he was when he engaged in wrongdoing. But even such exemplary repentance and satisfaction as Newton's cannot remove all the problems of guilt.

The highly divergent views of the respondents in Wiesenthal's *The Sunflower* can therefore all be justified. Those who argue in favor of the forgiveness of the dying German soldier are surely right. Forgiveness of him is obligatory, just as love is. But those who repudiate with fervor any forgiveness of him are also right, if we suppose that under the heading of "forgiveness" they understand the removal of guilt, reconciliation, and restoration to human community. Even a lifetime's worth of satisfaction, if the soldier had had another lifetime to complete it, coupled with heartbroken repentance, could not remove his guilt or restore him to his former place in human society. The damage and injustice he did were so great that their past effects on others and their ongoing effects on the soldier and others who remember what he did put the soldier at a distance of light-years from ordinary human community.

Anselm's account of the atonement of Christ is based on the idea that although human beings owe a great debt because of the evil they have done, they are unable to pay that debt. On Anselm's view, that is why Christ, who is both human and divine, is the only one able to pay this debt for them. Because he is human, he is a member of the species that owes the debt; and because he is God, he has the resources to pay what is owed. Consequently, as Anselm sees it, only Christ can make satisfaction for the debt incurred by human wrongdoing.

Anselm's account of the atonement of Christ is based on the idea that the debt in question is owed to God. Elsewhere I have argued against Anselm's account of the atonement, but what the reflections of this chapter show is that at least one part of Anselm's account is surely right. In consequence of grave evil, a human being may incur a debt of recompense so monumental that nothing he could do would ever repay it. Only, contrary to Anselm's account, the reflections of this chapter imply that the debt is owed to the victims of human evil. If there is an account of Christ's atonement on which Christ's satisfaction removes the guilt of human beings, then whatever else is contained in that account, it will have to portray Christ's atonement as including satisfaction made *to the victims of human evil.* Only human beings owe the debt to the suffering victims of their evil; but it may be true, as Anselm thought, that only God could pay so great a debt as that incurred by human evil—only, as the reflections of this chapter show, that debt is owed to suffering human beings, whether or not it is also owed to God, as Anselm supposed.

In this connection, I want to conclude by pointing out that, on Newton's own view of the matter, the story of Newton's satisfaction which I have told here is incomplete. Newton did not suppose that his own efforts at satisfaction were what had removed his guilt or enabled him to be reconciled to others, including even the victims of his slave trading. As his most famous hymn expresses his views of his own restoration, it was the amazing grace of God that found and restored him. Newton's work of satisfaction manifests his great gratitude for that grace and for the satisfaction of Christ, which did what Newton himself could not have done alone.

These theological considerations are too complicated to be dealt with briefly in passing. I mention them only to end on a more optimistic note than the reflections herein might otherwise give. Aquinas thought that there is no wrongdoing so evil that the wrongdoer cannot afterward be restored to an even more admirable condition in himself and in human community than he would have had before the wrongdoing; but Aquinas thought so because of the implications of the account of Christ's satisfaction which Aquinas himself accepted. On that account, it is right to see Newton as a hero in the history of the slave trade, as many people (me included) do. And, on that account, even the dying German soldier can be not only forgiven but in fact restored in reconciliation and community with all others. But such optimistic conclusions are grounded in the theological doctrine of the atonement, which implies that what is owed to the victims of human evil and what is needed to heal the psyche of a wrongdoer are provided by the satisfaction of Christ, on a non-Anselmian account of atonement.

Whether this optimistic note regarding human evil is right, or whether the more pessimistic account of those who refuse reconciliation and forgiveness with the German soldier is right rests, then, in the end, on theological considerations.[49]

[49] I am grateful to Michael McKenna and Brandon Warmke for helpful comments on an earlier draft of this chapter. Because this volume was delayed in publication, this chapter has appeared after my *Atonement* (2018), instead of before it, as originally planned. Some portions of this chapter are taken from that book. In addition, some recent work relating to that book and the topic of forgiveness in it, including work of my own, is not referenced here because that work appeared well after the submission of this chapter.

9

Forgiving Evil

Eve Garrard and David McNaughton

Is there such a thing as evil? Some people think not, on the grounds that it is an essentially religious, supernatural, idea, and that these days we have no need of that hypothesis. But it is a notable feature of our moral discourse that even people who have no religious or supernatural commitments do quite often appeal to the idea of evil, and they understand each other perfectly well when they do so. We say things like "That wasn't just wrong, it was *evil*," and "He was different from just an ordinary bad man, he really was an evil person," and the only thing that people disagree about is whether we have made the attribution of evil accurately, rather than whether the term has any application at all.

Evil can be predicated both of actions and of persons, and there is a lively discussion about which (if either) has primacy, conducted by different theorists of evil. In this chapter we will be focusing on evil actions, primarily because we find it hard to see how we can understand the evil agent (and a fortiori the nonevil agent who nonetheless commits an evil action) without some understanding of the nature of the evil action. But nothing that we say here should be taken to imply any dismissiveness toward the project of understanding the evil agent.

There is general agreement that if there is such a thing as evil, then evil actions are especially terrible ones—they're immoral in peculiarly disturbing and dreadful ways. One issue that arises about them is the question of how we should treat such terrible actions (and their perpetrators): what is the appropriate response to them? Prevention, obviously, where that is possible; but after that, what then? One aspect of this issue is the question: are evil actions forgivable? Or are they so bad that they are beyond forgiveness, so that forgiveness of evildoers is itself morally reprehensible, even when the agent is fully repentant?

This question is the topic of Simon Wiesenthal's book *The Sunflower* (1997). Here he writes of an event during the Second World War that took place

Eve Garrard and David McNaughton, *Forgiving Evil* In: *Forgiveness and Its Moral Dimensions.* Edited by: Brandon Warmke, Dana Kay Nelkin, and Michael McKenna, Oxford University Press. © Oxford University Press 2021. DOI: 10.1093/oso/9780190602147.003.0009

while he, a Jew, was incarcerated in a Nazi concentration camp, where his life hung by a thread every day. He was on one occasion taken to the bedside of a blind and dying Nazi soldier, a young man who told Wiesenthal that he had taken part in the burning of a group of Jewish families in a locked building. He asked Wiesenthal, as a Jew, to forgive him. Eventually Wiesenthal left the room silently, having offered no forgiveness. After the war, Wiesenthal invited various academics, writers, people of a variety of religions, to comment on this event, and to answer the question, "What would you have done?" The responses ranged from strong commitment to forgiveness for the repentant, through various doubts about the appropriateness of forgiveness in these extreme circumstances, to the vehement, passionate insistence of the writer Cynthia Ozick that forgiving the evildoer is pitiless toward the victim: "the face of forgiveness is mild, but how stony to the slaughtered. . . . Whoever forgives the murderer blinds himself to the vastest letting of blood." (Ozick in Wiesenthal 1997: 204–210.) She sees the repentant, dying SS man as a man with a moral temperament, a man of conscience—but "though at heart not a savage, he [has] allowed himself to become one, he did not resist. It was not that he lacked conscience; he smothered it . . . I"t was not that he lacked humanity; he deadened it." The morally sensitive SS man goes on shoveling babies into the furnaces, in spite of his twinges of conscience. He is "possessed of a refined and meticulous moral temperament—so refined and so meticulous that it knows the holy power of forgiveness, and knows to ask for it." But, "Forgiveness, which permits redemption, can apply only to a condition susceptible of redemption." She concludes, "Let the SS man die unshriven. Let him go to hell. Sooner the fly to God than he." [1]

A distinction can be drawn between the normative moral question about whether it is permissible to forgive evildoers for their evil actions and the metaphysical or conceptual question about whether it is actually possible to forgive the evildoer for his evil action. Clearly, if the answer to the second question is negative, then we need not bother with the first question at all. But a negative answer to that question does not seem very plausible, since there are several notable (and no doubt many generally unknown) cases of victims who have forgiven those who inflicted evil actions on them. If we were to persist in claiming that there is a metaphysical or conceptual problem with forgiving evil, then we would have to tell those who appear to have succeeded

---

[1] I.e., Sooner let the fly that disturbs the dying SS man find safe harbor in God than this SS murderer.

in doing so that they misunderstand their own situation and are incapable of doing what they think they have done, since it is conceptually or metaphysically impossible. Insisting on such an account to the one who appears to have forgiven is not a morally attractive prospect. So we are left with the normative question only, about the permissibility of forgiving evil actions; it is this question that we will be focusing on in the rest of the chapter.

This is not a question about victim psychology; it cannot be settled by looking at what is psychologically possible for victims. In any case that is something which will vary from one person to another, and we already know that for some victims, forgiveness for evildoers is psychologically possible, because they have actually done it (see Lomax 1995). And the same goes for the psychological difficulty of forgiving evil—we can be fairly sure that it is almost always going to be psychologically difficult, but that really does not imply that it cannot be done, or that there are no reasons for doing it. If we are talking about empirical possibility, then empirical actuality settles the matter: evildoers can, perhaps with great difficulty, be forgiven. But that doesn't settle the more philosophical question of whether forgiving in these cases is morally legitimate or whether, given the nature of evil, there are moral reasons against so doing.

Another way of looking at this question is to say that given our general understanding of the nature of forgiveness, this question arises: are there any actions which are beyond its scope, or is it always morally permissible, even right, to forgive wrongdoers? Do we have reason to forgive every single wrongdoer, or are some of them, perhaps the ones whose actions are not just wrong but actually evil, beyond the reach of forgiveness because of the specially dreadful nature of what they have done?[2] One obvious answer to the question is that evildoers are indeed beyond forgiveness, because they do not in any way deserve it. But although it is true that they do not deserve forgiveness, that is certainly not enough to show that forgiveness is morally impermissible. Many, many wrongdoers do not deserve forgiveness, but that does not place them outside its scope—forgiveness is a gift, and it can legitimately be provided even where it is not deserved. It is often right to give people something that they do not really deserve, and if we all got our just deserts,

---

[2] Some, for example, Luke Russell (2007), have denied that there is anything qualitatively distinct about *evil* acts; they are simply acts that are very wrong and extremely harmful. For a full discussion of Russell, and our reasons for dissenting from his view, see Garrard and McNaughton (2018: 20).

who would escape whipping? We need to look rather further into our views about forgiveness if we are to address this question at all adequately.

The question that interests us here lies at the intersection of our theory of evil and our theory of forgiveness. And the answer to this question is going to be affected, perhaps even settled, by the content of these theories—at least, that seems to be a reasonable starting point for addressing the issue. So let us begin by saying a little about theories of evil. We are not going to be defending any particular theory, since none of the ones we are familiar with seem to us to be entirely satisfactory, and that includes our own efforts in that direction. Nonetheless, we can still consider how they deal with the issue of forgiveness, or at least what implications they have for that issue.

First, we'll briefly say what kind of phenomena we will be considering as falling under the concept of evil. It is fairly common ground that we use the term "evil" in at least three different ways: first, to refer to anything which produces bad outcomes for humans—so we can in this sense of the word refer to hurricanes and floods as "natural evils." Second, we can restrict the term to cases of human agency and use it to mean any kind of wrongdoing; not natural evils but moral ones—"the evil that men do lives after them." Third, we can use the term to pick out human actions that have a special quality of horror, ones which deeply disturb us, and seem to go beyond the normal run of wrongdoings. So we may say of a given action that some features of it were so dreadful that the act was evil; and everyone will have some sense of what that means. This third meaning is the one which we are interested in, partly because it is a very distinctive use of the term—we do not really have a synonym for it, unlike the first two meanings; and partly because it points to a special place on the moral spectrum which many, perhaps most, people feel is of considerable moral significance, a place of special horror and recoiling.

We will be focusing here exclusively on this third, restrictive meaning. So what light do our current theories of evil throw on the issue of whether we should respond to evil with forgiveness or with unyielding hostility? Many though not all theories treat the evil act as logically primary, with the account of what it is to be an evil agent deriving from the prior analysis of evil action—so in general an evil agent is taken to be one who frequently or regularly commits evil acts, or who has a strong disposition to do so, or some cognate claim; and we will follow this order of priority, since we thoroughly endorse it. (As we have seen, there are also theorists who deny that there are any evil acts, and hence any evil agents, often arguing that the positing of such phenomena is itself morally objectionable. See, for example, Cole [2006] and Clendinnen [1999]. But interesting though their position is, we are not going to address it at any further length here; we are just going to help ourselves to the existence of evil.)

Theories of evil action seem to fall into two broad classes: those which locate evil in the terrible outcomes of the acts in question; and those which locate it in some aspect of the psychological state of the evildoer. A (rather crude) example of the former is the view that evil actions are just those which are at the bottom of the utilitarian scale: they are the ones which cause the most suffering. More refined and complex examples would include those of Claudia Card, in whose view evil actions are foreseeable intolerable harms produced by culpable wrongdoing (2002: 3), and also Luke Russell, who focuses on culpable wrongs which are connected in some appropriate way to the production of extreme harms.[3]

An example of the second, agent-focused kind of theory is the view of Colin McGinn (1997: 62ff.), who proposes that an evil act is one committed by an agent who derives pleasure, noninstrumentally, from the pain of others—that is, her motive is to cause suffering for no reason other than that it provides pleasure to the agent. This is a very narrowly construed agent-focused theory of evil. A different and broader example of this kind of theory is Adam Morton's barrier theory of evil, according to which "a person's act is evil when it results from a strategy or learned procedure which allows that person's deliberation over the choice of actions not to be inhibited by barriers against considering harming or humiliating others that ought to have been in place" (2004: 57).

Card says, very persuasively, that outcome-focused theories of evil are ones which look at it from the victim's perspective, whereas psychologically oriented theories are ones which locate the nature of evil in the perpetrator's point of view. So let us consider what light, if any, the outcome-focused theories of evil throw on the issue of forgiveness. Are the perpetrators of acts with the very worst outcomes beyond the reach of forgiveness? Most people think that in some circumstances it is morally appropriate to forgive wrongdoers who have produced bad outcomes. Forgiveness, after all, is for transgressors, not for the blameless ones among us. So if we can justify or

---

[3] Russell's view is actually more complex than this summary reveals, since he is a conceptual pluralist about evil—see Russell (2014, esp. ch. 6)—but we can't do full justice to that aspect of his work here.

recommend forgiveness for those who commit acts with bad outcomes, what would prevent us from thinking that acts with worse outcomes (and hence, on a simple utilitarian theory, evil acts) can and should be forgiven, in the right circumstances? Perhaps it might be said that the increase in quantity of suffering caused by the evildoer amounts to a qualitative difference between him and the mere wrongdoer. But if that is so, again we would like to know why, since not all increases in quantity amount to qualitative differences. Absent such an explanation, we do not seem to have a reason for withholding forgiveness from evildoers in circumstances where we might be prepared to offer it to wrongdoers. Indeed, if we think that there is a default reason to forgive all wrongdoers (which we will say a little more about later), then we will hold out for some such explanation before agreeing that evildoers are beyond the reach of forgiveness.

But in any case, the straightforwardly utilitarian view of evil is not very convincing. There are too many cases where the production of terrible outcomes is not evil and may sometimes even be justified (such as just wars); and conversely, there are cases where the suffering produced by the evildoer is quite small, or even nonexistent, but where the action is intuitively an evil one (classic example: the sadistic voyeur). But if we take Card's much more complex, but still outcomes-oriented view that evil acts are foreseeable intolerable harms produced by culpable wrongdoing, then we seem to have a series of elements each of which can be found in merely wrongful acts, although not all together (since ex hypothesi that would make the act evil); and some, perhaps all, of these wrongful acts would be acceptable candidates for forgiveness. An act which involved the foreseeable production of harm might be forgiven, one which involved the production of intolerable harm might be forgiven, and so forth. And similar considerations can be raised about Russell's view of evil as culpable wrongs which are connected in some appropriate way to the production of extreme harms. It might be argued that although each of the aforementioned features does not by itself preclude forgiveness, nonetheless their coinstantiation does; and for all we know that's true. But so far nothing has been shown to *support* this claim, or to explain why it might be the case, and there also seem to be fairly obvious counterexamples, such as an episode of drunken driving which leads to the deaths of children. Foreseeable, intolerably harmful, and culpably wrong. But not evil, in the restricted sense which we are focusing on here. So it looks as if the harm account of evil does not by itself show that evil acts are unforgivable.

Turning now to the more psychologically oriented accounts, we find similar problems. If evil acts are ones in which the agent takes noninstrumental pleasure in inflicting suffering, why does that rule out forgiveness for such acts? Doubtless the agent is in a very terrible moral condition, but that alone does not show that he should not be forgiven. And the same, we think, is true of the barrier theory: if an agent possesses, and acts on, procedures for overcoming normal barriers against considering the infliction of harm on innocents, why does that rule him out of consideration for forgiveness? The natural answer here is something like: "Because what he did was so terrible, and his own moral condition is such a dreadful one," and though this claim is true, it is of course question-begging.

A somewhat different question is whether an evil person can be forgiven for being evil.[4] We are not sure that the notion of forgiving a person tout court, as distinct for forgiving someone *for* a particular act, makes sense. However, there seem to be the following possibilities.

1. Forgiving someone who is bad, but not thoroughly evil, and who commits a particular evil act, for that act.
2. Forgiving someone who is thoroughly evil, and who commits a particular act that is wrong, but not evil, for that act.
3. Forgiving someone who is thoroughly evil, and who commits a particular evil act, for that evil act.
4. Forgiving an evil person for being evil (if this makes sense).

It might be claimed (1) that someone who is not thoroughly evil could legitimately be forgiven for individual evil acts. But should we forgive the radically evil person? In the case of (2) it would seem implausible to suppose forgiveness is impossible. Suppose Hitler, that well-known animal lover, negligently ran over someone's dog. Filled with remorse, he apologizes and begs forgiveness. It seems fairly implausible to claim that the owner of the dog should not forgive Hitler *for killing the dog* simply because he is *Hitler*. What of (3)? Here, let us suppose, the evil act flows from the evil character of the actor. The claim that we should not forgive the evildoer for his characteristically evil act may seem more attractive. However, in determining whether forgiveness for

---

[4] As we earlier indicated, we are not going into the difficult issue of what it is for a person to be thoroughly evil. But we are assuming that to be thoroughly evil one need not always choose the evil deed whenever the chance arises. Hitler was an animal lover, and a vegetarian, but he was also thoroughly evil.

that evil act is morally acceptable, it is not clear that the prospective forgiver need take account of the whole history of the perpetrator's many crimes and the ingrained nature of his evil disposition. (4), assuming that it is conceivable, is the hardest case. But even here, it is not clear that the appalling character of the evildoer makes forgiveness morally reprehensible.

Jean Hampton (Murphy and Hampton 1988) offers an account that would certainly rule out the legitimacy of forgiving in (4). For her, when we forgive, we are affirming that, at bottom, the agent is not morally rotten.

> The forgiver who previously saw the wrongdoer as someone bad or rotten or morally indecent to some degree has a change of heart when he "washes away" or disregards the wrongdoer's immoral actions or character traits in his ultimate moral judgement of her, and comes to see her as still *decent, not* rotten as a person, and someone with whom he may be able to renew a relationship. When one has a change of heart towards one's wrongdoer, one "reapproves" of her, so that one is able to consider renewing an association with her. . . . [The forgiver] revises her judgement of the person himself— where that person is understood to be something other than or more than the character traits of which she does not approve. (1988: 83, 85)

But in (4), ex hypothesi, the evil agent is indeed morally rotten.[5] The difficulty with Hampton's account is that it seems too strong, for it forbids forgiveness in all cases except (1). Indeed, it seems to run together two distinct issues: forgiving someone for a particular *act*, and assessing a person's whole character, to see what attitude we should take to *him*.

A better suggestion might be that in forgiving the evildoer what we are affirming is not so much that the forgivee is not morally rotten, but rather that he is not ultimately *irredeemably* so. Obviously there is a religious construal of this claim, but there is also a secular construal available: we might believe that human nature is sufficiently plastic, and/or open to moral reason, that we are never justified in writing another person off as rotten—there is always the possibility that he might change.[6]

One of the reasons that are sometimes cited against any deployment of the idea of an evil person is that it is the concept of a moral monster, a creature

---

[5] Note that Hampton's account blurs the distinction between forgiving the evildoer for a particular evil deed and forgiving the evil person for being evil.

[6] Settling this question will require a treatment of the issue of human nature: whether there is indeed such a thing, and if so, what it is like—an issue beyond the scope of this chapter.

essentially unlike normal people, and hence one for whom the normal reasons for forgiveness fail—he is too remote from being a human being to be a candidate for forgiveness. And, so the argument sometimes continues, if there are no evil persons, then the idea of an evil act loses much of its interest. This rejection of the idea of an evil person has an interesting implication, namely that we have reason to think of all other people as sharing our common humanity, and that is why regarding people as monsters is wrong. We will return to this implication later. But as a view of evildoers the "monster" theory is profoundly implausible, as those who complain about it rightly emphasize. However, it is a mistake to think that the implausibility of seeing some people as alien monsters goes against any use of the concept of evil person. Evildoers, even those with a settled disposition to commit evil actions, are often alarmingly like the rest of us, as much empirical investigation has shown; in any case this is pretty obvious from the most passing acquaintance with the history of the twentieth century and, for that matter, the twenty-first century, too. But it is in fact possible to have an account of evil under which evildoers are people like the rest of us, and if they are monsters, that's because that monstrosity is one of the common human potentialities, which can in the right circumstances be realized by more of us than we care to notice. The evildoer who is too monstrous and alien to be a candidate for forgiveness is not a plausible creature, and so this putative reason for finding that evil is beyond forgiveness seems to us to fail.

So far as we can see, there is nothing in the concept of evil itself, whichever way it is construed in the various accounts of it, that shows why, or even that, the evildoer is beyond the scope of forgiveness. Nor do they show that he is within it. The question remains open.

Let us emphasize that we are not at this stage claiming that evildoers are always forgivable. They may very well not be, on these or perhaps on any accounts of evil. What we do want to claim, however, is that our current theories of evil do not entail this putative fact. So far as we can see, there is nothing in the concept of evil which either precludes forgiveness or legitimates it.

So we should turn now to theories of forgiveness, to see if we can find illumination there. There are many different accounts of forgiveness, and they can be grouped together in various ways. One taxonomy (derived from the work of Thomas Brudholm 2008: 52ff.) categorizes accounts of forgiveness along two dimensions. First, there is a dimension which runs from blurred conceptions of forgiveness, overlapping with other related concepts such as reconciliation, condonation, excuses, and forgettings, to ones which are very precise, clearly delimiting the concept of forgiveness and distinguishing it sharply from other concepts. Second, there is a dimension along which theories range from maximalist to minimalist, in terms of the restrictions placed by the account on legitimate forgiveness.

If we want to find out what our conception of forgiveness implies for the forgiveness of evildoers, then a blurred conception will not help us, since it will be contaminated, so to speak, with issues about reconciliation with, or condonation of, or excuses for, evil acts. (Consider, for example, the Rwandan genocide, where some of the surviving victims saw the need for reconciliation if communal life was to continue, but said that they did not want to go so far as to forgive the perpetrators.) So a precise conception of forgiveness, clearly demarcating it from other cognate attitudes, will be better for our purposes. One such account (which we think is plausible for reasons quite independent of the issue of evil) is the claim that forgiveness is the overcoming of hostile attitudes, especially resentment, hatred, or contempt, toward the perpetrator and the adoption of a broadly well-wishing stance toward him. With this fairly precise account of forgiveness in hand—that is, an account which claims that forgiveness is compatible with refusals to excuse, or condone, or even to reconcile, and hence is distinct from any of these cognate attitudes—we can consider what more or less maximalist accounts of forgiveness might imply for evildoers.

On some, relatively minimalist, accounts, forgiveness is only permissible if certain conditions are met, in particular that the forgiver is a direct victim, and that the perpetrator has repented of his deeds. The requirement that only the victim can forgive (not in our view an entirely plausible one) does not seem to have any particular implications for forgiveness of evildoers. It may rule out forgiveness of evil where the victims are dead, but that would also be true for the victims of mere wrongdoing. The second constraint, that there must be repentance before there can be forgiveness, may seem at first sight more promising. But that would be a mistake—the demand for repentance before forgiveness will certainly rule out forgiveness for unrepentant evildoers, but it might also rule out forgiveness for unrepentant wrongdoers. So it won't help us to see if evildoers are beyond the scope of forgiveness in a way in which wrongdoers are not.

So now let us consider a maximalist view of forgiveness, one which says that unconditional forgiveness—forgiveness independently of whether the perpetrator has repented—is legitimate. This is not currently a very popular view among forgiveness theorists, many of whom are strong conditionalists (e.g., Griswold 2007), and some of whom have spoken persuasively against forgiveness in certain cases even when there has been repentance (see, e.g., Murphy 2003; Brudholm 2008; Améry 1986; among others). Does it follow from the maximalist view—which holds that perpetrators may be forgiven whether or not they repent—that the forgiving of evildoers is always legitimate? Not necessarily: it could be true that where forgiveness is legitimate, it doesn't require prior repentance; but it wouldn't follow that forgiveness is always legitimate.

We seem to be no further forward: the theory of forgiveness doesn't seem to be any more decisive on this subject than the theory of evil. However, if we go deeper into the content of forgiveness theories, more conclusive results may follow. Theorists of forgiveness differ markedly on the reasons that they offer in support of forgiveness. Here are three possible candidates: (1) the supposedly therapeutic value of forgiveness to the forgiver; (2) the appropriateness of bringing the repentant perpetrator back into the moral community; and (3) the expression of human solidarity.

As Brudholm has forcefully pointed out, not all victims of atrocities find forgiveness therapeutic, especially if it is pressed on them as the only morally commendable response to their tormentors. And even if it is therapeutic, this may be insufficient to warrant forgiveness: not all victims are aiming at their own mental health above all else—sometimes they are more concerned to stand witness for those who are dead, and to seek justice for them; and it's not immediately obvious, to say the least, that this stance is morally defective (see, for example, the work of Jean Améry). So the therapeutic reason for forgiveness seems neither to support nor to rule out forgiveness for evildoers—it's going to depend on the details of each case. What does it mean to bring the perpetrator back into the moral community? There are two ways of understanding what it would be to be exiled from the moral community. The stronger account would conceive of perpetrators as moral outlaws or lepers: people who were no longer thought of as moral agents, nor as having the rights accorded to moral agents. Understood this way, the suggestion seems to be redundant. Forgiving a person is certainly a way of registering the person's membership of the moral community, but so is refusing to forgive the person—creatures outside the moral community are not candidates for either forgiveness or for the refusal to forgive. We don't think that we ought, or ought not, to forgive man-eating tigers. This supposed reason is unconvincing even with wrongdoers, let alone evildoers. The weaker account would allow that bad or wicked moral agents are still agents, and they have both duties and rights. Here, being exiled from the moral community might be understood as the withdrawal of certain alienable rights and/or exclusion from certain decencies of social intercourse—being sent to Coventry. Just as jailed criminals may rightfully be excluded from voting, and other participation in communal matters, so the moral wrongdoer might be thought of as being liable to shunning, censure, and so on. Forgiveness would involve the restoration of those rights.

There are two difficulties with this account. First, it seems not so much to be an account of forgiveness as a *consequence* of being forgiven. Second, like Hampton's account, it has difficulty making sense of being forgiven for a *particular* offence. It would seem that one either remains in Coventry or one is readmitted to polite society. What if the perpetrator is forgiven for some, but not all, of his wrongs? Is he wholly, or only partly, returned to the bosom of the moral community, and how is this to be spelled out?

The final reason we will look at is that of human solidarity. Here the thought is that our reason to forgive perpetrators is that we are all in the same boat together, so to speak: the human condition is a hard and morally dangerous one; we are all of us prone to wrongdoing; hence, we are all likely to be in need of forgiveness. Even where the wrongdoing is so severe as to amount to evildoing, it is still true that many of us—though we are not, let us hope, evildoers ourselves—are such that in other circumstances we could have committed evil acts or become the kind of people who do so. And this common human plight gives us a reason of solidarity to forgive the perpetrator—he is one of us, after all, and in need of forgiveness, just as we might be in his shoes. As we noted earlier, those who deny the legitimacy of the whole concept of evil, on the grounds that it is the concept of moral monsters unlike the rest of us, beyond the human pale; and who think that this is an objectionable way to regard other human beings, have adopted a position that implies that human solidarity is morally desirable, even with major wrongdoers. They reject the concept of evil because it seems to them (mistakenly, in our view) to imply that the evildoer is unlike the rest of us, and hence not worthy of our solidarity; but in truth, they think, all humans are appropriate objects of solidarity. The solidarity account of reasons for forgiveness takes that thought seriously, but still has room for the existence of human evil, since it also takes seriously the dark potential within many of us to do terrible things. Hence, it also has room for forgiveness for evildoers, since they, too, can be suitable targets for solidarity.

We'd like briefly to consider two serious objections to the view that there's a theory of forgiveness under which we have reasons of solidarity to forgive evildoers, and hence that it's morally legitimate to do so. The first of these is the claim that the victims of evil are entitled to maintain resentment and anger at the perpetrators, and hence are not obliged to forgive them. This seems to us to be absolutely correct—victims do indeed have reason to maintain hostility toward their tormentors. But that is compatible with there also being a reason to forgive them, and one which can be strong enough to outweigh the (perfectly legitimate) reasons for victims to maintain hostility. And it is also worth pointing out that the moral legitimacy of forgiveness for evildoers does not amount to a moral requirement to forgive. Forgiveness of evil has the quality of a gift; it is supererogatory, not obligatory; so a victim who does not forgive is not morally defective. Hence, commitment to the view that forgiving evildoers is morally legitimate does not involve any improper moral criticism of victims who cannot or do not forgive.

The second objection is one which we take even more seriously than the first. This is the thought that forgiveness has had a very good press, and resentment has not; and that this is no accident in a culture which has been so heavily influenced by Christianity, with its tremendous emphasis on sinners and on the importance of forgiveness. A religion which has as its central text a Gospel, a declaration of good news for sinners, saying that their sins have been *divinely* forgiven, is likely to be very focused on *human* sin and forgiveness, too. But, so this objection goes, this is to privilege the focus on the sinner at the expense of the victim, and that is morally problematic. Even from a secular point of view, we're quite prepared to believe that we are all sinners, and in need of forgiveness—indeed, the story we have been peddling about the human potential for evil and the need for human solidarity might easily be seen as the Christian account in secular guise, though that is not any intention of ours. But the worry is that it might involve some neglect of victims, and their need for justice—a need which might very reasonably be taken to outrank the need of perpetrators for forgiveness.

However, if there are reasons to forgive evildoers, and also reasons to refuse to do so and to maintain hostility toward them, we will at some point have to make a choice. And as Jeffrie Murphy, an outstanding defender of resentment as a morally serious stance, has nonetheless said, we would all in the end prefer to be inscribed in the Book of Love rather than the Book of Resentment (Murphy 2003: 86). If push comes to shove, forgiveness is better than resentment because love is better than hate, though if anyone asks us to justify that latter claim, we would not know how to—some things are just bedrock. But there does remain the troublesome question of whether we can do justice to justice, so to speak, while still retaining the view that it is possible, it is not morally objectionable, to forgive those who have done evil.

Finally, is forgiveness the end of the story? Some theorists of forgiveness see it as "wiping the slate clean" or involving "forgiving and forgetting," and on those theories forgiveness does seem to close the file on wrongful or evil actions, and hence to be the end of the story for them. We think there are good general reasons for rejecting such theories, and they seem particularly implausible for evil actions, especially the great moral catastrophes such as torture or genocide. How could we possibly forget what the genocidaires have done or wipe their slate clean? But the refusal to forget or wipe the record clean is compatible with overcoming hatred and adopting some form of well-wishing for the evildoers. However, even on that more plausible account of forgiveness, there seems to be some residue left in the case of evil actions. Eleonore Stump (2004) captures this problem very perceptively in her question: Supposing (as was never the case) Goebbels had fully understood and repented of his terrible actions in pursuit of the aims of the Holocaust and had been forgiven by those who had a right to give or withhold forgiveness. Would we feel perfectly comfortable inviting the forgiven Goebbels to come round for dinner? The fact that we so readily find a problem with that suggests that evil actions leave a residue behind on the evildoer's hands, so to speak, which even forgiveness does not expunge. Why this is so, and what if anything can expunge the stain of evildoing, are questions which are in need of further investigation if we are to have a satisfactory understanding both of forgiveness and of evil, and of the relation between them.

References

Améry, Jean, 1986, *At the Mind's Limits: Contemplations by a Survivor of Auschwitz and Its Realities*, New York: Schocken.

Brudholm, Thomas, 2008, *Resentment's Virtue: Jean Amery and the Refusal to Forgive*, Philadelphia: Temple University Press.

Card, Claudia, 2002, *The Atrocity Paradigm: A Theory of Evil*, New York: Oxford University Press.

Clendinnen, Inga, 1999, *Reading the Holocaust*, Cambridge: Cambridge University Press.

Cole, Phillip A., 2006, *The Myth of Evil: Demonizing the Enemy*, Edinburgh: Praeger.

Garrard, Eve, and David McNaughton, 2018, "How to Theorise about Evil," *Moral Evil in Practical Ethics*, Schlomit Harrosh and Roger Crisp, eds., New York: Routledge, 7–29.

Griswold, Charles L., 2007, *Forgiveness: A Philosophical Exploration*, New York: Cambridge University Press.

Lomax, Eric, 1995, *The Railwayman: A POW's Searing Account of War, Brutality, and Forgiveness*, New York: W.W. Norton.

McGinn, Colin, 1997, *Ethics, Evil, and Fiction*, Oxford: Oxford University Press.

Morton, Adam, 2004, *On Evil*, New York: Routledge.

Murphy, Jeffrie G., 2003, *Getting Even: Forgiveness and Its Limits*, New York: Oxford University Press.

Murphy, Jeffrie G., and Jean Hampton, 1988, *Forgiveness and Mercy*, Cambridge: Cambridge University Press.

Russell, Luke, 2007, "Is Evil Action Qualitatively Distinct from Ordinary Wrongdoing?" *Australasian Journal of Philosophy* 85(4): 659–677.

Russell, Luke, 2014, *Evil: A Philosophical Investigation*, Oxford: Oxford University Press.

Stump, Eleonore, 2004, "Personal Relations and Moral Residue," *History of the Human Sciences* 17: 33–57.

Wiesenthal, Simon, 1997, *The Sunflower: On the Possibilities and Limits of Forgiveness*, New York: Schocken.

10

Forgiveness, Self-Respect, and Humility

Margaret R. Holmgren

I have argued elsewhere that it is always appropriate and desirable from a moral point of view for the victim of wrongdoing who has sufficiently completed a process of addressing the wrong to forgive her offender, regardless of whether the offender repents and regardless of what she has done or suffered (Holmgren 2012, 2014). While I firmly believe that unconditional genuine forgiveness is the morally appropriate response to wrongdoing—the response that we should ultimately strive to attain—I also want to acknowledge that it can often be very difficult to forgive one's offender in cases of serious wrongdoing.[1] The victim who manages to forgive her offender under these circumstances exhibits a number of important virtues.

This chapter examines some of the virtues that enable the injured person to address the wrong and forgive her offender. Arguably several virtues come into play when we forgive an offender who has perpetrated a serious wrong against us, but in this chapter I will focus on the virtues of self-respect and humility. These two virtues may seem initially to be opposed to each other, or at least to pull in opposite directions. I argue, to the contrary, that they are fully compatible with one another, and that each has an important role to play in reaching a state of unconditional genuine forgiveness. However, it is important that each of these virtues be understood properly. In what follows I develop a position on how these virtues should be understood in the context of responding to wrongdoing.

In the following discussion it will be important to have a clear understanding of virtue. Given space constraints, I will simply explain without supporting arguments the conception of virtue that I will use in this chapter and acknowledge that any fault in this conception may well undermine the

---

[1] Here it should be noted that by endorsing unconditional forgiveness, I am endorsing the position that the moral appropriateness of forgiveness does not depend on the *offender* meeting any conditions. As I suggest later, the victim of wrongdoing may have work to do before she is ready to forgive her offender. I thank Brandon Warmke for drawing my attention to this point.

Margaret R. Holmgren, *Forgiveness, Self-Respect, and Humility* In: *Forgiveness and Its Moral Dimensions*. Edited by: Brandon Warmke, Dana Kay Nelkin, and Michael McKenna, Oxford University Press. © Oxford University Press 2021. DOI: 10.1093/oso/9780190602147.003.0010

line of argument I develop. Virtues, as I will understand them here, are morally worthy *attitudes* that have been sufficiently ingrained or internalized that they constitute a reasonably regular response to a given type of recurring situation. Attitudes, again as I will understand them here, have three components: a cognitive component, an affective component, and a motivational component. The cognitive component of an attitude consists of the recognition of the morally salient features of the kind of situation under consideration and of their importance relative to one another. It is the cognitive component of an attitude that is pivotal in determining whether or not the attitude is morally appropriate. The affective component of an attitude consists of the emotional response that accompanies the awareness contained in the cognitive component. And the motivational component consists of a desire to see the situation resolved in a particular manner. In the absence of specific contravening considerations, this desire will typically result in behavior designed to bring about this result. In the case of a morally appropriate attitude, the three components will be in harmony with one another. We will fully appreciate the morally salient features of the situation we are considering, and our emotions and motivations will respond appropriately.

The understanding of resentment and forgiveness that I adopt in this chapter is based on this analysis of attitudes. Let us first consider resentment. The cognitive component of an attitude of resentment typically includes the recognition that another individual has wrongfully harmed us (or someone close to us), that this individual is a moral agent who could have and should have done otherwise, and that he is now responsible for addressing the wrong. The affective component of this attitude consists of a feeling of moral anger, with which we are all familiar. Given that an attitude of resentment responds to situations in which an individual has violated a *moral requirement*, the motivational component associated with it takes on the character of a *demand* that the wrong be acknowledged and addressed. This demand is enforced with at least a temporary limitation of good will (and in some cases with more severe consequences). Strawson describes this attitude in the following passage: "Indignation, disapprobation, like resentment, tend to inhibit or at least limit our goodwill towards the object of these attitudes, tend to promote at least partial and temporary withdrawal of goodwill; they do so in proportion as they are strong; and their strength is in general proportioned to what is felt to be the magnitude of the injury and to the degree to which the agent's will is identified with, or indifferent to, it. (These, of course, are not contingent connections)" (1982: 77).

An attitude of forgiveness, as I will understand it here, involves overcoming an initial attitude of resentment toward the offender and replacing it with an attitude of respect, compassion, and real goodwill. When we adopt the attitudes of respect and compassion toward the offender, we of course recognize that his actions and attitudes were wrong, that he is a moral agent who could have and should have done otherwise, and that he is now responsible for addressing the wrong. However, the cognitive components of these attitudes recognize other features of the offender as being *even more salient* from a moral point of view. In adopting an attitude of compassion, we recognize that the offender is a sentient being who is capable of experiencing happiness or misery and who, like us, very much wants to be happy. We further recognize that like us, he is subject to various needs, pressures, and confusions, and is vulnerable to error. And when we adopt an attitude of respect toward the offender, we recognize that he is a person with a moral status and intrinsic worth equal to our own, and that he has the same capacity for moral choice, growth, and awareness that we have. We are all familiar with the feelings that constitute the affective components of the attitudes of compassion and respect. The motivational components of these attitudes converge in a desire that things go well for the offender. With compassion, we want the offender to be relieved of suffering and established in a state of happiness. With respect, we want him to flourish in his personal and moral development. We have an attitude of real goodwill toward the offender when we hold the attitudes of respect and compassion combined. In this case we desire for the offender's life to be as beneficial and meaningful as it can be compatible with like opportunities for all.[2] Let us now consider in turn the virtues of self-respect and humility, and the roles that these two virtues play in reaching a state of unconditional genuine forgiveness.

---

[2] The extent to which this desire appropriately results in action will depend extensively on the circumstances. In some cases, an attitude of unconditional genuine forgiveness will simply incorporate respect and compassion for the offender and an internal desire for his life to be as beneficial and meaningful as possible. In other cases it may involve action on the part of the victim, ranging from offering a small amount of aid to the offender to restoring a pre-existing relationship with him (when it is safe and rewarding to do so) in which the two parties interact extensively with one another. A full discussion of this matter is beyond the scope of this chapter.

Self-Respect and Forgiveness

I want to suggest here that there are two kinds of self-respect that are important in the process of addressing the wrong and forgiving one's offender. Both of them are forms of recognition self-respect. Stephen Darwall has distinguished between recognition respect and appraisal respect, identifying recognition respect as the respect we have for an individual in virtue of her basic moral status as a person and identifying appraisal respect as the kind of admiration we extend to an individual in virtue of her positive qualities or achievements (Darwall 1977). Different interpretations of recognition respect are possible. Here I will adopt a broadly Kantian construal of recognition respect as respect for persons as autonomous moral agents who possess equal intrinsic worth and who must be treated as ends in themselves.

Recognition respect for persons as autonomous moral agents has two significant components, which I will refer to as status respect and agency respect.[3] On the one hand, if we respect an individual as an autonomous moral agent, we will respect him as a person with an intrinsic worth and moral status equal to that of every other person, and as an end in himself. I will refer to this form of recognition respect as status respect. On the other hand, if we respect an individual as an autonomous moral agent, we will respect him as an individual who has valuable moral capacities, including the capacity to grasp morally relevant considerations, to deliberate about moral issues, to make moral choices, to assess the worth of various ends that he might pursue, and to develop and inculcate morally worthy attitudes in himself. I will refer to this form of recognition respect as agency respect. For our purposes here, these two forms of respect are coextensive—they are both properly accorded to all moral agents, and are simply correlative aspects of respect for persons as moral agents.[4]

Turning specifically to *self-respect*, status self-respect is the respect we have for ourselves as possessing an intrinsic worth and moral status equal to that of every other person, and agency self-respect is the respect we have for ourselves as possessing our basic moral capacities. Agency self-respect incorporates a more active orientation toward ourselves as moral agents, and

---

[3] It is important to note here that I am using the term "status respect" and a manner that is significantly different from Robin Dillon, who uses the same term to refer to social status (Dillon 2001).

[4] On some accounts of intrinsic worth (e.g., accounts that attribute equal moral status to all sentient beings), status respect will have a broader application than agency respect. We need not worry about this point in a discussion of forgiveness, however, because both wrongdoers and those who deliberate about whether they will forgive their offenders are moral agents.

it may also be described as an important form of self-confidence: a confidence in our abilities to exercise our own moral capacities in an autonomous manner.

Both status self-respect and agency self-respect are important as we attempt to address the wrongs that have been perpetrated against us. Given that it is generally very difficult being the victim of a serious offense, I have suggested that many persons in this position will need to undertake a process of addressing the wrong before they are ready to consider forgiving the offender. I have described this process in some detail elsewhere (Holmgren 2012). Briefly, the individual who has been seriously wronged may have to recover her self-esteem if it has been challenged by the degrading message implicit in the wrong: the message that it is acceptable for the offender to treat her in this manner. She should also recognize that the act perpetrated against her was wrong and understand why it was wrong, and she may need to allow herself to experience whatever reasonable feelings arise for her in connection with the wrong. In addition, she may need to assess her relationship with the offender, and then take the steps that are necessary to honor her own needs for protection and rewarding interpersonal relationships. The victim may also need to express her beliefs and feelings to the offender, and finally, she must decide whether she wants to seek restitution for the harm wrongfully inflicted on her and/or to press criminal charges.

It seems clear that status self-respect will play a crucial role in this process. The injured person must recognize that she has a moral status equal to every other person, that she therefore has certain rights, and that those who violate her rights wrongfully harm her. She must recognize that because of her intrinsic worth, her feelings, needs, and beliefs matter as much as everyone else's. And she must recognize that because of her equal moral status she is entitled to restitution for wrongfully inflicted harm (in the absence of specific contravening considerations). Perhaps less obviously, agency self-respect also plays an important role in the process of addressing the wrong. To successfully complete the process of addressing the wrong, the injured person must have confidence in her basic moral capacity to assess *for herself* both her own worth as a person and the wrongness of the act that was perpetrated against her. She must have confidence in her capacity to experience and assess her own feelings, however intense they may be. She must also have confidence in her capacity to determine what *she* wants or values in her relationships with others, and she must have confidence in her ability to express her moral beliefs and decisions to others. Finally, she must have confidence in her capacity to assess whether it is morally appropriate for her to seek restitution and/or press criminal charges.

Both of these forms of self-respect also have an important role to play in forgiving one's offender after the process of addressing the wrong has been completed. Once the process of addressing the wrong is sufficiently complete, the injured person has done what she needs to do for herself and is in a position to determine whether she wants to attempt to forgive her offender.[5] One of the central arguments that theorists have made for maintaining an attitude of resentment toward a perpetrator of a serious offense who has not acknowledged and repented of his wrong is that an attitude of resentment is required if we are to evince sufficient self-respect. The most compelling form of this argument is that we fail to evince sufficient self-respect in this case by failing to protest the disparaging message implicit in the wrong.[6] Pamela Hieronymi expresses this line of reasoning as follows: "resentment protests a past action that persists as a present threat . . . I suggest that a past action against you . . . makes a claim. It says, in effect, that you can be treated in this way, and that such treatment is acceptable" (2001: 546). By failing to maintain an attitude of resentment toward an unrepentant offender, then, we acquiesce in this wrongful claim.

I have argued in response that in this regard an attitude of resentment actually fails to evince a full measure of self-respect by assigning far too much power and importance to the offender's confused beliefs and too little importance to one's own judgment. The person who has sufficient self-respect will recognize her own worth *for herself.* She will not withhold her self-respect until the offender repents and acknowledges her worth for her. Nor will she engage in a power struggle with the offender in order to get him to acknowledge her worth or to dominate him in some other manner. Rather, she will put the offender's confusion into proper perspective and trust her own assessment of her own worth. It is important to recognize that both status self-respect and agency self-respect are required for the injured person to put the offender's confusion into perspective and to trust her own judgment here. Again most obviously, status self-respect is required: the

---

[5] Given that we have limited control over our feelings, it should be acknowledged that we cannot necessarily decide to forgive the offender, where forgiveness is understood as a genuine change of heart. The best we can do is to decide to attempt to forgive him.

[6] Other arguments that forgiveness is incompatible with the injured person's self-respect center on the claim that by forgiving the offender, the victim fails to evince sufficient respect for her own needs. Arguably, however, the victim who has sufficiently completed the process of addressing the wrong outlined earlier has addressed her own needs in the situation at issue.

injured person must recognize that she has the same moral status that everyone else has and that therefore others are obligated to treat her in a morally appropriate manner. But agency self-respect also plays a crucial role for the injured person at this juncture. She must have a full measure of respect for *her own* moral capacities to assess her own worth, regardless of what the offender, or others, may think.

Agency self-respect will be required in other ways as well if an injured person is to forgive her offender after the process of addressing the wrong is sufficiently complete. The victim of serious wrongdoing who forgives her offender chooses to replace her initial attitude of resentment toward the offender with an attitude of genuine forgiveness, which she has determined to be more worthy from a moral point of view. In doing so, she also chooses to turn her attention away from the fact that the offender wronged her and to focus instead on her own positive pursuits. In order to perform these tasks effectively, the injured person must respect her capacity to determine *for herself* what kind of character traits she finds worthy of cultivating in herself, independent of the various psychological pressures she may experience to maintain an attitude of resentment. She must also respect her moral capacity to decide for herself what she wishes to focus on from this point forward.

Further, and in many cases most importantly, agency self-respect will be required for the victim of serious wrongdoing to rebuild her life after the wrong. Without confidence in her ability to rebuild her life in a worthwhile manner, it will be very difficult (although not impossible) for the injured person to forgive her offender. Some forms of wrongdoing inflict very serious kinds of damage on the victim. For example, a drunk driver who hits a pedestrian may injure this person so severely that she is unable to work or to pursue the passions that meant a great deal to her before the accident. Significant agency self-respect will be required for an injured person to cope with a situation of this sort, in which her life has been greatly altered by the wrong. She must have respect for her own moral capacities to acknowledge and then manage her own emotions (which are likely to be intense), to assess the ends and purposes that she can now pursue in her new circumstances, and to persist through the difficulties that she will encounter as she pursues the ends she has chosen.

Agency self-respect, then, plays a significant role overall for the victim who forgives an offender who has perpetrated a serious wrong against her. Sufficient respect for her basic moral capacities provides the injured person with the confidence she needs to undertake the process of addressing the wrong, to cultivate morally worthy attitudes in herself, and to undertake the process of rebuilding her life in a manner that is truly worthwhile.

In this section I have argued that the virtue of self-respect, in the two forms of status self-respect and agency self-respect, enables the victim of serious wrongdoing to adopt an attitude of unconditional genuine forgiveness toward her offender. Of course, if the injured person is to exhibit unadulterated, genuine virtue in forgiving her offender, it must also be the case that forgiveness is the morally appropriate response to the wrongdoer under the circumstances in question, and further, that the injured person understands forgiveness to be the morally appropriate response. I have argued elsewhere that an attitude of unconditional genuine forgiveness is *always* appropriate and desirable from a moral point of view for the victim who has sufficiently completed the process of addressing the wrong, regardless of whether the offender repents and regardless of what he has done or suffered (Holmgren 2012, 2014). However, given that persons hold different beliefs about the morality of forgiveness, it is important to recognize that a victim of serious wrongdoing may fully respect herself and still decide to maintain an attitude of resentment toward her offender after she has sufficiently completed the process of addressing the wrong. This situation may arise when such a victim honestly believes (mistakenly, in my view) that it is morally appropriate, or even morally required, to maintain an attitude of resentment toward an offender under the circumstances in question (most commonly, when the offender has yet to repent, or when he is guilty of very serious wrongdoing). A victim who fully respects her own moral status and her own moral capacities exhibits no lack of self-respect if, after careful reflection, she comes to a mistaken view about forgiveness (either believing it is justified when it is not or believing it is not justified when it is).[7]

In concluding this section, I want to emphasize that the analysis presented earlier is not intended to disparage or undermine in any way those victims who have not yet forgiven their offenders. In fact, on the analysis I have developed here, the attitudes of respect and compassion that are embedded in an attitude of forgiveness are to be extended to all persons in virtue of their status as moral agents and sentient beings. These attitudes clearly indicate a supportive stance toward victims of wrongdoing, rather than a judgmental stance. As autonomous moral agents, victims have both the right and the responsibility to determine *their own* attitudes toward their offenders, and

[7] I thank Dana Nelkin for drawing my attention to the need to clarify this point.

we must respect them as they do so. Further, given that victims of serious wrongdoing generally experience significant suffering, the virtues of respect and compassion will lead us to offer these persons whatever appropriate and effective forms of support we can provide for them.

Humility and Self-Respect

Let us now turn to the virtue of humility. In the last section, I argued that two forms of recognition self-respect—status self-respect and agency self-respect—play an important role in enabling the victim of serious wrongdoing to forgive her offender. As noted at the outset, the virtues of self-respect and humility may seem initially to be opposed to each other, or at least to pull in opposite directions. In this section, I will outline a broad conception of humility, and argue that on this conception, the virtue of recognition self-respect (as explained earlier) and the virtue of humility are actually fully compatible with one another. In the third section of the chapter, I will examine the role that humility plays in enabling the victim of serious wrongdoing to forgive her offender.

In order to examine the questions at issue in the remainder of the chapter, we will need a clear understanding of the virtue of humility. In the past three decades, a strong body of scholarship has been generated on this virtue. For the purposes of our discussion here, it will be helpful to divide accounts of humility into two general categories, which I will refer to as narrow accounts and broad accounts.[8] These two kinds of accounts differ in their scope. Narrow accounts often use the terms "modesty" and "humility" interchangeably, and focus on either the way in which an individual regards himself in light of his achievements or the way in which he presents himself in social settings in light of his achievements. For example, Owen Flanagan has proposed a "nonoverestimation" account of modesty, in which "the modest person may well have a perfectly accurate sense of her accomplishments and worth, but she does not overestimate them," in spite of an empirically documented human tendency to overestimate one's accomplishments (1990: 424). Michael Ridge writes that a person is modest only if "she is disposed to de-emphasize her accomplishments" in virtue of

---

[8] A similar kind of division is articulated in Nancy Snow's early article on humility (1995) and by a number of other authors as well.

not caring, for morally appropriate reasons, whether others esteem her for her accomplishments or whether she receives everything that she is due in virtue of those accomplishments (2000: 281). He adds that this lack of caring must be for the right kinds of reasons. And Ty Ratterman writes that the modest person "takes the fact that she is so good to be, in many settings, and for the appropriate reasons, bad to harp on or flaunt" (2006: 228), where "to flaunt is to force or impose oneself without warrant or request, to display ostentatiously or imprudently" (2006: 229).

While several of the narrow accounts of humility are very insightful, for our purposes here we will need to adopt an account of this virtue that is wider in its scope. More specifically, we will need what I will refer to as a broad account of humility: an account of humility that focuses on a proper estimation of the importance of the self in relation to other beings, entities, or states of affairs that are of value in the world. Joseph Kupfer articulates a broad conception of humility as follows: "Humility inclines us to respect and appreciate what is objectively valuable in the world apart from ourselves" (2003: 256–257).[9] This is basically the conception of humility that I wish to endorse, although an important component of the argument I want to make here is that an attitude of humility does not conflict in any way with status self-respect or agency self-respect, as I have defined them earlier. Specifically, then, I will understand the virtue of humility as follows. The cognitive component of an attitude of humility incorporates the accurate recognition of the intrinsic worth of the self; an accurate recognition of the intrinsic worth of other beings, entities, and states of affairs outside of the self; and, in particular, an accurate recognition of the importance of these values in relation to one another. The affective component of an attitude of humility includes feelings with which we are all familiar. Perhaps we can identify these feelings most easily when we call to mind an instance in which we reach the kind of perspective outlined in the cognitive component, after struggling with an attitude in which we place excessive importance on the self. As we adopt an attitude of humility, we experience the feeling of being much more grounded in a proper perspective on what is important, all things considered. We also experience a sense of freedom, having been liberated from the pressures that result from overestimating our own importance, and we feel a kind of openness and expansion that results when we focus on what is truly of value

---

[9] For some other examples of a broad conception of humility, see Snow (1995), Flanagan (1990), and Roberts (2009).

outside of ourselves. Finally, the motivational component of an attitude of humility is again clearly explained by Kupfer. He writes that "People with humility . . . are motivated to work to promote worthwhile things in the world" (2003: 257).

I think there are a number of reasons to adopt the kind of broad conception of humility articulated earlier. For our purposes here, we can note that the broad conception, if it succeeds generally in explaining our intuitions or providing a persuasive reason to revise them, has more explanatory power than a narrow conception. If this broad conception of humility is successful, it will not only ground an adequate account of modesty, it will also illuminate other areas of our moral thought. In this case our conception of humility will be less likely to be ad hoc, or an accidental generalization of our considered moral judgments, and we will therefore be more warranted in accepting it. I will leave it to the reader to judge at the end of the chapter how well this account of humility illuminates the area of response to wrongdoing.

At this point in our discussion, it is important to recognize that both status self-respect and agency self-respect are fully compatible with the virtue of humility, as it has been explained earlier. Let us first consider status self-respect. At least for those of us who accept the broadly Kantian conception of recognition respect articulated earlier, status self-respect is based on the accurate recognition that we have an intrinsic worth and moral status equal to that of every other person. In recognizing our equal moral status with others, we do not exaggerate our own importance relative to other people. We simply recognize that we, like the billions of other people on the planet, have an intrinsic worth equal to others and should be treated as ends in ourselves. We also recognize that like billions of other people on the planet, we have a moral status as sentient beings who want very much to be happy. Therefore, others ought to take our happiness into account on this basis. It should be recognized that there are states of affairs that may well have more intrinsic value than we do as moral agents and sentient beings. For example, at this time preserving the planet in a condition that is habitable by future generations of human beings and a multitude of other species is of paramount importance, and this end may require significant sacrifices from some of us. However, recognizing our own intrinsic value as moral agents and sentient beings need not and should not conflict in any way with recognizing that some states of affairs may be more morally significant than we are.

The argument for the compatibility of agency self-respect and humility is equally clear. Agency self-respect is based on the accurate recognition that our basic moral capacities are valuable and warrant respect. In respecting our own capacities for moral agency, we recognize that we have both the ability and the responsibility to exercise our moral capacities in an autonomous manner. Further, if we truly respect our moral capacities, we will work to develop these capacities—our capacity to grasp morally relevant consider- ations, to deliberate about moral issues, to make moral choices, to assess the worth of various ends that we might pursue, and to develop and inculcate morally worthy attitudes in ourselves. In adopting an attitude of agency self- respect, we in no way exaggerate our own importance in relation to other beings or states of affairs. Indeed, it can be argued that if we do not respect our own capacities for moral agency, we are likely to *fail* to respect suffi- ciently the moral importance of other beings and states of affairs. Respect for our own moral capacities gives us the confidence we need to develop those capacities, and it is just through developing those capacities that we come to appreciate the true value of other beings, entities, and states of affairs outside of ourselves. If my reasoning here has been correct, then we can conclude that the virtues of humility and recognition self-respect (which incorporates both status self-respect and agency self-respect) are fully compatible with one another and do not pull us in opposite directions. Let us now consider the roles that the virtue of humility may play in forgiving one's offender.

Humility and Forgiveness

In this section, I will argue that the virtue of humility as I have defined it here will prevent us from adopting a judgmental perspective toward the offender that is often implicit in an attitude of resentment, and it will lead us instead to adopt an attitude of unconditional genuine forgiveness. It is important to recognize at this point that allowing esteem for the self to grow beyond status self-respect and agency self-respect, and into appraisal respect for one's own record of moral performance, may well undermine forgiveness. It is likely enough in the case of serious wrongdoing that the victim will have a record of moral performance that is superior to that of the offender. Here the victim may feel entitled to withdraw from the offender the respect, compassion, and goodwill that she would normally feel toward others, on the grounds that the offender does not deserve them. While she is the kind of person who honors and upholds moral standards, he is not. Until the offender acknowledges the importance of the standards he has violated, he does not warrant the victim's respect, compassion, or goodwill. In this case, the victim adopts what I will refer to as a judgmental perspective toward the offender. It is worth noting that many authors, some of whom are generally sympathetic to forgiveness, have argued that resentment toward an unrepentant wrongdoer who is guilty of very serious wrongdoing may be justified on these grounds—resentment expresses a deserved, negative judgment of the offender's seriously deficient moral character.[10]

It seems clear that the virtue of humility has more than one role to play in countering the tendency to resent the offender based on such an unfavorable judgment. I want to suggest here that while there are (at least) three *contingent* roles that humility may play in achieving a state of unconditional genuine forgiveness, there is also a fourth role that is not contingent. Let us first consider the contingent relationships between humility and forgiveness.

Several authors have argued that the virtue of humility requires us to fully acknowledge the role of moral luck in our moral performance. For example, Jeffrie Murphy writes that "our excellences are often to some degree a function of good luck, and our goodness may be at least in part a function of our good luck in never being in circumstances that present irresistible temptations to evil" (2017: 25). This point is undeniably significant in the domain of response to wrongdoing. It seems clear that the victim of wrongdoing who is fully mindful of the role of moral luck in her own record of moral performance will often be less likely to adopt a judgmental stance toward the offender. She is likely to be both more humble and more forgiving as she reflects on the fact that she may have been much more fortunate than the offender—both in encountering circumstances favorable to her moral development and in not encountering circumstances likely to challenge her moral resolve severely. However, although the virtue of humility will certainly operate in this manner in a significant number of cases, it is also possible for cases to arise in which the victim of wrongdoing manages to forgive her offender *in spite of* the fact that she has clearly achieved a far superior record of moral performance under much more difficult circumstances than those that he has encountered. The relationship between this particular type of humility and forgiveness is therefore contingent.

A number of authors have also identified an important kind of *epistemic* humility that is likely to render us more forgiving. For example, Murphy and Hampton (1988: Chapter 6) have noted that we must recognize that there

[10] For example, see Smith (1997: 37), North (1998: 27), and Griswold (2007: 64).

are limits to our ability to judge an offender's level of culpability. It is very difficult for us to know what is going on for another person internally, and it is therefore often not clear that we are adequately situated to pass judgment on the offender's moral performance. Again, this is an important point, but as Murphy and Hampton respond, there will be cases in which we *can* clearly identify an individual's moral performance as deficient. If Murphy and Hampton's latter observation is correct, then the relationship between this kind of humility and forgiveness will again be contingent.

Finally, Garrard and McNaughton have written that "as a group, as a species, we are morally pretty unimpressive; the human nature that we have in common includes some very dreadful propensities" (2003: 54). They add that this is not "a purely biological claim, but one about sharing a common psychology" (2003: 54n18). These authors hold, then, that reflection on the dreadful propensities in our shared human psychology should create in us a kind of solidarity with even an unrepentant offender, and that this solidarity can justify an attitude of unconditional genuine forgiveness.

It certainly makes sense that reflection on the dreadful tendencies in our shared human psychology will make us more humble than we would be without this reflection, and less inclined to judge the offender negatively. And this heightened reluctance to judge the offender negatively should then make us more forgiving. However, while these authors have identified an important factor that will no doubt tend to make us both more humble and more forgiving, the connection between this kind of humility and forgiveness is again contingent. There are clearly individuals who do not have dreadful tendencies, and who are very capable of forgiving those of us who do—for example, the Dalai Lama and Mother Teresa. Dreadful tendencies may be part of the general human condition, but they can be greatly reduced or eliminated with sufficient moral development. While the Dalai Lama, for example, has clearly forgiven his offenders (some of whom were unrepentant and guilty of extremely serious wrongdoing), he has done so for reasons other than those identified by Garrard and McNaughton.

I want to argue here that humility has a role to play in forgiveness that is not contingent. Rather than simply limiting the judgments we make of the offender in light of his past moral performance, genuine humility will prevent us from adopting a judgmental perspective toward the offender to begin with. To adopt a judgmental perspective toward another person is to attach too much importance and status to ourselves and to fail to recognize what is of great importance outside of ourselves, in a manner that is damaging and destructive.

To see this point, let us begin by considering the attitude of unconditional genuine forgiveness. When we hold this attitude toward the offender, we extend toward him the attitudes of respect, compassion, and real goodwill regardless of whether he repents and regardless of what he has done or suffered. I have already discussed here the importance of status self-respect and agency self-respect for the victim of serious wrongdoing. These forms of self-respect respond to both the intrinsic value of the victim and to the importance of her moral capacities. As I have noted earlier, this focus on the self is vitally important for the victim as she works through the process of addressing the wrong and considers whether she can forgive her offender without acquiescing in his implicit claim that it is acceptable to treat her in this manner. However, once these processes are sufficiently complete, an attitude of genuine humility is also needed if the victim is to transcend the focus on herself and recognize the value of other persons and states of affairs in the world.

The victim who adopts the attitude of humility as described earlier will appreciate that while her own moral and personal development is very important, equally so is everyone else's. (Recall that the cognitive component of this attitude incorporates an accurate recognition of the intrinsic worth of the self; an accurate recognition of the intrinsic worth of other beings, entities, and states of affairs outside of the self; and, in particular, an accurate recognition of the importance of these values in relation to one another. Recognition of the equal importance of all persons' moral development is therefore entailed by an attitude of humility, at least within the Kantian framework adopted here.) In adopting an attitude of humility, the victim will recognize that the offender has an intrinsic worth and moral status that is just the same as her own, and that he has the same basic moral capacities that she values in herself. In this case she will adopt the attitudes of status respect and agency respect toward the offender, just as she has adopted these attitudes toward herself. Accordingly, she will come to recognize and appreciate the intrinsic importance of the offender's personal and moral development. Whether or not he has yet acknowledged and repented of his wrong, and whether or not the attitudes he holds at this time are morally appropriate, she will recognize that it is important for him to acquire morally appropriate attitudes in the future, to address the wrongs he has committed in the past, and to go on to develop himself as fully as possible as a person with valuable moral capacities. She will then genuinely hope for him to achieve these things.

Further, as she transcends the focus on herself that was necessary as she completed the process of addressing the wrong, the victim who adopts an attitude of humility will recognize that the offender is, like herself, a sentient being who very much wants to be happy and to be relieved of his suffering. She will recognize that the offender's happiness has value, just as her own happiness has value, and she will genuinely desire for him to be happy. Overall, then, she will extend to the offender the attitudes of respect, compassion, and goodwill that constitute the attitude of unconditional genuine forgiveness.

It is important to emphasize here that the *virtue of humility* is what enables the injured person to transcend the focus on herself and to fully appreciate the intrinsic importance of the offender's personal and moral development. It is also important to emphasize that a full appreciation of the value of the offender's personal and moral development will lead the injured person to adopt a perspective of support and goodwill toward the offender, rather than the judgmental perspective toward the offender described earlier. If she truly recognizes and appreciates the importance of the offender's moral development, the injured person will not withdraw her goodwill from him. These two stances are intrinsically incompatible. A full appreciation of the intrinsic value of the offender's moral development will necessarily result in a positive stance toward the offender's moral development. Resentment, retribution, contempt, and in general, any response that involves a withdrawal or limitation of goodwill toward the offender will evince a lack of appreciation for the intrinsic importance of his moral flourishing.

It is also worth noting that on an intuitive level, when we adopt a perspective of judgment, we seem to adopt a status that is not rightfully ours—a status that attributes too much importance to ourselves. This point is perhaps seen most easily outside of the context of response to wrongdoing, when we simply imagine approaching any other person and saying, "Now I will judge you based on your current attitudes and your past moral performance." There is nothing special about ourselves that entitles us to adopt such a position, and it seems incompatible with the virtue of humility to think that there is. If we truly possess the virtue of humility, we will see others as equals. We will recognize that just as we are autonomous in and responsible for our own moral development, others are as well. And we will see others as persons like us who want to be happy and who have valuable moral capacities that it is important for them to develop. Rather than adopting a judgmental perspective toward others, then, we will want to do what we can, motivated by respect, compassion, and real goodwill, to support their happiness and their personal and moral flourishing.

If my reasoning here has been correct, then a person who attains an attitude of genuine humility will not adopt a judgmental toward the offender in the first place, and will therefore not resent him on the grounds that he does not deserve her forgiveness. Rather, she will simply regard the offender with respect, compassion, and goodwill, thereby adopting toward him an attitude of unconditional genuine forgiveness. It seems to me that this connection between humility and forgiveness is not contingent.

I want to emphasize that in rejecting the judgmental perspective described earlier, I am not rejecting all forms of judgment. I am simply rejecting a form of judgment that involves an orientation toward another human being that is incompatible with a recognition of the moral importance of his personal and moral flourishing—a perspective from which we might decide that the offender does not deserve our forgiveness or goodwill, or that he deserves to suffer. There are several kinds of judgments that we can endorse without adopting this kind of negative orientation toward the offender. First, as mentioned earlier, it is important for the victim (and for everyone else) to understand that the actions and attitudes involved in the offense were wrong. However, we can clearly recognize the wrongful actions and attitudes of others without withdrawing our (recognition) respect, compassion, and goodwill from these persons.

Second, it is clearly important for the victim (and others) to make judgments about the offender's trustworthiness. The victim of domestic abuse, for example, must determine whether her partner can be trusted not to repeat his offense, or she will jeopardize her personal safety. But again, she can make this kind of judgment without withdrawing her recognition respect, compassion, and goodwill for this individual. She can regard him with respect and compassion and wish the best for him at the same time that she decides to terminate her relationship with him.

Third, it is clearly important for us to make judgments about persons as we carry out our personal and social relationships. For example, we may choose not to cultivate a friendship with an individual who is highly prone to criticizing others, and we may choose not to hire a candidate who has demonstrated himself to be significantly dishonest. If we do not make judgments of this sort, the quality of our personal and communal relationships will be significantly diminished. However, once again, it is clear that we can make these kinds of judgments at the same time that we regard the persons we are assessing with recognition respect and compassion, and wish for their personal and moral development.

And finally, we must make decisions about how to allocate burdens and benefits among individuals in our political institutions. I have argued elsewhere that we should make such decisions in reference to a justice-based moral principle that enjoins us to secure for each individual the most significant interests in life compatible with like benefits for all, and that one of the significant interests we have in life is making the most of our lives through our own choices and efforts (Holmgren 2012). In this case we will make judgments about who is guilty or innocent in criminal cases, who should be held liable for making restitution in civil cases, and so on. But again, in making these judgments our orientation toward offenders will not be one of judging who does and who does not deserve our respect, compassion, and goodwill. Instead, we can extend respect, compassion, and goodwill to everyone, offenders included, at the same time that we reluctantly conclude that we must impose burdens on offenders in order to prevent even greater burdens from falling on others. Our aim here is simply to secure for each person the most fundamental benefits in life compatible with like benefits for all.

Of course, a victim who adopts an attitude of humility as described earlier must also consider whether there is any transcendent value in adopting a judgmental perspective toward her offender, such that a continuing attitude of resentment toward him may be morally appropriate. In this case an attitude of resentment would be either compatible with or required by an attitude of humility. Personally, I am unable to find anything of transcendent value in adopting this perspective. Several authors have argued that an attitude of resentment toward unrepentant offenders is required if we are to evince a proper respect for or allegiance to our moral standards. I have argued elsewhere that this argument fails (Holmgren 2012, 2014). We can maintain our allegiance to our moral standards and condemn and oppose wrong *actions* at the same time that we regard offenders *as persons* with respect, compassion, and real goodwill.

Perhaps most significantly, many authors have also argued that we must resent unrepentant offenders who are guilty of significant wrongdoing if we are to respect them as autonomous moral agents who are the authors of their own choices.[11] Again, I have argued that this argument is fallacious

---

[11] For example, see Haber (1991).

(Holmgren 2012, 2014). Although these authors point out that an attitude of resentment presupposes that we recognize the offender as a moral agent, they fail to show that we *respect* him as such by adopting an attitude of resentment. An act of torture undeniably presupposes that we recognize the individual we are torturing as a sentient being, but we certainly do not respect him as a sentient being by torturing him, nor do we behave in a morally appropriate manner toward him by doing so. More argumentation is clearly required to show that beyond simply recognizing that the offender is a moral agent, we actually respect his value as such when we adopt an attitude of resentment toward him. I fail to see how such an argument could be constructed.

Finally, as with self-respect, we should recognize that a victim of serious wrongdoing may sincerely possess an attitude of humility and at the same time choose to continue to resent her offender. This situation will occur when the victim believes (again mistakenly, in my view) that there *is* a transcendent value in maintaining an attitude of resentment, such that an attitude of resentment would be fully compatible with the virtue of humility. And as before, I want to emphasize that my purpose in this chapter is not to disparage the victim of wrongdoing who chooses not to forgive her offender. Not only is it very difficult to forgive one's offender in cases of serious wrongdoing, it is also very difficult to discern the appropriate attitude to adopt toward one's offender. I am simply suggesting here that as we strive to determine the morally appropriate attitude to adopt toward offenders, we consider the conception of humility described earlier and the connection I have tried to draw between this attitude and an attitude of unconditional genuine forgiveness.[12]

Before concluding the discussion in this section of the chapter, I want to suggest that the virtue of humility has one more significant role to play in enabling the victim to forgive her offender. It seems that an attitude of genuine humility would also be of great value *psychologically* to the victim of serious wrongdoing who seeks to forgive her offender. The victim who sufficiently completes the process of addressing the wrong and who adopts an attitude of humility is able to transcend the focus on herself and to recognize and appreciate that which is of value in the world beyond herself. In doing so she connects herself with all of the tremendous richness and value in the world beyond the wrong that was committed against her. She can then explore the many potential sources of meaning, fulfillment, and delight in her life. Empirical evidence would be required to validate this claim, but it stands

---

[12] Again, I thank Dana Nelkin for urging me to clarify this point.

to reason that the more the victim is able to immerse herself in the value that exists in her life beyond the wrong, the easier it will be for her forgive her offender. In this case although she will certainly recognize that the offense committed against her was wrong, her attention will no longer be dominated by the wrong, nor will she be tempted to dwell on the offender with an attitude of resentment.

To summarize, I have argued in this chapter that the virtues of self-respect and humility, as they have been understood here, each have an important role to play in the process of forgiving an offender who is guilty of serious wrongdoing. The victim of wrongdoing who reaches a state of unconditional genuine forgiveness exhibits both of these important virtues. Further, these two virtues are fully compatible with one another and do not pull us in opposite directions. Self-respect, understood in terms of the conceptions of status self-respect and agency self-respect articulated earlier, is important both in the process of addressing the wrong and in adopting an attitude of forgiveness once this process is sufficiently complete. Humility is the virtue that ensures that the injured person will fully respect the offender as a moral agent and sentient being, and that she will fully appreciate the intrinsic importance of his personal and moral development. If my arguments are correct, then these two virtues, when properly understood and fully developed, will consistently support an attitude of unconditional genuine forgiveness.[13]

References

Darwall, Stephen L. 1977. "Two Kinds of Respect." *Ethics* 88, 34–49.

Dillon, Robin. 2001. "Self-Forgiveness and Self-Respect." *Ethics* 112, 53–83.

Flanagan, Owen. 1990. "Virtue and Ignorance." *The Journal of Philosophy* 87, 420–428.

Garrard, Eve, and David McNaughton. 2003. "In Defense of Unconditional Forgiveness." *Proceedings of the Aristotelian Society* 103, 39–60.

Griswold, Charles. 2007. *Forgiveness: A Philosophical Exploration.* Cambridge: Cambridge University Press.

Haber, Joram. 1991. *Forgiveness.* Lanham, MD: Rowman and Littlefield.

Hieronymi, Pamela. 2001. "Articulating an Uncompromising Forgiveness." *Philosophy and Phenomenological Research* 62, 529–555.

Holmgren, Margaret R. 2012. *Forgiveness and Retribution: Responding to Wrongdoing.* Cambridge: Cambridge University Press.

[13] I would like to thank both Dana Nelkin and Brandon Warmke for their unusually careful and insightful comments on this chapter. The chapter has been significantly improved as a result of their philosophical acumen.

232 MARGARET R. HOLMGREN

Holmgren, Margaret R. 2014. "A Moral Assessment of Strawson's Retributive Reactive Attitudes," in *Oxford Studies in Agency and Responsibility*, Volume 2, edited by David Shoemaker and Neal A. Tognazzini. Oxford: Oxford University Press, 165–186.

Kupfer, Joseph. 2003. "The Moral Perspective of Humility." *Pacific Philosophical Quarterly* 84, 249–269.

Murphy, Jeffrie G. 2017. "Humility as a Moral Virtue," in *Handbook of Humility: Theory, Research, and Applications*, edited by Everett L. Worthington Jr., Don E. Davis, and Joshua N. Hook. New York: Routledge, Taylor & Francis Group, 19–32.

Murphy, Jeffrie G., and Jean Hampton. 1988. *Forgiveness and Mercy*. Cambridge: Cambridge University Press.

North, Joanna. 1998. "The 'Ideal' of Forgiveness: A Philosopher's Exploration," in *Exploring Forgiveness*, edited by Robert D. Enright and Joanna North. Madison: University of Wisconsin Press, 15–35.

Ratterman, Ty. 2006. "On Modesty: Being Good and Knowing It without Flaunting It." *American Philosophical Quarterly* 43, 221–234.

Ridge, Michael. 2000. "Modesty as a Virtue." *American Philosophical Quarterly* 37, 269–283.

Roberts, Robert C. 2009. "The Vice of Pride." *Faith and Philosophy* 26, 119–133.

Smith, Tara. 1997. "Tolerance and Forgiveness: Virtues or Vices?" *Journal of Applied Philosophy* 14, 31–41.

Snow, Nancy. 1995. "Humility." *Journal of Value Inquiry* 29, 203–216.

Strawson, P. F. 1982. "On Freedom and Resentment." *Proceedings of the British Academy* 48 (1962): 1–25. Reprinted in Gary Watson, ed. (1982), *Free Will* (Oxford: Oxford University Press), 19–36.

11

Forgiveness as a Virtue of Universal Love

Christine Swanton

Introduction

For Kant, forgiveness is a duty of virtue which he describes thus:

> It is . . . a duty of virtue not only to refrain from repaying another's enmity with hatred out of mere revenge but also not even to call upon the judge of the world for vengeance, partly because a human being has enough guilt of his own to be greatly in need of pardon and partly, and indeed especially, because no punishment, no matter from whom it comes, may be inflicted out of hatred.—It is therefore a duty of human beings to be *forgiving* (*placabilitas*). But this must not be confused with meek toleration of wrongs (*mitis iniuriarum patentia*), renunciation of rigorous means (*rigorosa*) for preventing the recurrence of wrongs by others; for then a human being would be throwing away his rights and letting others trample on them, and so would violate his duty to himself. (Kant 1996: 208)

What is a duty *of virtue*? And in particular what is it to think of forgiveness as a duty of virtue? Broadly speaking, a duty of virtue inherits in some way properties of the relevant virtue. As the quote suggests, in the case of forgiveness, this involves many things: acts from what Kant calls the incentive of love which prohibits acting from hatred or enmity, acting in a way commensurate with self-love and not from "meek toleration of wrongs," and not acting from a sense of superiority. The topic of this chapter is the nature of forgiveness as a virtue and as an expression or manifestation of that virtue. To express a virtue in action will be understood as acting from a state of virtue while aiming at the targets of that virtue; to manifest a virtue in action will be understood as implying some degree of success in attaining those targets.

This virtue-centered approach to forgiveness must be distinguished from contemporary orthodox treatments which think of forgiveness as a

Christine Swanton, *Forgiveness as a Virtue of Universal Love* In: *Forgiveness and Its Moral Dimensions*. Edited by: Brandon Warmke, Dana Kay Nelkin, and Michael McKenna, Oxford University Press. © Oxford University Press 2021. DOI: 10.1093/oso/9780190602147.003.0011

communicative act which according to Warmke (2016) essentially alters the norms of interaction between forgiver and wrongdoer. Such acts (paradigmatically utterances along the lines of "I forgive you") may or may not express or manifest the virtue of forgiveness: they are not seen as essentially duties *of virtue*. The essential or central properties of such acts as communicative acts are a matter of considerable controversy (Pettigrove 2012; Warmke 2016)— controversies which will not be discussed here. Suffice to say that acts of forgiveness seen as duties of virtue may have different properties from those of acts of forgiveness seen simply as communicative acts. For example, in the former case it is reasonable to think of forswearing resentment as essential to forgiveness, while in the latter case, as Warmke (2016) convincingly argues, this is not so.

If acts of forgiveness are seen as duties of virtue, we need to understand the nature of the virtue of forgiveness (called by Roberts [1995] "forgivingness"), and that presupposes a view about the nature of virtue in general. A virtue will be understood in the classic Aristotelian way as (in its best manifestations) an excellence of character embracing excellence in motivational and emotional states, practical wisdom, and excellence in action. This conception of virtue is very demanding, which motivates a view of virtue as a *satis* or threshold concept (Swanton 2003; Russell 2009) such that one has a virtue if one possesses it to a sufficient degree.

What kind of virtue is forgiveness? For Kant, forgiveness is a virtue of love by contrast with virtues of respect. Following Kant, I will think of forgiveness as one of the several virtues of *universal* love. Others are patience, kindness, being merciful, and being gracious, and notably for Kant, beneficence. Notice, too, that the virtue of forgiveness is not simply having a loving forgiving nature, because that disposition may not have to a sufficient degree the hallmarks of excellence. The nature of duties of virtue is constrained by the nature of the virtue. As we have seen, for Kant there are several such constraints, but in this chapter I shall focus mainly on the most controversial of Kant's conditions: the idea that forgiveness is a virtue of universal and unconditional love.[1]

In explicating this view, three broad questions are addressed:

(1) How can forgiveness be seen as a virtue of *love*, and in particular a virtue of universal love?

---

[1] The other conditions are discussed in Swanton (2011).

(2) How can forgiveness be seen as a virtue of love which is distinct from another of Kant's virtues of universal love—beneficence? In what does the difference consist?

(3) What is the relation between forgiveness as a virtue, and processes and acts of forgiveness?

The first question is the topic of the second section; the second the topic of the third section; and the third is addressed in the fourth section. In answering these questions I align myself with Kant, but my primary purpose is not to explicate Kant but to provide answers to the three questions specified earlier.

Much of the literature on forgiveness is devoted to answering questions about what counts as forgiveness in the case of actions, and what is necessary for forgiving actions to be required of one, or to be appropriate. For example, is it necessary that one be personally wronged for forgiveness to be appropriate? My primary focus is not on these issues, but rather on some puzzles about the *virtue* of forgiveness that Kant's understanding of virtues of universal love has introduced. These puzzles and their resolutions inform my answers to the three broad questions posed earlier.

Forgiveness and Universal Love

Our first question is: How can beneficence, forgiveness, grace, and so on all be seen as virtues of universal love? First, what in general is a virtue of love? We can speak of love itself as a virtue: a person with that virtue has excellent loving dispositions in general. However, there are many forms of love. Love as a virtue, then, is the most general name for a group of virtue types which we may call virtues of love. The types correspond to forms of love. A well-known taxonomy is that of C. S. Lewis (1977); what he calls the four loves of Affection, Friendship, Eros, and Charity. Each of these types admits of several specific virtues. For example, the virtues of affection include those of blood ties such as parental love and filial piety, and merit-based forms of love such as admiration and worship.[2] Friendship admits of, for example, Aristotle's typology of virtue, pleasure, and utility friendship. Charity (agape or universal

---

[2] It is not being claimed here that all manifestations of admiration or filial piety involve or even should involve affection. Rather, affection (as opposed to friendship or eros) is a characteristic manifestation of love in these cases.

love) is also a virtue type having more specific forms such as grace, human kindness, forgiveness, and gratitude. Universal love itself as a disposition is a preparedness to be, for example, gracious, forgiving, merciful, and grateful to *anyone* where appropriate, and a manifesting of that preparedness, to assignable individuals, as appropriate. Such love is not to be withheld on the basis of lack of virtue or other merits in the object of love, including lack of remorsefulness; unattractiveness of that object; lack of affection for that object; or absence of partialistic bonds. It is both universal and unconditional.

Why should the "Four Loves" count as love, and why in particular should universal love be thought of as a form of love? Much depends on what one takes to be the core concept of love. Theorists about the nature of love focus on a variety of features or criteria of love which they deem essential or important to love. Here is a list of at least many of these features.

(1) An indefinable kind of emotion or passion that is pleasurable (Hume)
(2) Compassionate concern for and benevolence toward another (Fisher[3])
(3) Forms of "coming close" to another (as opposed to respect, which is a "keeping distance") (Kant)
(4) Attachment or bond between individuals (cf. attachment theory in psychology)
(5) A passion for union or fusion of some sort (Soble,[4] Aquinas)
(6) A form of appreciation of another as an individual (Velleman)
(7) A form of openness to another (Levinas)
(8) Seeing the beloved as good (Pettigrove)

I do not argue that this list of criteria of love is either complete or accurate, but the list is long enough to illustrate the wide variety of features which theorists have deemed necessary, sufficient, or central to love. Theorists disagree about which putative criteria are genuine criteria and about their relative importance. Some of these criteria are broader than others. For Kant, love as coming close is not a passion for union; and it does not necessarily

---

[3] Fisher 1990. For Fisher, the defining feature of love is a "humble benevolence" "the desire that that the other person obtains what she desires" for her own sake and not for the lover's (20). For criticism see Hamilton 2006: 250.

[4] Alan Soble, "The Unity of Romantic Love," in *Sex Love and Friendship: Studies of the Society for the Philosophy of Sex and Love 1977–1992* (Amsterdam: Rodopi: Value Inquiry Book Series, 1997). This feature Soble claims is essential and central to romantic love, whereas Aquinas regards it as essential and central to all forms of love. See Hamilton for a critique of Soble's view.

involve affection. It is also weaker than a bond since benevolence/benefi-
cence for Kant is a form of coming close, but it need not involve a bond. Nor
does the idea of a bond with another entail a passion for union: an adult off-
spring may have a strong bond with a parent yet lead a very independent life.

I shall not in this chapter argue for a position on the nature of love. What
seems to be true and noteworthy, however, is that different virtues of love,
even those of universal love, focus on some criteria rather than others. As
noted, beneficence if seen as a virtue of universal love merely requires in
Kant's terms a "coming close"; it does not require a bond, let alone a passion
for union. I shall argue, however, that forgiveness as a virtue of universal love
requires more than this; it requires specific kinds of excellence in bonding
(bonds of humanity). Other virtues of love such as parental and filial love
also involve excellence in attachment or bonds of various types. Virtues of
romantic love may characteristically involve passion for union as a background emotional orientation, but I doubt that it requires seeing the other as
good. Nor do I think that the affections of pleasure friendship require this.[5]

We are now in a position to answer our question: How can beneficence,
forgiveness, grace, and so on all be seen as virtues of love? Kant provides
an answer. This answer lies in Kant's idea of love as a broad "moral force"
contrasted with respect. The two moral forces (respect and love) are
described thus:

> In speaking of laws of duty (not laws of nature) and, among these, of laws
> for human beings' external relations with one another, we consider our-
> selves in a moral (intelligible) world where, by analogy with the physical
> world, attraction and repulsion bind together rational beings (on earth).
> The principle of *mutual love* admonishes them constantly to come closer to
> one another; that of the *respect* they owe one another, to keep themselves at
> a distance from one another; and should one of these great moral forces fail,
> "then nothingness (immorality), with gaping throat, would drink up the
> whole kingdom of (moral) beings like a drop of water" if I may use Haller's
> words but in a different reference. (Kant 1996: 198–199)

The virtues of universal love—kindness, patience, beneficence, and so on—
are virtues of love insofar as they all enjoin forms of coming close as opposed

---

[5] Pettigrove defends his view that love involves seeing the beloved as good against Frankfurt's view
to the contrary 77ff. I do not assess these arguments here.

to the keeping distance of respect. There are many forms of emotional and physical coming close dependent on the type of love: for example, the closeness of sharing and social connection in friendship, the closeness of coming to someone's aid with compassion, the closeness of comforting, the intimate closeness of romantic love, the closeness of acts of kindness to a lonely individual, the closeness of forgiving someone in resuming some form of relationship, and the closeness of human connection in the patience shown to a stranger in trying circumstances.

But how can some virtues of love be seen as virtues of *universal* love? The notion of universal love is on the face of it problematic. Love is thought to be essentially partialistic, since it involves some sort of connection to individuals in their particularity. It is not love of humanity as such. Given the particularity requirement, it is thought that love cannot be universal: one cannot love all. However, the kind of coming close involved in universal love is not a love of attraction or a partialistic love; rather, it is what Kant calls "practical love," which must be extended universally. As dispositions of universal love, the various virtues of universal love are forms of preparedness to "come close" in ways that are proper to those distinctive virtues. As a virtue of universal love, forgiveness is understood as a preparedness to extend forgiveness, as a form of (universal) love, in an excellent way appropriate to forgiveness as a virtue.

How can love be both universal and particularistic? Universal love is universal in the sense that it is a *preparedness* to come close (on Kant's analysis) to *any* individual regardless of affections, delight, or pleasure the person brings, or regardless of her personal merits or partialistic relations to one. It is particular in that it requires an actual connection to a specific individual—(on Kant's view, for example) a coming close to that individual—appropriate to the forms of love as the situation demands. What is the nature of the preparedness? Insofar as the virtues of universal love are virtues of character, they require that this preparedness have emotional and motivational features. It is not just a preparedness to act in ways which satisfy the conditions of forgiveness as a communicative act (whatever these may be). At the emotional core of this preparedness is a background emotional orientation to the world at large, one that is loving. Of course, what this involves is dependent on the form of love; but as a minimum, it requires openness and receptivity to the other, a well-wishing, and some degree of warmth as opposed to coolness, indifference, aloofness. This background orientation is what Heidegger (1962) calls a *Grundstimmung* (fundamental emotional attunement). Such attunements are ways of emotionally construing the world as a whole in a fundamental way. A loving *Grundstimmung* is an emotional orientation opposed to the many that inhibit both our openness to the other and our coming close through exercising the various virtues of universal love. These inhibiting fundamental emotional attunements include hate, anger, profound boredom, pathological fear, shyness, self-centeredness, and arrogant pride.

Forgiveness, Love, and Beneficence

For Kant, as we have seen, both forgiveness and beneficence are virtues of universal love where love is understood very broadly as a coming close. I shall accept this position, but deny that forgiveness should be understood as a species of beneficence. We turn then to our second question: How can forgiveness be seen as a virtue of love which is distinct from another of Kant's virtues of universal love—beneficence? In short, why cannot forgiveness be understood as one of the virtues of universal beneficence? To see why not, we first need to consider what Kant says about the duty of virtue of beneficence. The virtue of beneficence fundamentally requires that one treat others' nonimmoral ends as one's own and that one act in a beneficent way for the other's sake appropriately. More specifically Kant says:

> I ought to sacrifice a part of my welfare to others without hope of return because this is a duty, and it is impossible to assign specific limits to the extent of this sacrifice. How far it should extend depends, in large part, on what each person's true needs are in view of his sensibilities, and it must be left to each to decide this for himself. . . . Hence, this duty is only a wide one; the duty has in it a latitude for doing more or less, and no specific limits can be assigned to what should be done. (Kant 1996: 393)

The claim that "no specific limits can be assigned to what should be done" does not mean that beneficence is everywhere optional; rather, Kant is claiming that specific limits cannot be described in advance by a maxim or principle of action. The reason for the latitude in beneficence is that it is rationalized by features of the objects of potential beneficence, their needs and what is good for them. Thus, one is beneficent for reasons (the unmet needs of individuals), but it is impossible for a given agent to respond to all the reasons that favor beneficence (it is impossible for an individual to respond to all the unmet needs in the world). Since one cannot act on all of these reasons, there is latitude concerning on which reasons one acts, as Kant claims. In the love of forgiveness, things are quite otherwise. Reasons of forgiveness applying to one (and the nature of these is controversial) are all reasons on which one should act in some appropriate way. (How, when, and in what way one should act is a question discussed in the fourth section). In that sense, forgiveness has no latitude.

If the love of forgiveness operates in a quite different way from Kant's broad "coming close" notion of the love of beneficence (call this love in the broad sense), we need to examine the nature of this distinctive notion of love. Forgiveness on my view is not a virtue of beneficence (a desire for another's good which manifests paradigmatically in helping; promoting welfare) for it is a virtue of relationship conforming to criterion (4) of love. It involves an attachment or bond between individuals. (Call this love in the narrow sense.) To show that forgiveness is not a virtue of beneficence but a virtue of love in the narrow sense, love in this sense and beneficence must be distinguished. Both beneficence and forgiveness are virtues of love in the broad sense of criterion (3), but on Hume's analysis sketched later beneficence need not conform to criterion (4) of love.

A philosopher who well recognized the profound difference between the "passion" of what he called benevolence and the passion of love is David Hume, in the *Treatise of Human Nature*. Here he distinguishes between benevolence as a "direct passion" and love as an "indirect passion." Benevolence is a "direct" passion, being simply the desire for the good of another and arising "immediately from good or evil, from pain or pleasure" (T 2.1.2.4/ 276). In particular, the good from which the passion of benevolence "arises" is the welfare of another. By contrast, for Hume love depends for its existence on the "conjunction of other qualities" (T 2.1.2.4/ 276). The relation between cause and object of love is indirect: the cause of love, for example, is an attractive or valuable property of an individual which is then associated with the individual possessing the property (the object of love) (see T 2.2.9.12/ 385). What is loved, then, is not the pleasurable property which initially causes the love. Rather, by an imaginative process, the "fancy" will "carry its view" to the property's possessor: one acquires a different passion (love) for the object of love (T 2.2.5.5/ 359). In this way, as Frankfurt argues (see later), love is not essentially a form of valuing someone on the basis of her valuable properties or those of the relationship, but is rather constituted by an attachment or bond

to an individual brought about by triggering properties such as blood relationship or the virtue or beauty of the beloved. These properties initiate or
trigger the imaginative processes which result in the bonds of love. Because
love is essentially a bond with a specific individual, it may survive the loss
of the attractive or valuable property or properties initially causing the love,
and one does not automatically love anyone who possesses the same property or combination of properties.

In the case of forgiveness, as in the case of love in general where properties of the beloved and the relationship can trigger the bonds of love, actual-
izing the preparedness to forgive, that is, initiating the process of forgiving,
is not necessarily within one's voluntary control. This should not be surprising: the bonds of love for one's infant are triggered by its birth; the bonds
of friendship-love can be triggered by a chance conversation. This triggering
is not constituted by recognizing reasons which rationalize the triggering of
the process of bonding. (We say more about this later.) As Frankfurt claims,
"circumstances of one's experience and character" such as chance meetings
can make forgiveness possible, in possibly quite dramatic ways, kick-starting
the process of forgiveness even in the case of enemies. Once the triggering has
occurred, the bonds of humanity and other types of bond (such as restored
collegiality or hitherto unthinkable friendship) can then develop. In the most
serious cases of hard-to-forgive actions, the triggering events result in what
Griswold (2007: 79) calls "recognition of shared humanity," or in less serious
cases of, for example, collegial enmity resulting from collegial wrongs, the
recognition of not only shared humanity but shared collegiality. This recognition initiates the imaginative process that is completed in a bond (possibly
restored) of agapic and potentially other forms of love. These bonds, which
are more or less powerful, in turn facilitate the process of forgiveness.

As Griswold describes, a life event, a meeting where they "weep, dine, con-
verse together" (77), allows the mortal enemies Achilles and Priam to recognize their shared humanity. Here "each is reminded by the other of loved
ones"; they "participate in analogous webs of human attachment"; and there
are analogous ties of concern, of misery, of rootedness in and love of one's
homeland (77). This recognition initiates an imaginative emotional process of bonding which in turn facilitates forgiveness. Griswold also cites
the case of a tortured prisoner of war, Lomax, whose experience of meeting
and subsequent forgiveness turned the object of forgiveness "from a hated
enemy, with whom friendship would have been unthinkable into a blood-
brother" (97).

The fundamental reason, then, that forgiveness should be seen as a virtue of universal love in the narrow sense as opposed to a form of universal benevolence is that forgiveness is a virtue of relationship involving a bond. A major point of forgiveness is that in appropriate contexts, in appropriate ways, and at appropriate times one restores relationship. This does not entail that the same relationship must be restored: trust, for example, may be broken so that one may no longer be able to employ a person who has stolen from you or live with someone who is abusing you. One may justifiably believe the transgression is expressive of character so that one needs to protect oneself from future transgressions.[6]

This fact is important and has implications for the analysis of forgiveness, casting doubt on some views such as that of Russell (2016). According to him, forgiveness involves an absence of a "behaviourally adversarial position" toward the one forgiven, and such a stance may be manifested in a "deliberate avoidance of the perpetrator" and a "refusal to act in a trusting way towards a perpetrator who thinks he ought to be trusted" (Russell 2016: 711). Russell is correct in thinking that from the perspective of the transgressor, the victim may not have forgiven; and he is also correct in thinking that some forms of avoidance, for example, show that forgiveness has indeed not taken place. My problem is the definition of *forgiveness* in terms of absence of "behaviourally adversarial position" since not only may such a position be justified but it is compatible with the restoration or strengthening of the bonds of humanity necessitated by manifesting the virtue of forgiveness as a form of universal love.

The relationship that is restored or strengthened essentially in forgiveness is the bonds of humanity, a foundation of universal love. Notice that this does not mean that only those with the virtue of universal love can forgive: communicative acts of forgiveness can still occur. As noted earlier, I am speaking of forgiveness as a duty of virtue where forgiveness is understood as an expression or manifestation of a virtue. As such, forgiveness is not just a commitment to see the other in benevolent terms; it involves something more, an openness to the restoration or strengthening of a bond that has been compromised or destroyed, or the formation of a new bond, whether a bond of collegiality, a bond of friendship, a neighborly bond, or a marriage bond, and where this is impossible or undesirable at least a bond of humanity. No

---

[6] See Pettigrove 2012 on the relation between forgiving transgressions and the perpetrator's character.

longer do you see the forgiven person as merely an enemy, as subhuman or barely human, as an "animal," an evil monster, and so forth. What is involved in the bonds of humanity is highly contextually dependent and variable. It does, however, essentially involve a positive attitude such as good will and positive behavioral dispositions (such as where appropriate the relinquishing of an adversarial stance) toward the transgressor (Russell 2016), and not just the forswearing of negative attitudes such resentment.[7]

Forgiveness as a Manifestation of Virtue

This section focuses on the last of our questions posed in the Introduction. This is question (3): How is forgiveness as a virtue related to processes and acts of forgiveness? In order to answer this question we need to know in more detail what it is for the virtue of forgiveness to be manifested. It is commonplace in our act-focused ethics to think of virtue as manifested in action. We might think, therefore, that duties of the virtue of forgiveness are *acts* of forgiveness (whatever these may be). However, a virtue V may be manifested in other ways—in particular, by working through processes, emotional and behavioral, which may or may not terminate in what one may call V-acts (acts of forgiveness, say). Thus, for example, a virtuous manifestation of the virtue of forgiveness need not be a virtuous act of forgiveness. Notice that Kant claims in the passage on forgiveness cited earlier that we have a duty to be "forgiving," which involves for him having attitudes constituting what he calls the incentive of love to be contrasted with, for example, "meek toleration of wrongs."

Processes of forgiveness manifesting the virtue of forgiveness may be attempts (possibly anguished) in seeing the transgressor as human like oneself, moderating anger, not wishing the wrongdoer unspeakable harm, and so on. During this process we may become forgiving and that in turn may result in specific acts of forgiveness. What is required by the virtue of forgiveness is initiating and progressing (even through fits and starts) the work of forgiveness, where forgiveness is hard, or where immediate acts of forgiveness may be inappropriate or shallow. As mentioned earlier, successful termination of this process may not be within one's voluntary control: the right triggering events for the needed transformation simply may not occur.

---

[7] See Russell 2016 for further discussion on the necessity of positive dispositions for forgiveness.

In short, the analysis of forgiveness as a virtue should be distinguished from that of acts of forgiveness such as the performative utterance "I forgive you." An important point is that actions expressing the virtue of forgiveness are not simply performative actions such as "I forgive you"; they have to express or work toward expressing agapic love in the narrow sense, in ways distinctive of forgiveness.

What is distinctive of forgiveness as a virtue of universal love in the narrow sense? Forgiveness does not simply involve having a loving orientation; rather, it is characteristically constituted by a retrieval of such an orientation after it has been disrupted by anger subsequent to certain sorts of wrongdoing. Hence, the virtue of forgiveness has anger within its field or domain of concern; more specifically, the point of the virtue of forgiveness is the restoration or strengthening of bonds with the transgressor compromised in the face of anger or resentment at wrong done by him to you or to those with whom you identify. In the more noble cases of forgiving, there may be an admirable failure to have the angry orientation in the first place when such an orientation would be expected.[8]

Let us now look at the nature of the virtue of forgiveness in more detail. A very useful structure for assessing the nature of a virtue is provided by Aristotle's notion of the mean. In virtuous action Aristotle says a virtuous agent aims at the mean[9] and exhibits wisdom in doing so, although she may not necessarily attain it. We may call the mean aimed at the target of the virtue. The mean itself is constituted by rightness or correctness in relation to both feeling and action. In the case of action the mean is constituted by acting in the right manner, for the right reasons or motives, in relation to the right objects, in the right circumstances, to the right extent, at the right times, and with the right instruments (Aristotle 1976: e.g., 1106b 18–23).

We may call an action right even though that action does not attain the target of the relevant virtue(s) to an optimal extent on all dimensions of the mean. Theorists differ markedly about which elements of the mean are salient in given circumstances, and which elements are relevant or necessary at

---

[8] According to Roberts, "forgivingness is the disposition to abort one's anger (or altogether to miss getting angry) at persons one takes to have wronged one culpably, by seeing them in the benevolent terms provided by reasons characteristic of forgiving" (1995: 290). Griswold has a stronger position: "If one felt *no* resentment in response to someone's injurious action against oneself, it would make no sense to forgive them for their deed" (2007: 40). Resentment for Griswold is moral anger (2007: 39).

[9] "Virtue aims to hit the mean" (Aristotle 1976: 1106b16–24).

all. For theorists such as W. D. Ross, for example, good motives are not necessary for rightness (as opposed to goodness) of acts at all.

Obviously the idea that right action is action that hits the mean of relevant virtues on relevant dimensions of the mean does not provide a blueprint for action. It is a structure or framework only which alerts us to just how many types of factor are involved in acting rightly. Many of these are routinely neglected such as manner of acting and the instruments deployed in acting. In the remainder of this chapter, I will discuss aspects of the virtue of forgiveness by focusing on several dimensions of the mean of forgiveness as a virtue.

Right Objects

In the extensive literature on forgiveness, there is considerable debate about the objects on which forgiveness is properly bestowed. What kinds of actions is it proper to forgive? For some, it is proper to forgive only those whose actions have wronged the forgiver; for others, one can forgive those whose actions have wronged people other than oneself on the assumption that one has somehow identified with the perpetrators or empathized strongly with their victims. For example, despite hideous wrongs, the wrongdoers are seen as all members of the human race, or European like oneself, or members of one's nation. Or the victims have been children tortured and killed by their caregivers,[10] and one identifies strongly with the children. I shall not in this chapter adjudicate on these issues but have simply for the sake of argument assumed the truth of the latter, more permissive view.

The issue addressed here is the view that forgiveness is unconditional in the sense that one must not exclude anyone from forgiveness based on his deserts understood in various ways. The opposing view (call this the restrictive view) claims that forgiveness is properly bestowed only on those who satisfy certain desert-related conditions such as taking responsibility for their wrong, repudiating the wrong, being regretful or remorseful for having wronged, and where possible communicating that fact to the victim (Griswold 2007: 49–50).

---

[10] Very recently the torture and killing of a three-year-old boy, Moko, in New Zealand by his caregivers so outraged people that very many in several towns and cities were brought out on the streets in forms of protest. It does seem odd to claim that the caregivers' brutality is not a proper object of forgiveness for such people because the child is not their own.

The view that forgiveness is unconditional brings to the fore another puzzle associated with forgiveness. How can forgiveness be unconditional when we might think that forgiveness is conditional on various kinds of deserts of the wrongdoer?

On the view that forgiveness is a virtue of universal love, actions expressing that virtue have to express or work toward expressing agapic love. Now if one were to forgive on the condition that the one who has wronged one has shown remorse or has repented, would the act of forgiveness express a virtue of love? In particular, does one express the virtue of love of forgiveness for reasons, such as the transgressor is deserving of forgiveness? This question raises the general question "Are there reasons for love?" Frankfurt's idea that one does not love for reasons (Frankfurt 2001, 2004, 2006) suggests otherwise. If forgiveness is a virtue of love, and if Frankfurt is right about the nature of love, one does not forgive for the reason that inter alia the person forgiven has somehow deserved it. On the restrictive position, by contrast, forgiveness is not a virtue of love but rather a virtue more akin to desert conceptions of justice.

Frankfurt's position has been criticized, however, so let me try to defend it. Criticism of his position has been based on confusion about the notion of a reason. Frankfurt, in at least three different places, claims that one does not love *for* reasons by which he means that "love is not the outcome of any process of reasoning." Loving commitments "are not based upon deliberation" and are not "responses to any commands of rationality" (2004: 29). A fortiori love is not bestowed or withheld *for* the reasons of desert or lack of desert. Rather love is "shaped by the circumstances of individual experience and character."[11] This view is completely consistent with the idea that relationships or features of the beloved such as her character and wisdom constitute reasons of love in the sense of an explanation for love,[12] or in the sense that such reasons favor love. In the former of these two latter senses of reason, the reason makes an agent's action intelligible even if she has not acted on the basis of it. In the sense of reason where a reason is a fact that favors an action or an emotion, we can assess the love as fitting, worthy, admirable, virtuous, foolish, and so on. There is no reason for Frankfurt to deny

---

[11] Frankfurt 2001: 7. See also his *Taking Ourselves Seriously and Getting It Right* (Stanford, CA: Stanford University Press, 2006), where he says that loving cannot be "the rationally determined outcome of even an implicit deliberative or evaluative process" (40–41).

[12] See further Silverman 2010: 22.

that love has reasons in either of the latter senses.[13] Frankfurt's position does not imply that forgiveness cannot be assessed as appropriate or inappropriate to the circumstances, for example one's forgiveness may be shallow, insincere, overly quick or overly slow, based on lack of appreciation of the seriousness of the wrong perpetrated, an overestimation of the seriousness of the wrong, or a lack of understanding of surrounding issues and explanations.

One might argue that even if one does not forgive *for* reasons, reasons that favor forgiveness demand that the person forgiven somehow deserve forgiveness as a requirement for forgiveness. This view goes against the nature of love in general. Love is not something that is deserved or undeserved. It may be foolish, unwise, or imprudent because of the lack of, for example, remorse or virtue in the beloved; but desert is not a *condition* of love. If forgiveness that is deemed unmerited can properly be assessed as foolish, we may think that in a particular case the forgiveness is indeed foolish, unwise, or unvirtuous. This is a coherent position, but usually I believe forgiveness in such circumstances is regarded as particularly admirable or noble.

Hume's idea that love is the product of an imaginative process rather a process of reasoning sits well with Frankfurt's view that love is not the outcome of a process of deliberation on the basis of assessing reasons for and against love. This is not to say that the imaginative process leading to the passion of love cannot be assessed as rational or reasonable or otherwise, as I have claimed and as Hume recognizes.[14] Beneficence, by contrast, is essentially a form of responsiveness to a specific property of the object of beneficence, namely another's needs in relation to her good. Love in the narrow sense at issue here is not *essentially* a form of such responsiveness. Nonetheless, as Hume points out, benevolence and love are closely associated.

The duty of forgiveness on this analysis is not discharged by attention to features which make the forgiveness somehow deserved or merited and which rationalize the forgiveness by assessment of reasons on the basis of which one acts. Rather, recognition of the duty is constituted by an ongoing preparedness to forgive *all* who have wronged one or those with whom one identifies and manifestation of the virtue as appropriate in the variety of ways associated with the process of forgiveness.

---

[13] It is thus wrong to claim (as does Silverman 2010: 21) that Frankfurt's position entails that one cannot evaluate love as virtuous or admirable; his view that a person cannot be accused of acting unreasonably if she maintains her love for her child in the face of (justifiable) contempt for that child (for one does not love one's child for reasons) does not have the implication that the love cannot be evaluated.

[14] For further discussion, see Swanton 2015.

Right Manner

The manner of forgiveness must for Kant express the incentive of love; most importantly we cannot forgive in an arrogant or superior manner displaying contempt or hatred or which humiliates the one forgiven. This aspect of what Kant calls the duty of the virtue of forgiveness is crucial for the restoration of bonds that is central to forgiveness as a virtue of love. Attention to the aspect of the mean "right manner" helps to resolve another puzzle of forgiveness: one that also concerns the relation between the virtue of forgiveness and its manifestations. How can it be that even if one has forgiven from a virtuous state, the virtue of forgiveness (on Griswold's view) may not have been fully manifested? This issue shows the importance of manner of forgiveness in the optimal expression of forgiveness, given a plausible view about the nature of the target of the virtue of forgiveness.

Let us first try to understand Griswold's position. When speaking of the ways in which the virtue of forgiveness may be manifested, we must distinguish between the process of forgiveness and acts of forgiveness. Griswold at times speaks of forgiveness as a process that requires completion if it is to be paradigmatically or ideally successful as a process (2007: 42). A similar point applies to Noddings's (1984) analysis of caring as a relationship that is "completed" in the cared-for's appropriate acknowledgment of the one-caring's care. She is not speaking of caring as a virtue in the one-caring: a virtue which may be expressed in exemplary praiseworthy fashion without proper uptake from the cared-for. Indeed, the virtue may be expressed in a particularly admirable way if the cared-for persists in ingratitude and obstructiveness.[15] Similarly on the present analysis of forgiveness as a virtue of love, the virtue of forgiveness may be expressed in a particularly admirable way if the forgiven abjures reconciliation or fails to be remorseful or take responsibility.

Griswold suggests much more controversially that the *virtue* of forgiveness is not fully manifested or not manifested "at its best" unless the ends of the virtue are achieved: "restoration of mutual respect and recognition between the two parties" (2007: 49). He says "the offender depends on the victim in order to be forgiven, and the victim depends on the offender in order to forgive" (49). This feature is "part of the logic of forgiveness," a feature which may render forgiveness "unique amongst the virtues" (49).

---

[15] A good example from real life is given in Pettigrove 2012.

This view is counterintuitive since (we tend to think) a fully virtuous agent should be in control of the exercise of her virtue. Nonetheless several thoughts lend plausibility to Griswold's claim.

(a) Whether or not a virtue is manifested "at its best" depends on whether or not the targets of the virtue are attained.

(b) The target of forgiveness is or centrally includes features that are essentially relational and social. The target is the completion of a process, in an excellent way, in line with the virtue, and the "dyadic character of the process permeates it from start to finish" (48).

(c) Hence, the manner of forgiveness is particularly salient: one must in one's manner of forgiveness facilitate the right response in the one forgiven. For example, one's acts of forgiveness cannot show contempt or one's sense of superiority.

The plausibility of Griswold's position is enhanced if we distinguish between two notions of "virtue at its best": *manifesting* in an optimal way a virtue, and *possessing and exercising* a virtue to an optimal degree. There is plausibility to the claim that one *manifests* a virtue in an optimal way only if one is successful in attaining the target of a virtue; which, if Griswold is right in the case of forgiveness, is completion of the process of forgiveness by, for example, restoration of an appropriate relationship. By contrast, having a virtue at its best requires only that one possess excellent character and, on Aristotle's view, wisdom, but the exercise of these excellences is often insufficient for attaining the targets of a virtue for which cooperation of the world is necessary. Such cooperation may well be beyond the power of the possessor of the virtue.

In short, Griswold's view is plausible on two main assumptions. First, he is speaking of forgiveness as a virtue "at its best," and by this he means *manifesting* in an optimal way a virtue. Second, failure to complete the process of forgiveness (where completion requires suitable uptake of the one forgiven) is compatible with an exercise of a virtue of forgiveness being particularly admirable and praiseworthy.

Finally is acceptance of Griswold's view understood as described earlier compatible with forgiveness being a virtue of universal love? Indeed, it is. Recall that a virtuous agent *aims* at the targets of the virtues whether or not she attains them. The "right objects" of forgiveness may be unrestricted as far as aims are concerned: these objects need not be remorseful or deserving in any way. Though the chances of completion of the process of forgiveness may be relatively slim in these cases, the admirability of the attempt may be high and the rewards great where any success is achieved.

Right Extent

Consideration of the extent of forgiveness raises a question that constitutes a final puzzle: How can forgiveness not have latitude (unlike beneficence which for Kant does have latitude) and yet it is possible (on my view) that one has not acted wrongly if one has failed to forgive someone to whom forgiveness is appropriate? Why, in short, cannot the extent of forgiveness be limited to some degree as Kant claims by the agent's inclinations or "sensibilities" where it is "left to each to decide . . . for himself," and if it cannot be so limited, how can it sometimes not be wrong not to forgive? There are two aspects to this worry; the first of which is dealt with here and the second under "right time."

On the view of forgiveness as a virtue of universal love, we are to forgive (or at least initiate the process of forgiveness) regardless of attractiveness to the agent, connection to her, or the merits of the person forgiven. The process may not be completed in cases where there is lack of merit in the form of repentance or apology, but the virtuous agent does not refrain from starting the process even if there is little expectation of something like reconciliation.

The relation between proper objects of forgiveness and the extent of forgiveness is complex. Assume for the sake of argument that the proper objects of forgiveness include all and only those who have wronged one, or those with whom one identifies (such as one's children). One might assume that given that forgiveness is a duty of virtue, one is required to forgive anyone who is within this category of proper objects of forgiveness. However, in both Kant's ethics and virtue ethics, the relation between duty and required action is much more complex. Let us explore these complexities.

As we have seen, both beneficence and forgiveness are for Kant duties of virtue of love, but the relation between these duties and requirements to perform specific acts of forgiveness and beneficence differ. The latter duty has latitude: we do not have a duty to be prepared to aid all the needy in the world, let alone aid them. The former duty I have claimed does not have latitude. But how can this be so if it is sometimes not wrong to fail to forgive?

It may be thought that because the duty of virtue of forgiveness has no latitude one has a duty to *forgive* all who fall within the scope of the virtue of forgiveness. It may be thought, then, that the general duty of virtue of forgiveness entails that we have a *requirement* to forgive *anyone* who falls within the scope of the virtue.

There is no such entailment. Given that duties of forgiveness (on the Kantian view) attach to the virtue, one has a duty at the very least to conform to virtue if not to act from a virtuous state. However, it does not follow from the fact that something conforms to the duty of virtue that it is required, even if the duty of virtue has no latitude. First, it is conceded that given that the duty of virtue of forgiveness has no latitude, we have a duty of virtue to conform to that virtue in relation to *all* who are proper objects of forgiveness. We cannot pick and choose. But it does not follow that we must actually forgive all. As we have seen, not all things conforming to or expressing a virtue V are V-acts. In particular, it does not follow that we must complete the process of forgiveness in acts of forgiveness.

Second, some V-acts conforming to virtue may be admirable but not required; some may be merely optional; some may be desirable but not required. The view that there is a requirement to forgive all that fall under the general duty of the virtue of forgiveness has plausibility on the assumption that what I shall call "The Simple View" is true. On that view, if according to a duty of virtue it is *best* to A, we are *required* by duty to A. According to Crisp (2013), this is Aristotle's view of the relation between duty and virtue: there is for him no supererogation in Aristotle's ethics. On this view a duty of virtue (a duty to conform to virtue) is a duty to do what is most virtuous, so we are required to behave heroically or in a saintly way when that is the most virtuous action. However, the Simple View, if true at all, may apply only to virtue manifested at its best. Many factors may militate against our discharging the putative duty to forgive all in a complete process of forgiveness of the kind envisioned by Griswold. In given circumstances it may be humanly impossible to forgive, as Griswold concedes, or even to start the process. We may be required only over time to reorient ourselves emotionally so that we might be in a position to offer forgiveness to a given transgressor at a later time. In short, the duty of virtue of forgiveness requires only that we be prepared over an appropriate time to forgive all who fall within the scope of the virtue and to manifest that virtue in processes of forgiveness—emotionally and behaviorally—in a timely manner. As of now, the preparedness and manifestation may require only the enhancement of a capacity to reorient oneself emotionally over time.

The observation that the Simple View, if true at all, applies only to virtue manifested at its best helps take care of Griswold's objection to Garrard and McNaughton's (2003) view of unconditional forgiveness. According to Griswold (2007: 64):

> what their argument fails to register is that as a communicative or bilateral act, "forgiveness" that requires nothing of the offender (putting aside submission to judicially mandated punishment) does communicate to her, as well as everyone else, that she is not being held accountable.

However, the forgiver may believe that it is not up to her to *require* accountability to her or others as opposed to thinking it desirable, a good thing, or to be hoped for. She may think that punishment is the task of the appropriate authorities. She may think that having forgiven or initiated the process of forgiveness, repentance, remorse, even apology may come later with a change of heart, something that may not be within the complete control of either party. In short, given that forgiveness is a manifestation of a virtue of love, Griswold has too strong a view of what the communicative or bilateral act *requires*.

Right Time

There is another aspect to the claim that forgiveness has no latitude and yet it may not be wrong to have failed to forgive. This aspect, as suggested earlier, is the issue of time. Forgiveness is a dynamic virtue whose manifestation is a work in progress, as the phrase "letting go of anger" suggests. Where the perpetrator of a wrong is unrepentant and the wrong is very serious, the work of forgiveness may be difficult and protracted. Aristotle's notion of the mean is apt here: one must let go in the right way, at the right time, and so on. Inasmuch as virtue involves correct emotional states, attaining the mean in relation to emotion may be something not attainable within a lifetime.

The view that forgiveness is not a virtue of beneficence is compatible with the claim that on a particular *occasion* of manifesting the virtue of forgiveness the (relative) benevolent attitude of the forgiver arising from the forswearing of anger and hostility may be the only emotion proper to forgiveness that is evident. In the early stages of the process, the transgressor may still be seen as merely an enemy, but the benevolence extends to no longer wanting the transgressor to suffer and even perhaps to actively wishing him well. The work of love and restoration of some kind of bond may take some time and indeed may never occur in a particular case. As already suggested, the life events that trigger the process of forgiveness proper, events not necessarily aimed at or within one's control, may simply never occur. To say that forgiveness is a virtue of love in the narrow sense on this account is only to say that the *Grundstimmung* at the basis of the preparedness to forgive is a loving emotional orientation to the world at large understood (as applied to forgiveness) in terms of a *preparedness* to bond. It is not to say that any manifestation of the virtue is itself a form of interaction, let alone bonding.

Indeed, the failure to complete the process of forgiveness even over a long period of time may be intelligible, perhaps even fitting in a particular case. The imaginative work required to forgive may be impossible. Consider the following kind of example. A killer has raped, tortured, and murdered one's child. The bond of humanity is broken because he has so seriously wronged one's loved one. This bond is not restored or mended precisely because of the continued construal of the offender as alien, evil, and so forth. However, over time one forgives in the limited sense that as Roberts (1995) puts it, anger is aborted or moderated and one has construed the offender in more benevolent terms: at least one no longer wishes him ill. Perhaps over time a more robust forgiveness may occur. However, upon release, the killer commits crimes at least as heinous. No further more benign shift in construal of the offender can take place: it is psychologically impossible as the original victim relives the murder of her own child and is extremely anguished about the other murdered children. It is still possible that she has the virtue of forgiveness; the preparedness to restore the bonds of humanity through forgiveness may still be present. It is just that for quite intelligible and normatively acceptable reasons it cannot be actualized in this case.

Finally, it may be thought that unconditional forgiveness is incompatible with justified anger and is therefore weak. It may even be thought that Aristotle suggests this, for according to Aristotle, the virtue whose field is anger requires that we be angry on the right occasions, to the right degree, toward the right people, and in the right way. He does not say that the mean state with respect to anger is a disposition of no anger. Yet is not forgiveness a letting go of anger? Indeed, it is, but the letting go need not be complete: anger may merely be moderated. It means that the anger cannot harden into bitterness. Aristotle could still have the correct view of the virtue of "patience," the mean with respect to anger, which supposes that a disposition of inirascibility or imperturbability (where that does not mean simply slowness to anger), is a vice.

The idea that forgiveness is a work in progress suggests that premature acts of forgiveness for which one is not strong enough for those acts to constitute a genuine form of agapic love may be a form of vice. Nietzsche's idea that apparent virtuous behavior may be expressive of weakness suggests that forgiving actions can be the manifestation or expression of vices of lack of self-love where one feels unworthy and even deserving of the wrong done to one; hatred; or contempt. [16] In such cases, as Kant claims, one would not be fulfilling one's duty of *virtue*.

Conclusion

This chapter has discussed forgiveness as a virtue of universal love from the point of view of answering three broad questions:

(1) How can forgiveness be seen as a virtue of *love*, and in particular a virtue of universal love?

(2) How can forgiveness be seen as a virtue of love which is distinct from another of Kant's virtues of universal love—beneficence? In what does the difference consist?

(3) What is the relation between forgiveness as a virtue, and processes and acts of forgiveness?

These questions were addressed with the aim of resolving several associated puzzles. The focus on forgiveness as a virtue of universal love and acts of forgiveness as expressions or manifestations of that virtue is different from orthodox treatments of forgiveness as a communicative or performative act. Hence, I have not entered the many debates about what kind of communicative act is forgiveness, for example whether such acts essentially have declarative force (Warmke 2016), are acts of private commitment, commissive acts (Pettigrove 2012: 12–17), exercises of a normative power, or are simply

---

[16] Nietzsche's views on the role of strength and weakness in virtue (such as his view that compassion is a virtue but pity (which he understands as having certain psychological concomitants of forms of weakness) is a vice are discussed in my *The Virtue Ethics of Nietzsche and Hume*.

acts of forswearing or withdrawing resentment, forswearing blaming, or forswearing punishment.[17]

References

Aristotle. 1976. *The Nicomachean Ethics*. Translated by J. A. K. Thomson and revised by H. Tredennick. New York: Penguin.

Crisp, Roger. 2013. "Supererogation and Virtue." In Mark Timmons, ed., *Normative Ethics*, Vol. 3. Oxford: Oxford University Press, 13–34.

Fisher, Mark. 1990. *Personal Love*. London: Duckworth.

Frankfurt, Harry. 2001. *Some Mysteries of Love*. Lawrence: University of Kansas Press.

Frankfurt, Harry. 2004. *The Reasons of Love*. Princeton, NJ: Princeton University Press.

Frankfurt, Harry. 2006. *Taking Ourselves Seriously and Getting It Right*. Stanford, CA: Stanford University Press.

Garrard, E., and D. McNaughton. 2003. "In Defence of Unconditional Forgiveness." *Proceedings of the Aristotelian Society* 104, 39–60.

Griswold, Charles L. 2007. *Forgiveness: A Philosophical Exploration*. Cambridge: Cambridge University Press.

Hamilton, Richard Paul. 2006. "Love as a Contested Concept." *Journal for the Theory of Social Behaviour* 36, no. 3, 239–254.

Heidegger, Martin. 1962. *Being and Time*. Translated by John Macquarrie and Edward Robinson. London: SCM Press Ltd.

Hume, David. 1968. *A Treatise of Human Nature*. Edited by L. A. Selby-Bigge. Oxford: Clarendon Press.

Hume, David. 2000. *A Treatise of Human Nature*. Edited by David Fate Norton and Mary J. Norton. New York: Oxford University Press.

Kant, Immanuel 1996. *The Metaphysics of Morals*. Edited and translated by Mary Gregor. Cambridge: Cambridge University Press.

Lewis, C. S. 1977. *The Four Loves*. London: Harper Collins.

Noddings, Nel. 1984. *Caring: A Feminine Approach to Ethics and Moral Education*. Berkeley: University of California Press.

Pettigrove, Glen. 2012. *Love and Forgiveness*. Oxford: Oxford University Press.

Roberts, Robert C. 1995. "Forgivingness." *American Philosophical Quarterly* 32, no. 4, 289–306.

Russell, Daniel C. 2009. *Practical Intelligence and the Virtues*. Oxford: Clarendon Press.

Russell, Luke. 2016. "Forgiving While Punishing." *Australasian Journal of Philosophy* 94, no. 4, 704–718.

Silverman, Eric J. 2010. *The Prudence of Love: How Possessing the Virtue of Love Benefits the Lover*. Lanham, MD: Lexington Books.

Soble, Alan. 1997. "The Unity of Romantic Love." In *Sex Love and Friendship: Studies of the Society for the Philosophy of Sex and Love 1977–1992*. Amsterdam: Rodopi: Value Inquiry Book Series, 385–401.

---

[17] Many thanks to Brandon Warmke, Dana Nelkin, and Glen Pettigrove for their very helpful comments on this chapter.

Swanton, Christine. 2011. "Kant's Impartial Virtues of Love." In Lawrence Jost and Julian Wuerth, eds., *Perfecting Virtue: New Essays on Kantian Ethics and Virtue Ethics*. Cambridge: Cambridge University Press, 241–259.

Swanton, Christine. 2015. *The Virtue Ethics of Hume and Nietzsche*. Malden, MA: Wiley Blackwell.

Velleman, J. David. 1999. "Love as a Moral Emotion." *Ethics* 109, 338–374.

Warmke, Brandon. 2016. "The Normative Significance of Forgiveness." *Australasian Journal of Philosophy* 94, no. 4, 687–703.

12

Frailty and Forgiveness

Forgiveness for Humans

Lucy Allais

The central commonplace that I want to insist on is the very great
importance that we attach to the attitudes and intentions towards us
of other human beings, and the great extent to which our personal
feelings and reactions depend upon, or involve, our beliefs about
these attitudes and intentions.

—Strawson 1962: 5

Introduction: A Paradox of Forgiveness

Forgiveness has sometimes been thought to be paradoxical or at least very
puzzling, and many attempts to give an account of forgiveness involve
trying to answer or avoid supposed paradoxes, often by giving up on one of
the competing considerations that seem hard to reconcile.[1] In this chapter
I take seriously both sides of the competing requirements responsible for one
way in which forgiveness seems so puzzling, and I suggest that they bring
out something important about a central way forgiveness functions for us.
I focus on the idea of forgiveness as involving a change of heart and the ways
in which this has been thought to lead to paradox. While it is in fact my view
that this change of heart is central to forgiveness, I do not argue for this here;
rather, my aim is simply to *characterize* a change of heart that could feature in forgiveness in a way that avoids paradox while taking seriously the
considerations that seem to lead to paradox. I present this argument in the

---

[1] See, for example, Atkins (2002); Derrida (2001); Kolnai (1977: 217); Murphy and Hampton
(1988); Calhoun (1992); and Hieronymi (2001).

Lucy Allais, *Frailty and Forgiveness* In: *Forgiveness and Its Moral Dimensions*. Edited by: Brandon Warmke,
Dana Kay Nelkin, and Michael McKenna, Oxford University Press. © Oxford University Press 2021.
DOI: 10.1093/oso/9780190602147.003.0012

context of beginning to develop a Kantian account of what forgiveness is and why we need it. My aim is to use materials from Kant's moral psychology to make sense of forgiveness rather than to analyze the few things he directly says about it. Further, I use these materials to characterize a change of heart rather than to give a Kantian account of reasons to forgive or forgivingness as a virtue.[2]

Not much has been written on forgiveness within the context of Kant's moral philosophy and moral psychology.[3] Kant himself does not say much directly about forgiveness, and it may be that his retributivism, as well as his emphasis on obligation, on autonomy, and on the universality of moral reasons don't, on the face of it, seem fertile ground for a concept like forgiveness, which seems personal, possibly at odds with retributivism, and (arguably) elective. However, I will argue that Kant's account of human frailty and his understanding of the nature of agency are helpful for making sense of forgiveness. The other central (and related) philosophical resource I draw on is P. F. Strawson's famous account of reactive attitudes, which I take to characterize something central to our seeing people as responsible. I take as my starting point his emphasis on "how much we actually mind, *how much it matters to us*, whether the actions of other people—and particularly of some other people—reflect attitudes towards us of goodwill, affection, or esteem on the one hand, or contempt, indifference, or malevolence on the other" (Strawson 1962: 5, my emphasis).

Strawsonian reactive attitudes are *affective* attitudes; they essentially involve feeling. Their targets are persons and they are *reactive* in the sense that they are responses to other persons, specifically, to attitudes other persons express, typically through their actions. As I understand Strawsonian reactive attitudes, it is crucial to their content that, in central cases, they are responses to the good or ill *will* expressed by others in their actions toward us, in the light of a legitimate expectation of a certain amount of good will.[4] When you resent someone, on this view, you affectively see them as having done something they are responsible for and which you were entitled to expect them

---

[2] See Bloser (2018) for an account of the latter.

[3] This seems recently to be changing. See Bloser (2018); Moran (2013); Satne (2016); Sussman (2005); and Ware (2014).

[4] I follow Goldie (2002) in thinking of emotions, and emotion/feeling-involving attitudes, as having content that is both essentially intentional and essentially affective—that is, in rejecting the idea of breaking emotions down into cognitive content with an add-on of nonintentional feeling or affect.

not to do.[5] You see this as reflecting their willing: their willing expresses their responses to requirements of value, including value they wrongly failed to regard. Thus, reactive attitudes are centrally an affective evaluative view of a person's willing; they affectively evaluate a person in the light of the way they expressed good or ill will toward you.[6]

The apparently paradoxical nature of forgiveness, as I understand it, is generated by a conjunction of features often thought to be central to it. First, there are a cluster of ideas with respect to norms of forgiveness: the thought that forgiveness is virtuous, that it can be generous, that it can be in some way like a gift—something that is, at least often and in some way, at the discretion of the victim, and not something the wrongdoer is in a position to demand. Second, there are ideas that seem central to characterizing what forgiveness is: that forgiveness is centrally given for unexcused, unjustified wrongdoing, that it is given without a change in judgment about the wrongdoing (it is not a matter of coming to see that the action was in fact excusable, justifiable, or otherwise acceptable, which are ways of coming to see that there is nothing to forgive), yet it involves a change in which the wrongdoing is somehow no longer "held against" the wrongdoer. Characterizing this change, which is often taken to be a change "of heart" (feeling), is taken by many to be central to understanding forgiveness but also seems puzzling.

One way of putting the apparent paradox is that it seems that when we try to characterize this change, forgiveness always turns out to be either, on the one hand, unnecessary and trivial or, on the other hand, irrational and maybe even impossible. If forgiveness involves ceasing to see a wrong as attaching to a wrongdoer but without changing a judgment about the wrongdoer's culpability and the wrongness of the action, it seems irrational; it seems to involve seeing a person incorrectly. On the other hand, if a change in how you see them is warranted—perhaps they have repented, atoned, and done what is possible to undo the wrong—it seems there is nothing more to be done than recognize this: there is nothing more for forgiveness to do. The idea here is that if we should see people in the way their actions warrant seeing them, forgiveness either involves seeing them in an unwarranted way, or it involves merely recognizing something we ought anyway to recognize, which does not seem virtuous or in any way discretionary. More

---

[5] In my view, this means you see them as having done something you think they could have not done, and therefore you see them as having what Kant calls the causality of freedom.

[6] I develop this in more detail in Allais (2008a, 2008c, 2014).

specifically, forgiveness is often discussed in a context in which a starting point is that that wrongdoing justifies resentment (or other blaming reactive attitudes),[7] so resentment can be justified, warranted, or appropriate.[8] But if wrongdoing warrants resentment and makes it appropriate, then it seems that giving up resentment would be failing to have an appropriate attitude toward the wrongdoer. If, however, the wrongdoer has done what they can to change the situation that makes resentment appropriate, then giving up resentment is simply what is required in order to have appropriate attitudes. This is hard to reconcile with thinking that forgiveness can be something praiseworthy and at least partly discretionary, that makes an important contribution to relationships, and that goes beyond simply accurate calibration as to exactly how much blame people are due. In summary, resentment (and other blaming reactive attitudes) involves an affective view of the wrongdoer; forgiveness involves a change in this affective view. Can we characterize this change in a way that explains what makes it morally and rationally permissible, perhaps praiseworthy, yet without making it generally obligatory?

One way to deal with the paradox of forgiveness is simply to deny that forgiveness centrally involves giving up warranted resentment. There are a few ways this can be done. One is to question whether *resentment* is always at issue with respect to forgiveness. Another way is to see forgiveness as the giving up of *unwarranted* (extreme, vicious, inappropriate) resentment and to see it as compatible with holding on to *warranted* resentment.[9] One

---

[7] Two classic accounts are Jeffrie G. Murphy and Jean Hampton, *Forgiveness and Mercy* (Cambridge: Cambridge University Press, 1988) and Joseph Butler, "Upon Resentment," in *Fifteen Sermons Preached at the Rolls Cathedral* (London: Macmillan and Co., 1913).

[8] One strategy for dissolving the supposed paradox would be simply to hold that the emotions involved in forgiveness don't have intentional content of the sort that could make them in tension with beliefs about culpable wrongdoing. (I simply want the person to stop raging at me, not to change her views about my having done wrong.) I will not discuss this option directly here as it seems that almost all participants in the philosophical debate assume that emotions have content and that this content can be assessed at least as appropriate or inappropriate, proportional or disproportionate.

[9] See Garcia, who argues (presenting this as an interpretation of Butler) that forgiveness does not require that we forswear any resentment, but rather that we resent in the right way, steering between the two extremes of showing insufficient concern for our own well-being by not being resentful enough and having the vices of malice and revenge (Garcia 2011: 2). A related view in the vicinity of this view is to emphasize that saying that emotions can be warranted is not to say that they are obligatory, so the fact that wrongdoing warrants resentment does not mean it makes resentment obligatory and therefore that there is a rational and moral mistake involved in giving up resentment. This is in fact part of the view I will defend, but I think we need to be careful not to get to it too quickly. There are a variety of ways in which some belief or view could be warranted but not obligatory which do not help. Possibilities include that there may be evidence for the view, but you may not have considered this evidence, and it may not be obligatory for you to have considered this evidence, and there may be other evidence that counts against the view. The problem with this is that the question of forgiveness arises when you *have* considered the evidence, and you *do* see it as supporting a particular view of the wrongdoer. Feeling resentful or hurt is not obligatory when it is warranted, but, in my view,

version of this strategy makes forgiveness dependent on apologies and re-morse that demonstrate that a change in attitude is warranted.[10] Yet another strategy is to say that forgiveness is simply something else: such as giving up a demand for punishment, giving up a demand for recompense, or going through a ritual of having an apology stated and accepted, perhaps as part of reconciliation. In contrast to these approaches, my view is that we need to make sense of forgiveness as centrally involving a change of heart in which we give up blaming reactive attitudes that are warranted by unjustified, unex-cused, unacceptable, and culpable wrongdoing. In this chapter, I do not argue against these alternative views, but rather aim to give an account of a change of heart that avoids paradox while doing justice to central features of forgive-ness and its role. My argument is therefore compatible with this change of heart's being merely one part of forgiveness.

My aim is to give an account of a change of heart that involves giving up warranted blaming-reactive attitudes and to say something about the impor-tance of this in our lives. In my view, what is powerful about forgiveness is undermined if we situate it in a context of keeping track of everything the wrongdoer has done in order to calibrate precisely what is his due. In con-trast, I hold that forgiveness involves giving people more than their due. Some further general features of my approach are that I assume that an ac-count of forgiveness should make it plausible that forgiveness is generally a good thing (that forgiveness is generally virtuous) and is something that we need for human relationships. I am assuming that forgiving is, paradigmat-ically, something with respect to which the forgiver has a good deal of dis-cretion and which the wrongdoer is not in a position to demand or assert an entitlement to (though I do not argue that it is never obligatory to forgive). Finally, I assume that this change of heart is to some extent under our con-trol, but this does not mean thinking it is something we can choose to do

forgiveness is centrally at issue when we *do* feel resentful or hurt and this feeling is warranted. (I dis-cuss some of these issues in Allais [2014].)

[10] An extreme example of this is given by Griswold's highly demanding account, according to which the conditions necessary for forgiveness are a series of reasons for giving up resentment, where these are "conditions of a moral nature" which warrant a change in belief (Griswold 2007: 54). He says that "taken together these conditions ensure that in forgiving the offender we have accu-rately targeted that for which the offender is being forgiven, and that we are right to forgive the of-fender for those deeds" (2007: 51). The meeting of these conditions is supposed to justify forgiveness by showing that resentment is no longer warranted. A similar though less demanding account is Hieronymi's argument that apologies can undermine the warrant for resentment and thereby justify forgiveness (Hieronymi 2001: 535–536).

instantly (it may involve undertaking to start a process of change), it doesn't mean that we can always succeed, and it is compatible with being mistaken in thinking we have forgiven and then realizing that we haven't.

It is worth noting that seeing forgiveness as centrally and paradigmatically involving a change of heart (a change in how one affectively sees the wrongdoer) is entirely compatible with seeing the central role of this change in heart in the context of relationships. Warmke and McKenna argue that in what they call exemplar cases forgiveness aims to communicate with the wrongdoer (Warmke and McKenna 2013). In my view, this is compatible with seeing forgiveness as centrally involving a change of heart: it is this change of heart that the person who wants to be forgiven wants to have communicated.[11] This shows that emphasizing a change of heart—focusing on one person's internal feelings rather than actions and interactions—is not inappropriately individualistic.[12] Our affective views of one another in response to our actions are central to what it is to relate to other human beings and how we see one another. Having these reactive responses is part of caring about people, and we care, in particular, about the reactive responses the people we care about have to us.

Why Blame?

As I noted in the previous section, one strategy for avoiding the apparently paradoxical nature of forgiveness questions whether forgiveness involves giving up warranted resentment by arguing that emotions other than resentment could be at issue in forgiveness; I agree with this. It seems to me there are a number of emotions that could be involved when forgiveness is at issue, including, for example, a number of forms of hurt feelings and some forms of disappointment. It may be that the forgiveness literature is too focused on resentment at the cost of other relevant emotions; in this chapter I will focus more on hurt feelings. However, I hold that there is something which

---

[11] Further, seeing a change of heart as central is fully compatible with this having many implications for actions—blaming, resentful, angry, and forgiving feelings all have implications for action. Having committed oneself to undertaking to forgive commits one to certain actions, and having told someone that you have forgiven them commits you to certain actions, including the fact that your account of your feelings should be honest and will be inconsistent with continuing to express blaming feelings.

[12] As is argued by Atkins (2002), who presents an account of forgiveness as a kind of mutual rebuilding of trust and objects that emphasizing an individual change of heart underestimates the importance of mutual reflection in relationships.

resentment and (the relevant forms of) hurt feelings have in common that is central to the emotions at stake with respect to forgiveness: they involve seeing someone as *at fault*. They involve blame. I have previously called them retributive reactive attitudes, but this is potentially misleading as it may suggest a necessary link to punishment or a desire for punishment. I will here call them blaming reactive attitudes. Blaming reactive attitudes involve an affective evaluation of a person's willing that sees this willing as at fault in the way it valued or treated some other person or persons.

Characterizing and understanding the giving up of blaming attitudes requires some account of their point and role. Why should we have blaming attitudes? Martha Nussbaum (2016) has recently argued that anger, forgiveness, and guilt are all morally problematic, and they should rather be replaced by unconditional love. She argues that while anger may involve a correct evaluation of wrong having been done, it is also accompanied with a morally indefensible desire for the wrongdoer to suffer, where this suffering is seen either as payback which will supposedly assuage and compensate for one's own pain or expresses a desire to lower the wrongdoer's relative status in response to a change in status created by the wrong: to take away the humiliation of the first hit (Nussbaum 2016: 5, 15, 24, 25). The desire to make the wrongdoer suffer is always problematic, she argues, because it mistakenly imagines that the suffering of the other would make things better, while in fact this suffering does nothing to undo the harm done or fix anything. The desire for status lowering of the wrongdoer rests, in her view, on distorted values (she says that relative status should not be so important and reveals narcissistic concerns), and she argues that reversing positions through down-ranking does not create equality but rather substitutes one inequality for another (Nussbaum 2016: 15, 29, 31).

Nussbaum also finds forgiveness problematic. She sees it as situated within a viewpoint that starts with anger that is allowed to be appropriate, which she thinks is always a normative mistake. She thinks it reveals a narcissistic focus on the self (Nussbaum 2016: 11). She argues that in what she calls its "transactional" form, which requires apologies, forgiveness requires wrongdoers to grovel and abase themselves, in a way which can itself express payback, and "exhibits a mentality that is all too inquisitorial and disciplinary" (Nussbaum 2016: 10, 11, 33). She argues that it is too backward looking and insufficiently focused on future welfare. And she argues that the forgiveness process is violent toward the self: "[f]orgiveness is an elusive and usually quite temporary prize held out at the end of a traumatic and profoundly intrusive process of self-denigration. . . . To engage in it with another person (playing, in effect, the role of the confessor) intrudes into that person's inner world in a way that is both controlling and potentially violent towards the other person's self" (Nussbaum 2016: 72–73). She says that "[t]he offer of forgiveness, though seemingly so attractive and gracious, all too often displays . . . a list-keeping, inquisitorial mentality that a generous and loving person should eschew" (Nussbaum 2016: 12). Rather than enter into the realm of anger and forgiveness, she argues that we would be better in a realm of unconditional love in which the negative feelings we have toward wrongdoing are confined to grief (a pained recognition of loss which does not take the person as its target) and thoughts about how to make things better (Nussbaum 2016: 47, 48).

In my view, Nussbaum mistakenly sees the pain involved in blaming reactive attitudes as extrinsic, as something separate from the possibly appropriate content of an affective evaluation. This may be easiest to see with guilt. She sees guilt as involving the desire to impose suffering on oneself through mistakenly thinking that this would help or make the situation better, and mistakenly thinking that this is necessary to motivate people to act well (Nussbaum 2016: 130–131). But the reactive attitudes analysis sees guilt as involving pain because guilt essentially *is* a painful recognition of one's being at fault: that one has done wrong. Pain does not come in because of a false belief that inflicting suffering on the self would make things better but because properly grasping one's wrongdoing is intrinsically painful; this is what it is to feel sorry. One is not feeling *sorry* if one is not grasping one's wrongdoing with some pain.

While, on Nussbaum's account, the negative emotions in anger involve the desire to make things even by making the wrongdoer suffer or lowering her status, in my view, blaming reactive attitudes involve an affective appraisal of another's willing—of what their willing expressed about their valuing of some person or persons. If another is genuinely at fault (has expressed ill will) blaming reactive attitudes are ways of registering this and caring about it. To expand on this, I draw on Miranda Fricker's (2014) account of what she calls "communicative blame." Fricker's aim is to explain a central positive role interpersonal blame plays for us, which she argues need not be implicated in the various pathologies of blame that give it a bad name (such as including blaming too much, blaming cynically, blaming inappropriately, blaming when there's no point, etc.).[13] She argues that the basic point of communicating blame to a wrongdoer is to inspire remorse in them, where remorse is

---

[13] She shows how understanding the positive role of blame in fact gives us insight into what is going on in the various ways blaming can go wrong.

understood as "a pained moral perception of the wrong one has done," and where, in the best case, this remorse "effects an increased alignment of the wrongdoer's moral understanding with that of the blamer" and "an increased alignment of too of their motivationally live moral reasons" (Fricker 2014: 3). Here we can see an alternative to Nussbaum's account of a desire for suffering that may be involved in a blaming attitude: the desire can be for the wrong-doer to understand what she has done, where this understanding will be painful.

Appropriate blame, on Fricker's account, requires that the blamed party is in some way at fault—the person has failed with respect to reasonable expectations. As its name suggests, *communicative* blame aims to get the wrongdoer to understand something, and it does this in a way that involves emotions: "[i]n virtue of the fact that Communicative Blame's purpose is to jump-start the uncomprehending and/or uncaring wrongdoer's moral understanding, its proper form is *reasoning with emotional force*" (Fricker 2014: 9). Blame accuses the wrongdoer of fault, with an aim of getting them to understand that they are being blamed, to feel sorry for what they have done: "to see or fully acknowledge the moral significance of what they have done or failed to do" (Fricker 2014: 9). It is therefore, she argues, aimed at promoting greater alignment between the moral understandings of the blamer and the blamee. Blame, as she sees it, can be aimed at a person who already recognizes the reason you want them to recognize and also at one who does not, and in the latter case, if they care about your respect, blame can move them to begin to recognize the reason. Thus, she argues, "at least our paradigm of blame is not an expression of anything bad, but rather aims at bringing the wrongdoer to see things from the wronged party's point of view, thereby enlarging her perception and altering her reasons" (Fricker 2014: 13). Communicative blame, she argues, is therefore essential to "the interpersonal normative energy that perpetually regenerates and develops shared moral consciousness" (Fricker 2014: 3). I would add that this is part of how we help each other to stay sane and caring.

Fricker's account is of blame as an interaction, whereas my focus here is on reactive attitudes as blaming attitudes. The two are distinct: one can communicate blame without feeling anything, and one can have a blaming attitude without communicating it. However, they are also closely related; blaming attitudes frequently are communicated. As I understand them, blaming reactive attitudes have the content that Fricker's communicative blame communicates: seeing someone as at fault, being pained by this, and wanting them to feel sorry (which is an intrinsically painful realization of fault), centrally as part of wanting them to understand, care about, and respect you.[14] On this account, blaming attitudes can be appropriate or warranted: where there is genuinely fault and it would be good for the wrongdoer to feel sorry because this would involve their properly grasping their failure to respond properly to some value. It is not necessary to this account to think that we always ought to feel or always ought to communicate blaming attitudes, even when they are warranted, something Fricker stresses.

On this account, blaming reactive attitudes are central to a participant view in which we care about others' willing toward us. Consider feeling hurt by someone. As I see it, this can be a blaming reactive attitude: it can see the other as being at fault for the way they thought about you or the way they failed to consider you in what they did. Further, insofar as it involves a desire for them to grasp this, it involves wanting something which will be painful for them. But this is not because, as in Nussbaum's account, you want to impose extra suffering on them as payback, but rather because you want them to understand and care about how they disregarded you, and (assuming your judgments of fault are correct) this understanding will be painful to them if they care for you. Being hurt by someone involves a painful view of them (their willing) as having not regarded you in the way you want them to; similarly, recognizing that you have hurt someone involves a painful recognition of the quality of your willing. The apparently vindictive desire for someone who has wronged you to have some pain may therefore not, in fact, be vindictive (though, of course, it could be), but rather may express a desire for recognition (recognition of your value and the way it was disregarded) and concern from the wrongdoer. Wanting someone to recognize that they have hurt you need not involve problematic thoughts of metaphysical payback, it need not involve a desire that they abase themself, and it need not involve thoughts of judgment, superiority, and intolerance (though, of course, it might—there are possible pathologies in the vicinity of all these feelings). Rather, wanting someone to recognize that they have hurt you can simply be wanting them to understand why what they did disregarded you and wanting them to *care* about this.[15] As with Fricker's communicative blame,

---

[14] Here I am concerned only with other-directed blaming attitudes; guilt is a blaming reactive attitude that already involves feeling sorry.

[15] My focus here is on interpersonal blame and hurt, but we can see here how this could transfer to a political case: wanting to change a way in which a group is being disrespected and wanting this to be understood.

the desired outcome is increased understanding, alignment of values, and being known. On this view, never having blaming reactive attitudes to others would involve either never seeing them as responsible or not caring about the quality of their willing toward you.

Consider, in contrast, Nussbaum's suggestion that the only morally un-problematic emotion to feel in response to another's wrongdoing is *grief*, which does not take the *wrongdoer* as its target (and which we should combine with a focus on future-welfare-oriented action). Nussbaum thinks this takes us out of the problematic territory of judging others and wanting to impose suffering on them. In my view, feeling grief but not hurt takes us out of the interpersonal vulnerability involved in *caring* for others and *caring about their caring* for us. One is sad that harm was caused, rather than concerned with the particular other person, the person's willing toward you and your feelings about each other. Rather than being a narcissistic concern with the self, feeling hurt is based on an interactive concern with the other person: it is because you care about the person that you care about their caring for you. As Strawson notes, this is part of what it is to be a *participant* in relationships. If someone you care about has genuinely wrongfully disregarded and failed to care about you, but what you feel is merely a painful registering of loss with no desire for the person to understand your feeling or for the person to understand why you think it wronged you, it seems to me that you have given up on the person's caring for you.[16] Against Nussbaum's concern that blaming attitudes descend into narcissism and isolation, it seems to me that this is more clearly true of feeling only grief and never hurt or other blaming attitudes.[17]

A final note about blame: blame is a backward-looking response to what a person has culpably done, and in this respect might be considered retributive. However, I distinguish this interpersonal emotion response, including the desires for the wrongdoer to have a painful realization of what she has done, from a retributive justification of punishment, and, in particular, state punishment, and see this distinction as crucial to a Kantian account of

---

[16] Note how Nussbaum's description of the role of grief focuses on the self: "[m]oving on without grief means having a disjointed or patchwork life, and so the most important reason for grieving is forward-looking: it draws attention to a very important commitment that should remain embedded in the narrative understanding that a person has of her own life, and communicates to others. It expresses a deep aspect of who that person is" (Nussbaum 2016: 48).

[17] This is, of course, compatible with it sometimes being appropriate to feel grief rather than blame; it seems to me that the most central cases of this will be where one is giving up on a relationship or some aspect of a relationship; thanks to Helga Varden (personal correspondence) for clarifying my thinking on this.

responsibility. On Kant's account, interpersonal blame and legitimate state punishment are importantly separate, grounded in a crucial separation of virtue (what we are obliged to do) from right (what we are entitled to co-ercively impose).[18] Further, my understanding of Kant's retributive view of state punishment follows Ripstein in seeing punishment as fundamentally grounded in its being how the state upholds the law. On this version, punishment should not be understood as an attempt to promote a state of affairs in which happiness and suffering are distributed proportionately to worthiness for happiness and suffering; this is something that the state lacks both an entitlement to impose and sufficient knowledge to impose (since people could behave legally without morally worthy motives). Thus, neither in interpersonal blame nor in state punishment, on this account, is there an extrinsic desire or aim to make the wrongdoer suffer.[19]

Frailty

So far I have defended the importance and possible appropriateness of blaming reactive attitudes. I now want to argue that there are parts of Kant's account of agency that are helpful for understanding what can be involved in overcoming these as well as why the possibility of overcoming them is so important to human life. In previous work I have argued that Kant's contrast between the empirical and the intelligible self, which involves seeing empirical causal explanations as fundamentally different types of explanations from reasons explanations, is helpful to making sense of forgiveness.[20] This distinction (and, as I understand it, Strawson's correlative distinction between what he calls the objective view and the participant view of reasons-responsiveness) is helpful in bringing out part of the content of reactive attitudes: the fact that they involve seeing an action as reflecting the agent's *willing*. This is a crucial difference between participant, reasons-explanations and merely empirical causal explanations, such as making a judgment about the internal causal workings of a car that sees it as liable to break down. Seeing a car as unreliable does not involve seeing this as reflecting on its willing—its

---

[18] It does not follow merely from the fact that someone is morally obliged to do something or from the fact that it would be good for the person to do something that anyone else is entitled to force the person to do it.

[19] This is compatible with there being roles for the communication of blame and anger in social life and in politics.

[20] Allais (2014).

response to value—whereas this is central to the way reactive attitudes see persons.

Elsewhere I have suggested that this difference in the content of empirical and intelligible causal explanations, and the close connection between this and the way the content of reactive attitudes includes a view of the agent as free and responsible, is necessary to explain how we can rationally give up affective evaluations of an agent's willing when they are warranted.[21] If we see actions only as the empirical causal outcomes of complicated empirical causal systems, then there will be a fact of the matter about the kind of causal result this system is likely to lead to in the future. There will be relevant similarities between the way you should form your attitudes to a person who has let you down and the way you should form your attitudes to a car that has let you down. It may be that you have evidence that the internal causal mechanisms of the car that led to the problem was such that it is unlikely to be repeated, in which case you should not form an attitude toward the car that sees it as generally unreliable. It may be, in contrast, that the reasonable thing to think is that what happened was an indication of a flaw which is likely to lead to repeated problems; the rationally supported view of the car is that it is unreliable. It may be that the car was previously unreliable but has now been changed (maybe a mechanic fixed it) in such a way that it used to be reasonable to see it as unreliable, but you should now change your view and see it as reliable. Or it may be that you simply lack evidence in all of these respects and should simply withhold your judgment about how reliable it is. Understanding human agency in terms of this kind of empirical causal explanation is one way in which obsessively conditional accounts of forgiveness, such as that of Griswold, can be understood. In the context of a view of human action which sees it only in terms of empirical causal explanations that are relevantly like those involving the inside of the car, it will be rational to require detailed evidence of a change in internal causal structure—and therefore a change in the outputs it is reasonable to expect—before reevaluating the wrongdoer. And on this view there will be a way of seeing the wrongdoer that is rationally required, and we should simply apportion our judgments to the evidence about their internal causal structures (including in cases where we don't know enough and should withhold judgment).

I have appealed to the idea that participant views involve seeing action in terms of something other than the output of a complex empirical causal

---

[21] Allais (2014).

system, but this is not yet enough to explain why their content should be more optional. After all, I have also argued for the legitimacy of blaming attitudes by arguing that we are entitled to see an action as reflecting an agent's willing; this surely requires thinking that there is a warranted way of seeing the agent's willing or, in Kantian terms, her intelligible self. Kant thinks that we are entitled to take people's actions as reflecting their responses to reasons and to hold them responsible on the basis of their actions, and in fact, our only ways of judging other people's willing are on the basis of their actions.[22] Never taking a person's wrong actions as reflecting badly on their willing would involve failing to see them as responsible and as a person, and it may involve failing to care for them. This might make us wonder why we should not simply fix our affective evaluations of each other by the quality of willing we express in each of our actions, and wonder why we need forgiveness, rather than simply accurate evaluations of each other's willing. I may be an imperfect calculator, navigator, and runner, and liable to do these things badly in many ways. I don't need you to see me as better, in any of these respects, than the evidence of my actions supports seeing me as being. It might be positively harmful to all of us if you do. I suggest that Kant's pessimistic account of the human condition has materials for making sense of why our views of each other's willing are relatively different from these other kinds of abilities.

In Kant's late work *Religion within the Bounds of Mere Reason* (1793; hereafter, *Religion*), he presents a dark account of human agency in which he holds that all of us "even the best" have an innate propensity for evil. He seems to argue that if we take our transgressions seriously, the only evaluation we could make of the structure of our own and other people's willing is that it is not good. This seems to suggest that our evaluations of everyone's willing should be low. He then, as I understand him, presents a view of human willing that enables us to avoid this conclusion—to give a different account of what it is to see a person as good—in the context of making sense of grace. His discussion of grace is based in the first-person perspective of reflecting on one's own transgressions and the idea of God's perspective on a human's life as a whole,[23] but I will suggest that it gives us materials for

---

[22] And our central criterion for holding people responsible involves judging them to have (empirical) cognitive capacities required for understanding reasons which were not interfered with in the circumstances. See Frierson (2014, ch. 5) for a very helpful discussion of Kant's account of the empirical markers of responsibility.

[23] This could, in my view, be developed as an account of self-forgiveness.

making sense of a (secular) account of forgiveness in interpersonal relations.[24] My aim here is not to try to make sense of all of Kant's claims about
what he calls humanity's radical evil; it may be that he has rhetorical concerns
here which are not ours, some of which may be separable from the central
commitments of his practical philosophy.[25] My interest is in how his account
of the frailty of the human condition can help make sense both of what forgiveness is and of why we need it. The important part of Kant's account for
our present purposes is his view of human agents as not simply finite and im-
perfectly rational, but corrupted or deeply and systematically flawed.[26]

There is debate in the literature about Kant's account of the basis of human
evil, as well as the basis of his claim that evil can be known to be universal in
humans.[27] My interest here is in the nature of the flawed agency he attributes
to us rather than his argument for its universality. One of the many seemingly puzzling features of the way Kant presents our propensity to evil is
his saying that I am evil if I recognize the moral law but allow occasional
deviations from it (*Religion* 6: 32); even just *one* deviation is supposed to reveal the evil structure of our willing. In the first stage of evil, which Kant calls
frailty, we recognize moral reasons but are not strong enough to always act
on them (*Religion* 6: 37). It seems strangely harsh to see me as *evil* because
I occasionally get it wrong and am not strong enough to always act on all the
moral reasons I recognize—doesn't this just make me less than perfect, rather
than evil? But Kant thinks that taking our transgressions seriously presents
a view of ourselves which suggests that our willing is fundamentally not

[24] See Sussman (2005) for a fascinating approach to forgiveness in Kant as approached through his
conception of grace.

[25] Allan Wood argues that Kant's aim in this work is to convince his audience of late eighteenth-
century Christians, especially Lutherans in Germany, "that there need be no fundamental conflict
between their religious beliefs and their moral and scientific ones" (Wood 2010: 32).

[26] And which is not simply a function of our sensuous natures and inclinations, but rather is rooted
in our free agency.

[27] On my reading, part of the explanation of this is that we are born into situations in which we
are implicated in injustice and in which there are often no morally untainted options available, and
we develop our moral agency in these conditions, guided by other flawed and problematically situated people. See Allais (2018). Our basic patterns of inclination and interpretation are formed in
imperfect situations which do damage to the health of our capacity to be whole agents in ways that
are not always easy for us to see. Kant thinks that this means that, for humans, the attempt to be
morally better will always be an uphill struggle, requiring constant vigilance and effort. Further, he
sees our flawed agency as inevitably involving self-deception, in a way that means that even our best
efforts at moral improvement may be corrupted and be caught up in vices (such as self-righteousness
and complacency) that it is not possible for us to entirely avoid. As Kant puts it, our flawed natures
corrupt the ground of all maxims (*Religion* 6: 37). See Grenberg (2010); Morgan (2005); Muchnik
(2010); Papish (2018); and Wood (2010) for alternative accounts.

good or well ordered.[28] An important part of making sense of this is seeing that he holds that our wills must be governed by some higher-order commitment. This is not an implausible requirement on agency—to avoid being a Frankfurtian wanton. Kant thinks that at the most fundamental level the metaprinciple governing our willing will be either the moral law or self-love. Crucially, frequently acting in accord with the requirements of morality will not show that the moral law is my metaprinciple, since it is possible that my inclinations frequently line up with the requirements of morality. However, if I occasionally—or even once—act against the moral law, this seems to show that I have not incorporated it into my will as my metaprinciple. This is why occasional transgressions reveal actually badly structured willing in terms of our higher-order commitments.

To illustrate, consider my failure to be a vegetarian. Suppose I recognize that I shouldn't eat factory-farmed meat and decide not to (and possibly congratulate myself on never cooking meat at home) but occasionally order meat in restaurants or eat it at other people's houses. I recognize the moral reason but allow occasional deviations from it. Why do I occasionally eat factory-farmed meat? Not because I will otherwise starve, but because it is sometimes easier or convenient, and I am sometimes in places in which the meat dishes seem appealing. In this case, it seems that the principle I am actually committed to—the principle actually governing my willing—is one of not eating factory-farmed meat so long as I don't have strong inclinations to do so or find it convenient. This is like having a principle of acting in accordance with morality so long as it is reasonably convenient and fits in with what I want to do, and acting against it when this is not the case. In this case, the basic structure or order of my willing is not good. This is precisely what Kant thinks our flawed natures consists in, and he thinks that it can be something that seldom shows up, if we are lucky enough to have inclinations that are frequently in line with what morality requires,[29] just as my having strong

---

[28] See Frierson (2014, ch. 7) for a very interesting and helpful discussion of a Kantian account of weakness of will as involving disunity of the self.

[29] He says: "[t]his is how so many human beings (conscientious in their own estimation) derive their peace of mind when, in the course of actions in which the law was not consulted or at least did not count the most, they just luckily slipped by the evil consequences; and [how they derive] even the fancy that they deserve not to feel guilty of such transgressions as they see others burdened with, without however inquiring whether the credit goes perhaps to good luck, or whether, on the attitude of mind they could well discover within themselves if they just wanted, they would not have practiced similar vices themselves, had they not been kept away from them by impotence, temperament, upbringing, and tempting circumstances of time and place (things which, one and all, cannot be imputed to us). This dishonesty, by which we throw dust in our own eyes and which hinders the establishment in us of a genuine moral disposition, then extends itself also externally, to falsity or

vegetable-oriented inclinations may result in my eating meat very seldom. The worry is that seriously contemplating my failures, even if they are occasional, to act on moral reasons I recognize seems to show that my fundamental commitment is not to doing what morality requires, but rather to doing what morality requires when it is not too difficult or in conflict with self-interest; in other words, it seems to show that my fundamental commitment (the fundamental structure of my willing) is to self-love.[30]

We can make a similar point in the context of having hurt someone in a relationship. Suppose you have disregarded someone you care about and let them down, and this willing of yours has hurt them. You might want them to see that your failure to regard them was justified or excused or not really that bad. But suppose they and you both think it was not justified or excused. Your saying sorry indicates that you see that it was wrong, but it does not change the fact that this is in fact what you willed and it doesn't give them a reason to think of your willing as generally better or more ordered. (As Kant says: "if improvement were a matter of mere wishing, every human being would be good" [*Religion* 6: 51]). Note that they don't have to think badly of you in a general way, or even to think that you are likely to hurt them often; they merely needs to think that there are particular circumstances under which you failed to consider them in a particular way; your willing was not ordered with respect to them as it should have been. Even if you are truly remorseful and feel terrible about what you did, it is not obvious why this should change their evaluation of your willing. Yes, they may say, you get it now, but still, *you* were prepared to do *that* to *me*; why shouldn't I simply keep this in mind in my tracking of your character and your willing?

As we have seen, Kant holds that our willing is structured and in particular that it is fundamentally structured by one of two opposed metaprinciples: the moral law and self-love.[31] However, it seems to me that, as the earlier two examples illustrate, we can also make sense of the same structural account

deception of others. And if this dishonesty is not to be called malice, it nonetheless deserves at least the name of unworthiness" (*Religion* 6: 38).

[30] What exactly it is to have willing structured by the principle of self-love is complex. See Papish (2018) for a helpful account of this (ch. 1), as well as interesting discussion of how the problematic structure of the evil will could involve trying to give both the concerns of morality and those of self-love simultaneous motivational force, in ways that ultimately satisfy neither (ch. 4).

[31] While this may sound like a simplistic opposition, both these have complex content. Having the moral law as metaprinciple means treating the humanity of each other as a constraint on what counts as a reason for action, and what this means will vary. See Papish (2018, ch. 1) for an excellent discussion of the complexity of what is contained in Kant's account of self-love.

with respect to more particular instances of structured willing, such as whether my fundamental commitment is to not eating factory-farmed meat as opposed to eating what I feel most inclined to eat. Thus, I do not think we need Kant's specific account of the opposition between two fundamental metamaxims to make use of his thoughts that our willing must have some structure (some relatively ordered hierarchy of principles) and our actions reveal our priorities and our values. As I see it, in paradigm cases the blaming reactive attitudes relevant to forgiveness are specific and not targeted on the overall structure of your willing: you can be hurt by a particular instance of someone's failure to consider you without seeing the person as overall a bad person. The blaming reactive attitudes are affective evaluations of a person's willing in some specific respect.

Kant's view that occasional transgressions reveal the bad structure of your willing holds only on the assumption that your willing has some order or structure. Neither resentment nor forgiveness would be issues for wantons, since if you were a wanton your inconsistent actions would not reveal the overall structure of your willing, because you would lack one (and arguably would not be a responsible agent). The idea is that if you do have a structured will with higher-order commitments, transgressions reveal that your willing is structured in a bad way. Earlier I suggested that one way of making sense of highly conditional accounts of forgiveness such as Griswold's is in terms of a view of agents as complex empirical causal structures with respect to which we need evidence that they have changed before it is rational to judge that they are likely to produce different kinds of outputs. We can now see another way of making sense of Griswoldian conditions: they can be seen as an attempt to demonstrate that the wrongdoer now really has a properly ordered, good will (with respect to the kind of action in question). This shows why it is appropriate for his conditions to be so demanding—it is not enough simply to be sorry (never mind simply saying sorry) because this doesn't prove that my willing is any different and that I won't act in the same way in similar circumstances in the future. Far from being simply an obscure Kantian commitment, I suggest that the idea that our wills are structured in terms of higher-order commitments that transgressions reveal can explain why forgiveness seems puzzling. The suggestion is that it is because it is natural to think of our willing in terms of this kind of order or structure (higher-order commitments), that it is natural to think that our transgressions reveal something problematic about our willing which could only be reevaluated with serious evidence that the structure of willing has changed, while such evidence would make the rational reevaluation mandatory and/or trivial.

As I understand the Kantian picture of practical reason, the very structure of practical reason makes it central to our making sense of ourselves as agents that we can interpret ourselves as basically good (well-ordered, unified selves). This is because, as I read him, Kant thinks that acting for reasons commits you to seeing what counts as a reason for action as governed by the constraint of respecting the humanity of others. This means that making sense of yourself as an agent, as acting, requires being able to see yourself as committed to recognizing the humanity of others as a higher-order constraint on action—seeing yourself as having an ordered, unified will fundamentally committed to the moral law. The need to interpret yourself as good and ordered is deeply embedded in practical reason. Concern about what our transgressions reveal is therefore deep, and it is unlike recognizing, for example, my limitations as a runner or navigator; it threatens my understanding of myself as an agent and my ability to make sense of myself to myself. Further, as we have seen, Kant takes the human condition to be one in which we all have, to some extent, disordered, fundamentally and structurally flawed selves. In these conditions, it seems like the possibilities open to us are self-deception and despair. This, in my view, is why Kant thinks our flawed agency is characterized by a propensity to moralized self-deception: self-deception enables us to avoid despair by seeing ourselves as better than we are and not taking seriously what our failures really say about our willing. But this undermines our moral agency (it corrupts all maxims). But if self-deception is the only alternative to despair, moral agency seems impossible; Kant thinks that moral hope is a necessary condition of being engaged with morality.

So far, it might seem that the Kantian picture I am sketching makes the problem of forgiveness harder, or at least doesn't help solve it. However, I will suggest that Kant's account of the flawed nature of human agency gives us a way of making sense of what forgiveness is, as well as of why we need it. In response to his account of our flawed nature, Kant brings in the idea of grace, which seems to involve (at least) there being a possible (God's-eye) perspective on our overall willing (our life seen as a whole) from which our flawed strivings can be seen as oriented toward good willing. My suggestion is that this gives us materials to develop a Kantian account of forgiveness, which would be (in some respects) an interpersonal secular version of the kind of possible view on our agency contained in grace.

As I have presented Kant's account of the structure of our willing, it might seem as if there are two ways in which our willing can be ordered. On the one hand, we could be properly ordered moral agents with the moral law as our governing metaprinciple. On the other hand, we could subordinate the moral law to the principle of self-love. As we have seen, Kant thinks our occasional deviations show that we have not made the moral law our metaprinciple: he says that if a human being is good in one part he has in-corporated the moral law into his maxim, but if he had done this he would never act against morality (*Religion* 6: 25–5); this seems to show that we have the latter, evil, structure to our willing. Thus, it might be thought that Kant's view is that the possibilities for moral agents like us are to have one of these two forms of order, and that humans in fact have the latter one. However, it seems to me that Kant in fact holds neither of these two forms of order to be possible for us. Being entirely ordered evil agents is not a possibility because we always recognize the claims of the moral law; being inclined to wrong-doing always involves some incoherence, possibly some inner turmoil, rather than being a form of order. Kant also holds that being well-ordered virtuous agents in the sense of classical virtue theory—agents who do the right thing easily and with pleasure and for whom virtue is not a struggle—is not a pos-sibility for humans in the actual human condition. The ways in which we are systematically flawed mean that the forms of virtue attainable by us will in-volve constant struggle against human frailty, including constant effort not to deceive ourselves. But Kant holds that there is a way for humans to be good, where this involves being in a situation of struggling to improve, a process of "incessant labouring and becoming" (*Religion* 6: 48). Presumably a situ-ation of struggling and laboring toward improvement—which is the way in which goodness is a possibility for humans—is one in which we sometimes deviate from what morality requires. But this is just what he said would show that we are evil. My suggestion is that the way around this apparent tension is to see that the condition of virtue that is possible for us in the actual human condition involves not having a properly or fully ordered self. Human agents are not fixed, determinate characters, but rather messy, only partially unified works in progress, constantly determining themselves by their choices, and therefore, at best, constantly engaged in a struggle of trying to be better, in-cluding a struggle to be honest with themselves.

As I understand Kant's account of grace, the idea is that it is possible for there to be a view of our agency (a God's-eye perspective) from which we can be interpreted as overall oriented to good, despite our failings. My suggestion is that this is possible because we are not fixed, stable characters. Further, we can understand the change of heart involved in forgiveness in a related way. In my view this change of heart involves coming to affectively see someone as better than their wrongdoing indicates them to be: there is an affective evaluation of the wrongdoer that their wrongdoing warrants, and the change of heart in forgiving involves overcoming or ceasing to have this blaming affective evaluation. Though it is far more specific than grace (taking a view of an agent in relation to some specific act rather than an overall character), it is like grace in evaluating the agent as oriented to better willing than their transgressions indicate, where this evaluation is neither rationally ruled out nor mandated. This is the puzzling change of heart we started with. As I see it, there are two parts of Kant's picture that are helpful for making sense of this change of heart.

A crucial part of this picture is the idea that we are always to some extent disordered or not properly unified agents. If we were fully ordered and unified, our transgressions would make an interpretation of us as oriented to the good rationally impermissible; our transgressions would reveal that we have a bad will.[32] This is one side of the worry we started with—that the change of heart forgiveness involves looks irrational. On the other extreme, if we were wantons we would not be responsible agents. But if we are neither fully ordered nor wantons, but flawed agents struggling to get it right (to be oriented toward good), there may be space to interpret us in the light of better willing than our wrongdoing indicates. In my view, it is flawed agents, works in progress, without an entirely fixed and stable character, for whom forgiveness is a live option and a need; this is the context in which forgiveness has an important role. If the possibilities for human agents were the two forms of order with which Kant starts in the *Religion*, then we would either need to be in a position to demonstrate, Griswold-style, that we are now properly ordered or we should be judged on the basis of our worst actions, since these reveal the structure of our will. If becoming the properly ordered, unified agents of virtue theory were an option for us, and we were able to demonstrate this, we would not need forgiveness. However, if the only alternative is that our wrongdoings reveal our actually badly structured willing,

---

[32] See Frierson (2010) for a very helpful discussion of ways in which our assessments of agency are systematically affected by how optimistic or pessimistic a view of this we start with, and how the literature on situationism starts with the optimistic virtue theory view and proves less than what it is sometimes taken to prove if we start with a more pessimistic view.

then forgiveness is never rational.[33] Neither of these possibilities has space for forgiveness. However, if we allow the possibility of systematically flawed, never entirely ordered agents who may be engaged in a constant process of attending to trying to be better-ordered, we have the possibility of seeing a wrong as willed by an agent (a free action for which she is responsible), yet not reflecting a bad structure of their will, without requiring that they be able to prove that they have become properly ordered. On this picture we take seriously a transgression as having revealed a failure of good willing, while interpreting the wrongdoer as oriented to better willing, where this does not require seeing them as having a perfectly ordered will with respect to whatever is at issue, but as being committed to and caring about striving toward or being oriented toward one, while being flawed. This means that we can interpret someone in terms of good willing without evidence that they have a perfectly ordered will or proof that they have changed (which seems to make forgiveness pointless).

Another part of Kant's picture that I think is helpful (and maybe necessary) is something like the distinction between the empirical and the intelligible self (or between empirical causal explanation and reasons explanations),[34] where a crucial part of this is that the intelligible character is not a fixed causal system with a determinate output, but rather, something with respect to which the agent is constantly able to choose and is in fact choosing. It is constantly being renewed and changed in each choice. Our choices reflect what we take as reasons for action, or our responses to value, and our intelligible character is a matter of the structure of our willing: our higher-order orientation to value. Interpreting an agent as acting does not involve working out which of their inclinations was causally dominant but rather what value they chose to respond to: what they chose to take as a reason for willing. An agent's actions reflect their willing, and where we have judged wrongdoing to be culpable, unexcused, unjustified, and unacceptable, we judge them to have displayed bad willing. However, a free agent is someone who permanently has the possibility of choosing better willing.

---

[33] The paradoxical nature of forgiveness can therefore be seen as an antinomy driven by the natural, but false assumption of the human will as properly ordered.

[34] An agent's empirical character can be understood to include their inclinations, dispositions, the kinds of desires they have, their tastes. Just as with their external context, these constitute part of the choice set within which people act (and which make good action harder for some than others, in ways we may not be in a position to know). Our empirical characters are partly something that we are simply landed with, and partly something we are responsible for, since our choices influence how these features of ourselves develop.

This account explains the epistemic possibility of interpreting someone's willing as better than some particular transgression indicated it to be. Kant's concern is with the whole structure of the will (whether it is oriented toward the moral law or self-love), but I think we can make a similar point with respect to particular actions and willings, such as, for example, seeing someone who has hurt you as oriented toward better willing toward you with respect to the kind of thing that hurt you. Suppose that in a close relationship you have hurt someone in a way that was unexcused and unjustified. Your willing was not good. Suppose constructive communicative blame takes place. The person communicates to you their anger or hurt or resentment, because they want you to understand how what you did disregarded them. You do, painfully, understand this. This will involve understanding of each other, as well as, in Fricker's terms, growth in the development of shared personal moral consciousness. Suppose this is enough to enable the person to forgive you.[35] How is it that they are now seeing you? I submit that they need not see you as having demonstrated that you are never going to fail to regard them properly again—as having proved that your willing is now perfectly ordered (in the specific regard at issue). On the contrary, in continuing with you in a relationship they are being willing to open themself again to the possibility that you may fail them again, trusting or hoping that when you do you will care about this. In seeing that you care about having disregarded them, they are seeing you as oriented toward regarding them, as caring about regarding them, as committed to trying to regard them.[36] They are interpreting you in the light of good willing, despite your having demonstrated inadequate willing, and without your having demonstrated that you have perfectly fixed your willing and that it is now properly ordered.

Since, on this account, being forgiven is being seen as flawed yet oriented to better willing, rather than being seen as fully well-ordered (with respect to the wrong at issue), we can see why optimistic classic virtue theory would not see forgiveness as important for human life (something Nussbaum is keen to stress), and we can see why the pessimistic Judeo-Christian view of the human condition as somehow fallen was a historically more fertile ground for the development of the idea of forgiveness. However, against Nussbaum, this is not centrally a function of hostile and inappropriately moralizing

---

[35] This may be partly a psychological question.

[36] They might even be seeing you in the light of trust that you will come to understand and care about the transgression in the future. Thanks to Helga Varden (in correspondence) for this point.

religious prescriptions but rather of a more pessimistic view of how easy it is for humans to have well-ordered coherent selves.[37]

My account might be understood as saying that in forgiving we are evaluating someone's willing in an optimistic, future-oriented way. I think there is something in the vicinity of this that is correct, and it is no accident that forgiveness has its most central role in going forward with someone in a relationship; however, the future-oriented implications of optimism may be misleading. The affective evaluation of a person's willing that I see as involved in the forgiving change of heart is, in my view, compatible with deathbed requests for forgiveness and with forgiving the dead. In both these cases it obviously does not make sense to talk about an optimistic view of the agent's future willing. Rather, the idea is simply that we are evaluating their overall willing, with respect to the kind of wrongdoing in question, as better than the action indicates. We are seeing them as oriented toward good willing (in the particular way at issue with respect to the wrongdoing) despite their wrongdoing. So the sense in which forgiveness is optimistic need not be understood in terms of expectations for the future, but rather in terms of a positive interpretation that goes beyond the evidence.

On this account, we can see why apologies, remorse, and recompense are standard grounds for forgiveness but also why forgiveness is possible in the absence of them. (I have said nothing about reasons for forgiveness, which I take to be various; in particular, I do not hold that forgiveness is a change of heart of a particular sort undertaken for moral reasons.) As ways of acknowledging and expressing concern about the wrong, apologies, remorse, and recompense express an attempt to be oriented to better willing. However, they do not demonstrate or prove that the wrongdoer is oriented to better willing. In my view, both where there are apologies, remorse, and recompense and in unconditional cases, where there are not, the victim goes beyond the evidence in evaluating the wrongdoer as having better willing than their wrong action supports thinking. This therefore allows that forgiving is possible in a wide variety of cases, including extreme unconditional cases.[38] And since forgiving is centrally a change in *attitudes*, it is compatible with still expressing protest at wrongdoing where not doing so would be morally problematic, so even unconditional forgiveness need not be compromised.

---

[37] Classical virtue theory was initially developed by comfortable free citizens whose lives were systematically dependent on the unfreedom of others, in ways that may allow them to overestimate how easy it was for them to act in ways that seemed right.

[38] Garrard and McNaughton's (2003) opening case.

This account also shows why we need forgiveness. The possibility of an optimistic view of the self from which our actions can be understood in terms of our striving/attempting to be good is a condition of moral agency because we need it to avoid self-deception or despair. (Like all aspects of human agency, this very mode of optimistic interpretation will be subject to its own problems and pathologies; it seems to me to be part of the explanation of what may keep people in abusive relationships.) In forgiving, we express this optimistic, hopeful view to others: we give them the gift of affectively evaluating them as better than their wrong actions indicate them to be (and in a way in which it is possible for them to be). Like trusting each other, despite knowing that we are going to fail, this is a way in which we can help each other to actually be better.[39] (It will also, like trust, be subject to temptations to abuse, as well as to the temptation of "pious wishing," where we want to be forgiven so that we, incorrectly, can think of ourselves as already being better without making any effort.) Nussbaum, as we saw, worried about forgiveness being intrusive, and we can see here some grounds for this: there is a loss of control and an interpersonal vulnerability in there being something central for our engaged agency that we need from other people.

The paradox with which we started was driven by the concern that forgiveness involves a change of heart in which the wrongdoer is affectively regarded in a changed way but without a change in the judgments that warrant blaming affective attitudes—the judgments that there was culpable wrongdoing which reflects their willing. This makes forgiveness seem either irrational (when blaming attitudes are warranted) or pointless (if blaming attitudes are not [or no longer] warranted, then we simply ought not to have them). On the account I am sketching, (at least a central part of) forgiveness involves taking up a view of a person that affectively sees them as oriented toward better willing than their wrongdoing indicates (without changing your

[39] Thinking that we help each other in our moral agency does not make our *freedom* dependent on others: we have the capacity to do the right thing, independent of whether other people are hopeful about our doing so. But we are not disembodied noumenal agents: we have the capacity to initiate actions in a way that is not a determined function of previous states of the universe, but we can of course use this capacity only within the constraints of nature, including laws, and the situations in which we find ourselves, with the abilities we have. We are dependent on each other in many ways for our animal needs, which are of course necessary for our agency; it is not surprising if help from other people, and responses from other people to our agency, makes a difference to our development of our moral capacities. In the introduction to the *Metaphysics of Morals* Kant speaks of moral anthropology as something "which, however, would deal only with the subjective conditions in human nature that hinder people or help them in *fulfilling* the laws of a metaphysics of morals" (MM 6: 217).

evaluation of their wrongdoing).[40] Part of what makes this rationally possible is that they are not just an empirical causal system with respect to which there is a fact of the matter (or objective randomness) about what causal result will flow from their internal causal workings: the content of reactive attitudes includes a view of persons as free and responsible. Further, I have suggested a view of human agency within which we can see an action as having expressed an agent's bad willing but also see the same agent in the light of better willing. Seeing people as deeply flawed, slightly deluded, and partly ignorant does not rule out the possibility of seeing them as trying, within these limitations, to do what's right and being basically oriented toward good willing, basically committed to moral reasons, and recognizing the humanity of others.[41] Finally, I have suggested that this is something we need because of the frailty of the human condition: our need to hold onto the possibility of being better despite the evidence of our failings.

Communicative blame, as Fricker defends its positive uses, is a way in which we help each other stay sane and good, and can grow in understanding and shared moral consciousness when we fail. Blame need not be unloving; we help each other keep on track by holding each other to standards to which we are committed. Like blame, forgiveness involves recognizing wrong-doing, but it is a different kind of way of being loving: an emotional openness to flawed individuals as people who, perhaps in difficult circumstances, are getting it wrong but trying to be better, who subjectively need the possibility of being seen as better without being able to prove that they deserve this. In the optimistic world of classical virtue theory, good agents could restrict their relationships to well-ordered others, and if these others ever fail, require that they demonstrate that they have become well-ordered again before changing evaluative orientation toward them. In the isolated world of Nussbaumian agents, we could orient ourselves to future welfare and focus on feeling sad about the course of events in the world when we are let down. Those of us flawed humans who are in relationships with other flawed humans need

---

[40] This does not mean seeing the person in exactly the way you would have seen them had the wrong act not taken place; being hurt and being forgiven can lead to being closer than you would have been had the wrong act not taken place.

[41] Even in those who are very deluded, the *moralized* nature of the delusion itself speaks to their having this commitment and "germ of goodness." He says: "Surely we must presuppose in all this that there is still a germ of goodness left in its entire purity, a germ that cannot be extirpated or corrupted" (*Religion* 6: 45).

forgiveness to move forward with optimism and hope with people who have let us down and who we let down, whose willing we deeply care about.[42]

References

Allais, L. 2008a. "Wiping the Slate Clean: The Heart of Forgiveness." *Philosophy and Public Affairs* 36, no. 1: 33–68.
Allais, L. 2008b. "Forgiveness and Mercy." *The South African Journal of Philosophy* 27, no. 1: 1–9.
Allais, L. 2008c. "Dissolving Reactive Attitudes: Forgiving and Understanding." *The South African Journal of Philosophy* 27: 1–23.
Allais, L., 2013. "Elective Forgiveness." *The International Journal of Philosophical Studies* 21, no. 5: 637–653.
Allais, L. 2014. "Freedom and Forgiveness." In *Oxford Studies in Agency and Responsibility*, volume 2, edited by Neal Tognazzini and David Shoemaker.
Allais, L. 2018. "Evil and Practical Reason." In *Kant on Persons and Agency*, edited by E. Watkins. Cambridge: Cambridge University Press.
Atkins, Kim. 2002. "Friendship, Trust and Forgiveness." *Philosophia* 29, no. 1–4: 111–132.
Bloser, C. 2018. "Human Fallibility and the Need for Forgiveness." *Philosophia*.
Butler, Joseph. 1913. "Upon Resentment." In *Fifteen Sermons Preached at the Rolls Cathedral*. London: Macmillan and Co.
Calhoun, Cheshire. 1992. "Changing One's Heart." *Ethics* 103: 76–96.
Derrida, Jacques. 2001. *On Cosmopolitanism and Forgiveness*. London: Routledge.
Fricker, Miranda. 2014. "What's the Point of Blame? A Paradigm Based Explanation." *Nous*: 1–19.
Frierson, Patrick. 2010a. *Kant's Empirical Psychology*. Cambridge: Cambridge University Press.
Frierson, Patrick. 2010b. "Kantian Moral Pessimism." In *Kant's Anatomy of Evil*, edited by S. Anderson-Gold and P. Muchnik. Cambridge: Cambridge University Press.
Garcia, Ernesto. 2011. "Bishop Butler on Forgiveness and Resentment." *Philosopher' Imprint* 11, no. 3.
Garrard, E., and McNaughton, D. 2003. "In Defence of Unconditional Forgiveness." *Proceedings of the Aristotelian Society* CIII: 39–60.
Goldie, Peter. 2002. *The Emotions: A Philosophical Exploration*. Oxford: Clarendon Press.
Grenberg, Jeanine. 2010. "Social Dimensions of Kant's Conception of Radical Evil." In *Kant's Anatomy of Evil*, edited by S. Anderson-Gold and P. Muchnik. Cambridge: Cambridge University Press.
Griswold, Charles. 2007. *Forgiveness: A Philosophical Exploration*. New York: Cambridge University Press.
Hironymi, Pamela. 2001. "Articulating an Uncompromising Forgiveness." *Philosophy and Phenomenological Research* LXII: 529–555.

[42] Thanks to Katy Abramson, Adam Leite, Helga Varden, Eric Watkins, and the editors of this volume for reading and making very helpful comments on this chapter. Thanks also to the UCSD moral philosophy reading group. And thanks to Patrick Frierson for conversations which very much helped develop my thoughts.

Holmgren, Margaret R. 1993. "Forgiveness and the Intrinsic Value of Persons." *American Philosophical Quarterly* 30: 341–352.

Hughes, Paul. 1997. "What Is Involved in Forgiving?" *Philosophia* 25: 33–49.

Kolnai, Aurel. 1977. "Forgiveness." In *his Ethics, Value, and Reality*. London: The Athlone Press.

Lang, Berel. 1994. "Forgiveness." *American Philosophical Quarterly* 31: 105–117.

McGary, Howard. 1989. "Forgiveness." *American Philosophical Quarterly* 26: 343–351.

Moran, Kate. 2013. "For Community's Sake: A (self-respecting) Kantian Account of Forgiveness." *Proceedings of the XI International Kant Congress*: 433–444.

Morgan, Seriol. 2005. "The Missing Formal Proof of Humanity's Radical Evil in Kant's Religion." *The Philosophical Review* 114, no. 1: 63–114.

Muchnik, Pablo. 2010. "An Alternative Proof of the Universal Propensity to Evil." In *Kant's Anatomy of Evil*, edited by P. Muchnik and S. Anderson-Gold, 116–143. Cambridge: Cambridge University Press.

Murphy, Jeffrie G., and Jean Hampton. 1988. *Forgiveness and Mercy*. Cambridge: Cambridge University Press.

Novitz, David. 1988. "Forgiveness and Self-Respect." *Philosophy and Phenomenological Research* 58: 299–315.

Papish, Laura. 2018. *Kant on Evil, Self-Deception, and Moral Reform*. New York: Oxford University Press.

Satne, P. 2016. "Forgiveness and Moral Development." *Philosophia* 44: 1029–1055.

Sussman, David. 2005a. "Kantian Forgiveness." *Kant-Studien*: 85–107.

Sussman, D. 2005b. "Perversity of the Heart." *The Philosophical Review* 114, no. 2: 153–777.

Sussman, D. 2005c. "Kantian Forgiveness." *Kant-Studien* 96: 85–107.

Sussman, D. 2010. "Unforgivable Sins?: Revolution and Reconciliation in Kant." In *Kant's Anatomy of Evil*, edited by S. Anderson-Gold and P. Muchnik, 215–235. Cambridge: Cambridge University Press.

Sussman, D. 2015. "Grace and Enthusiasm." Paper presented at the Pacific APA conference in Vancouver, 2015.

Strawson, Peter Frederick. 1962. "Freedom and Resentment." *Proceedings of the British Academy* 48: 1–25.

Ware, O. 2014. "Forgiveness and Respect for Persons." *American Philosophical Quarterly* 51, no. 3: 247–260.

Warmke, B., and M. McKenna. 2013. "Moral Responsibility, Forgiveness, and Conversation." In *Free Will and Moral Responsibility*, edited by I. Haji and J. Caouette, 189–211. Cambridge: Cambridge Scholars Press.

Wood, Allan. 2010. "Kant and the Intelligibility of Evil." In *Kant's Anatomy of Evil*, edited by S. Anderson-Gold and P. Muchnik. Cambridge: Cambridge University Press.

13

Forgiveness and Consequences

Richard Arneson

Recent philosophical accounts of forgiveness are steeped in deontological, anticonsequentialist views about morality. In this chapter I discuss an act-consequentialist approach to forgiveness with the aim of exhibiting its moral attractiveness. Act consequentialism holds that one morally ought always to do an act that would lead to an outcome no worse (impartially assessed) than the outcome of anything else one might instead have done; doing anything else is morally wrong. But a possibly more important divide is between those moral views that do, and those that do not, include at the level of fundamental principle a significant beneficence component. Along the way the merits of a thin or spare account of the nature of forgiveness are considered. These two aims—advancing a spare account of what forgiveness is and defending an act-consequentialist position as to when one should and should not forgive—are independent of each other. The act consequentialist will hold that whatever forgiving turns out to be, one should forgive just in case doing so will bring about best consequences.

The Spare Account

Discussion of the conditions that must be satisfied for forgiveness to be justifiable cannot get off the ground until it is specified what forgiveness is. Here we find many competing specifications. To be useful, an account of forgiveness should have some resonance in ordinary usage, but usage varies, and it is doubtful that how competent speakers use the term will single out one account to the exclusion of all others. That there are different ideas in play comes out when people say such things as "In a sense he forgave his brother, but at another level he did not really forgive him."

This chapter works with a spare account of what forgiveness is but makes no grand claims to the effect that other accounts are illegitimate or rest on

Richard Arneson, *Forgiveness and Consequences* In: *Forgiveness and Its Moral Dimensions*. Edited by: Brandon Warmke, Dana Kay Nelkin, and Michael McKenna, Oxford University Press. © Oxford University Press 2021. DOI: 10.1093/oso/9780190602147.003.0013

some mistake. On the spare account, forgiveness is the extinguishing of certain negative reactive attitudes in a person toward another, these attitudes being directed at what is perceived to be that individual's wrongdoing (or at least subpar behavior) that constitutes a wrong or offense either to the person harboring the attitudes or to others with whom that person specially identifies. The negative reactive attitudes that forgiveness eliminates include resentment, indignation, anger directed at a person, and blame insofar as blame involves dispositions to feel and not only to judge adversely. These attitudes all centrally involve dispositions to have the feelings associated with the particular attitude; they can also involve secondary dispositions to act in ways that express the negative feelings and to act in ways that harm the person who is their object. There is also an occurrent feeling dimension to forgiveness: If I now feel resentment or the like toward you, I have not fully forgiven you, whatever my dispositions in this regard might be. Also, I shall stipulate that if someone gives up the judgment that a person has done him wrong, but still sustains a resentment-like hostile feeling and attitude directed at what the person has done, having this emotional residue means that forgiveness has not occurred.

Some take it to be essential to forgiveness that in forgiving one retains with full force the negative moral judgments about the person's conduct that brought about in one the negative reactions one is overcoming. On the spare account, this need not be so. Forgiveness might typically be accompanied by a weakening of these negative judgments, and something that feels very much like forgiveness can even be prompted by their disappearance. Whether the dilution of negative judgment is desirable or not, many will think, hinges on the degree to which one's adverse judgments were correct in the first instance. It is true that if one entirely gives up one's adverse judgment on someone's conduct that prompted negative reactive attitudes and still harbors residual negative feelings toward the person which one subsequently seeks to extinguish, what one is now seeking to eliminate is not any longer a negative reactive attitude, so it would be incorrect to call what one is now doing "forgiving." But this does not rule out forgiving a person for what one takes to be a wrong done to one but that is not really so. It is also possible that forgiveness of a person for some act or omission might give rise to heightened adverse judgment on the person's conduct or on the character of the person as seen in light of the episode.

Forgiving can be an action, something an individual does. On the spare account, forgiving can also can be something that happens, and can happen independently of the will or activity of the one who forgives, and even against the will of the forgiver. It can happen that you have forgiven someone for something you had not intended ever to forgive, even for something you regard as unforgivable and strenuously tried to keep resenting. Forgiving is a transition between a state of affairs in which one has ill will or other negative reactive attitudes directed toward an individual who has (as one believes) wronged one or harmed one or let one down in some way to a state of affairs in which these negative reactive attitudes are extinguished.

The spare account seems to be revisionary in this respect. A dictionary I consulted does not include any entry under "forgive" that allows forgiving to be passive (in a way that bypasses one's agency) rather than active. Still, it sounds idiomatic to say, "I tried not to forgive Sam, given his horrible behavior to me that night, but I could not sustain my ill will toward him; it is entirely dissipated; forgiveness has occurred despite my efforts to stay hostile." Forgiveness, according to the spare account, the state in which the relevant hostile reactive attitudes have dissipated, can be reached in alternative ways, by acts of trying to forgive, but also by psychological processes not intended by the agent, or unintended byproducts of the forgiver's actions. In another range of cases, one might notice a psychological process going on in oneself that is gradually diminishing one's resentment toward some offender, and one might then do nothing to stop the process. There are various possibilities here. One might deliberately do nothing because one is glad that resentment is fading, or because one would prefer that resentment continue but one is not willing to accept the costs that would be incurred in sustaining it. Or one might not make up one's mind as to how one regards this fading of resentment, and just passively do nothing about it. Many insist that forgiving must issue from intentional action aimed at overcoming resentment, and deny that, for example, forgetting about an injury and an injurer amounts to forgiving. But the spare account partly agrees. Forgetting all about an injury is compatible with staying resentful, which involves a disposition to feel negative emotion toward the injurer when prompted. The disposition can remain even if no prompts ever trigger it.

If the spare account involves revision of our ordinary notion, the revision has a point. Acts of forgiving are always acts of trying to forgive, which might or might not succeed. If an attempt to forgive succeeds, what occurs is that the negative reactive attitudes directed at the target individual as characterized earlier disappear. One can say in performative mode, "I hereby forgive you," but whatever the performance, ill will may still remain in its aftermath. A wholehearted, sustained attempt at forgiveness may yet fail.

In contrast, one can utter, "I hereby forgive you" as a performative that forswears debt, compensation, and perhaps apology that the forgiven person had owed to the forgiver. Directed duties owed to an injured person can, perhaps within some limits, be forgiven by the injured person or by someone authorized to act on her behalf. But to my ear this is all more accurately described as pardoning (but see Nelkin 2013 and the discussion of her view later). At least, it is not forgiving according to the spare account. This becomes immediately clear if the person makes the expanded statement, "I hereby waive my right to the $1000 compensation you owe me for wrongfully smashing my leg, but be it noted that I will continue to resent you for what you have done to me." There is no hint of inconsistency in the expanded statement.

Since forgiving involves the elimination of negative reactive attitudes, it can vary by degree. One can forgive someone a little, a lot, or entirely. These attitudes involve dispositions, which can be hard to detect, in oneself or in others. A disposition to experience resentment and the like can vary depending on (1) the strength of the stimulus that would be required to trigger occurrent resentment feeling and also on (2) the degree of vehemence of the resentment that a stimulus of a given strength would rekindle. For example, my mother was rightly resentful of mean-spirited comments I made to her during the years when we were prone to arguing about the War in Vietnam and other American social problems. Years later, we are getting along famously; we suppose all this past hostility is inert; at some point we think it safe to recall old times and revisit those conversations. But this turns out to be like pouring hot water on instant coffee; the brew of emotion returns. Surprising herself, my mother is now angry at me for what I did years ago. She had forgiven me—to a degree.

Forgiveness can involve dispositions to avoid behavior that might trigger rekindling of negative reactive attitude feelings. It might be correct to say I forgive someone even though under very intensive or extensive stimulation my negative feelings would arise in me again, provided I am also steadily disposed to avoid placing myself in situations in which these rekindlings of the negative would occur. Of course, this situation is only compatible with forgiveness at the margins.[1]

---

[1] If I am bursting with latent negative reactive attitudes toward Sally, but by dint of enormous effort of will and constant surveillance avoid the huge variety of minor stimuli that would trigger feeling responses stemming from these attitudes, we would not say I have really forgiven Sally.

The Act-Consequentialist Stance toward Forgiving

Since according to the act consequentialist, a candidate act of forgiving (really, attempted forgiving) can be either mandatory, if doing it would bring about the best reachable outcome impartially assessed, or forbidden, if it would not bring about the best reachable outcome, and since acts of forgiving can also be either apt or inapt, we have four possibilities—right and apt, right and inapt, wrong and apt, and wrong and inapt. In broad terms, forgiving is apt (or fitting) when it is appropriate in virtue of some relation between the person targeted for forgiveness and her enmity-arousing offense or in virtue of some other feature of this person—for example, that she has already suffered enough and declining to forgive would pile extra suffering on her. People disagree about what relations and features render forgiveness apt; I help myself to one specification that I find plausible in the next sentences.[2] The problematic cases, which will provoke a raised-eyebrows response on the part of many deontologists and other nonconsequentialists, are the right and inapt and the wrong and apt forgivings. In the former, the act of forgiving is morally right, and required, even though the person to be forgiven is not distanced from his wrongful act by repentance, reparation, apology, and atonement. The person forgiven does not merit or deserve forgiveness, because he has not effectively repudiated his wrongful act. So forgiving in such circumstances would be inapt, and it looks to be wrong.[3] The act consequentialist disagrees; hence, her stance needs some explanation and justification.

The other suspicious category of forgiving consists of acts of forgiving deemed wrong by the act-consequentialist standard, even though forgiving in these cases would be apt—the person who might be forgiven has had a change of heart and has effectively repudiated his wrongdoing that is the target of the negative reactive attitudes that forgiving would seek to overcome. The person in this case merits or deserves to be forgiven, so here refraining from forgiving looks to be wrong. Or rather, since some deontological views

---

[2] Insight on what are plausible appropriateness conditions for forgiving can be gleaned by considering what are deemed to be the conditions for true or genuine apology. On apology, see Bovens (2008).

[3] Some nonconsequentialist accounts of forgiveness and of the conditions for justified forgiveness make room for inapt forgiving. See, for example, Garrard and McNaughton (2003). In contrast, Griswold argues that there are necessary and sufficient conditions for the propriety of forgiveness, and "When satisfied, these conditions qualify the offender for forgiveness and entitle the victim to forgive" (2007, 47). According to Griswold, forgiveness at its best is afforded only when the offender's attitudes change, thus satisfying the conditions. In the terminology used in this chapter, forgiving is then apt.

will hold that acts of forgiving are always or usually morally optional but not morally obligatory, the apparent difficulty for the act consequentialist is that she rigidly holds that acts of forgiving that would fail to bring about the best reachable outcome are one and all morally impermissible, rather than sometimes either morally mandatory or at least morally permissible.

To make headway on this issue, the next few sections of this chapter explore some examples of forgiving and refraining from forgiving that involve mismatch. These turn out to be familiar occurrences that are acceptable or not depending on their consequences—or so it will be urged.

An important further point emerges from this discussion of mismatch cases. Not only act consequentialists will concur in the judgments that, by virtue of good consequences to be obtained, forgiving inaptly and refraining from apt forgiving can be and often are morally justified all things considered. Any morality, including a deontological morality that upholds constraints and options, can reach these verdicts, provided the morality contains a significant beneficence component—a general duty to improve the world by acting so as to bring about better not worse outcomes. Just to have a name, let us refer to this family of views as *deontology with beneficence.* Here as elsewhere it turns out that the boundary between act consequentialism and nonconsequentialist rivals may not be the most important moral boundary line from either a theoretical or a practical point of view.

A companion thought that is of crucial importance to the character of a morality is the degree of significance it attaches to the duty of beneficence so construed. Here as elsewhere in morality what matters is not so much that there is a distinction to be made but how strong the reasons are that shelter on one side or the other of the distinction.

Dangerous Resentment

Persevering in resentment, indignation, or hatred of those who have (as one thinks) done one wrongful injury can readily motivate one to acts that aim to injure the wrongful injurers. Nothing guarantees that reasonable and appropriate degree of resentment rightly shaped to the specific injury that occasions it will motivate only morally appropriate acts of retaliation. To avoid acting wrongly in response to provocations and slights and wrongful injuries, sometimes the most effective technique, and occasionally the only technique that offers a reasonable prospect of success, may be to bring about in oneself the extinguishing of the negative reactive attitudes directed toward the person in view of these wrongs to oneself. One should, in other words, forgive even the unrepentant wrongdoer, and one should perhaps forgive the unforgiveable (wrongs, if such there be, that are so horrendous that forgiveness of them would never be apt in any circumstances).

Persevering in apt resentment can be dangerous in ways that need not involve the risk that one will jump over the moral fence and indulge in wrongful revenge and retaliation. That one harbors resentment might be unavoidably manifest to others with whom one is interacting, the resented person and others as well. The resented person might reasonably or unreasonably fear retaliation, and the fear might impede trust and useful cooperation. Providing reassurance might be difficult or even impossible. "My continuing resentment of you will not, I assure you, provoke me to smash your face wrongfully" may not provide much helpful reassurance. Moreover, persevering in resentment can impede mutually beneficial cooperative relations in subtler ways. Interacting with someone who harbors resentment of one may provoke anxiety or mild dread, and so one avoids interactions. Much the same goes for others who might interact with the parties locked in resentment relations. In many situations, the best way forward for all affected parties is overcoming resentment. Of course, it would be nice if the resented person repented and apologized and made amends and reformed his character, but in the absence of this nice scenario, inapt forgiving may still be the best available way forward.

Dangerous Vicarious Resentment

Even if one is oneself saintly in being able to prevent oneself from acting wrongly from apt resentment feelings and masterful in being able to communicate the message that one has this saintly disposition to others, still, one's resentment may be infectious, and be toxic for social relations in indirect ways. I may not be disposed in the least to retaliate against Smith, my work colleague, for wrongfully breaking my legs, but my brother might do so, or his friend, or his children, or some of their associates and acquaintances. Again, there will be in such cases sometimes decisive moral reasons of good consequences in the offing to overcome one's apt resentment.

Resentment as an Obstacle to Harmony

In some cases merely becoming appropriately resentful at mistreatment and sustaining the resentment in the face of continued mistreatment may impede the unfolding of a process that promises good consequences. One should sometimes quash the resentment one feels, depending on the magnitudes of harms and benefits at stake in the short term and the long run.

Jean Hampton (in Murphy and Hampton 1988, 39) has described a familiar example. The in-laws have come to town and are mistreating their son's wife. The wife is righteously angry, but the husband pleads with her not to spoil the holiday gathering and show forgiveness. This is a generic scene, and in many versions, a row now will pay off in future better relations or at least avoidance of further wrongful impositions. In some cases, showing forgiveness may do the trick of restoring family harmony and need not even involve deception if one's in-laws are emotionally thickheaded. But in some such cases, we should accept that the credible appearance of forgiveness is the best way to restore desirable holiday harmony and cheer, and the only way to achieve the credible appearance of forgiveness is actually to forgive, so forgive one must, if one can.

Prudent Self-Healing

Consider Sally, who was brutally raped. Her resentment and anger and even hatred of her assailant are perfectly appropriate, we can readily imagine. Moreover, the utter indifference to her plight and contempt of her shown by her unrepentant assailant at trial is etched, she fears indelibly, in her mind, and torments her. Sally tries to "get over it" by contributing assiduously to rape awareness and rape prevention campaigns, all good causes. But none of this stops her brooding, which is making life miserable for her and impeding any effective progress toward gaining for herself a rich and fulfilling life. In this situation overcoming resentment and other negative reactive attitudes may be utterly beyond her capacity, and understandably so. But if she can undertake some psychic regimen that will expunge the negative reactive attitudes and emotions stemming from this traumatic wrongdoing she suffered, prudence and morality may well unite in heartily endorsing this inapt forgiving. She forgives for her own sake, and rightly so.

Good Cause

Terrible things have happened to our country, we can imagine. Our country has divided into tribal and factional squabbles, which led to ethnic cleansing, civil war, seriously destructive attempts at genocides, and further atrocities. Guilty wrongdoing was not evenly spread across the population; some groups maliciously wronged others; some were for the most part innocent victims; some groups fought and killed only in proportionate ways for just causes. An uneasy peace has been restored. Renewed cooperation across the lines of bloody conflict is in sight. Apt and just resentment, indignation, and hatred cloud these prospects. A moral realpolitik is in order. If those who suffered wrongs, or sufficient numbers of them, can manage a generalized inapt (or mostly inapt) forgiveness, civil peace and harmony may be restored, and if this forgiveness does not occur, the prospects for a tolerable outcome for all are greatly diminished. Here gritting one's teeth and making good-faith efforts to overcome all resentment against the wrongdoers may be the best way forward and, in fact, morally mandatory. This is so even if we should be disposed to be tolerant and forgiving of people who cannot summon up this effort at heroic inapt forgiveness.[4]

Abused Spouse

Jane has suffered grievous wrongs at the hands of her abusive husband. She has freed herself from the bad marriage and extricated her children and herself from further danger. Meanwhile her former husband has done a complete about-face. He regularly attends Alcoholics Anonymous meetings, and he does volunteer work counseling men struggling to stop abuse and women struggling to end abusive relationships. He is an exemplar of remorse and contrition and has thoroughly amended his ways. He does not seek to resume the relationship with his former wife; he recognizes encounters with him stir up bad memories and are painful. He seeks forgiveness and is an apt candidate for its receipt. All of this is consistent with Jane, while recognizing the changes in her husband, having good forward-looking reasons to sustain

---

[4] But, of course, there will be a secondary act-consequentialist calculation as well; perhaps some inapt blamings of those who are excusably dragging their feet at the forgiveness effort are also called for in view of the bad consequences of refraining from inapt blaming.

resentment and anger at him. She has some residual distrust of her ability to avoid sliding into some similar abusive situation in the future; retaining negative reactive attitudes armors herself against this possibility. Perhaps her case has gained media attention and any forgiving of her former spouse is bound to leak into news reports in a way that may have the unintended effect, despite all she might try to do to forestall it, to weaken the gathering resolve of other women to end abusive relationships or block their blossoming.

Girding One's Loins for Struggle

Although so far I have described forgiveness as overcoming negative reactive attitudes prompted by wrongdoing done to oneself or to those near and dear to one, with whom one is personally identified, there can be cases of forgiveness in which the persons forgiven have no personal connection at all to the person doing the forgiving. Perhaps the background for forgiveness has to include emotional identification with the victims of wrongdoing. One reads about the Nazi regime and feels indignant and angry on behalf of its victims. One hears stories about slavery and Jim Crow and feels angry at racist oppressors of African Americans throughout US history. One knows, some Nazis became profoundly remorseful, and so have some racists. Some have become apt candidates for forgiveness. Of course, it would be horribly presumptuous to imagine that I could by myself forgiving an oppressor remove any grounds for continued resentment and hostility his actual victims might have felt and might still feel. But I can still quash the angry resentment I myself feel toward these perpetrators of injustice. In some but not all cases I should do so. Anger at perpetrators might help fuel current struggles of injustice, and such anger directed at those apt for forgiveness might be part of the most effective feasible strategy for serving this moral purpose. In light of the consequences for possible victims of injustice, some apt forgiving is morally wrong just as some inapt blaming is morally right.

One might well wonder exactly what is supposed to be going on in some of these inapt blaming and forgiving episodes. Forgiveness theorists point out, perfectly correctly, that overcoming negative feelings toward the perpetrators of wrongs toward oneself and those near and dear to one can coexist without any inconsistency with holding adverse judgments about the person's conduct and about what the conduct reveals about his character. Forgiveness has to do with feelings, not judgments. A related view is that forgiveness is the overcoming of negative feelings directed toward the person who wronged one but not necessarily of feelings toward the deed itself. Hate the sin but love the sinner, Saint Augustine admonishes us.

But loving the sinner, if that is indeed desirable, is compatible with continuing to resent the person for the wrong done to one, to have ill will or anger, or maybe to have directed irritation specifically with respect to the person qua doer of that deed. This resentment could persist even if overall one loves the person. Maybe all things considered we should love everyone if we can. Maybe not. That issue is different from the question of whether we should drop resentment for a particular wrong done to us, or let it slide, or allow it to be sustained, or actively nurture it.

On the spare account, the fact that in particular circumstances forgiving would be apt, and the fact that in other particular circumstances refraining from forgiving would be apt, at most indicates the presence of one type of reason for forgiving or refraining from forgiving. There are other reasons to consider. On a consequentialist view, these reasons, indeed all reasons for choice and action, ultimately boil down to forward-looking considerations; one should do what will bring about the best reachable future outcome, impartially assessed. There is nothing paradoxical or untoward about inapt forgiving or inapt refraining from forgiving.

Restoring Relations

According to some views, forgiveness is essentially bound up with restoring relationships with those who have done one wrong (Murphy and Hampton 1988). Forgiveness heals the rupture that wrongdoing brought about and enables something approximating a return to the status quo ante in the interactions between the one who forgives and the one who is forgiven. On views of this sort, it would be morally inappropriate for a woman abused by her romantic partner to forgive her abuser if he has not reformed his character to the point that restoring relations with him will not continue the cycle of abuse (or, a possible if unlikely scenario, forgiving him will not in itself bring about a transformation that ends his abuse).

On the spare account being considered here, restoring relations is not necessarily an element in forgiveness, though such restoration might be a consideration favoring forgiveness or an end that forgiveness will expectably achieve in some situations. Forgiveness on the spare account is elimination

of negative reactive emotions and attitudes toward the person who is forgiven, nothing more or less. Forgiveness so understood can coexist with retention of adverse judgments toward the wrongdoer regarding his conduct
or the character his conduct has revealed. Forgiveness can coexist with a determined unwillingness to renew a special relationship with the person being
forgiven, if one had a significant relationship with him prior to the wrongdoing and rupture, and indeed can coexist with determination to forego any
interaction with that individual.

Restoring relations, though not necessarily an element in forgiveness,
might on the spare view be its full justification. Restoring relations with those
who have wronged one might expectably bring about good consequences, in
a variety of ways, such that forgiving is permissible or even mandatory. One's
associates are wrongly mistreating one in the nonprofit agency to which one
is dedicated, but forgiving them might be a needed component of a strategy
of carrying on one's work in the agency, which promises much good to distant needy strangers. If no alternative strategy that involves directing anger
and indignation against the wrongdoing one suffers will do as much good
overall, one ought to forgive and bear the wrongs patiently.

In all these cases, the spare account of forgiveness yoked to an act-
consequentialist account of when forgiving is morally forbidden or required
strikes me as eminently sensible. However, readers who disagree might still
go part-way with this account. One might accept the spare account of forgiveness even if one holds utterly different views about the conditions under
which forgiveness is permitted, forbidden, or required. More important,
one might have nonconsequentialist convictions, involving allegiance to
constraints and options, which dictate that one sometimes ought not to forgive, or is permitted not to forgive, even when doing so would be maximally
beneficent, and dictate also that sometimes one ought to forgive, or is permitted to forgive, even when forgiving would be maximally beneficent.

With all that on board, one might still allow that sometimes, the
consequences of not forgiving might be sufficiently bad that one ought all
things considered to forgive even when the forgiving would be morally inapt
in light of the disposition of the person who might be forgiven and sometimes, the consequences of forgiving would be sufficiently bad that one ought
all things considered not to forgive even when forgiving would be perfectly
morally apt in light of the dispositions of the person who might be forgiven.
If the deontologist gives significant weight to bringing about morally good
outcomes impartially assessed, the act consequentialist and she might be

close comrades on many controversial practical issues, in the domain of forgiveness and in other moral domains.

Trying to Forgive

Used to refer to an exercise of agency, *forgive* is a success verb. One has not forgiven unless one has succeeded in eliminating one's negative reactive attitudes directed toward the person one is trying to forgive. Trying to forgive is then an action or a course of actions one might take, and it is separate and independent of forgiving and can be assessed as apt or inapt and as morally permissible, impermissible, or mandatory in its own right. The concept of forgiving rules out the possibility of trying to forgive when one knows, or believes one knows, that there is nil chance of success, but one can try to forgive even when the chances of succeeding are small.

Moreover, a wholehearted, sincere attempt to forgive may have significant good (or bad) consequences that differ from the consequences that would come about if the attempt were successful. Perhaps sometimes in the wake of civil war and grievous crimes directed at a certain ethnic group, making a sincere sustained attempt to forgive, if one is a wronged member of the criminally wronged ethnic group, would have good consequences in signaling a likely lessening of hostility and consequent prospects for renewed mutually profitable cooperation, whereas actually fully forgiving would inexorably suggest to former oppressors that they could probably get away with similar misdeeds in future without suffering retaliation.

It goes without saying that for an act consequentialist there is always in principle the option of pretending to forgive or pretending to try to forgive, as alternatives to making sincere efforts in this direction. Pretending to forgive might have good consequences, better than any alternatives, including successfully forgiving. Notice that pretending to forgive might have good consequences even if the person to whom the pretense is directed recognizes it for what it is.

Other Views

Recent philosophical discussions of forgiveness tend to weave together accounts of what forgiveness is and what determines whether forgiveness is morally acceptable. The accounts tend to be nonconsequentialist. There are many of them. The next sections of this chapter survey some interesting views with a view to shedding some contrasting light both on the spare account and on the act-consequentialist position on the acceptability of forgiving.

The Views of Lucy Allais

As its title suggests, Lucy Allais's essay "Wiping the Slate Clean: The Heart of Forgiveness" (2008) works to make sense of the idea that a core element in forgiving is what is often referred to as wiping the slate clean or as ceasing to hold it against a person that she has culpably committed a wrong against the one who forgives. There are puzzles here, because if one retracts the judgment that the person one is forgiving has culpably committed a wrong against one, there is nothing to forgive, and if one retains that adverse judgment, wiping away the resentment that it justifies might seem unmotivated, irrational, and even morally wrong. A further puzzle is that according to Allais forgiving can make sense even when the offender is not penitent, apologetic, or remorseful, nor in other ways repudiating and repenting the wrong done to the now forgiving victim.

Allais's solution is to distinguish sharply between adverse blaming judgments directed against the wrongful act done to the victim and retributive attitudes and feelings directed against the wrongdoer with respect to that wrongful act. In forgiving one retains the former but gives up the latter, and in particular a special type of directed attitude that she characterizes: Forgiving at its core, according to Allais, involves ceasing to regard the person as having bad character in the specific way her wrongdoing toward you seems to reveal. Forgiving involves wiping the slate clean: After forgiveness of one who has wronged you, so far as your estimation of the person is concerned, it is as though the wrong had never occurred, though your judgment of the offense and its quality remains intact. The attitude that changes when you forgive someone "concerns the way you feel about the offender as a person as a result of the offense."

But shouldn't your estimate of the person's character be shaped by the ensemble of evidence you have regarding her, including the wrong she has done you? Even if not itself a judgment, a feeling or emotion can have cognitive appropriateness conditions. Allais responds by appealing to the epistemic slack that always accompanies estimations of character. The evidence may rule out some estimations but always permits a range. This feature of our feelings about other people's character permits one rationally to forgive, with forgiveness understood as wiping the slate clean, even if there is no evidence at all of remorse, repentance, reform, and reparation forthcoming from the one who has wronged one.[5] Of course, a change of heart on the part of the wrongdoer can facilitate forgiving and can be a reason to forgive.

Forgiving so understood might be a gift, not something the remorseful wrongdoer can claim from his victim (and those identifying with the victim) as an entitlement. It is compatible with Allais's account of the heart of forgiveness to maintain that forgiving is always optional and never required.

Allais is seeking to interpret as coherent the position of some women involved in Truth and Reconciliation proceedings in South Africa, which were conducted in the wake of apartheid and criminal wrongs undertaken in its defense. The women on whom Allais's account focuses express a willingness to forgive those responsible even for heinous crimes provided only that those undertaking forgiveness know whom they are forgiving. (I suppose that on her view it can make sense, and might sometimes be justifiable, to forgive even unknown perpetrators of culpable wrongs done to one.)

An act-consequentialist account of when forgiving is justified will agree with Allais that forgiving can be justified even when there is no evidence of change of heart on the part of the perpetrator and might indeed sometimes be specially admirable in such circumstances. But for the consequentialist the justification for forgiving undeserving perpetrators will always rest on careful weighing of the likely outcomes of forgiving compared to alternative courses of action. Also, for the consequentialist, forgiving strictly speaking is never optional for the potential forgiver (unless consequences are exactly balanced). It is either required or forbidden.

On some views, forgiving is never required, but rather either always optional or sometimes optional and sometimes forbidden. But consider an offense that happened in the past and a victim who continues to harbor negative reactive attitudes toward the perpetrator. With a long enough passage of time, continuing in this stance appears objectionable. But why should time

---

[5] It should be noted that Allais is making a point about the concept of forgiveness. She does not intend to be taking a stand as to the conditions that render forgiveness morally permissible, prohibited, or mandatory all things considered. These further questions are normative issues not to be settled by conceptual fiat. She wants to make the significant point that those victims who would forgive heinous criminal wrongdoers in the absence of any evidence of change of heart on the part of the perpetrator are not necessarily either confused about what they are doing in forgiving or morally wrong to engage in such inapt forgiving.

matter in this way? The act remains wrong and culpable, just as wrong and culpable one or ten or fifty years later as at the time it occurred. The act consequentialist has a suggestion. Anger and resentment directed at those who wronged you, proportionate to the magnitude of the offense and of the harm incurred, are often productive of good consequences, notably deterrence of similar wrongs, but nurturing these attitudes long after the offense is usually (though not always) counterproductive. Time makes a difference to the strength of the reasons for having reactive attitudes because time is a generally reliable indicator of the goodness or badness of having these attitudes. As the consequences become less good, at some point forgiveness becomes required, not optional. At what point? Again, the act consequentialist has a clear account of where to draw the line.

Allais agrees in broad terms that forgiving involves overcoming resentment but insists that a core element in forgiving is giving up the specific attitude of (affectively) seeing the offender as lesser, as having bad character in the specific way the wrongdoing appears to reveal. But it seems there can be cases of wrongdoing in which there is no epistemic slack regarding assessment of the character of the wrongdoer of the sort Allais takes to be necessary for forgiving, yet forgiving is justified. One can forgive Hitler without ceasing to see him (affectively) as incorrigibly having bad character as revealed in his wrongdoing. Whether one should forgive in such a case depends on what forgiving will bring about. But this sort of judgment about this type of case presupposes that what Allais proposes as the heart of forgiveness is not best regarded as that, and not necessary to forgiveness more usefully construed. To my mind the lesson we should draw is that Allais is right to interpret forgiveness as centrally involving overcoming resentment and allied negative reactive attitudes directed toward a wrongdoer for his wrongdoing, but her further interpretation of the metaphor of wiping the slate clean in terms of more precisely specifying the type of feeling involved is more problematic.

Also, it is far from clear that wiping the slate clean as Allais characterizes it should occur, and hence doubtful this can be the core of forgiveness. How persons behaved toward you should play a role in determining what behavior you expect from them in the future, and in your regard for their characters. As a wrongdoer, it is understandable I would want the slate wiped clean in the Allais sense, but what is written by my conduct stays written. I am the person who committed that particular wrong to those particular people. Allais seeks to register this, by distinguishing the forgiver's cognitive judgment of the person qua perpetrator of that particular wrong and the forgiver's feeling toward the person's character regarding that wrong. But should the feeling float free of the judgment?[6] If I tried to murder Tom with an ax, unless Tom is utterly (and correctly) convinced this was an aberration that will not recur, or will not be followed by related outbursts, he should be on guard in my presence and adjust his emotional stance as well as his beliefs about the kind of person I am, given what I did. Such a shift in Tom's emotional stance toward me is fully compatible with forgiving me if forgiving is understood as overcoming of resentment and related hostile attitudes.

Eve Garrard and David McNaughton on Unconditional Forgiveness

Whereas the act-consequentialist account says that there can be situations in which it would bring about the best impartially assessed reachable outcome, and hence is morally required, to forgive, even if there are no particular features of the person being forgiven that provide reasons for doing so, Eve Garrard and David McNaughton go further. They maintain that forgiveness is always and everywhere morally admirable and morally permissible, even if never mandatory, no matter whether or not the person being forgiven is repentant, contrite, remorseful, has made genuine apology, has made compensation or restitution, or anything along this line. They defend unconditional forgiveness.

On their view, forgiving an offender involves giving up hostile feelings toward the person, being open to restoring one's prior relationship (if there was one) with the offender when that is possible and desirable, and waiving one's complaint against the wrongdoer that one has been wronged. They defend the view that there are no conditions the offender must meet, to be eligible for such forgiveness, in part by noting that forgiving someone is compatible with continuing to find the person blameworthy, insisting on compensation or restitution, endorsing or seeking the person's punishment, not condoning the person's wrongful action, cutting off one's relationship with the individual, and being mindful of the wrong in one's future dealings with that

---

[6] Allais flags and sets to the side the question of what is involved in restoring trust on the part of the forgiver, who might have dealings with the wrongdoer being forgiven in the future. She allows that forgiving someone in her sense might be compatible with not regarding the person as trustworthy in future dealings with him. What makes trust reasonable is a further issue not settled, she holds, by her proposed conception of forgiveness. And to reiterate, her account by design does not address the question, when forgiveness is justifiable all things considered.

person. If we take an overly broad view of what forgiveness is, the idea that unconditional forgiveness is always permissible and even admirable would be harder to defend and perhaps indefensible.

Why always forgive? There is always a sufficient justification for forgiveness as they characterize it, they maintain. This is human solidarity based on common species membership. Our species is prone to bad acts, and being human also, the thought "there but for the grace of God go I" or a secular equivalent is always appropriate. Even if you would not have done the wrongful deed had you been in the shoes of the person who wronged you, you might have been or become this sort of person, had circumstances been different. Luck beyond one's power to control always at some level explains why the person wronged you and not the reverse (or the doing by you of something equally bad and wrong). One might take this claim about luck to rule out as inadmissible the thought that anyone is ever truly morally blameworthy or culpable for doing bad deeds or omitting to do good ones. The familiar claim here is that one can be morally responsible, hence morally blameworthy or praiseworthy for one's acts depending on their quality, at most for what lies within one's power to control, and on the moral luck thesis, nothing we do lies within our power to control. Garrard and McNaughton take the different line that moral blameworthiness attaches to people who wrong others, but if one is wronged, forgiveness is never inappropriate, always permissible and admirable.

The act consequentialist has a simple riposte. Let us assume for the sake of the argument that sheer luck beyond one's power to control always explains why you are the wronged person contemplating forgiveness rather than in the position of the person who culpably did wrong and might be forgiven. But forgiving is an act with consequences, which might be good, bad, or ugly. Agreeing that the person's unrepentant or even heinous character with respect to the wrong done is never a bar to the acceptability of forgiving someone, the act consequentialist denies that forgiveness is admirable or even permissible when the consequences of forgiving are sufficiently bad. In that stance the act consequentialist travels in the company of a broad array of nonconsequentialist doctrines that include a significant beneficence component in the set of principles that together are deemed to determine what should be done. The consequences of forgiving a wrongdoer might be excessively bad, so forgiveness in that circumstance is wrong. The act consequentialist pushes this line further: If better consequences would be brought about by refraining from forgiving rather than forgiving, one morally ought not to forgive. There but for the grace of God go I, and if I went there, I, too, should not be forgiven, if holding a grudge against me would improve the world by impartial moral assessment.

Jeffrie Murphy on Forgiveness

Jeffrie Murphy succinctly defines forgiveness as "forswearing resentment on moral grounds" (1988, 24; see also his 2003). These must involve perception of separation between the wrongdoer and the wrongdoing. If "the wrong-doer is intimately identified with his wrongdoing," forgiveness will involve condoning or acquiescing in wrongdoing, and so be incompatible with "self-respect, respect for others as moral agents, and respect for the rules of morality." According to Murphy, the required separation need not involve a change of heart on the part of the wrongdoer; sometimes it suffices that the wrongdoer had good motives, or has had good relations with the victim in the past, or even that the wrongdoer has suffered enough. On this view forgiving must be intentional, so losing one's resentment by forgetting the injury or distracting oneself will not count as forgiveness, and overcoming resentment to bring about good consequences is not acting with the right sort of reason and so is not (true) forgiving. On Murphy's view, overcoming resentment, to quality as forgiving, need not be apt or appropriate in the narrow sense identified earlier in this chapter.

A problem with Murphy's view is that since overcoming or just losing resentment as such is always compatible with continuing to judge that the one being forgiven has committed an unexcused wrong against one and is culpable for doing so, it does not seem that forgiving ever need involve condoning the conduct being forgiven. Also, overcoming resentment for the reason that in the circumstances doing so is singled out as morally right by act-consequentialist standards will be incompatible with maintaining proper respect for oneself, other people, and the rules of morality only if act consequentialism is an unsound moral doctrine.

Dana Nelkin's Debt Release Account

As already noted, the social phenomena that get classified under the heading of "forgiveness" are heterogeneous. Different accounts of forgiveness are oriented toward different bits of the phenomena. For example, contrast the spare account and the debt release model of forgiveness (Nelkin 2013; see also Warmke 2016 and Twambley 1976). On the spare account, forgiveness is like love, in that neither is directly under the control of the will.

In contrast, on a debt release model, forgiveness is not essentially a matter of feeling a certain way or being disposed to feel a certain way. Nelkin summarizes the debt release idea in these words: "In forgiving, one ceases to hold the offense against the offender, and this in turn means releasing them from a special kind of personal obligation incurred as the result of committing the wrong against one"—such as obligations to apologize, to make reparations, to atone, to pay compensation for wrongful damage inflicted. Forgiving so construed is quite similar to a promisee releasing a promisor from the obligation to do what has been promised. In forgiving, as in releasing someone from a promise, one is exercising a moral power that persons have. Like promising, forgiving (in this sense) is what used to be called a performative verb, as is signaled by the fact that one can sensibly say "I hereby forgive" just as one can say "I hereby release you from your promise to me," and when one sincerely utters these words in the presence of the right background circumstances, one thereby brings it about that the obligations owed by the person addressed to the speaker are dissolved.

Regarding forgiveness and resentment, Nelkin identifies three components, or perhaps subtypes, of this negative reactive attitude: protest against a wrong done to one,[7] feelings of ill will, and the desire to be in a position of power over the offender. She suggests that on the debt release model, overcoming resentment on any of these construals is neither necessary nor sufficient for forgiveness, but there is a close association between forgiving and overcoming resentment: in standard circumstances the former will often bring about, or accompany, the latter. She also suggests that in forgiving one might relinquish the right to resent. This does not rule out sustaining boiling resentment after (debt release) forgiving, but the resenting forgiver will be internally conflicted.

---

[7] For an account that takes resentment to be "protest against a past action that persists as a present threat," see Hieronymi (2001, 546). Overcoming resentment on this view is only appropriate when the threat is removed. The threat is posed by the wrongdoer and maybe others continuing to leave standing the statement implicit in the act against the victim that what was done to this victim was acceptable. But it seems one could relinquish all resentment (hostile feeling) against a wrongdoer who is unrepentant, even in the face of support for the wrongdoer's stance by others, while affirming one's judgment that what was done was wrong and unacceptable. In this way, resenting and protesting against wrong can come apart, and on forward-looking views of the justification of forgiveness, should sometimes come apart.

One who elaborates the spare account and one who elaborates the debt release account are explicating two different concepts. At the beginning of this chapter I suggested that "pardoning" would be a preferable word to use in connection with the debt release concept, but of course the word "forgiving" is used for both. Is there more than verbal disagreement between one who advocates the spare account (or other accounts that identify the core of forgiving with overcoming of resentment) and one who advocates the debt release account (or others that make something other than overcoming of resentment central to forgiving?

There might be empirical disagreement here—one might claim the standard or ordinary meaning of forgiving is debt release (or relinquishing resentment, or something else entirely). Or there might be background normative disagreement—one might claim the morally significant element in the social practice of forgiving is debt release (or some alternative). The latter might remind one of *persuasive definition* as introduced by Charles Stevenson (1963 [1938]). Persuasive definition surely sometimes is not disreputable. One might be pursuing a sound moral agenda and find that appropriating a term used in various ways in common speech and insisting it has one correct, or truly correct use, which one then stipulates, might be useful for advancing the desirable agenda. And if one rightly has certain moral commitments, some concepts and some conceptions of concepts may be useful, and others not, for elaborating and deploying the moral commitments.

However, in the case at hand, it does not seem that the act consequentialist has a stake in favoring the spare account over the debt release model. The act consequentialist could ride along with a wide variety of proposals about what is the core idea or ideas in forgiving. Whatever the answer, the act consequentialist will have a particular line on the further issue, what makes it the case that forgiving (or trying to bring it about that forgiveness occurs) is mandatory, permissible, or required in given circumstances.

Why then favor the spare account of forgiving? I simply believe that in ordinary life, our practices involving forgiving (and apologizing) are mainly centered on feeling and emotion. If I have done something wrong to someone, and her response is to the effect that "I release you from the obligations to me that your wrongful conduct to me brought into being, but I still harbor angry resentment directed at you, and expect to sustain that hostile feeling toward you, and probably to nurture it," I do not consider myself forgiven. The simple idea to which I am appealing here is that forgiveness involves a change of heart on the part of the one who is forgiving.

Assessing Forgiveness Norms from the Standpoint
of Multilevel Scalar Act Consequentialism

All the accounts under review regard forgiving as presupposing the background thought that the person being forgiven is blameworthy for having committed a moral wrong against the victim who is doing the forgiving. The target of forgiveness has violated an obligation owed to the one who forgives. Can the act consequentialist accept this agreed background? The answer is Yes, but this complicates her response to the deontological norms woven into accounts of forgiveness.

The act consequentialist holds that we always have just one fundamental obligation, to act for the best. This obligation is not directed, owed to particular persons with whom one is interacting. However, since humans tend to be variously not well informed, not good at integrating such information as they have into decisions about what to do, and anyway not motivated to do what is impartially for the best, we need what R. Hare once called levels of moral thinking.[8] We need simple rules and norms for practical guidance, these ideally being such as to lead us toward choices of action that are on the whole closer to the choices than act consequentialism would dictate for the circumstances we face than the choices that we would reach if we tried to follow the act-consequentialist principle in each separate decision.[9] On a multilevel view, practices and norms that establish rights and duties as ordinarily understood can be good rough guides that point us toward doing what is right and also shift expectations and so change what it is right to do in particular circumstances. An act-consequentialist assessment might approve or disapprove of existing established practices and norms to varying degrees. On this approach, the reason-giving normativity of norms such as tell the truth and keep your promises is derivative and instrumental to achieving the

---

[8] Hare (1981); also Railton (1984).

[9] A scalar act consequentialist regards as morally important not so much whether what one does is right or wrong, but rather the amount of shortfall between the best outcome one might have brought about and the actual outcome of what one chose (here we are assuming that choice of one or another action brings about a particular outcome for certain). Acts are more or less wrong, depending on the amount of shortfall. On this view, it is not troublesome if following a norm such as "Don't cheat!" often leads one to do wrong acts provided their shortfall is not too great and trying to guide choice directly by calculating overall consequences would do worse. But as an act consequentialist one's commitment to any secondary norm will be hedged; one should be alert to large shortfall. See Railton (1984) and also the canonical statement of utilitarianism at the beginning of chapter 2 of Mill (1979 [1861]).

best reachable outcomes. But this sort of normativity attaches to some not all practices and norms and variably to them.

Now consider the proposal that one ought to forgive only wrongdoers who repent, make reparations, apologize, and atone (or alternatively that only forgiving when these conditions hold is true forgiveness and one ought to strive only for true forgiveness). Taken as a candidate fundamental-level norm, this proposal must conflict with act consequentialism, which adherents of the doctrine affirm as the sole fundamental moral principle, not one among several. But at a derivative or secondary level, the act consequentialist could sign onto this norm in the same way that she presumably signs on to ordinary norms such as tell the truth and keep your promises.

The arguments advanced in this chapter are to the effect that signing on to this and other conceptions of forgiveness advanced by philosophers would be misguided. This means that whereas in many circumstances I will do best by act consequentialist lights to forego deliberating from scratch about what would best bring about good consequences on the whole when I am considering telling a lie, and instead just follow the rule against lying, it is not generally the case that when I am considering forgiving, I am likely to do better according to the standard of bringing about best consequences if I just follow some one of the various proposed norms to the effect that one should forgive if and only if the person to be forgiven truly deserves it. Instead, I should consider broadly the moral value of the outcomes that will ensue depending on whether I forgive or not (try or not) and choose what will bring about the best outcome. All the forgiveness accounts canvassed here, and others as well, point to what are in many circumstances relevant considerations bearing on decisions to forgive, but each one demands narrowing the relevant range or reasons, and thereby goes wrong.

The disagreements between the act consequentialist and the advocate of one or another directive conception of forgiving that specifies when one ought to forgive will be in a way direct and obvious and in another way indirect and subtle. The consequentialist will deny that it is in itself wrong, even just pro tanto in itself wrong, to forgive the undeserving or decline to forgive the deserving. But it will always be an empirical question, and often not a clear or easily answerable one, whether at the level of secondary, derivative norms, the act consequentialist should embrace a norm for its instrumental value, in light of the consequences of internalizing it and following it in ordinary circumstances. Act-consequentialist dismissal of some candidate idea about the morally appropriate conditions for forgiving should standardly be tentative and provisional, not dogmatic.

References

Allais, L. 2008. "Wiping the Slate Clean: The Heart of Forgiveness." *Philosophy and Public Affairs* 36: 33–68.

Bovens, L. 2008. "Apologies." *Proceedings of the Aristotelian Society* 108: 219–239.

Garrard, E., and D. McNaughton. 2003. "In Defense of Unconditional Forgiveness." *Proceedings of the Aristotelian Society* 104: 39–60.

Griswold, C. 2007. *Forgiveness: A Philosophical Exploration.* Cambridge: Cambridge University Press.

Hare, R. 1981. *Moral Thinking: Its Levels. Method, and Point.* Oxford: Oxford University Press.

Hieronymi, P. 2001. "Articulating an Uncompromising Forgiveness." *Philosophy and Phenomenological Research* 62: 529–555.

Mill, J. 1979. *Utilitarianism.* Edited by G. Sher. Indianapolis: Hackett. (Originally published 1861).

Murphy, J. 2003. *Getting Even: Forgiveness and Its Limits.* Oxford: Oxford University Press.

Murphy, J., and J. Hampton. 1988. *Forgiveness and Mercy.* Cambridge: Cambridge University Press.

Nelkin, D. 2013. "Freedom and Forgiveness." In *Free Will and Moral Responsibility*, edited by I. Haji and J. Caouette, 165–188. Newcastle upon Tyne: Cambridge Scholars Press.

Railton, P. 1984. "Alienation, Consequentialism, and the Demands of Morality." *Philosophy and Public Affairs* 18: 134–171.

Stevenson, C. 1963 [1938]. "Persuasive Definitions." In *Facts and Values: Studies in Ethical Analysis*, edited by C. Stevenson, 32–44. New Haven, CT: Yale University Press.

Twambley, P. 1976. "Mercy and Forgiveness." *Analysis* 36: 84–90.

Warmke, Brandon. 2016. "The Normative Significance of Forgiveness." *Australasian Journal of Philosophy* 94: 687–703.

Index

For the benefit of digital users, indexed terms that span two pages (e.g., 52–53) may, on occasion, appear on only one of those pages.